797,885 Books
are available to read at

Forgotten Books

www.ForgottenBooks.com

Forgotten Books' App
Available for mobile, tablet & eReader

ISBN 978-1-330-05181-8
PIBN 10013684

This book is a reproduction of an important historical work. Forgotten Books uses state-of-the-art technology to digitally reconstruct the work, preserving the original format whilst repairing imperfections present in the aged copy. In rare cases, an imperfection in the original, such as a blemish or missing page, may be replicated in our edition. We do, however, repair the vast majority of imperfections successfully; any imperfections that remain are intentionally left to preserve the state of such historical works.

Forgotten Books is a registered trademark of FB &c Ltd.
Copyright © 2017 FB &c Ltd.
FB &c Ltd, Dalton House, 60 Windsor Avenue, London, SW19 2RR.
Company number 08720141. Registered in England and Wales.

For support please visit www.forgottenbooks.com

1 MONTH OF FREE READING

at
www.ForgottenBooks.com

By purchasing this book you are eligible for one month membership to ForgottenBooks.com, giving you unlimited access to our entire collection of over 700,000 titles via our web site and mobile apps.

To claim your free month visit: www.forgottenbooks.com/free13684

* Offer is valid for 45 days from date of purchase. Terms and conditions apply.

English
Français
Deutsche
Italiano
Español
Português

www.forgottenbooks.com

Mythology Photography **Fiction**
Fishing Christianity **Art** Cooking
Essays Buddhism Freemasonry
Medicine **Biology** Music **Ancient Egypt** Evolution Carpentry Physics
Dance Geology **Mathematics** Fitness
Shakespeare **Folklore** Yoga Marketing
Confidence Immortality Biographies
Poetry **Psychology** Witchcraft
Electronics Chemistry History **Law**
Accounting **Philosophy** Anthropology
Alchemy Drama Quantum Mechanics
Atheism Sexual Health **Ancient History**
Entrepreneurship Languages Sport
Paleontology Needlework Islam
Metaphysics Investment Archaeology
Parenting Statistics Criminology
Motivational

YALE

LAW JOURNAL

VOLUME VI

OCTOBER, 1896—JUNE, 1897

NEW HAVEN, CONN.:
PUBLISHED BY THE YALE LAW JOURNAL COMPANY
1897

INDEX.

ARTICLES.

	PAGE
ACTIONS ON FOREIGN JUDGMENTS. *Ernest Knaebel*	71
BRIEF FOR THE UNITED STATES IN THE CASE OF THE UNITED STATES OF AMERICA *v.* THE TRANS-MISSOURI FREIGHT ASSOCIATION. *Hon Judson Harmon.*	295
CONSTRUCTION. *Thomas Thacher*	59
FEDERAL JUDGES AND QUASI JUDGES. *Edward B. Whitney*	20
INJUNCTION IN FEDERAL COURTS. *Hon. William A. Woods*	245
INTERNATIONAL JUSTICE. *President David Jayne Hill, LL.D.*	1
ON A PERMANENT ARBITRATION TREATY. *Edward V. Raynolds, D.C.L.*	66
PARTY FEELING IN 1796 AND 1896. *John Loomer Hall*	149
PERSONAL INJURY LITIGATION. *Hon. Eli Shelby Hammond*	328
PERSONAL TRADE NAMES. *Francis W. Treadway*	141
RECENT LEGISLATION AFFECTING PATENTS. *Charles A. Terry*	333
SEEN AT THE JAMESON TRIAL. *Professor John Wurts*	32
SOME RECENT DEVELOPMENTS OF THE LAW OF PATENTS. *Hon. William K. Townsend, D.C.L.*	179
SOME QUESTIONS RELATING TO THE MEASURE OF DAMAGES IN STREET OPENING PROCEEDINGS IN NEW YORK CITY. *Henry de Forest Baldwin*	263
THE CONCLUSIVENESS OF DECREES OF DISMISSAL. *Thomas Mills Day Jr.*	341
THE HAWAIIAN JUDICIARY. *Hon. W. F. Frear*	213
THE LAW AND PRACTICE OF CONNECTICUT CONCERNING HEARING IN DAMAGES ON DEFAULT, OR DEMURRER OVERRULED. *John W. Alling*	121
THE LAW OF ICY SIDEWALKS IN NEW YORK STATE. *Loran L. Lewis, Jr.*	258
THE PRESUMPTION OF INNOCENCE IN CRIMINAL CASES. *Professor James Bradley Thayer, LL.D.*	185
THE PROMOTION OF UNIFORM LEGISLATION. *Hon Lyman D. Brewster*	132
WHEN MAY A RAILROAD COMPANY MAKE GUARANTIES? *Hon. Henry C. Robinson, LL.D.*	252

EDITORIALS.

ARBITRATION TREATY BETWEEN GREAT BRITAIN AND THE UNITED STATES	158
BIMETALLISM	38
CHICAGO PLATFORM	40
CIVIL SERVICE LAW	229

	PAGE
IMMIGRATION LAWS	230
INSURANCE LEGISLATION IN CONNECTICUT	279
LIBRARY PROCEDURE	352
NEW YORK MARRIAGE BILL	228
PEACE IN SOCIETY, EVOLUTION OF	102
PERMANENT INTERNATIONAL COURT OF ARBITRATION	104
POLITICS AND PATRIOTISM	38
POWER OF PUBLIC SPEAKING	41
PROLIXITY OF LEGAL OPINIONS	155
SECTIONALISM IN AMERICAN POLITICS	106
SIMILARITY OF NATIONAL AND INTERNATIONAL DEVELOPMENT	103
STATUTE OF LIMITATIONS IN INTERNATIONAL LAW	157
TESTAMENTARY CAPACITY, CONNECTICUT BILL CONCERNING	160
THREE YEAR'S COURSE IN THE YALE LAW SCHOOL	41
UNANIMITY OF THE JURY IN CIVIL CASES	350
UNCERTAINTY OF LEGISLATIVE ENACTMENTS, CAUSE OF	279
UNITED STATES v. THE TRANS-MISSOURI FREIGHT ASSOCIATION	277

COMMENTS.

ANSWER TENDING TO INCRIMINATE WITNESS	43
CASE OF "THE THREE FRIENDS"	283
DOCTRINE OF ADDITIONAL SERVITUDE APPLIED TO STREET RAILWAYS	356
EFFECT OF PASSAGE OF WILSON BILL UPON GOODS IMPORTED AND PLACED UNDER BOND UNDER THE MCKINLEY BILL	162
ELECTRIC LIGHT COMPANIES AS "MANUFACTURING INDUSTRIES"	231
ENDORSEMENT OF BILLS TO FICTITIOUS PERSONS	43
HABEAS CORPUS	163
INJUNCTIONS AGAINST PRIVATE CORPORATIONS	354
INTERSTATE COMMERCE LAW	284
IRRIGATION LAWS	161
PART PAYMENT AS FULL SATISFACTION	356
PATENTS. RIGHT OF PATENTEE TO SELL HIS ARTICLES	231
PROCUREMENT OF BREACH OF CONTRACT, ACTION ON	355
PROTECTION OF ONE MAN CORPORATIONS	108
SOUTH CAROLINA DISPENSARY ACT	232
UNITED STATES v. TRANS-MISSOURI FREIGHT ASSOCIATION	281

YALE LAW JOURNAL

VOL VI   OCTOBER, 1896   No. 1

INTERNATIONAL JUSTICE.

The dogs of Constantinople, we are told, have their own territorial limitations. They follow a stranger to the limit of their wards, but invariably halt upon the frontier with as much deference to the boundary as a French soldier at an outpost of the German Empire. It is not difficult to understand how these limits have been established. Originally, the hungry animals roamed everywhere, seeking after food; but, in time, they fell into habitual rounds, and became attached to certain places where there were exceptional chances for a dinner. Newcomers were attacked and driven away, and these in turn established themselves in less desirable quarters, repelling invasion with a similar ferocity. Thus originated a division of the city into canine wards, or, to change the figure, tribal aggregates were formed, and territorial limits were established by frontier battles, which fixed lines of permanent compromise between the bands of contestants.

Every sensitive being tends to exercise its native powers and gratify its native appetites. This brings it in conflict with other creatures; and, if it survives, it must adopt a course of behavior toward its fellow-creatures of the same and of different species which will insure its escape from their rapacity or revenge. Thus, for every order of beings, a course of conduct is marked out which is most advantageous in the struggle for existence. The formula descriptive of this course—that is, the rule according to which the being acts—is the natural law of that being's life.

Man has had no exemption from these universal conditions of existence; and, when he reached the level of reflective capacity, he found himself already a member of a society shaped for him by the forces of nature, and was compelled to conform to certain rules of action which had been unconsciously introduced. Society is the creature as well as the creator of custom; and, in its natural sense, "law" is the parent rather than the child of social existence. "Long before any supreme political authority has come into being," says Sheldon Amos, "a series of practical rules determine the main relations of family life, the conditions of ownership, the punishment of the more violent forms of moral wrong-doing, and the adjustment of contracts. The mode in which such rules are formulated seems to be the following: A spontaneous practice is first followed, and, if good and useful, is generally copied over and over again, the more so as habit and association always render the imitation of an old and familiar practice easier than inventing a new and untried one."[1]

But at last a stage is reached in the social evolution of man at which a distinct verbal formulation of custom in precepts or maxims becomes desirable; and, when law has attained this expression in propositions, all that is necessary to modify or create it is the power to enforce compliance with new requirements upon the individuals who form the community. When this point of development is reached, a new force enters into society. From that moment it becomes possible to transcend actual custom by setting up ideals of justice, which shall henceforth react upon practice with the elevating power and logical consistency of principles of equity rationally applied. All that is then needed to establish *theoretically* the dominion of reason over human action is the transfer of legislative authority from the hands of arbitrary individual rulers to the sovereign people, or their direct representatives, by constitutional provisions. For the accomplishment of this task many centuries have been required, but the growth of legislative privilege has been, in late years, more rapid than the development of legislative capacity. For the *practical* perfection of the work of legislation, however, there is still needed a higher development of popular intelligence, which alone can raise the standard of the law-making power.

Parallel with the evolution of law as an institutional growth, there has been a corresponding development of the idea of justice. Primarily, this idea arises from the experience of inequality, and at first appears in the negative form of equalizing inju-

---

[1] The Science of Law, p. 49.

ries inflicted. Deprivation of the common objects of desire by the exercise of superior force was an early human experience. The impulse to regain that which was taken away or, if this was impossible, to make an equal reprisal led to a state of warfare which was rendered the more intense the longer it continued. The communistic or tribal nature of primitive property made every invasion of individual rights a tribal insult, to be avenged in kind. The murder of a man involved his next of kin in the obligation, extended at last to the entire tribe, to slay the murderer, and every lesser injury required a corresponding retorsion. Thus grew up the *lex talionis*, universal at all the lower levels of humanity. So far there was absolutely no idea of justice, except as the equipoise of injuries. This conception is far from being outgrown in the present civilized States of Christendom, and runs through our statutes, our codes, and our theology, wherever the idea of retributive justice appears. It is essentially a purely negative notion, an equation of evils and injuries, not a positive conception of indestructible obligations binding men and nations to deeds of mutual beneficence.

The early and negative notion of justice is wholly material, and expresses a relation between measurable things and quantities. According to this idea, there is no debt of injury that cannot be paid, and none that should not be. Duty consists in inflicting an equal injury upon an enemy. A little extra damage may safely be done, as he will be certain to retaliate, and whatever is done against him now will be so much to our credit on the next account. Such a conception, of course, contemplates perpetual antagonism as following from a law of nature, and therefore, to be expected. There is no logical stopping-place in a series of settlements upon this theory, where every truce is only a rest in preparation for a new aggression.

But the positive and modern idea of justice is at every point in opposition to this crude compensation of evil with evil. It is a rational conception, based upon the idea of personality as a power of infinitely expansive tendency. *Every human being has an inherent right to become all that his nature and capacities permit of his becoming, as he develops toward the realization of his own ideal.* Unnecessary restriction of this development cannot be justified on any rational ground. The only interference that can be permitted is that which necessarily results from the conflict of rights in the process of individual expansion. The freedom of the individual is absolute, except as it interferes with the equal freedom of other individuals, and to find, determine, and fix with authority the limits of this freedom, as restricted by the equal freedom of all, is the problem of justice.

This conception applies equally to men and nations. Like every human individual, every free, independent and sovereign State has a tendency to expand, to exercise its powers, to develop its resources, and to realize its national destiny as apprehended by itself. International justice is the problem presented by the moral and physical necessity of finding, determining, and fixing with authority the limits of this freedom of growth and expansion as restricted by the equal freedom of all independent and sovereign States. It is a problem of colossal magnitude and of supreme importance to human welfare. Within a few months we have seen the two greatest nations of the earth, speaking the same language, accepting the same religion, animated by the same legal, institutional, and humanitarian traditions, counting their battle-ships, enumerating their available forces of men and artillery, and estimating the extent of their financial credit if, in an expected crisis, there should be a declaration of war between their respective governments. Prior to the appearance of the morning newspapers which sent a thrill of astonishment and dismay through more than a hundred millions of human beings, there was not on either side of the Atlantic the faintest suspicion that war was a possibility. And, in reality, it was not possible except through a criminal blunder; for the good sense and friendly spirit of these two peoples were such that deliberation alone was needed to show to both that such an enterprise is unnecessary, unwise, and unreasonable. But the bare possibility that two civilized nations could be flung into the arena of battle by the accidents of diplomatic mismanagement or misunderstanding over a question which does not seriously affect the interest of either country shows that it is not untimely to consider deliberately the condition of those international relations which could be so easily disturbed, and whose disturbance would involve the best part of humanity in the barbarities and atrocities of primitive tribes of savages seeking to efface one another from the surface of the earth.

The establishment of international justice upon a basis as secure and peaceable as that of municipal justice in civilized states would not seem to be a chimera, and yet it is invested with difficulties of considerable magnitude. Three conditions at least must be fulfilled before a system of perfect international justice can be created and rendered fully effective: (1) a code of Internationl Law must be formulated, and recognized as binding upon sovereign states; (2) a method of adjusting differences by the application of this code must be devised; and (3) a means must be discovered of enforcing the decisions arrived at through the method of adjustment. These three conditions involve quite unequal degrees of inherent difficulty, and present different stages of approach to realization. For the sake of clearness, it may be well to consider them in the order of statement.

I. THE CODES OF INTERNATIONAL LAW.

1. The recognition of international rights has been almost exclusively confined to modern times and Western civilization. The ancient absolute monarchies of the Orient, even more than those of the present, were intolerant of all national pretensions except their own, and lived in a state of almost uninterrupted warfare with their neighbors. Their ignorance of distant nations and their feuds and quarrels with adjacent peoples rendered peaceable intercourse almost impossible, and the idea of justice between States was therefore unborn.

The Greeks recognized the independence of other States, both Hellenic and non-Hellenic, and had diplomatic intercourse with them to a limited extent; but they were accustomed to regard all foreigners as barbarians. Their customs in war were extremely cruel, and their policy in peace did not extend beyond the unification of Greece against the barbarian world. In their domestic alliances, dictated by community of blood and civilization, they attained a conspicuous degree of federation. "Among the Greek cities and States a certain recognition of international justice was shown by the action of the Amphictyonic Council, an institution more religious than political, for the pacific adjustment of disputes. That council had doubtless some influence in restraining the savagery of intestine wars by binding its members not to destroy any of the Amphictyonic towns, not to turn away their running waters, and not to commit theft in the temple of Delphi, the common center of the confederacy."[1] But the authority of the council was confined to the twelve Hellenic nations associated in the worship of the same gods.

The Romans established far wider foreign relations than the Greeks, but in their treatment of other nations they were not governed by any body of justice. "Blinded by the desire for universal dominion," says Leone Levi, "the Romans did not see that any International Law did or could exist, and, if they apprehended its existence, they certainly did not acknowledge its

---

[1] Leone Levi, "International Law," p. 10.

authority nor observe its doctrines."[a] The *jus gentium* was, indeed, better known to them than to any other nation of antiquity, but they understood by it those natural principles of justice that underlie all national customs in common, and are, therefore, applicable to all men and countries. But they did not apply these great principles as between States, probably for the reason that they did not distinctly recognize the equal and reciprocal rights of all nations, especially as against themselves. Their *jus feciale*, applied by the *collegium fecialium*, was intended to control the conduct of their armies toward other nations during war, and the declaration of war was in the power of this college. But the fecial law was not founded upon the *consent* of other nations, and was, therefore, in no proper sense, a form of international law.

During the whole of the period between the downfall of the Roman Empire and the close of the Dark Ages some of the Mediterranean cities maintained more or less intimate commercial relations, and the first movement toward the formation of codes of law applicable to foreign intercourse seems to have originated from the requirements of maritime commerce. Everywhere upon land there was some kind of local authority, but the sea, "that great common of mankind," beyond the jurisdiction of any king, was the open field of piracy and plunder. What the Christian religion, originally so full of peace and the spirit of human unity, had failed to do when rendered a political power by official adoption, the interests of trade attempted to accomplish, and justice upon the sea was the first step toward justice among the nations. "The Jugements of Oléron" was a body of regulations governing the navigation of the Western seas, believed to have been drawn up in the eleventh century. It was long recognized in most of the Alantic ports of France, and was afterwards incorporated in the maritime law of Louis XIV. "The Consolato del Mare," or "Customs of the Sea," was a more pretentious collection of rules pertaining to commerce and navigation both in peace and war. Its provisions regarding prize law long prevailed in the maritime code of Europe, and have been reaffirmed in many treaties. Other sea laws, such as the "Guidon de la Mer," the "Laws of Wisbuy," and the "Ordinances of the Hanseatic League," mark the wider extension of the maritime laws and policy of the Mediterranean. All of them are believed to contain elements extracted from the oldest known maritime code, the "Rhodian laws."

---

[a] International Law, p. 11.

Among the causes that contributed to the development of International Law we must mention the decay of feudalism. Dating back to the migration of the Teutonic tribes into Western and Southwestern Europe, in the third and sixth centuries, this system of land tenure was unfavorable to the existence of sovereign States. The fiefs had been at first precariously held, being without any guarantee except possession. By the connivance of the more powerful chiefs, titles had become annual, then for life, and at last hereditary. At the height of feudalism the kings held only a nominal and military jurisdiction, and, in assuming hereditary crowns, they had sanctioned an hereditary partition of territory which rendered them dependent upon their feudal barons. With the emergence of the modern States system from the ruins of feudalism, sovereignty became concentrated in the hands of a few powerful rulers; and really sovereign States began to assert their rights, and to secure them by treaties and conventions.

The institution of chivalry originated the code of knightly honor, and was permeated, sentimentally at least, with principles of courtesy and justice. It was indirectly promotive of the development of International Law by creating a universal comity among members of the knightly profession, and by securing the better treatment of slaves and captives, and the keeping of faith with strangers and enemies.

The most potent influence upon the early period of International Law was undoubtedly the Roman Church. As the political power of Rome declined the Church grew into an organization of great central authority and influence, practically universal throughout Europe, and gradually assumed the imperial functions of the decayed empire, strengthened by spiritual pretensions that gave it command over every individual mind in Europe. The Roman law, the greatest system of jurisprudence that the world has ever known, universalized and adapted in the Canon Law, continued its sway over the greater part of Europe. The history of the Holy Roman Empire records the absorption of the political power of its temporal head by the originally coördinate spiritual head, until the Pope came to be recognized as the embodiment of imperial jurisdiction. He became the arbitrator of international disputes, and his representatives were the omnipresent agents of a united Christendom. The œcumenical councils, were, in a sense, international congresses, which served to preserve the peace of Europe. With the breaking out of religious wars, in which Catholicism and Protestantism were arrayed against each other, and the consequent subdivision of Europe into Catholic and Protestant States, the papal influence in the settlement of disputes gradually subsided, and has now almost vanished from the earth. The necessity of securing international rights by other means than war, however, was undiminished; and the formulation of the principles of equity between sovereign States became the more imperative.

Where religion had failed, science was invoked, and Hugo Grotius, a Protestant jurist and publicist of great experience and noble genius, in 1623 published the first systematic work on International Law, under the title *De Jure Belli et Pacis*. The Law of Nations was based by Grotius upon the eternal principles of natural justice, but he was a profound student of the Roman Law, and his work may be considered as resting upon historical as well as natural foundations. His treatise has been translated into all languages, and "has elicited the admiration of all nations and of all succeeding generations." As Halleck has said, "Its author is universally regarded as the great master-builder of the science of International Jurisprudence."

2. It is easy, in the light of the foregoing sketch, to see what are the sources of International Law, although, as Leone Levi has said, "As it is now recognized, it is the creation of comparatively recent years—the result of the combined influence of philosophy and ethics, religion and civilization, commerce and political economy, to say nothing of the action of accelerated means of communication, such as railways, steamships and electric telegraphs."[4]

Following the order of certainty in the determination of what International Law at the moment actually is, we may say that its first source is treaties and conventions. As nothing can be internationally binding which does not have the *consent* of nations, voluntary and written compacts are the most certain and efficacious in securing rights. Whether or not these embody the highest conception of justice often depends upon the strength or weakness of the signatory powers which have given their assent to treaty provisions. Whenever the obligations are reciprocal, the presumption is that they are mutually regarded as just.

The decisions of municipal courts upon international questions and the municipal statutes of sovereign States are, of course, authoritative for these States upon the ground which they definitely cover; as, for example, laws relating to naturalization,

---

[4] International Law, p. 1.

extradition, neutrality and piracy. As these differ widely in different countries, there arises the important branch of jurisprudence known as the Conflict of Laws, for which provision should be made in the formation of a code.

Another source of International Law is the judgments of international tribunals, or courts of arbitration. These may fairly be regarded as precedents which may be invoked by sovereign States, as municipal decisions are by individuals.

Still another source is to be found in diplomatic correspondence and other State papers as related to particular subjects of dispute. These are often inaccessible, being regarded as confidential and sometimes as containing State secrets. Most civilized countries now publish large portions at least of this class of documents.

Next in authority, perhaps, is the Roman Law, especially in those countries whose municipal codes are based upon it. In England and the United States, whose municipal law is influenced by English custom as expressed in the Common Law of England, and not so deeply affected by the Roman Law as that of the Continent—a tendency to reject its distinctive maxims has often appeared, and the text-writers on International Jurisprudence have, accordingly, been grouped into two schools, the Continental and the Anglo-American. This distinction is, however, now passing away, and the text-writers are approaching uniformity upon the cardinal principles of the Laws of Nations.

For the non-professional student of the subject these text-books are the chief source of information; but they have only that authority to which the recognized ability of their authors entitles them. It is a notable fact that two of the most able and most widely accepted text-writers of International Law have been Americans, Wheaton representing the North and Calvo the South American Continent.

Lastly, to complete the sources of International Law, mention must be made of what may be called the Divine Law, which includes those ultimate principles of reason and those fundamental ethical conceptions upon which the whole system of human justice finally reposes. Because it is the most general, it is the least certain as a source of definite prescription; for it is the *application* of these great principles, not their reality or obligation, that divides opinion and generates dispute.

3. The definite codification of International Law has been undertaken by several competent hands. In 1867 Mr. David Dudley Field brought before the British Association for Social

Science a proposition to frame an international code. Mr. Field was personally qualified for such an undertaking by long experience as a codifier of municipal law. He produced what is in reality a complete treatise on the subject, although it bears the modest title "Outlines of an International Code." One feature of Mr. Field's code is the introduction of the principles of arbitration in the settlement of international disputes. His work attracted great attention in Europe, and has been translated into French and Italian. In 1873 he assisted in forming an international association for the purpose of reforming and codifying the Laws of Nations, with special reference to the substitution of arbitration for war. He had also been a member of the peace conference at Washington in 1861, and presided at the great peace convention in London in 1890.

The celebrated Swiss jurist, John Kaspar Bluntschli, famous throughout the world as a writer of works on jurisprudence, has also undertaken the preparation of an International Code, published in 1874, under the title "Le Droit International codifié."

In 1887 the same task was undertaken by Leone Levi, the well-known Jewish economist of London, whose work as a law reformer extends to other branches of jurisprudence. His book on "International Law" in the "International Scientific Series" is, in reality, a code, although it is designated in the subtitle as "Materials for a Code." Its scope is wider than that of Field or Bluntschli, who confined themselves to the natural portion of the Law of Nations. Levi includes also the positive portion, supporting his code with a digest of treaties. He also presents a plan for the settlement of international disputes, which will be considered in another connection.

None of the codes described above has been officially adopted by any nation, so that, in the technical sense, there is at present no absolutely authoritative code of International Law in existence. And yet it would not be correct to say that the Law of Nations is a mere branch of ethics or collection of moral precepts. Treaties and conventions have created a body of definite and binding obligations which may be regarded as strictly legal in their effects. The time has come, however, when an international commission should be authorized to prepare a code; and this should be made binding by a general treaty among civilized States giving it authority as International Law.

II. THE METHODS OF ADJUSTING DIFFERENCES.

It is evident that the mere existence of a body of rules and maxims recognized as applicable to international relations, however equitable and elaborate, is practically useless unless there is an efficient method of applying it to the conflicting interests and disputes of nations.

1. The first and most obvious method of adjusting differences is that of diplomatic negotiation. The right of legation is one of the oldest and best established of international usages. Embassies for making agreements and conventions with foreign powers were employed by the most ancient States, and in a rudimentary form are customary even among barbarous peoples. The extent to which a sovereign State maintains permanent legations in foreign countries is an evidence of its political wisdom. The idea of permanency of representation through ambassadors and ministers has grown with the development of means of communication, until it has become the universal custom of civilized states to maintain legations in all the countries with which they have intimate relations of trade or general intercourse. The mere fact that a State is thus represented often secures it against discrimination that would otherwise be exercised; and the value of a diplomatic agent consists less in what he may be able to adjust than in what he may be able to prevent. The diplomatic history of every country would illustrate the utility of the personal presence of a qualified representative at each of the great capitals of the world. This advantage, however, depends largely upon the intellectual, social and linguistic qualifications of the envoys chosen. It is also seriously diminished by sending out diplomatic agents of lower rank than those accredited by other powers to the same government, thus condemning them to juniority and subordination in the diplomatic corps, and stripping them of the social dignity and influence which might be serviceable to their government. Still another impediment to this means of adjustment is a chauvinistic temper in the foreign office, where ignorance or discourtesy may cost a country valuable rights or bring upon it humiliation and contempt.

2. A second method of adjusting differences is that of voluntary or invited mediation by a third party. At the Congress of Paris, in 1856, the representatives of Austria, France, Great Britain, Russia and Turkey, recommended that "States between which serious disagreements might arise should, before appealing to arms, have recourse, as far as circumstances admit, to the good offices of friendly powers." This is a very moderate and highly qualified recommendation; but it indicates a growing love of peace and a sense of responsibility for war.

3. A third way of avoiding the sacrifice of national rights

without incurring the consequences of battle is arbitration, which differs from mediation in the degree of judicial formality with which it is conducted.

Arbitration of disputes between governments was practiced to some extent by the ancient Greeks, and it is thought that the Athenian Symmachy had from the beginning a common tribunal at Delos, where the treasury of the allied States was located. But the range of this method of attaining justice was certainly very limited in ancient times.

During the Middle Ages the Pope often intervened as arbitrator, and was frequently the referee of the ecclesiastical councils which deposed and excommunicated princes, settled questions of tolls and taxes, and decided rights of sovereignty.

Among modern States the application of arbitration has not been extensive, although Vattel about the middle of the eighteenth century commended it as a "reasonable and natural mode of deciding such disputes as do not directly affect the safety of a nation." About seventy modern international cases have been settled by arbitration, nearly half of them between the United States and other countries. The most important of these was the settlement of the Alabama claims against Great Britain. Provision for this settlement was made by the Treaty of Washington, in 1871, which provided for a commission of five arbitrators, before whom the case of each nation was argued by distinguished counsel. The commission rendered a decision in which both countries acquiesced, awarding an indemnity of $15,500,000 to the United States.

Distinguished sovereigns and military men have been earnest advocates of arbitration and able jurists have proposed plans for extending its application. General Grant once wrote, "I look forward to an epoch when a court recognized by all nations will settle all differences." General Sheridan said in a public address, "I mean what I say when I express the belief that in time arbitration will rule the whole world." According to Sir Lyon Playfair, the late Emperor Alexander of Russia was so impressed with the importance of the peaceable settlement of international disputes that "he rose from his bed in the night, and wrote a plan that all crowned heads should join in a conclusion to submit to arbitration whatever differences might arise among them instead of resorting to the sword."

On October 31, 1887, a memorial, signed by more than one-third of the members of the British Parliament, and representing more than seven hundred thousand workingmen, was presented to President Cleveland, requesting his good offices in behalf of peace. The President sent the memorial to Congress, and on the 4th of April, 1890, a concurrent resolution was adopted by the Senate and the House "that the President be, and is hereby, requested to invite, from time to time, as fit occasions may arrive, negotiations with any government with which the United States has or may have diplomatic relations, to the end that any differences or disputes arising between the two governments, which cannot be adjusted by diplomatic agency, may be referred to arbitration, and be peaceably adjusted by such means." As Sir Lyon Playfair has said: "To the United States the lovers of peace look with hope and confidence that she will take a leading part in the promotion of peace by international arbitration. Her growth is the great fact of modern history. She is a country of boundless resources, and has shown that she can carry on great and successful wars, so that her intervention as a peacemaker could not be misinterpreted."

We may now examine briefly the plans that have been proposed for a wider extension of this method.

(1) The plan of David Dudley Field embraces the following programme. When an agreement cannot otherwise be effected, a Joint High Commission of ten, chosen in equal numbers by the litigants, shall report within six months their efforts to reconcile their principals. This is merely preliminary. If they are unsuccessful these parties shall give notice of the result to the other nations that have accepted the code, and the latter shall provide for a High Tribunal by the nomination of four persons each, from whom the contestants may eliminate, by successive rejections, those whom they do not approve, until the number is reduced to seven. These seven are to compose the court. The code provides for a compulsory resort to this procedure. If any State accepting the code shall begin a war in violation of it, the others are bound to resist the offending nation by force.

(2) The programme of Leone Levi proposes a Council of International Arbitration, to which each State adopting the code is to nominate a number of members selected from persons of high reputation and standing, to serve for a fixed period of years. The council is to be declared existent as soon as any two States have concurred in its organization. When organized, other States will be invited to nominate members. On the occurrence of any dispute between the States the council will call a meeting and offer its assistance. When the contending States have accepted the services of the council, this body will nominate some

of its members, and each of the litigant States will nominate other persons, to form a High Court of International Arbitration for adjudicating the dispute; and the award shall be binding upon the States.. The High Court shall be constituted with regard to the character and locality of the dispute, and shall exist for the one case only. Physical force is not to be resorted to, either to compel reference to the council or to enforce compliance with the award. The dispute, however, whether referred or not, is to be considered by the council, and its judgment is to be communicated to all the States represented by it. The council will make rules of procedure for itself and for the High Court. The seat of the council is to be a neutral city, such as Berne or Brussels. The cost of maintaining the council shall be borne equally by the concurring States, but the cost of the High Court by the contesting parties in equal shares.

III. THE MEANS OF ENFORCING JUDGMENT.

The evident weakness of these plans of arbitration is their inefficiency in securing compliance with judgment when rendered. Municipal law is enforced by definite penalties, which are applicable by the executive branch of government. Both of the schemes just described for the establishment of an International Court leave it absolutely powerless to enfore its decisions. And here it becomes evident that sovereign States differ essentially from any other parties at law, and this distinction is seen to lie in sovereignty itself. Here arises the most difficult problem in the task of instituting international justice.

1. A solution that has been many times urged, but which is practically as chimerical as it is ideally perfect, is the universal federation of States. Castel St. Pierre contemplated a perpetual alliance or league, of which all the States of Europe should be members. War was to be rendered impossible, except in case of revolution, and all nations were to be united as the guardians of peace. Jeremy Bentham, the great English jurist, toward the close of the eighteenth century sketched the plan of a General Congress consisting of two deputies from each State. Military establishments were to be reduced in some fair ratio, colonies were to be abandoned in order to eliminate a frequent cause of strife, and refractory States were to be put under the ban. A fixed contingent of troops was to be at the command of the Congress to enfore its decrees. About the same time the great German philosopher, Immanuel Kant, published an essay entitled "Zum Ewigen Frieden," proposing that no State should be

merged by sale, exchange, gift or inheritance in another state; that no State should interfere with the affairs of another, that standing armies should gradually cease, and, finally, that all States should adopt republican constitutions and enter into a confederation, conferring upon every man a citizenship of the world.

Such speculations are dreams rather than plans, and yet when we consider that as late as 1818 Lord Ellenborough declared the right of English litigants "to settle their disputes by combat," it would be adventurous to predict the impossibility of equal advances in the social sense of nations. Still, it is hardly credible that sovereign States will in any way abridge their sovereignty by a mode of federation that would deprive them of independence. As Sheldon Amos has said, "The States of Europe do not at present wish to submit themselves to any central force, nor even to create such a force out of their own body by the most adequate representative system imaginable." And yet he feels compelled to add that all indications "point to the gradual elaboration among States of what may be properly called a supreme political authority. What form this authority will take," he continues, "it may be impossible for us, in this generation, so much as to guess; just as the members of an early, spontaneously developing village-community had no materials from which to construct a notion of civil government in its later sense."[1]

2. Another proposed mode of securing the acceptance of the decisions of an international court is the voluntary disarmament of nations, rendering the resort to war less probable by diminishing the military spirit. A nation preoccupied with industry, devoid of military ambition, and temporarily unfitted to engage in military operations, it is argued, will be more readily disposed to accept a judicial decision than a State which is constantly prepared for war, influenced by the martial spirit, and confident of success in case of a conflict. This is undoubtedly true; but the fact is also an argument against disarmament to a State surrounded with enemies, and liable to be exposed to foreign aggresion if its standing army is reduced.

There are, however, so many reasons for the reduction of military forces, that a just convention based upon the plan of proportionate reduction would be an inestimable blessing to mankind. The enormous taxes required to maintain the standing armies of Europe, the abstraction of so many productive agents

---
[1] Science of Law, p. 327.

from industrial pursuits to serve in the army, and the constant menace to peace which military ambition inevitably offers are certainly good reasons for at least a relative disarmament of nations. But there can be little hope of this so long as the perpetuation of dynasties is esteemed a matter of importance, for it is on this account rather than for national security that standing armies are required. A general adoption of republican constitutions is a step in political evolution which must precede any considerable reduction of standing armies. This aid to the enforcement of the judgments of international courts belongs, therefore, to the future rather than to the present, and cannot be counted upon in the formation of immediate plans for arbitration. And so it becomes evident since nations will not abrogate either their sovereignty or their means of self-defence, that reliance must be placed upon the moral and the social means of enforcing such decisions. As the movement is an ethical one, it is probably in every way best to attempt to advance it by purely ethical considerations, which have at least one great advantage—that they appeal to what is best in men universally, and are most effective when they are addressed to the reason and the conscience in whose interest they are urged.

In conclusion, the following plan of procedure seems to commend itself as not altogether hopelessly impracticable for securing to civilized nations the administration of justice without resort to the costly and frequently unjust arbitrament of battle:

(1) The negotiation of a general treaty extended to all sovereign States willing to enter into it, but primarily adapted to the requirements of England and the United States, having for its sole object the establishment of a permanent International Court, and requiring no other signatory powers to give it effect than the two named above.

(2) The appointment of an expert commission by the powers accepting the treaty to codify in separate codes the Laws of Nations, (a) as a body of rational jurisprudence or abstract justice, and (b) as a body of positive law now existing in treaties and conventions.

(3) The adoption of a plan for the formation of a permanent International Court, with jurisdiction covering all forms of dispute between the contracting nations which do not involve the sovereignty or independence of these States.

The International Court should of course be constituted upon lines to be determined by a representative commission of experts after the most deliberate discussion. The following propositions, however, seem to be sufficiently well established to deserve the respectful consideration of such a commission:

(1) All the sovereign States having a part in the treaty should have an equal number of representatives in court. This follows directly from the sovereign character of the States which may be signatory to the treaty. To apportion representation would abolish equality before the court. This principle has been recognized in the formation of our Senate, in which Rhode Island and Delaware have an equal number of Senators with New York and Pennsylvania, although the former are comparatively insignificant in territory and population. The questions adjudicated by a court are not questions of power, but of justice; and a small State may have as good a cause as a great one.

(2) The judicial office should be held for life, providing for removal in case of corruption, incapacity or extreme old age. This would render possible the creation of a judicial body minutely conversant with International Law, precedent, and political history, and at the same time would place the court above selfish considerations.

(3) The court should have jurisdiction over all cases not affecting the autonomy of the contracting States. Provision should be made for private as well as public redress, under proper conditions of preliminary attempts at mediation. All questions effecting the autonomy of States should be beyond the jurisdiction of the court, otherwise it might become the medium of depriving States of their sovereignty, and the suspicion of this would make the establishment of the court impossible.

(4) The court should sit in a neutral territory. This would facilitate justice by rendering impossible, or at least difficult, the attempt to influence the court by public opinion or otherwise. Both Switzerland and Belgium are neutralized by existing conventions, and one or the other could be chosen, as the character of the case might require, for the holding of the court.

(5) The transactions of the court should be open and public, and all its proceedings should be recorded and published. Justice is fond of the light, as injustice is of secrecy. A greater care is taken in reaching a decision when all the grounds and conditions of it are universally known.

(6) All petitions, pleadings, and decisions should be in writing. This accords with the practice of the highest courts, and rules out ambiguity of statement, the effect of personal influence, and appeals to the feelings, while it conduces to precision, deliberation, and permanence.

(7) Refusal to submit to the court a case within its jurisdiction, or to comply with its decision, should be followed by the permanent exclusion of the offending State from its privileges and protection. This is a provision of the utmost importance, for it will solve the problem of enforcing the decisions of such a court. In effect, it outlaws the lawless. It presents to every State a choice between obedience to the code and deprivation of its obvious advantages. The effectiveness of this provision undoubtedly depends, in a egrat degree, upon the extent to which the code is accepted; but it cannot be doubted that, if the most powerful nations were united under the jurisdiction of the court, it would become a moral impossibility to refuse or violate its requirements.

When we consider how jealous the German and Italian States were of one another and of any supreme authority, much less than a century ago, and follow the history of German and Italian unity to its present consummation, we learn two important lessons. The first is that, when the ambition of monarchs is checked by constitutional limitations, wars become less easy and frequent; for the people are able to restrain public ministers from courses of conduct hostile to the welfare of the masses. Another lesson is that, with the growth of popular intelligence, traditional claims to sovereignty fade into smaller proportions and less flaming colors, and industrial and commercial well-being becomes the prime consideration of statesmen. We may, therefore, confidently expect that, with the development of constitutional government and experience of its benefits, there will follow a gradual breaking down of those merely local conceptions of sovereignty which are so powerful in the cruder states of society; and universal equity, secured by legal institutions, will continue to become dearer to the minds of men. The law of political evolution seems to be that larger areas and populations tend to be unified under homogeneous constitutional forms, whose inner analogy or hidden identity is ever becoming more apparent. To the vision of the poet there has already appeared "the parliament of man, the federation of the world." Such foregleams of coming events are never realistically accurate; but the spontaneous activity of the imagination is always controlled by the existence of elements that are about to combine, not, indeed, as in the dream of the poet, but according to nature's own law of change and progress.

All that has yet been said or written upon this great problem probably constitutes little more than the rude scaffolding of that great temple of international justice whose dome will yet shelter the nations of the earth from the wrongs of oppression and the horrors of battle. But its foundations are laid in the moral nature of humanity; and, although—like a vast cathedral grown old with passing centuries—it is still uncompleted, we may bring our unhewn stones to lay upon its rising walls, in the faith that its invisible Builder and Maker will shape them to a place in the permanent structure.

David Jayne Hill.

FEDERAL JUDGES AND QUASI-JUDGES.

Chief-Justice Jay, three years after the adoption of the Constitution, laid down the proposition "that by the Constitution of the United States, the Government thereof is divided into three distinct and independent branches, and that it is the duty of each to abstain from and to oppose encroachments on either."[1] These branches are the legislative, executive and judicial. The distinction has always been treated in theory as fundamental, and for a long time its preservation was treated in actual practice also as an object of great solicitude. The early amendments to the Constitution gave additional guarantees that the judicial sphere should not be invaded by the legislature or by the executive. The judiciary, on the other hand, maintained their right to exemption from non-judicial work. The Chief-Justice, in the case just quoted, laid down the further proposition: "That neither the legislative nor the executive branches can constitutionally assign to the judicial any duties but such as are properly judicial and to be performed in a judicial manner." Upon the same principle the executive departments claimed, and the judiciary conceded that the executive discretion should not be guided nor interfered with in any way by judicial process. Even when the duties of the executive were of the simplest and clearest character, the right of the judiciary to compel their performance was stoutly resisted. The controversy, which was commenced by Jefferson and Marshall at the beginning of the century, was not settled until the time of Van Buren.[2] No student of our form of government can afford not to read the vigorous exposition of this fundamental distinction by Postmaster-General Kendall and Attorney-General Butler in the lower court in Kendall's case, its more qualified statement by the Attorney-General in the same case at the bar of the Supreme Court, or the opinions of the Supreme Court Justices in this case and in that of Secretary Paulding which immediately followed, and which have resulted in confining the remedy of *mandamus*, in the Federal

---

[1] Hayburn's Case, 2 Dall. 410, note.

[2] Marbury *v.* Madison, 1 Cr. 137; United States *v.* Kendall, 5 Cr. C.C. 163; Kendall *v.* United States, 12 Pet. 524; Decatur *v.* Paulding, 14 Pet. 497.

courts, within limits narrower, probably, than those recognized in any other system of jurisprudence of English origin.

In order to secure the entire independence of the judiciary, its members were given practically a life tenure. They were not even to be retired compulsorily for old age. They were to be removed from office only by a two-thirds vote of the United States Senators, sitting as a Court of Impeachment. It was intended thus to ensure fearlessness in the performance of judicial duties, by providing that the tenure of judicial office should be made secure before its incumbent should be called upon to render any decision.

It may be interesting to consider how thoroughly this constitutional theory has proved complete. It will be found that all Federal Judges, except the justices of the Supreme Court of the United States, are practically removable; that among one class of them removals are of continual occurrence; and that it is even not impossible for a man to occupy the highest judicial position in the nation, and then to lose it by reason of an unpopular decision. It will be found that all judges may be charged with some duties strictly executive in nature, while some judges may be charged with executive duties to an indefinite extent. It will be found that a large department of work strictly judicial in its nature may be confided either to the judicial or to the executive branch, at the will of Congress; which has gone even so far in practice as to grant a right of appeal from the judiciary to the executive or *vice versâ*.

Mr. Justice Curtis has defined judicial acts, in an "enlarged" sense, as "all those administrative duties the performance of which involves an inquiry into the existence of facts and the application to them of rules of law."[1] He instances among such acts that of the President in calling out the militia; but this gives the term an enlarged definition indeed, for when the President, having been asked to call out the militia, has ascertained the facts and satisfied himself about his legal powers, there still remains a question of expediency to be determined, and this element of expediency makes the case one calling rather for executive than for judicial discretion, although a discretion sometimes exercised by courts, as in the care of trust property or of property attached. The definition would become a stricter one by excluding the element of expediency and postulating "all the elements of a civil case—a complainant, a defendant, and a judge—*actor*,

---

[1] Murray's Lessee v. Hoboken Land and Improvement Co., 18 How. 272, 280.

reus et judex."[4] It is not necessary to the essence of a judicial act that it be performed by a person bearing a judicial title. Thus the Constitution expressly provides for a Court of Impeachment composed of United States Senators, and provides, also, that each House of Congress shall be "the judge of the elections, returns, and qualifications of its own members."

Passing by these exceptional instances and those afforded by military and naval tribunals, judicial discretion, as above defined, in our Federal Government, is exercised by at least three classes of officers; first, judges appointed under the judiciary article of the Constitution; second, judges appointed under the territorial provision of the Constitution; and, third, *quasi*-judicial officers deputed by Congress for the decision of controversies to which the United States is a party. These classes will now be considered separately.

I. *Judges appointed under the judiciary article.*—In theory, as we have said, these officers are irremovable except upon conviction in a Court of Impeachment. They hold by a tenure whose dignity is now very rare. They are commonly spoken of as holding for life.

Nevertheless, in every court save one, if a sufficient number of the judges become obnoxious to the other branches of the Government, they can be got rid of. The Constitution provides that the judicial power "shall be vested in one Supreme Court, and in such inferior courts as the Congress may from time to time ordain and establish." As the Constitution has been practically construed, Congress may abolish an inferior court as well as establish it. This has actually been done in two noted instances. The first occurred in 1802. In the last weeks of the Federalist administration, a bench of United States Circuit Judges had been established by law, and had been filled by Federalist appointments. The political effect of this, so far as we may judge from the Congressional debates, had been overlooked in the excitement of the pending contest for the Presidency between Jefferson and Burr. The immense power which the Federal judges could exercise is construing the constitution and laws was, however, coming into general recognition, and the Republican party, on assuming the control of the legislative and executive branches of the Government, saw what a weapon had been placed, perhaps for a generation to come, in the hands of the opposition. The new judges could not be removed. The new court, therefore, was

---

[4] Fong Yue Ting *v.* United States, 149 U. S. 698, 729.

abolished, after a great constitutional debate. The judges united in a memorial protesting against the proceeding; but they were even denied a resort to *quo warranto*.[1] In 1863 a similar method was adopted for the purpose of getting rid of the judges of the United States Circuit Court for the District of Columbia. Again the constitutional question was raised in Congress. Some claim was made that this was only a territorial court, and, therefore, not protected by the judiciary article of the Constitution; but Senator Ira Harris of New York, who was in charge of the measure, and had himself long held high judicial office, put it squarely on the ground that Congress had the right to abolish any inferior court. The bar of the District protested; but the court was abolished, and the present Supreme Court of the District of Columbia, composed of new judges, took its place.

The Supreme Court of the United States was established by the Constitution itself, and therefore cannot be abolished. Its membership can be diminished only by voluntary retirement, by impeachment, or by death; thus giving Congress the power, as in 1866, to make the diminution permanent. Congress, however, may increase the membership, as was done in 1807, 1837 and 1869. In this respect it is similar to the highest British tribunal, the House of Lords. If popular feeling against its members or their decisions at any particular time become sufficiently strong, it can be "packed" by increasing its numbers sufficiently to control its vote. The House of Lords, although sometimes threatened, has not been actually "packed" for nearly two centuries; and the Supreme Court has never even been openly threatened, so far as I am aware, although it has been often charged that President Grant in effect "packed" the court in 1870 in order to obtain the overruling of one of its decisions, and although such an intent during the present year has been claimed to be hidden in the wording of the platform of one of the great political parties. The writer has elsewhere argued that the chief bulwark against this danger has been the general practice of the court in adhering to its decisions upon political questions notwithstanding changes of membership.[2] It is possible, however, that a man may sit for a while upon the Supreme Court as upon any inferior court, and yet be without the consti-

---

[1] Annals of Congress, January 27 and February 3, 1803, pp. 30-32, 51-78, 427-441.

[2] Political Dangers of the Income Tax Decision. "The Forum," July, 1895, p. 529.

tutional guaranty of independence. Whatever offices become vacant during a recess of the Senate, the President has power to fill "by granting commissions which shall expire at the end of their next session." Under this provision John Rutledge of South Carolina was appointed Chief-Justice of the United States Supreme Court by President Washington during a recess of the Senate, and actually presided at the August term, 1795. The Senate subsequently refused to confirm his nomination, some say on the ground of insanity, some say for political reasons. The precedent has been attacked as dangerous and as violating the spirit of the Constitution; but it has not infrequently been followed, at least in the case of inferior courts.

Space does not permit a discussion here of the limits within which the courts may interfere with Federal executive officers by *mandamus*, by injunction or otherwise. Curious questions have arisen as to how far Congress may go in imposing *quasi*-executive duties upon the judges. The first and second Congresses attempted to impose upon the Circuit Courts the duty of examining into applications for invalid pensions and reporting their conclusions thereon to the Secretary of War, to whom appellate jurisdiction was given. The judges held unanimously that such business was not judicial, and that the statutes were nullities.[1] Congress subsequently provided that the United States District Judge for Florida should adjudicate upon certain claims of the United States in that District, the adjudication, however, to be subject to review by the Secretary of the Treasury. The Supreme Court unanimously held that this was not judicial business, being "entirely alien to the legitimate functions of a judge or court of justice;" and that if the judge could properly act under the statute at all, he "could not act in a judicial character as a court nor as a commissioner." Grave doubt was expressed as to the constitutionality of the law, but this question was not presented and therefore not decided.[2]

Similar laws are now upon the statute book, and are administered by the judges without question. Thus it is common for a district judge to take evidence upon the question of good faith after the imposition of a penalty or forfeiture for violation of the tariff laws; his findings of fact being transmitted to the Secretary of the Treasury, who is not, however, bound thereby.[3] So,

---

[1] Hayburn's Case, *supra*; United States *v.* Yale Todd, 13 How. 52, note.

[2] United States *v.* Ferreira, 13 How. 40, 51.

[3] Anti-Moiety Act of June 22, 1874, §§ 17, 18.

also, the district judges often report the facts upon applications of district attorneys for compensation even for services rendered out of court.[10] Under a similar statute, however, whereby the judge is called upon to certify the value of an informer's services, subject to review by the Secretary of the Treasury, Judge Maxey of the Western District of Texas has recently held that the power attempted to be conferred is not judicial, and that the judges accordingly are without jurisdiction in the premises.[11] No attempt appears to have been made to obtain a review of this decision.

The Constitution itself recognizes, however, that the courts may properly perform duties of an executive nature, and accordingly provides expressly that Congress may vest in them "the appointment of such inferior officers as they think proper." The United States Commissioners and the Clerks of Court, who belong to the executive branch of the government, are appointed under this provision, and District Attorneys and Marshals receive in the same way *ad interim* appointments. A controversy recently arose over the right of Congress to call upon the judges to enforce the attendance of witnesses before administrative officers. In the lower courts the existence of this power was denied.[12] It was sustained, however, in 1894, in the Supreme Court by a vote of five to three in the case of the Interstate Commerce Commission.[13] Notwithstanding that decision, one of the district judges still maintained that he could not be required to enforce the attendance of witnesses before special examiners of the Pension Bureau, but the Supreme Court, on application of the Commissioner of Pensions, granted a writ of *mandamus* compelling him to do so.[14]

II. *Territorial Judges.*—The judicial power of the United States is placed by the Constitution in the hands of judges who "shall hold their offices during good behavior." Nevertheless the people of the Territories and the vast properties there situated are under the protection of judges who are appointed for four years only and who are removable by the President. This

---

[10] *In re* District Attorney, 23 Fed. Rep. 26; United States *v.* Bashaw, 152 U. S. 436.

[11] *Ex parte* Riebling, 70 Fed. Rep. 310.

[12] *In re* Pac. R. R. Commission, 32 Fed. Rep. 251; *In re* McLean, 37 Fed. Rep. 648; *In re* Interstate Commerce Commission, 53 Fed. Rep. 481.

[13] Interstate Commerce Commission *v.* Brimson, 154 U. S. 447.

[14] *In re* Lochren, 163 U. S. 692.

practice has existed since the earliest days, and has been repeatedly approved by the Supreme Court." These judges have been termed "legislative courts" as distinguished from "constitutional courts." Their existence is justified under that sweeping constitutional provision which gives to Congress "power to dispose of and make all needful rules and regulations respecting the territory or other property belonging to the United States." For the same reason that these judges are not protected with a life tenure, they are also not protected from the imposition of duties non-judicial in nature. They are not judges at all in the constitutional sense of the term, but are officers to whom are delegated such judicial powers as must necessarily be performed by somebody within the Territory.

A similar constitutional provision authorizes Congress "to exercise exclusive legislation in all cases whatsoever over such district (not exceeding ten miles square) as may by cession of particular States and the acceptance of Congress become the seat of the Government of the United States." It is an unsettled question whether it is this provision, or the judiciary article of the Constitution, which lies at the basis of the Supreme Court and the Court of Appeals of the District of Columbia. That District, unlike the Territories, is not in a mere period of transition, expecting soon to become a self-governing State. It has a large population, and that population ought to receive as complete protection as any other part of the Union. It ought, therefore, to be possible for Congress to establish a constitutional court in the District of Columbia, whose judges, like the judges of the other inferior Federal courts, can be removed from office only by the abolition of the court itself. There is much indication in the laws establishing these courts that Congress actually intended to accomplish this result.

A peculiar court recently established[16] for a temporary period has also an unsettled *status*. This is the Court of Private Land Claims, established for the ascertainment and confirmation, under the Treaty of Guadalupe Hidalgo, of Mexican land grants within the territories of New Mexico, Arizona and Utah, and the States of Nevada, Colorado and Wyoming. The law establishing the court provided that it should expire December 31, 1895, and the terms of the judges were to expire with the court. The court was given a limited term because the work for which it

---

[15] McAllister *v*. United States, 141 U. S. 174, and auth. cit.

[16] Act of March 3, 1891, c. 539.

was established was expected by that time to be completed. Doubts have been expressed as to the constitutionality of this legislation, especially with respect to the three States mentioned. Jurisdiction over the Territories has been sustained under the territorial clause of the Constitution." The writer is unable to perceive why it is not sustainable as to the States also. The court does not exercise that branch of judicial power which can be granted under the judiciary article of the Constitution alone. The cases which it adjudicates are claims against the United States, and are for the legislative branch of the Government to decide, unless the jurisdiction be deputed.[18] Moreover, the terms of the judges were made to run until the expiration of the court, and, since Congress can abolish inferior courts as well as institute them, there seems no reason why a court should not be instituted for a limited term, to dispose of some temporary class of business.

III. *Quasi-Judicial Officers.*—Chief-Justice Taney in his last opinion said: "The Constitution of the United States delegates no judicial power to Congress. Its powers are confined to legislative duties."[19] There is, however, a great deal of power in Congress which is judicial in its essence; the power, namely, to hear and decide claims against the United States itself. However complete may be the analogy between such claims and similar demands against an individual, they have never been regarded as coming within the judiciary article of the Constitution or the Bill of Rights.[20]

In early days such claims could only be presented to Congress, and always required special legislation. They are still adjudicated sometimes by a special act; but more often they are heard and decided by the forms of judicial procedure. For this purpose, in 1855 a judicial or *quasi*-judicial body was established by Congress under the name of the Court of Claims,[21] and its jurisdiction has since then from time to time been enlarged. Its judges, according to the terms of the statute, are to hold office during good behavior, but whether or not these statutory provisions are repealable is an undecided question. The tribunal might equally well have been styled the Board of Claims, and

---

[17] United States *v.* Coe, 155 U. S. 76.
[18] Astiazaran *v.* Santa Rita Land and Mining Co., 148 U. S. 80, and auth. cit.
[19] Gordon *v.* United States, 117 U. S. 697, 705.
[20] McElrath *v.* United States, 102 U. S. 426, 440.
[21] Act of Feb 24, 1855, ch. 122.

its members styled commissioners or auditors. In essence its work is nowise different from that of the accounting officers of the Treasury. As remarked by Chief-Justice Taney: "Neither of them possesses judicial power in the sense in which those words are used in the Constitution. The circumstance that one is called a court and its decisions called judgments cannot alter its character nor enlarge its power."[22] Yet, as already remarked, a hearing and decision by such a court is strictly judicial in nature when Congress does permit the United States to be sued; and when its decision is unreviewable by the executive it may be made reviewable by the superior courts. Hence, although the Chief-Justice rightly said that the Supreme Court's power "is exclusively judicial, and it cannot be required or authorized to exercise any other,"[23] nevertheless that court for thirty years past has had and constantly exercised power to review decisions of the Court of Claims when appealed; and by the recent Tucker Act[24] the Circuit and District Courts of the United States now exercise a jurisdiction concurrent with that of the Court of Claims. As the latter is not a constitutional court, it may be, and often is, charged with the duty of investigating questions of fact and law for the benefit of Congress or of executive officers, who are not bound to act upon its conclusions. Claims against the United States come commonly first before one of the Auditors of the Treasury; then on appeal before the Comptroller of the Treasury; then by petition before the Court of Claims or a Circuit or District Court; and, finally, before the Supreme Court or the Circuit Court of Appeals. It was recognized by Madison in the first Congress that such duties, when cast upon the Comptroller, are as judicial in nature as those of the courts, and for this reason he endeavored to obtain legislation giving the Comptroller a tenure during good behavior."[25]

Another *quasi*-judicial tribunal, passing upon questions as to which the United States is one of the parties interested, is the Board of General Appraisers sitting at New York. The decisions of this Board as to the valuation of imported goods are final; upon questions of classification they are subject to review by the courts. Their opinions are printed in the Treasury publication entitled "Synopsis of Decisions."

---

[22] Gordon *v.* United States, *supra*, at p. 699.
[23] *Ibid.* at p. 700.
[24] Act of March 3, 1887, c. 359.
[25] Annals of Congress, June 29, 1789, pp. 611, 614.

Other claims or *quasi*-claims against the United States, whose disposition is under the control of Congress, have been referred by general laws to executive officers, who decide them by judicial methods. Among the various classes of pecuniary claims against the Government, by far the largest number are claims for pensions. These arise from acts of Congress which are based upon the war power. They are passed upon by the Commissioner of Pensions, subject to review by the Secretary of the Interior. Congress also has the right to dispose of the public lands of the United States. This power, by general laws, has been deputed to the officers of the General Land Office, subject to review by the Secretary of the Interior. Claims to public lands based upon treaty provisions are sometimes placed by Congress in the hands of tribunals specially constituted, such as the well-known Board of Land Commissioners in California, and the Court of Private Land Claims above mentioned. Applications for letters patent by inventors are passed upon by the Commissioner of Patents, whose decisions thereon are not reviewable by any executive officer. The opinions rendered in pension, land and patent cases are regularly reported.

These powers have also been exercised directly by Congress itself through special legislation—including that of granting patents for inventions.[26] Yet even this power is so judicial in nature that a direct appeal is allowed from the decisions of the Commissioner to the courts of the District of Columbia;[27] or a bill in equity may be filed in any United States Court, in case the applicant is unsuccessful upon appeal, praying an adjudication that he is entitled to a patent.[28] Contrariwise, as has been already pointed out, rulings of the judges in similar instances have often been made reviewable by executive officers, and the constitutionality of such legislation has never yet been overthrown by a decision of the Supreme Court.

Decisions of these *quasi*-judicial officers, when acting within their jurisdiction, are, as a rule, unreviewable by the courts. They rank, however, no higher than the decisions of courts of limited jurisdiction, and when the officer has passed the bounds of his jurisdiction in rendering a decision, it is void or voidable.[29]

---

[26] Act of Jan. 21, 1808, c. 13.

[27] Act of Feb. 9, 1893, c. 74, § 9.

[28] Rev. St., § 4915; Gandy v. Marble, 122 U. S. 432.

[29] Noble v. Union River Logging R. R., 147 U. S. 165, 173; Mullan v. United States, 118 U. S. 271; Butterworth v. Hoe, 112 U. S. 50.

It is also binding only upon the claimant, the United States, and parties claiming under them. Thus, a person claiming prior title is not bound by decisions of the General Land Office, but may bring suit in equity to compel a conveyance of the land thus granted.[20]

In some of the bureaus at Washington these decisions are but nominally made by the officer to whom the case is confided by Congress. His signature stands for work performed entirely by the clerical force of his office. This is unavoidable. The work is so immense that it must be divided up among very many persons. Decisions are thus made by mere clerks which affect vast property interests and would well deserve the attention of high judicial tribunals. Systems of appeal within the departments for the same reason fail to effectuate their purpose. Thus the Attorney General, joined with the Secretary of the Interior, "acting as a board," was given certain appellate jurisdiction over the Commissioner of the General Land Office,[21] but through press of other business his personal attention is an absolute impossibility. A bill was recently introduced in Congress for a court of departmental appeals, that these cases might be actually decided by the men whose names are affixed to the decisions, and that these men should be of greater standing in the community; but it met with no favor.

The system of adjudication by clerks has reached its most formidable development in the Pension Office. All pension certificates are supposed to be over the signature of the Commissioner of Pensions, and in theory represent adjudications made by him as a special *quasi*-judicial tribunal. As a matter of fact, the work is done by an immense clerical force. Thus during the fiscal year ending June 30, 1892, the number of pension applications passed upon was 459,611. This represented about 1,500 for every working day, and, as the working day in Washington is only six and one-half hours long, represented one "adjudication" every fifteen seconds. In fact, the Commissioner did not even sign his name. It was affixed to the certificate by a rubber stamp. These clerical "adjudications," made largely upon *ex-parte* statements, have recently been much referred to with veneration such as is given to decrees of a Lord Chancellor. Bills have been pressed in Congress to render them unreviewable except upon proof of actual fraud, even this issue to be left to the slow

---

[20] Widdicombe v. Childers, 124 U. S. 400, 405.

[21] Rev. St., § 2451.

processes of an action at law. Claims have been pressed in the courts that the present legislation has this effect. A test case was decided adversely to this contention in June, 1895, by the Court of Appeals of the District of Columbia.[32] The decision came up for review in the Supreme Court of the United States, where Mr. James C. Carter appeared (as was understood) on behalf of the great organization known as the Grand Army of the Republic. Other important questions also were involved in the case. The Supreme Court ordered a reargument, and before it was again reached the proceeding abated by the appointment of the defendant, Commissioner Lochren, to the position of United States Judge for the District of Minnesota. No proceeding has been instituted against his successor, and this interesting question thus remains unsettled.

The limits of this article will not admit of further illustrations, but it is believed that enough has been said to show that the boundary between the executive and judicial work of the Government affords interesting ground for exploration.

Edward B. Whitney.

---

[32] Lochren v. Long, 6 App. Cas. D. C. 486.

SEEN AT THE JAMESON TRIAL.

The great State Trial was on. The witnesses for the Crown had willingly or unwillingly told with fatal certainty the story of Jameson's raid from organization to defeat. The relentlessly exact reports of the testimony had frayed the cloak of chivalry which public opinion had hung upon the shoulders of the accused, and the suspicion was gaining ground that the raid was a bold stroke for wealth planned and carried out in detail by selfishness and greed. The Boer witnesses nightly proclaimed the wrongs of the Transvaal in the smoking-rooms of the hotels. They openly asserted their belief that Jameson and his officers could not be convicted in an English court. Their distrust provoked them, and their self-confidence permitted them, to use the boldest language in discussing the situation in mixed gatherings. The Chief of the Transvaal Mounted Police had exclaimed to a company of Englishmen: "I hope Jameson will be acquitted! I hope he will be acquitted! Then the Transvaal will abrogate the Convention, and that will mean war with England! And we can defeat any army that England can send against us!"

Admission to the court room was only by invitation, or by card, issued in the name of the Lord Chief-Justice. A card was only good for one entrance. No more cards were issued in a day than there were seats in the court room. The pressure to obtain admittance was said to be great, the number of applications, unprecedented. If a professional member of the American contingent at that time in London was fortunate enough to have the doors of the court room opened to him, it was perhaps in this wise: A business-like note through the mail informed him that by permission of the Lord Chief-Justice of England, his Lordship's Secretary would give him a seat "on the bench" during the remainder of Dr. Jameson's trial at the bar.

To an American, to whom a seat on the bench by the courtesy of the judge is a thing almost unheard of and only to be mentioned with bated breath, the prospect might be deterrent. But the opportunity was not to be thrown away lightly, and the door of the Lord Chief-Justice's private room in the law courts was reached shortly before court opened. The private secretary was as business-like as possible He simply said, "Oh, yes;" and, stepping into a recess, pulled aside a portiere and pushed the visitor out into the full blaze of the footlights. He was on the bench. The court-room was already full. Counsel, defendants, peers, diplomats, ladies of high degree—all were expectant. A court attendant in a short black gown stepped up and gave the visitor a very small chair against the wall on the left of the Justices' desk and about twelve feet away from it. It was a seat on the dais—on the bench; but it was not with the Justices. No appalling dignity was thrust upon the occupant, who simply had the distinction of being the spectator who had the best seat. The dais reached the full length of the room. In the middle was the Justices' desk, on either side of which was a space of about fifteen feet in which were placed a dozen small folding chairs. These were "seats on the bench," reserved for guests of the presiding Justice—generally professional visitors. These private boxes, so to speak, were partially separated from the audience, on the one side, by a raised jury box, on the other, by a similar box for the stenographers, and the witness stand. The Master of the Crown had a small table in front of the Justices' desk. The entire remaining space was occupied by two rows of benches, narrow and straight-backed, like church pews, each with a narrow running desk-board in front of it. The two rows were separated by an aisle and the benches were placed on a slight incline, rising to the back of the room.

On the front bench on one side sat Dr. Jameson and his co-defendants; behind them were the senior counsel for the defense, backed by junior counsel, and behind these again were the juniors of the juniors—in all about eighteen lawyers. On the other side, the front bench was occupied by Treasury officials, behind whom were the counsel for the Crown—seniors, juniors and juniors of juniors—about eighteen in all.

Attorney-General Webster was the leader for the Crown. Sir Edward Clarke led for the defense. Every barrister in the room, including the onlookers, was black-gowned and wigged. There was no barrier or any mark of separation between the benches occupied by counsel and the benches in the rear occupied by the public. Facing the bench was a large gallery for the public. At one end was a small gallery reserved exclusively for distinguished ladies, guests of the Lord Chief-Justice. The entrance doors were kept locked and were carefully guarded by attendants in uniform, who stood on the outside. Light came exclusively from lofty sky-lights. The acoustic properties of the room were perfect.

At 10:30 a gowned attendant stepped on the bench and cried, "Silence!" Everyone rose to his feet and the portieres divided disclosing the three Justices, a vision in crimson. In profound silence the Justices advanced. Each was seated by an attendant, the Lord Chief-Justice in the middle, Mr. Baron Pollock on his right, and Mr. Justice Hawkins on his left. Everyone else then sat down. The scene was striking, impressive. In the background was a brilliant company of spectators; in the middle, the somber gathering of lawyers; in the foreground, the three mediæval crimson figures, calm and impassive, expressing, to an ideal degree, the embodiment of the Law—cold, relentless, implacable.

The costume of the Justices was a crimson robe falling straight to the heels, encircled at the waist by a voluminous silk sash. A cape of the same color just cleared the shoulders, and over this was a hood of grey silk. So far as could be seen, the only distinguishing mark in the costume of the Lord Chief-Justice was three small bows of narrow, scarlet ribbon, tacked to his hood. The wigs of the Justices were uniformly crimped. They were admirably adapted to lend severity to the features. The wigs of the barristers, on the other hand, softened the features. In these, the hair was drawn straight back from the forehead, curled in horizontal rolls at the back, and then brought together in a short queue, which was tied with a black ribbon.

Throughout the trial, the proceedings were mainly conducted by the leaders. Consultations among the seniors were frequent. Occasionally a junior leaned over and hazarded a suggestion in a whisper, but the youngest of counsel, who sat on the rear benches, apparently understood little of the details of the proceedings. They were all extremely youthful in appearance and were evidently associated in the case more for the name of the thing and as a matter of favor to them than for any support which they could give. There was no formal opening of court, only the announcement, deferentially made:

"My Lords: The Crown against Jameson and others."

The Attorney-General was on his feet between the benches. After calling one witness to prove certain entries in Dr. Jameson's diary, he announced that the Crown had completed its case with the exception of the proof that Pitsani Pitlogo, the place where the raid was planned, and Mafeking, the point from which the expedition started, were, or one of them was, within the limits of the British Empire, and that the operation of the Foreign Enlistment Act extended over these places. Then was read the

Act of Parliament authorizing the acquisition of new territory and prescribing the steps to be pursued in order to extend British sovereignty over new territory; that portion of the Foreign Enlistment Act which prescribed the conditions precedent to the operation of the act in new territory; and then were introduced exemplified copies of proclamations, treaties with native African chiefs, commissions, orders in council, and acts of the Legislature of Cape Colony, defining the status of British Bechuanaland (in which is Mafeking), and the territory immediately to the north, in which Pitsani Pitlogo is situated. Printed copies of these documents had previously been furnished to the Justices and to the defense. No time was lost in inspection or reading. By direction of the court the jury were simply told the character and purport of each document as it was offered.

The Crown announced closed. Sir Edward Clarke moved the discharge of the defendants upon the ground that no infringement of the Foreign Enlistment Act had been shown, inasmuch as it did not appear from the evidence that Mafeking and Pitsani Pitlogo were British territory, or that the Foreign Enlistment Act extended to Pitsani Pitlogo. His point was that a certain proclamation by the Governor of Cape Colony had not been made in accordance with the Act of Parliament. To state the point was to make the non-comformity apparent. It was a technicality which would have carried the day in most of the criminal courts of this country if proof of sovereignty *de jure* were required. But in England the quality of justice is not so strained.

Sir Edward Clarke's argument was an intellectual treat. It was a marvel of ingenuity, lucidity and logical strength. The speaker's voice was low and beautifully modulated; his tone, conversational; his manner, quiet but earnest. There were no gestures, nor was there any of the intenseness, the reaching after effect, so characteristic of American oratory.

The Attorney-General's reply was a strong argument; but he closed with an appeal to common sense. This gave Sir Edward Clarke, in his concluding argument, a chance for a thrust. He said that whenever a man failed to understand the point at issue he always appealed to common sense. This was the Lord Chief-Justice's opportunity, which he improved thus, by way of interruption:

"Yes; I have always understood that common sense had nothing to do with a point of law." At which the barristers all smiled dutifully.

The motion was overruled by the court in a masterly opinion by the Lord Chief-Justice in which he refuted the arguments of Sir Edward Clarke. The Associate Justices concurred, but Mr. Baron Pollock alone gave his reasons. He utterly disregarded the arguments of Sir Edward Clarke, and his opinion could be summed up thus:

"We are only concerned with the question, Does British sovereignty extend over these places? not How was that sovereignty acquired?

The defense had no evidence to offer, and court adjourned to give time for the preparation of the arguments to the jury. Throughout the day's proceedings, three things could not fail to attract the attention of an American lawyer—the impassive demeanor of the Justices; the extreme deference and respect exhibited by counsel to the Court; and the absence of bustle, the perfect order and quiet maintained in the court room.

The arguments to the jury can not be summarized here. *De jure* sovereignty over Mafeking and Pitsani Pitlogo was argued as matter of fact, as were *de facto* sovereignty and the operation of the Foreign Enlistment Act. Then, marking a new era in international law, came the charge of the Court by the Lord Chief-Justice, at the conclusion of which he propounded to the jury seven questions, six of which related to the acts of the defendants, while the seventh left to the jury the question of sovereignty *de facto* over Pitsani Pitlogo. Sir Edward Clarke endeavored to interpose an objection to the propounding of these questions, but he was silenced in the most peremptory manner by the Lord Chief-Justice, who said that he would permit no interruption at that stage. The jury were then told that they were only requested by the court to answer the questions; they could not be compelled to answer them. They could, if they chose, bring in a general verdict of guilty or not guilty; but, in refusing to answer the questions, they would be assuming a grave responsibility, inasmuch as questions of law were involved.

There was a tightening of lips and a holding of breath as the jury filed back to their seats with averted eyes. As each question was read to the foreman and his answer came adverse to the defendants, a shocked expression plainly grew on the faces of the audience. It was the realization that hopes were baffled, that the worst had come.

By direction of the Court the jury then rendered a general verdict of guilty, but they coupled with it a recommendation to mercy in the shape of a rider: "The jury consider that the state of affairs in Johannesburg presented great provocation."

The Justices retired to give the defense time for deliberation. There was an earnest exchange of views between prisoners, counsel and friends. The spectators were too stunned for discussion, but the whole place was instinct with silent questionings: Is it final? Is there no possibility of a new trial? Can there be no appeal?

The Justices returned and amazement succeeded consternation when Sir Edward Clarke announced that the defendants had determined to accept the verdict and to submit to the judgment of the Court.

"Let the defendants stand up," said the Lord Chief-Justice; and five men with faces typical of a dominant race, came to their feet. The voice was as impassive as ever; but the arraignment was terrible. The waste of human life, the private sufferings, the public wrong committed in endangering the peace of nations, the aggravation of the offense by reason of the high social position, the superior education and intelligence of the accused, and the official character of some of them—all these were pointed out. And then came the sentences of imprisonment, ringing down the curtain on the last act of the tragedy. Foreign wrath was appeased; English Law was vindicated.

John Wurts.

YALE LAW JOURNAL

SUBSCRIPTION PRICE, $2.00 A YEAR   SINGLE COPIES, 35 CENTS

EDITORS:

ROGER S. BALDWIN, *Chairman.*
HUGH T. HALBERT, *Treasurer.*

CHRISTOPHER L. AVERY, JR.   HENRY W. MERWIN,
MICHAEL GAVIN, 2D.   JOHN MACGREGOR, JR.
GEO. JAY GIBSON,   SAMUEL F. BEARDSLEY.

Published six times a year, by students of the Yale Law School
P. O. Address, Box 1341, New Haven, Conn.

If a subscriber wishes his copy of the JOURNAL discontinued at the expiration of his subscription, notice to that effect should be sent; otherwise it is assumed that a continuance of the subscription is desired.

SELDOM has the mission of political parties been so clearly defined; seldom have Politics and Patriotism been more widely separated than in the present presidential campaign. Political parties as the means by which the people may express their will deserve the highest respect and honor; but political parties as the demagogic leaders of unwilling constituents should be regarded with the greatest distrust. The reason and excuse for party organizations are the advantages which they present for expressing and enforcing the will of the people. They are political instruments and nothing more. Their mission is to bring out the main question in issue, to harmonize as far as possible minor differences in order to unite upon a great principle, and, in a word, to subordinate the less to the greater. So long as this is the limit of their authority and so long as their members are united on the great question in issue, so long do these organizations deserve support. But when disagreements are not on minor but on major points, not on details but on principles, then the excuse and reason for their existence are gone and *cessante ratione, cessat ipsa lex*. Duty to party in this campaign is of a very peculiar character, but if duty to party is placed above duty to principle the future of democratic government is by no means certain.

*

ONE of the avowed objects of bi-metallism is to secure as far as possible an unchanging standard of values for the payment of long contracts. Dissatisfaction with the present gold standard is expressed by bi-metallic advocates because of an alleged appreciation of gold in the past and because of their fear of a further and greater appreciation in the future. If the volume of the present gold standard were enlarged by the addition of silver it is claimed that an increase or reduction in the total amount of the two metals would be less noticeable and less productive of a change in their relative values than a corresponding increase or reduction in the volume of a single standard, while a demand for one would cause such an abatement in the supply of the other as to bring the value of the two metals together.

In applying this theory to the United States it appears that the evil has been exaggerated and that the remedy is worse than the evil. The appreciation of gold, according to statistics, has been very small, if at all. Wages are higher than they used to be, and products, eliminating the results due to increased competition and improved facilities for transportation, sell for practically as much to-day as they did when silver was demonetized. On the other hand, silver has most certainly depreciated, and during the last twenty years has fallen to about one-half its former value. The proposed remedy, then, for this ephemeral evil, is the addition of a depreciated and depreciating metal to an approximately unchanging measure of values in order to render the latter more constant. There can be little doubt as to the result of this plan if adopted.

But without becoming liable to a charge of perversion or misstatement of facts it may be most fairly asserted that the appreciation of gold, if there has been any, has been much less than the depreciation of silver, and while it is most difficult to make out even a *prima facie* case for the former theory, it is apparent to all that silver has had a tremendous fall. Regarding then the subject in this light and assuming that it is possible for these two metals to circulate side by side, on a bi-metallic basis, we are even then forced to admit that the standard of values as it would exist under bi-metallism would be far more changing than the standard of values under the present system. If during the past twenty years our standard had consisted of two metals, one of which had appreciated an almost inappreciable amount, while the other had depreciated to almost half it former value, it is certain that the fluctuation in the value of our medium of exchange would have been far greater even than that fluctuation which is claimed to have taken place by the enemies of the present standard. Long contracts made in the past would be paid in a medium of exchange whose numerical value had remained the same, but whose real value had greatly fallen, while long contracts, payable in the future, would be made with the greatest temerity or, most likely, not at all. The plan of bi-metallism which this country is urged to adopt is as reasonable as would be an attempt to purify a stream of water by making it a repository for sewage. An aggravation of the very evil which bi-metallism aims to avoid would be the first result of its adoption.

*

ONE of the fundamental doctrines of our Government finds expression in the separation of its legislative and judicial departments; one of the greatest safeguards of our highest judicial tribunal is the principle of life tenure. And yet the platform of one of our political parties in the present campaign declares that it is "opposed to life tenure in the public service," and urges Congress to use "all constitutional power" to cause the reversal of one of the United States Supreme Court decisions.

The conditions, of which these expressions are evidence, are even more serious than the money question, for while the latter is a question of policy the former is a question of constitutional and national integrity. It may be argued that the clauses directed against our highest judicial authority are not now endorsed, that if the Chicago platform were to be revised these clauses would not be incorporated in the new edition, and that they would have been rejected before the adoption of the platform had it not been for the all-pervading haste that characterized the convention which gave them birth. But these reassurances do not reassure. According to the principle that a written instrument should be construed as a whole we must look to the entire platform as adopted for a full expression of its principles. The discharge of an obligation by a payment only half as large as contracted for is regarded lightly, if not endorsed. The use of federal powers to enforce federal rights is discouraged and denounced. A method of taxation, which has been declared unconstitutional, is recommended, and the revolutionary principle adopted that if the court's judgment does not coincide with their wishes, they will take means to change the judges, the means being another unconstitutional measure, the abolition of life tenure.

Such is the document which we are told to receive as our articles of political faith and to endorse as an expression of our principles! The disposition of this document, taken as a whole, is undoubtedly antagonistic to honest and conservative government, and a menace to the peace and good order of society, while the spirit which pervades it compels the belief that its result if not its aim would be to impair the integrity of the Supreme Court of the United States.

THOSE who have heretofore depreciated the power and value of public speaking at the present day, must by this time be thoroughly convinced of their error. The occurrences of the past few months have certainly demonstrated that masses may still be controlled by the force of one man's individuality, and have caused the fables concerning the achievements of Greek and Roman orators to seem less fabulous and more real than before. The nomination of the Presidency of the United States and the Republican gubernatorial nomination of New York State were both mainly obtained by reason of an ability to say what others had often thought but had seldom so well expressed. No peculiar power besides that of public speech was necessary, no learning but that possessed by average educated men. The toil and success of years counted as little when weighed against the inspiration and impulse of the moment. Few better examples of the force and power of public speaking, whether for the good or for the bad, could be found. If this force is used for the good, no one can gainsay its usefulness; if used for the bad, there should be an equal force to oppose it. The opportunities in the Law School for public debate are many and by those who hope to practice in the courts or to enter public life they should be most highly prized and zealously cultivated. The recent success of Yale in debating was due to persistent and hard work; the success of the individual has been and will be due to the same causes.

THE extension of the course at the Yale Law School from two to three years marks a stage in its progress. It is not only that a degree from its faculty is hereby made more valuable but it is also evidence that the resources of the graduate and undergraduate departments have been developed and increased. The advisability, however, of pursuing the three years' course or of combining the work so as to graduate in two years must depend mainly upon the circumstances and the individual. To the Junior class the JOURNAL offers its congratulations upon the increased opportunities which they are to enjoy and hopes that their relation to the school will be as instructive and profitable as has been that of their predecessors. To those Seniors who expect to practice law in the State of New York the course on New York Practice offered by Mr. Charles W. Pierson will be most necessary and valuable.

* * *

WE note with pleasure the nomination of the chairman of the last editorial board of the JOURNAL for Judge of Probate for the District of Stamford, Connecticut, on the Republican ticket. As a lawyer and as a man Mr. Taylor stood high in the estimation of the faculty and of his fellow students, and we feel certain that he will prove worthy of any confidence, public or private, which may be placed in him. His election would be a cause for congratulation to the Law School and to his constituents.

COMMENT.

When a witness refuses to answer a question upon the ground that it will tend to incriminate him the question often arises as to who shall determine whether his answer will have this effect, and the case of *Ex parte Irwine*, 74 Fed. Rep. 954, recently decided by the United States Circuit Court rules upon this point.

In a trial upon indictment for violating interstate commerce laws, the witness refused to answer several questions and was committed to jail for contempt of court. He applied for a writ of habeas corpus and in rendering judgment the Circuit Court stated that it would be subversive of every principle of right and justice to allow a witness to evade answering a question upon the bare statement that his answer would tend to incriminate him, and held that "it is for the trial judge to decide whether an answer to the question put may reasonably tend to incriminate the witness, or furnish proof of a link in the chain of evidence necessary to convict him of a crime. It is not enough that the answer may furnish evidence which upon some imaginary hypothesis would supply the missing link, but it must appear to the court from the character of the question and other facts adduced in the case, that there is some tangible and substantial probability that the answer of the witness may help to convict him of a crime. If once the fact of his being in danger be made to appear, great latitude should be allowed him in judging for himself the effect of any particular answer, and if he says upon oath that he cannot answer without accusing himself, he cannot be compelled to do so."

The very interesting and important question of the effect of endorsement of bills to fictitious persons, recently came before the Supreme Court of Tennessee, in *Chism, et al.*, v. *Bank* (36 S. W. R. 387). The facts were as follows: A firm of cotton factors innocently issued and endorsed a draft to a fictitious person or order, whom their warehouseman fraudulently represented to them to be a real person and consignor of cotton. The warehouseman, using the name of the fictitious person, indorsed the draft to himself or order, collected it and absconded. On discovering the fraud practiced the drawer sued the defendant bank for wrongful appropriation of the the draft and refusal to account for the proceeds.

It seems from a note to Bayles Bills, page 179, that the controversy over the effect of endorsement of bill to fictitious persons grew out of the bankruptcy of Linsay & Co. and Gibson & Co., London merchants, who negotiated bills with fictitious names upon them to the amount of nearly a million sterling a year. A great many cases grew out of these endorsements in the various courts of England, one of which, *Meriet* v. *Gibson* (1789), 3 Term. R. 481, was carried to the House of Lords. But in all those cases the drafts were *purposely* drawn in favor of non-existing parties, and the decision established the doctrine (which has been followed in subsequent cases) that where the drawer or maker of a bill of exchange knows that the payee is a fictitious person at the time he makes the draft, a bona fide holder may recover on it against him as upon a bill *payable to bearer* (*Satlock* v. *Harris*, 3 Term. R. 174; *Gibson* v. *Hunter*, 2 H. Bl. 187).

But where the drawer innocently issues or endorses the draft in favor of a fictitious person, believing him to be real, as in the case at hand (36 S. W. R. 389), another element is introduced into the controversy. The questions arising out of the case and submitted to the Supreme Court of Tennessee have arisen and been discussed in but few of the American courts, and the conclusions reached by them have been various. Some of the authorities hold that it will be no defense against a bona fide holder for the maker or drawer to set up that he did not know the payee to be fictitious, even though he was free from any negligence in drawing or making the draft. Others hold that it is a defense where drawer or maker was ignorant of the non-existence of the payee, provided that drawer was guilty of no negligence.

On the one hand, in this country, among text writers, Mr. Daniel states the rule as general that, "In the case of a note payable to a fictitious person it appears to be well settled that any bona fide holder may recover on it against the maker, as upon a note *payable to bearer*. It will be no defense against such a bona fide holder for the maker to set up that he did not know the payee to be fictitious." The case of *Kohn* v. *Watkins*, 26 Kansas 691, involved the precise questions which were brought up in the Tennessee case, and the Kansas court followed the authority of Mr. Daniel. Hatton, C. J., in his opinion, said: "When a drawer issues a bill to a fictitious payee, although ignorant of that fact at the time, and parts with the possession thereof, ought he, in fairness and justice, be allowed to say that such bill is void?" Where one of two innocent parties must suffer from the wrongful or tortious acts of a third party, the law casts the burden or loss upon him by whose act, omission or negligence such third party was enabled to commit the wrong which occasions the loss" (*Bank* v. *Rld. Co.*, 20 Kan. 520) All of these cases hold that the drawer is estopped from setting up as a defense that he did not know such payee to be fictitious (*Cooper* v. *Mayer*, 10 B. & C. 468; *Schutz* v. *Astley*, 2 Bing. N. C. 544).

Upon the other hand we have several well-considered cases which in effect adopt the English rule, to wit, that only such paper as is issued to a fictitious payee or endorsee by the party sought to be bound, with full knowledge of the fact, shall be treated as payable to bearer. This seems to be the better law, and was followed by the Tennessee courts.

Supporting this view in *Armstrong* v. *Broadway Nat. Bk.*, 22 N. E. R. 866, it was held: "Where by the fraud of a third person a depositor of a bank is induced to draw his draft payable to a non-existing person or order, the drawer being in ignorance of the fact and intending no fraud, the bank on which the draft is so drawn is not authorized to pay it, and charge the amount to the account of its customer, on the endorsement of the party presenting it, although it appears to have been previously endorsed by the party named as payee. Such endorsement is in effect a forgery, and the payments thereon by the bank confers no right on it as against the drawer of the draft." In this case the authorities are carefully reviewed. See, also, the cases of *Dodge* v. *Bank*, 20 Ohio St. 234; *Shipman* v. *Bank*, 27 N. E. 371; *Byles* on *Bills*, p. 82; *Forbes* v. *Epsy*, 21 Ohio St. 483.

O'Brien, J., in one of the cases, says: "The maker's intention is the controlling consideration which determines the character of such paper. It cannot be treated as payable to bearer unless the maker knows the payee to be fictitious and actually intends to make the paper payable to a fictitious person."

A bank holds a depositor's funds to be paid out to such persons as the depositor directs. It is its duty to pay to the person named or his order, and to withhold payment until it is satisfied as to the identity of the payee and the genuineness of his signature (Morse. Bank, Sec. 474). If a bank pursues any other course it does so at its own peril.

It is a saying frequently repeated in "The Doctor and the Student," says Minshall, C. J., that "he who loveth peril shall perish in it." In other words, where a person has a safe way, and abandons it for one of uncertainty, he can blame no one but himself if he meets with misfortune.

RECENT CASES.

CONSTITUTIONAL LAW.

Impairment of Contracts—Extending Time for Redemption—State, ex rel., Thomas Cruse Sav. Bank v. Gilliam, Sheriff, 45 Pac. Rep. 661 (Mont.). An act extending the time for redemption of premises sold under mortgage, as applied to mortgages executed before its passage, impairs the obligation of the contract, and is unconstitutional.

Interstate Commerce—Norfolk & W. R. Co. v. *Commonwealth,* 24 S. E. Rep. 837 (Va.). A state may in order to secure and protect the lives or health of its citizens, or to preserve good order and the public morals, legislate for such purposes, in good faith, and without discrimination against interstate or foreign commerce, without violating the commerce clause of the constitution of the United States, although such legislation may sometimes touch, in its exercise, the line separating the respective domains of National and State authority, and to some extent affect foreign and interstate commerce. A state law prohibiting the running of freight trains on Sunday is such legislation and does not conflict with the interstate commerce clause of the federal constitution.

CRIMINAL LAW.

Burglary—Breaking.—Pressley v. *State,* 20 South. Rep. 647 (Ala.). Where a building is made of logs and rests upon the ground without a floor other than the ground itself, digging a hole under the lower log and thus entering the house is a breaking sufficient for the crime of burglary.

Homicide—Dying Declaration.—State v. *Parham,* 20 So. Rep. 727 (La.). A declaration made by a person with full consciousness of approaching death which has been reduced to writing by his attending physician, signed by the declarant and his signature attested by a Justice of the Peace, is admissible in evidence as a dying declaration.

INSURANCE.

External, Violent and Accidental Means—Exceptions of Policy.— American Accident Co. of Louisville v. *Carson.* 36 S. W. Rep. 169

(Ky.). A person who is unexpectedly shot by another without cause or provocation is injured by "external, violent, and accidental means," and a policy insuring against such injuries which provides that it shall not cover intentional "injuries" inflicted by the insured or any other person refers only to non-fatal injuries.

Condition of Policy—Waiver by Agent, what Constitutes—Forfeiture—Reinstatement.—Concordia Ins. Co. v. *Johnson,* 45 Pacific Rep. 722. A general agent of a company issuing a policy may waive its conditions, although the policy denies him that power. To constitute a waiver there must be more than mere knowledge on part of the agent. His language and conduct must be such as to reasonably imply an intention on his part to consent to the improper use of the insured property. If policy is void on account of the breach of its condition, it is not reinstated and made effective by the mere fact that conditions are complied with again before the loss occurred.

RAILROAD COMPANIES.

Carriers of Passengers—Ejectment from Car.—McGhee, et al., v. *Drisdale.* 20 South. Rep. 391. Action brought for damages alleged to have been sustained by reason of being put off a train. A passenger, offering an expired ticket as fare, was told by conductor that he would have to pay his way. Upon refusing to do so, he was gently led from the car, but returned and paid his fare. Evidence tended to show that the passenger had knowledge of time limit indorsed on back of ticket before purchasing it, and of the fact that it was out of date. Court held he had no cause of action against the railroad company.

Carriers—Ejection of Person from Train—Declarations of Brakeman.—Lyons v. *Texas & P. Ry. Co.,* 36 S. W. Rep. 1007 (Tex.). A person was forced to jump from a rapidly moving train at the point of a pistol presented by the brakeman who, at the same time, said, "The boss ordered me to put you off," and was injured. The declaration of the brakeman was held inadmissible to prove that the passenger was put off by the order of the conductor as being against the theory upon which declarations are admissible as part of the *res gestæ.*

Carriers—Wagonway in Freight Yard—Negligence.—Curtis v. *De Coursey,* 35 Atl. Rep. 183 (Pa.). The duty which a railway company owes to persons delivering or receiving freight in the care of a passageway for wagons from the public highway to its freight yard does not differ from that which it owes to passengers in the care of its platforms and stations. Such persons do not enter and use the yard by the mere permission or passive acquiescence of the company. They are there by invitation, in its technical sense, and by right. A passageway for wagons must therefore be kept in a reasonably safe condition.

Street Railroads—Injuries to Passenger—Negligence—Alighting from Moving Car.—McDonald v. *Montgomery St. Ry.*, 20 Southern Rep. 317. The plaintiff in attempting to get off a moving car was injured and brought suit to recover damages The court held that a passenger jumping from a car in motion assumes the risk of alighting safely and cannot recover for injuries unless they were occasioned solely by the defendant.

Railroads—Crossings—Injuries—Contributory Negligence—Willful Negligence.—Birmingham Railway and Electric Co. v. *Bowers*, 20 South Rep. 345. A deaf person crossing a railroad track by way of a path used for public convenience, is guilty of negligence by not looking out for approaching train. An engineer running a train at a rapid rate of speed is justified in thinking that a person whom he sees in the path some distance from and approaching the track will not attempt to cross in front of the train, so that his failure to attempt to stop the train until it is too late to prevent it striking such person will not constitute willful negligence.

MISCELLANEOUS.

Injunction—Scope of Order—Violation.—Jeweler's Mercantile Agency, Limited, v. *Rothschild, et al.*, 39 N. Y. Supp. 700. Injunction granted to restrain defendants from using previous as well as subsequent publications of the plaintiff. Plaintiff's business consisted in obtaining information with regard to the names, places of business, etc., as to individuals, firms, etc., in the jewelry trade for the benefit of their subscribers. The interest in the case lies in the fact that this is a different situation than that where a person is restrained from using the literary property of an author. These reports were not literary works. Court held that a fine of nearly $2,000 and imprisonment for two months was not excessive.

Exemptions—Tools of Trade.—Davidson v. *Hannon, et al.*, 34 Atl. Rep. 1050 (Conn.). Where a statute exempts "implements of the debtor's trade" from attachment, and a liberal construction in favor of the debtor has been adopted, a photographer may be considered as engaged in a trade and a photographic lens used by him in his business will be exempt.

Partnership—When Relation Exists.—*Winne* v. *Brundage, et al.*, 40 N. Y. Supp. 225. Defendant and R. entered into an agreement whereby the latter agreed to negotiate the sale of the defendant's promissory notes, receiving as compensation a commission, a brokerage, and 25 per cent of the net profits of the defendant's business. R. was to have no part in the management of the business, and his share in the profits was to cease when his employment terminated. Held, that this agreement did not create a partnership, so as to render R. liable for debts incurred by the defendant in the business.

Assignment for Benefit of Creditors—Estoppel to Claim.—*In re Sawyer, et al*, 40 N.Y. Supp. 294. A firm doing business in New York made an assignment there, and on the following day a Tennessee creditor, without notice of the assignment and before its registration in Tennessee, attached property of the firm in Tennessee. This attachment was sustained on the ground that the assignment had not taken effect on the property attached. Held, that inasmuch as the attachment was not in hostility to the assignment the creditor was not estopped from claiming a share of the assigned estate, but was entitled only to the balance of his *pro rata* share after deducting the amount realized on the attachment.

Charitable Institutions—What Constitutes—Exemptions from Taxation.—*City of Louisville* v. *Southern Baptist Theological Seminary*, 36 S. W. Rep. 995 (Ky.). Under a constitutional provision exempting from taxation "institutions of purely public charity," an institution confessedly a pure charity is also purely public although the management and organization are private and denominational, provided no one is excluded by reason of denominational connection or preference.

Conditional Sale—Rights of Seller—Forfeiture of Payments.—*Vaughn, et al.*, v. *McFadyen*, 68 N. W. Rep. 135 (Mich.). When property is sold with the agreement that the title shall remain in the seller until the full price is paid, and in case of default in payment, the property may be taken back by the seller and all payments made shall be deemed payments for its use, although the seller elects to take the property after default, he cannot refuse to accept the amount due until he has taken actual possession.

Municipal Corporations—Rejection of Bid—Liability to Bidder.—Talbot Paving Co. v. City of Detroit, 67 N. W. Rep. 979 (Mich.). Where a city charter requires contracts to be awarded to the lowest bidder this provision is for the protection of the public and not for the benefit of the bidder. Hence, the lowest bidder under such a contract, whose bid is rejected, has no right of action against the city for profits which he might have made had his bid been accepted.

Limitation of Actions—Waiver.—State Trust Co. v. Sheldon, et al., 35 Atl. Rep. 177 (Vt.). The maker of a note may, at the time of its execution, waive the statute of limitations. In which case he will be estopped from setting up the statute as a defense. This is an exception to the general rule that no contract or agreement can modify a law and is valid because no principle of public policy is violated, the statute being designed for the benefit of individuals.

Life Tenant—Room in House—Eviction—Measure of Damages.—Grove v. Yonell, 68 N. W. Rep. 132 (Mich.). A bond recited that the defendant, being indebted to the plaintiff for certain lots, would pay a stated sum within a certain time, and that the plaintiff might "occupy any room that is in the house on said lots during the remainder of her natural life." The plaintiff selected a room and took possession of it. Afterwards she was asked by the defendant to take a room in another part of the city, and refused. Whereupon, the defendant leased the house and grounds for a term of years without any reservation of the plaintiff's room, and during the plaintiff's absence told the lessee she might use the room. Upon the plaintiff's return the lessee refused to allow her to go to her room. Held, that there was an eviction of the plaintiff by procurement of the defendant, and that the measure of damages from the date of eviction to the commencement of the action was the fair rental value of the room, and after that the rental value computed on the expectation of life of the plaintiff as based upon the mortality tables.

BOOK NOTICES.

Handbook on the Law of Torts. By William B. Hale, LL.B., author of "Bailments and Carriers," "Damages," etc. Law sheep, 636 pages. West Publishing Co., St. Paul, Minn., 1896.

The list of text books on the subject of Torts has received an exceedingly valuable addition in this work of Mr. Hale's, one of the most recent of the "Hornbook Series." Though written, as the author states in his preface, merely as an abridgement in a single volume of the more extended treatise of Mr. Jaggard, the language and mode of treatment in many parts are the writer's own. This is true especially of the chapters on "Negligence" and "Master and Servant," which are exceedingly well written. The tendency of the entire book is toward clearness and accuracy in the statement of the legal principles involved, and the effect of this is supplemented by the typographical arrangement common to all the "Hornbook Series," the principles being printed in conspicuous bold-faced type, and the discussion and explanation of these in ordinary print. The notes and references are copious, and conflicting authorities carefully indicated wherever they occur.

The Law of Passenger and Freight Elevators. By James Avery Webb of the St. Louis and Memphis Bars. Half law sheep, 128 pages. The F. H. Thomas Law Book Co., St. Louis, Mo., 1896.

Mr. Webb, who is already well known to the legal profession as the editor of the last edition of "Burrill on Assignments," "Pollock on Torts," and "Smith on Negligence," has produced a very instructive monograph on the law of elevators. The subject is concisely and yet fully treated, and the volume forms a complete digest of the existing law in respect to this class of carriers. At the end of the book is a collection of the statutory provisions in the different States regulating the construction and operation of elevators.

Studies in the Civil Law. By William Wirt Howe, formerly Justice of the Supreme Court of Louisiana. Cloth, 329 pages. Little, Brown & Co., Boston, Mass., 1896.

Judge Howe, while occupying the position of W. L. Storrs Professor of Municipal Law in Yale University in the year 1894, delivered a very able series of lectures on the study of the Civil Law, and on its connection with English and American law. These lectures he has revised and expanded and published for the first time in book form. The first part of the volume is devoted to the historical side of the subject, treating of the early condition of the Civil Law and its influence in England. Next is taken up the more technical part, the origin and the extinguishment of "obligations"; then the Roman mode of procedure is dealt with, and the book closes with an interesting and beautifully written sketch of the famous Louisiana jurist, Judge Martin. This group of lectures will be of great advantage to those beginning the study of the Civil Law, and the value of the work is enhanced by the fact that it is from the pen of so eminent an authority.

Elements of the Law of Torts. By Melville M. Bigelow, Ph.D., LL.D. Cloth, 386 pages. Little, Brown & Co., Boston, Mass., 1896.

It gives us great pleasure to note the appearance of the sixth edition of Mr. Bigelow's well-known work on Torts. It is written in the same careful style as the former editions and with the same broad treatment of the subject. The author in the first part of the book starts with the consideration of a tort as a breach of a duty owing by one to his fellows, and in the remainder of the volume classes all torts under three heads: breaches of the duty to refrain from fraud or malice; breaches of absolute duty, and breaches of the duty to refrain from negligence. This arrangement allows the student a view of the entire subject at the outset, and reduces to a minimum the difficulties attendant upon the study of so intricate a subject.

Jurisdiction, Practice, and Peculiar Jurisprudence of the Courts of the United States. By Benjamin Robbins Curtis, LL.D. Cloth, 316 pages. Little, Brown & Co., Boston, Mass., 1896.

The second edition of this work of Judge Curtis is the result of a careful revision and annotation of the former edition, which was rendered necessary by the changes in the United States Statutes in regard to jurisdiction and procedure in the Federal Courts. Though it is intended primarily for students the book will undoubtedly be of great assistance to the skilled practitioner on account of its accuracy of statement and its broad scope, which make it a most reliable index to this branch of the law.

The Law of Charitable Uses. Trusts, and Donations in New York. By Robert Ludlow Fowler. Law sheep, 198 pages. The Diossy Law Book Co., New York, 1896.

Mr. Fowler has traced the course of the law of charitable donations from its origin in England through all its changes until it reached its present condition under the laws of New

York State. Every step in its growth has been distinctly noted, and the whole subject is handled with unusual skill. The treatise provides the reader with an immense amount of information both as to the historical aspect and as to the present state of the law on these points.

International Law. By Freeman Snow, Ph.D., LL.B., late instructor in International Law in Harvard University. Law sheep, 172 pages. Government Printing Office, Washington, D. C., 1895.

The course of lectures on International Law delivered by Dr. Snow at the Naval War College in 1894 was so valuable that it was ordered by the Secretary of the Navy to be revised and published. The book is intended chiefly for naval officers, but will reward richly a perusal of its pages by the civilian.

Handbook on the Law of Persons and Domestic Relations. By Walter C. Tiffany. Law sheep, 512 pages. The West Publishing Co., St. Paul, Minn., 1896.

The last publication in the "Hornbook Series" is fully up to the high standard set by former issues. Mr. Tiffany has handled the subject in an able and systematic manner. In four parts out of the five into which the book is divided he treats at length of the rights and duties growing out of the four domestic relations. The fifth part has been supplied by Mr. William L. Clark, Jr., and in it are discussed the subjects of Infants, Persons Non Compotes Mentis, and Aliens. The whole forms a most valuable treatise on the subject.

A Treatise on the Law of Personal Property. By James Schouler, LL.D., Professor in the Boston University Law School. Law sheep, two volumes, 732 and 720 pages. Little, Brown & Co., Boston, Mass., 1896.

Dr. Schouler has already made valuable contributions to modern legal literature by his treatises on Domestic Relations, Bailments, Executors and Wills. The first edition of his work on Personal Property filled a want long felt by the legal profession of a text-book dealing with that subject in the same thorough and exhaustive way in which many books have treated of Real Property. The third edition has been produced lately under the personal supervision of the author, and shows in every part the skill of the veteran text writer. The foot notes contain an unusually complete and extensive compilation of cases and decisions of the courts of last resort. We predict for the book in its present form increased popularity and success.

MAGAZINE NOTICES.

The Green Bag, August, 1896.

    William Sampson Grant (with portrait), . . Irving Browne.
    A Tribunal Under the Terror, ... George H. Westley.
    Spes (verse), ... John Albert Macy.
    The English Law Courts, VI. The Ecclesiastical Courts.
    An Astral Partner (concluded), . . Hon. A. W. Tourgee.
    The Ordeal of Battle.
    The Lawyer's Easy Chair, ... Irving Browne.

September, 1896.

    Sergeant Smith Prentiss (with portrait), . . A. Oakey Hall.
    Female Gamblers, ... Andrew T. Sibbald.
    The English Lawyer in English Public and Social Life, Edward Porritt.
    The English Law Courts (illustrated): VII. The Probate
        and Admiralty Division; VIII. The County Courts.
    The Courts at Bar.
    London Legal Letter.
    The Lawyer's Easy Chair, . . , . . Irving Browne

October, 1896.

    McKinley and Bryan as Lawyers (with portraits), . A. Oakey Hall.
    The Trial of Dr. Jameson in its Legal Aspect.
    The Muswell Hill Murder.
    The English Law Courts (illustrated), IX. Courts of
        Criminal Jurisdiction.
    The Anglo-Saxon and Roman Systems of Criminal Juris-
        prudence, . . . Hon. M. Romero, Mexican Minister.
    The Right of Sanctuary, ... George H. Westley.
    The Vice-President—What to do with Him, . . Hon. Walter Clark.
    The Lawyer's Easy Chair, ... Irving Browne.

Albany Law Journal, 1896.

    July 4. The Advocates of Greece and Rome, . J. E. R. Stephens.
    July 11. The Next Step in International Arbitration,
                                                Alexander Porter Morse.
    July 18. The Real Property Law, . . Theodore F. C. Demorest.
    July 25. John Marshall, ... Gen. John C. Black.
    Aug. 1. Life and Character of Hon. Allen G. Thurman,
                                                Hon. George K. Nash.
    Aug. 8. Selection of Juries, Grand and Petit, Hon. R. E. Jenkins.
    Aug. 15. Samuel Johnson on Law and the Lawyers, N. W. Sibley.
    Aug. 22. International Law (Annual Address before the
            American Bar Association), The Rt. Hon. Lord Russell.

Aug. 29. The Uses of Legal History,   Montague Crackenthrope.
Sept. 5. Noteworthy Changes in Statute Law,   Moorfield Story.
Sept. 12. Noteworthy Changes in Statute Law,   Moorfield Story.
Sept. 19. Legal Education in England, .   George Henry Emmett.
Sept. 26. Report of Committee on Uniform System of Legal Procedure.
Oct. 3. Legal Tender Acts and the Gold Clause in Contracts,
                                               J. J. H. Hamilton.

Central Law Journal.

July 3. The Vendor's Lien, ... B. R. Webb.
July 10. Substituted Service, . . . James L. Hopkins.
July 17. Evidence. Admission of Testimony from Former Trial when Witness is Absent,   George Kroncke.
July 24. Railway Fires, . . . Seymour D. Thompson.
July 31. Blackmail, ... Samuel Maxwell,
Aug. 7. Unofficial Entries by Third Persons, . Irving Browne.
Aug. 14. Stipulations in Policies Against Additional Insurance. . . . . . W. C. Rodgers
Aug. 21. The Legal Effect of a Promise to Pay a Specific Kind of Money, . . Walter D. Coles.
Aug. 28. The Right of a Party to Impeach His Own Witness, ... John F. Doherty.
Sept. 4. Proceedings to Obtain Sick and Distress Benefits of Societies and Fraternities,   Eugene McQuillin.
Sept. 11. The Treaties of the United States and Alien Land Laws of Illinois and Other States of the Union, . . . G. W. Duwalt.
Sept. 18. Execution Levy on Personalty as Satisfaction—Stay of Collateral and Other Action,   Newton Wyeth.
Sept. 25. An Exposition of the Laws Pertaining to Wheelmen. . . . . W. L. Woodward.
Oct. 2. Passenger and Freight Elevators,   James Avery Webb.

American Law Review, July and August, 1896.

Proof by Comparison of Handwriting—Its History,   John H. Wigmore.
The Forgery of Fictitious Names, . . . T. W. Brown.
Rights of Material and Supplymen in Railroad Foreclosures, ... Charles O. Dickson.
Citizenship of the United States Under the Fourteenth Amendment, ... Marshall B. Woodworth.
A Question as to Paraphernalia, . . . T. F. Uttley.

MEMORABILIA ET NOTABILIA.

Professor James Bradley Thayer of the Harvard Law School, will be the Storrs lecturer this year.

* * *

Edward D. Robbins of Hartford, and W. F. Foster, '94, have been added to the list of instructors in the school.

* * *

Ernest Knaebel, '96, has been appointed Registrar of the Law School and E. T. Buckingham, '97, Assistant Librarian.

* * *

At the session of the American Bar Association held at Saratoga in August, the following gentlemen connected with the Law School Faculty were present: Dean Wayland, Professors Phelps, Watrous and Beers, Judge Shipman, Mr. Sharpe and Judge Gager. Professor Phelps was unanimously elected president of the section on legal education for the coming year.

* * *

Professor Baldwin has prepared a series of selected cases on the subject of railroad law, designed, primarily, for the M. L. course. They are being published by the West Publishing Co.

* * *

Professor George E. Beers has been appointed by the Mayor of New Haven to represent the city at Tennessee's Centennial Exposition, to be held in Nashville next Summer, and has been elected by the committee its Secretary and Treasurer.

* * *

At a meeting of the Kent Club held Monday evening, October 5th, the following officers were elected for the Fall term: C. L. Avery, '97, President; G. V. Smith, '98, Vice-President; Faust, '98, Secretary; H. M. Burke, '97, Assistant Treasurer; Candee, G. V. Smith and Arnot, Executive Committee.

* * *

For the office of Probate Judge, Livingston W. Cleaveland, Carlos H. Storrs, '89, and T. M. Callahan, '94, have been nominated by the Republicans, Gold Democrats and Silver Democrats respectively.

* * *

1893. Homer S. Cummings has been nominated by the Silver Democrats for Secretary of State.

1894. W. R. Adams is studying for the degree of Ph.D. at Yale.

Maher, '94, and Conman, '95, have opened a partnership office in the Exchange Building.

1895. F. L. Averill has been nominated for the Legislature by the Republicans of New Haven.

J. S. Green is in the office of Wright & Hotchkiss, New Haven.

1896. A. J. Brumder, who was compelled to go to Florida last Spring on account of his health, will join '97 about November 15th.

The marriage of Mason L. Decker to Miss Stewart occurred at the home of the bride in Peekskill, N. Y., on October 14th. J. J. Hickey, '97, and M. L. Hatcher, '97, acted as ushers.

Winthrop E. Dwight is studying at Oxford.

E. J. Garvan is in the office of J. G. Calhoun of Hartford.

C. C. Gilbert has entered the office of Henry G. Newton of New Haven.

J. L. Hall and O. S. Seymour are with Watrous & Buckland, New Haven.

P. W. Harrison is in the office of his father, Judge Lynde Harrison, New Haven.

F. J. Kearful is taking postgraduate work and is in Professor Beer's office.

S. G. Meeker is secretary and attorney of the North American Investment Co., with an office at Bridgeport.

F. C. Taylor is the Republican nominee for the office of Probate Judge, District of Stamford.

W. L. Tibbs is in the office of Moran, Kraus and Mayer of Chicago.

PRIZES AWARDED IN YALE LAW SCHOOL, JUNE, 1896.

Townsend Prize, $100, Class of 1896—John Loomer Hall, B.A. Yale University 1894.

Jewell Prize, $50, Class of 1896—Ernest Knaebel, B.A. Yale University 1894.

Munson Prize, $50, Class of 1896—Ernest Knaebel, B.A. Yale University 1894. With special honorable mention of Francis Joseph Kearful.

Betts Prize, $50, Class of 1897—Christopher Lester Avery, B.A. Yale University 1893.

Wayland Prizes (Yale Kent Club) Class of 1896—First Prize, $50, Herbert Humphrey Kellogg, B.A. Yale University 1894. Second Prize, $30, Ernest Grey Smith, Ph.B. Lafayette College 1894. Third Prize, $20, William Luther Tibbs, Ph.B. Colorado College 1894.

HONORS, GRADUATE COURSE.

Degree of D.C.L., *cum laude*—William Frederick Foster, LL.B. Yale University 1894, M.L. 1895.

Degree of M.L., *cum laude*—Tokichi Masao, LL.B. University of West Virginia; A. I. Moriarity.

Senior Class.

Degree of LL.B., *Summa cum laude*—Ernest Knaebel, B.A.

Degree of LL.B., *Magna cum laude*—Winthrop Edwards Dwight, B.A., Ph.D.

Degree of LL.B., *cum laude*—Raymond Holbrook Arnot, B.A., Edward Marvin Day, B.A.; Bibb Graves, B.C.E. University of Alabama; James Ashworth Howarth, Jr., John Hill Morgan, B.A.; John Stephenson Pullman, B.A. Wesleyan University.

Junior Class.

Christopher Lester Avery, B.A., Roger Sherman Baldwin, B.A., Samuel Fayerweather Beardsley, B.A., Nehemiah Candee, B.A., Michael Gavin, B.A., George Jay Gibson, Jr., B.A.; Michel Ambrose Kilker, M.E. Keystone Norman College; Harry Warner Minor, David Edward Moulton, Francis Parsons, B.A. Charles Frederick Peterson; John Walcott Thompson, B.A. Dartmouth College; Henry Waterman, Ph.B., Cornell University; Arthur Ashford Wilder.

YALE LAW JOURNAL

CONSTRUCTION.

This title will, perhaps, serve as well as any other to suggest the two-fold subject of this article. Construction, as applied to a writing, usually means to a lawyer the bringing of the intended meaning out of the words used. To quote from Jones on the "Construction of Commercial and Trade Contracts," "the construction of a contract is the ascertainment of the thought which its language expresses"; or, as Lord Chelmsford puts it, "the construction of a contract is nothing more than the gathering of the intention of the parties to it from the words they have used." To the lay mind the construction of a writing may as naturally mean its creation, the making of it, or the putting together of the necessary words to express the meaning intended. This is not mere coincidence of forms. The two verbs "construct" and "construe" have the same derivation; and a little reflection will bring out the similarity of the processes of construction in the two senses. To construct a writing is to put together words, being unlimited in the choice, to express a given meaning. To construe a writing is to make out or, it may well enough be said, to construct a meaning out of words given. It is obvious that the art of constructing writings and the art of construing them are closely akin. Skill in the one can hardly be acquired without acquiring at the same time some skill in the other. Ignorance of the one implies ignorance of the other. Training in the one is necessarily, to some extent, training in the other. To emphasize the importance of some systematic training in both these branches and to suggest the feasibility and utility of the study of the two together, are the purposes of this article.

I doubt whether I have anything to say which is new or original—anything which is not fairly obvious. But the obvious is peculiarily apt to escape consideration. What we see every day too rarely sets us thinking.

Now, if we take up first the art of construing writings, it will not be necessary to argue the proposition that it is an art as frequently required as any in the work of the lawyer. Writings are of many kinds. There are statutes, codes, wills, deeds, contracts and other documents. How much of the time of the courts is taken up in construing them may be fairly appreciated by taking down at random a volume of current reports and examining the cases. It would hardly be hazardous to wager that one-half of the cases will be found to involve construction, that in one-half of the cases some question is presented as to the mere meaning of written words, as distinguished from questions of legality or validity. Take into consideration, also, the opinions of courts and the necessity, under the doctrines of precedent and *stare decisis*, of construing the language previously used by the judges, and the estimate of the amount of construction in the courts will rise much higher.

But, speaking generally, only a comparatively small part of a lawyer's work is in the courts. In an active practice hardly a day passes in which the lawyer is not called upon, in his office or in conference or negotiations, to determine the meaning of some provision of a statute, will, deed, contract, decision or other writing.

Again, as to the making of writings, for various purposes and in connection with interests present and future, large and small, simple and complex, the lawyer's skill in this line is demanded daily.

The magnitude of that part of a lawyer's work, in the office, at the bar and on the bench, which involves construction in one sense or the other, is obviously such as to demand more attention than it seems to have received in connection with legal education.

Furthermore, the nature of this work peculiarly demands training. Much can be done in the law, with fair results, by undisciplined industry not backed by learning. The dull plodder, without much learning or mental discipline, may find an authority which answers his client's question or wins his case in court. A much higher order of skill is required to draw a will or contract, or to construe an agreement or a statute the effect of which has not been judicially determined. Decided cases give aid only indirectly. It is practically hopeless to seek for a precedent as to construction, or a form to follow in drafting an instrument, which exactly fits. If the same language shall be found to have been construed, the surroundings will not be found to be the same. A form book will more probably lead astray an unskilled draftsman. There is the need of judging whether or how far the precedent or the form fits the case in hand. This requires the same order of skill, perhaps in less degree, as drafting or construing without the aid of precedent. And this skill can be acquired only by training, and by training which cannot be got in a day or a week, training which not only gives a working knowledge and appreciation of the meaning of words and the structural rules of language, but develops habits of thought, including the easy use of the imagination.

Is it asked, "Are lawyers generally so trained?" Certainly not, in any satisfactory sense, before they begin practice. Only in their practice, as a rule, and then not systematically but only as the training comes in their professional work. In their collegiate education some have acquired part of the necessary knowledge and discipline—especially in the study of the classics. But of conscious training for this branch of work, either before admission to the bar or afterwards other than in their practice as it has developed, very few lawyers have had the benefit. There are, of course, many things which go to make the thoroughly equipped lawyer, which only experience can give. But whatever can be, should be given in the preparatory education. And the training now referred to can, I believe, be better got, or at least better started (the education of a good lawyer never ends until he quits) by systematic study than by chance experience.

The layman may ask, in view of what has been said: "Why go to a lawyer to have a will drawn, or an agreement?" There may be some question of law, as to the power to dispose of property by will or as to the mode of execution, or as to the validity of what is proposed to be embodied in the agreement. If there is no such question but it is only necessary to express clearly, without ambiguity, and fully, with a view to possible contingencies, a known intention, it would require some boldness to assert that the work would be better done by the average lawyer, not having had special experience in this line, than by a layman of the same intelligence and general education. The same thing substantially is true as to construing a writing. Certainly it is safe to say that there would be little choice, for such work, as between the ordinary lawyer just admitted to practice and a business man of like age and general education. I can think of no study, prior to admission to the bar, which seems to have been of special benefit to me with a view to these branches of work (excluding the questions of law arising in the connection), except the general study of languages, and especially the study of Latin because of its orderly structure.

And yet work of this kind is apt to be of the most responsible kind, and a lawyer trained for it can render to his clients services the most important and the most valued. In this line lies the most remunerative work and that which involves the greatest amount of personal confidence, of the kind which binds the client most firmly to his lawyer. Reputation for skill in expressing what is intended so that there can be no mistake about it, and in construing language so as confidently and correctly to declare its meaning, is worth more, pecuniarily, than reputation for any other of the talents or acquirements of a lawyer. Millions are often invested in reliance upon a lawyer's opinion of the meaning of a statute. Investments and business enterprises of great magnitude are made or entered upon, with confidence, because the agreements upon which they rest have been drawn by lawyers of known skill in such work. It is unnecessary to enlarge. This is as obvious as the other things to which I have called attention.

There is no more fascinating work in the law than construction. There are moments of irritation because of the slovenly work of the draftsman, his verbosity perhaps, his lazy effort to clear one obscurity by adding another instead of removing the first. There are times when we may well recall the remark of Sir Robert Peel, whom Dr. Lieber quotes as saying that he "contemplates no task with so much distaste as the reading through an ordinary act of Parliament." But still the work is fascinating, of shaking out the words and letting in the light, comparing one phrase with another, seeking to put one's self in the attitude and surroundings of the writer, testing one hypothesis and another and finally reaching a conclusion which can be asserted with confidence and backed by logic. It would be cause for grief to lawyers who have enjoyed such work to think that the occasion for it might soon cease. And so it is no hardship to agree with Dr. Lieber when he says, in his very interesting work on "Hermeneutics," that "the very nature and essence of human language * * * renders a total exclusion of every imaginable misapprehension, in most cases, absolutely impossible." Improvement in the use of language may go on then indefinitely. And yet, while there are courts and lawyers, they will be furnished with plenty of the pleasure of construction, or, as Dr. Lieber himself would say, of interpretation and construction, since he gives to construction a different meaning from that given it by the writers quoted at the beginning of this article.

But still a study of the cases involving construction cannot but leave a strong impression that the art of expressing thought in words so that ambiguity and uncertainty are avoided, has been sadly neglected, and that training in this art is needed among lawyers. If such training were what it should be, much of the work of construction would be done away with. Of course, it would be unfair to assume that all or nearly all the writings which come before the courts are the work of lawyers. But enough of them are to point the moral. And until it shall be the rule that lawyers are experts in this art, it will hardly do to criticise the layman, except in special cases, for drawing his own agreements, when no question as to what he may agree or other question of law is involved. The layman has often lost by his lawyer's lack of skill. In the present conditions, it is not always easy for him to discover what lawyer within reach is expert in this line.

Let us briefly look at the work involved in the drawing of a writing and at the same time observe how much akin this work is to the art of construing. It will, I think, become clear that the two arts may best be studied together. Suppose, for instance, a will is to be drawn. Put aside all questions as to any restraints of the law, assuming that the intention of the testator is entirely permissible and only needs to be clearly stated. There is need at the outset of some construction of words, not, however, without outside aid. The client states what he wishes to provide. What he states must be construed, made plain and certain; and so put to him for confirmation or correction. When his purpose in a general way is apprehended, a rough sketch of the will may be made. Then, especially, comes in the work of the imagination. Imagine the various possible happenings in the meantime which may produce various conditions when the will shall take effect. Suppose a wife, a son or a daughter dies, will the will accord with the testator's purpose? If the estate is disposed of by giving fixed sums to certain persons and the residue to others, will it operate aright if the testator's fortune should be considerably increased or diminished? The consideration of present circumstances and also of various possible sets of circumstances at the testator's death in this case, finds it parallel when the task is reversed and we are called upon to construe. An instrument is always to be construed in the light of the attitude and surroundings of him or those who made it. After such questions as above are settled, not by construction but by reference to the client, the will will be substantially completed. Thereafter, the careful lawyer will examine the language in detail. And this examination will proceed in large part in the same way as if the same will were brought to him for construction after it had become operative. He will seek for ambiguities, not now to solve them but to remove them. He will bear in mind the recognized rules of construction, not now to find out what the testator's intention was, but to see whether the application of such rules may mislead as to the intention which is known to him. He may find that different expressions have been used in different paragraphs when the intention was the same, and change the one or the other to make the paragraphs conform. He may find that he has used a word in a technical sense, and will either add something to make this clear or substitute words which in their plain and ordinary sense convey the meaning intended. He may see a possible ambiguity prevented only by punctuation, and change the order of the words so that punctuation may be disregarded and yet the sense be certain. In general, as in construing he would put himself back in imagination to the time and amid the surroundings of the testator; so, in putting the will in final shape, he will put himself forward and look at the document as though it were presented to him for construction after the testator's death.

Careful study of language, both as to the ordinary meaning of words and as to proper arrangement of words and clauses, will aid the lawyer alike in drawing and in construing; although in construing he must at the same time recognize that comparatively few persons write according to rule.

But enough has been said as to the importance of training in these two branches of work and as to the relation between them. Certainly so, if it is all as obvious as it seems to be. It remains only to make one or two practical suggestions. It is not altogether easy to map out a scheme of class-room study in these two subjects. Much will depend on the teacher. But, whether with a teacher or not, I venture to suggest that fair training in these branches may be acquired in some such way as the following. Read Jones on the "Construction of Commercial and Trade Contracts," a book which is pleasant and interesting reading, simply as such, without any ulterior purpose; or Lieber's "Hermeneutics," which, though more profound, will easily hold attention when once begun; or Sedgwick on the "Construction of Statutes." The rules of construction are not arbitrary rules like the provisions of a code of practice. There is no need of memorizing them. It is necessary only to appreciate them. They are derived from observation of the ordinary usages of men. They are acknowledged by common sense when stated, and when acknowledged they are practically learned. If they were not so acknowledged by persons of average intelligence they would lack their only foundation. So a rather hurried reading will put the mind of the reader into very fair relation with the subject, though the words of all the rules be forgotten. Here, again, we are dealing with the obvious. Then, take cases cited here and there by the author. Take the writing before the court. Examine it to discover where the ambiguity lies. Redraw it to express the one possible meaning and then the other, in such a way as to make doubt impossible. Then read the opinion and revise the work. In this connection, have some regard for brevity. After the writing has been robbed of ambiguity, see if it cannot be cut down, expressed more simply and more briefly without loss or even with increase of certainty. Brevity and simplicity are at a premium in these days. Nothing pleases clients more (especially intelligent business men) than to see an agreement put so simply and briefly that it is no task to read it and take in its meaning. Writings are not now estimated by the yard or by the learning implied in the use of unusual words.

A law student who works on these lines with some thoroughness will be better qualified at graduation to draw and construe writings than many lawyers who have been in practice for years; although experience only will make an expert.

Much attention is paid in our universities in these days to debating, to training in the oral use of language to convince; much also to the study of the proper use of English in writing generally. It is fitting that in our law schools especial attention be paid to the use of language to express intentions, in wills, statutes, agreements and other writings with which the practice of the law has to do, with simplicity and brevity and especially with the utmost possible certainty. It may be that this has already been done to an extent unknown to me. I should certainly be very glad to be convicted of ignorance in this respect, especially as regards the Law School of Yale University.

Thomas Thacher.

ON A PERMANENT ARBITRATION TREATY.

In the latest message of the President to Congress, in addition to the information that a definite and final settlement of the controversy over the Venezuelan boundary has been reached, the fact has been made public that "negotiations for a treaty of general arbitration for all differences between Great Britain and the United States are far advanced, and promise to reach a successful consummation at an early date." It still remains unknown to the public what are the details of the proposed treaty, or whether it is in contemplation to establish a permanent arbitration tribunal, or merely to agree to arbitrate in all cases of disagreement. Probably in either case, in spite of the fact that the President speaks of "all differences," the treaty will be found to contain certain reservations, as there is a substantial consensus of opinion that cases do sometimes arise in which arbitration between independent nations is inadmissible.

If it shall prove that the governments of President Cleveland and Lord Salisbury have actually succeeded in forming between the two peoples a durable alliance which shall assure that for the future all questions arising between them shall be settled peaceably and honorably, without derogation from the independence or dignity of either nation, they will surely achieve a fame which the greatest of the world's conquerors might envy, but in view of the evident and apparently insuperable obstacles, it is as well not to be too confident, at least until the treaty is before us, that such a desirable consummation is actually within reach.

Perhaps the anticipated treaty will be found to be no more than a mutual agreement that the two nations will hereafter settle by arbitration all differences which have failed of solution by diplomatic methods, presumably with reservations of questions affecting the sovereignty, independence or honor of either, but with no attempt to provide beforehand for any permanent court of arbitration or any invariable method to be followed in the selection of arbitrators. It would not be easy to pass any criticism upon such a treaty, except that it would be a disappointment to whose who are expecting something more. It would be of value as an expression of the present mutual good will of the two powers, and would probably have some tendency to perpetuate that good will, but it would after all amount to little more in fact than the assurances of lasting peace and amity contained in many an existing treaty, and would be but a feeble bulwark of peace in any future clash of real or supposed interests.

It may be that the attempt is to be made to provide in advance for the manner in which future differences are to be laid before the arbitrators, for the mode of selecting these and of giving effect to their decision. This would be going a little farther, but only to encounter difficulties without compensating advantages. It is not the constitution or procedure of the tribunal that is the critical matter when any international question threatens a rupture of friendly relations, for such points are comparatively easy of settlement when once the governments have agreed that arbitration and not war shall end the dispute, and such an agreement could not be helped and might be hindered by an already existing treaty regulating the subsequent procedure. Should it happen on any future occasion that one of the governments considered the provisions of the general arbitration treaty likely to prove prejudicial to its interests in the particular case it would form a temptation to refuse arbitration rather than a reason for consenting to it.

General expectation, however, goes far beyond this, and looks for the establishment of a permanent High Court, to be at once the means of reconciliation of all disputes and a visible evidence to all mankind that two great nations have forever repudiated the savagery of war as the *ultima ratio gentium* and have substituted for it, as between themselves, the peaceful rule of international justice. It is at least a beautiful dream, and until we know better we may hope that it is to prove something more than a dream, but the difficulties to be overcome are disheartening. For, in the first place, how could such a court be satisfactorily constituted? If it were to be composed of an equal number of members from each nation there would be little probability of agreement. Absolute impartiality is too rare a quality to permit of reasonable expectation that the judges could wholly divest themselves of national bias where their national interests were involved. It must be remembered that in most disputed questions there is much to be said for both sides, and that it is seldom that either party to a controversy is so clearly in the right that upright and intelligent men cannot differ in their judgment. If impartiality could be expected from any body of men in the world it could surely be from the Judges of the Supreme Court of the United States, yet we all remember how they divided as members of the Electoral Commission of 1876. If, in order to secure a majority decision, one or more members of the court are to be foreigners, then he or they will in reality give the decision and the American and English judges will be only the more relieved from any duty to be impartial, as the presence of foreigners would in effect be an admission that the others were expected to be partisans and in the guise of judges to be in fact advocates. It is perhaps theoretically possible, though it would certainly be somewhat anomalous, that a permanent Anglo-American court should be composed entirely of foreigners.

But the obstacles in the way of devising and organizing a court are insignificant in comparison with those which would impede its successful working. How is it to be determined when and how an issue is to be submitted to its adjudication? If this is to be left to the agreement of the governments in each case, if they are to be as free as now to arbitrate or not to arbitrate, then there is no gain whatever; there is positive disadvantage in the existence of a permanent court. As already said, the agreement to arbitrate is the critical matter which when settled leaves subsequent details relatively easy. But the existence of a court would in no case tend to promote such agreement, while it might often hinder it, should either nation suspect, with or without reason, that the court as constituted was likely to decide adversely to its claims in any particular case. If, on the other hand, the court itself is to be clothed with power, either on its own motion or on application of one of the governments concerned, to take jurisdiction in case of disputes without the consent of both parties, then it is more than likely that the first attempt to exercise this authority would also be the last, for the only possible power to compel obedience would lie in the armed force of the other nation. It is almost uniformly admitted that certain questions must be exceptions to any scheme of permanent arbitration; who shall decide whether any question in dispute is within these exceptions? Each nation for itself, always and necessarily, unless they have surrendered their status as independent states, and a refusal to agree upon arbitration would almost surely be based upon such a claim, which would equally be made the ground for refusal to submit to the nominal authority of the court to take jurisdiction on demand of the other party. Suppose such a court to have been in existence one year ago, when the President's message about the Venezuelan boundary dispute suddenly brought us to contemplate the possibility of war over a matter which few of us had ever thought of as one in which we had any interest whatever. It is precisely that threat of war which has stirred up the demand that some means shall be found whereby lasting peace shall be assured, at least between ourselves and England, but what could the court have done in that case? Nothing whatever; there was no question between England and America upon which it could have claimed jurisdiction or which could be decided by arbitration in any form. The boundary question was between England and Venezuela, the question of our right to intervene and to demand of England a certain course of conduct in relation to that dispute was no question of right in the legal sense at all; there was no law, international or otherwise, to give to, or withhold from, the United States such a right. It was a matter of national interest alone, a political question pure and simple, which only the supreme government of the nation could decide. What was true of the Venezuelan question is true of nearly all questions which could possibly need the intervention of arbitration to prevent war. The questions about which nations will fight are generally questions of their own national or dynastic interests or antipathies; they will rarely fight over disputed facts or claims for damages unless they are in a temper to reject all settlement and to fight because they prefer war to peace. It is, perhaps, conceivable that England and America might set up some common authority which, by the consent of both, should be endowed with power to consider and determine not only issues submitted by agreement in each case, but as well all questions where the interests or policy of the two peoples were opposed. If that were done, however, it would not be a court that was established but a supreme government over a confederacy of the English-speaking peoples; but a confederacy the most fragile that it ever entered the mind of man to establish, with a government destitute of the most essential attribute of government, the power to enforce its authority. If such a confederacy proved durable it would prove that we were ready in fact for a far closer union, for the reunion of the severed branches in one vast Anglo-Saxon empire. There are some who dream of such a union, and possibly the future may bring it forth, but it certainly is not yet desired by the mass of the people on either side of the ocean.

Most men who have given the subject careful thought have found themselves forced to the conclusion that a permanent court of arbitration between two nations alone is impracticable, but many have believed that such a court might be established by several nations, and have hoped that the principal states of Europe and America may be brought to enter into such a plan. It would seem that the difficulty of constituting an impartial court might be lessened if the parties to the agreement were numerous, and it also appears, at least at first sight, as if the problem of how to secure obedience to its decrees might be solved by the pledge of every state to unite to execute them, by force of arms if need be, against a recalcitrant member. But in truth this project is more hopeless than the other. Such a combination would be as truly the formation of a new confederacy as if only two nations were included, and the greater the number of the members and the greater the diversity of their interests the more certainly would it be fore-doomed to failure. The different states would be no less jealous of each other, no less determined to decide for themselves wherein their interests lay and to further that interest by hook or crook, than before; it might even be that their jealousy would only be increased by the claim of alien states to an increased right of interference. Faith in the prospect of any such league of peace would seem to indicate either an ignorance of modern European history, or an unquenchable hopefulness that what human nature has been in the past it will not be in the future if only it can be shown a better way. If we can be assured that the rulers of mankind will hereafter prefer the general welfare to the satisfaction of their own ambitions, the peace of the world to the aggrandizement of their own states; if we can be sure that no treaties are made with the secret intention that they shall be broken when it is safe and profitable to break them; that no alliance which is proclaimed to the world shall be undermined by other treaties kept secret from the partners in the alliance; in short, when we may be sure that statesmen have adopted the Golden Rule as the actual rule of politics; then we can confidently hope for the brilliant success of a permanent international agreement for arbitration—only, it will be wholly superfluous.

Edward V. Raynolds.

ACTIONS ON FOREIGN JUDGMENTS.

Munson Prize Thesis.

The term "foreign judgment," as used in the books, applies indiscriminately to judgments rendered in a foreign country and those rendered in sister States of the Union, and it is not unusual for text-writers to treat the two classes conjointly. The limits of this paper, however, force us to confine our discussion to those judgments which are foreign in the stricter sense. There is an obvious and fundamental distinction between these and the judgments of a sister State, both in respect of their inherent force and of the basis underlying it, which, in the case of the former, is comity, absolute reciprocity, or individual obligation, and, in the case of the latter, a provision in the federal Constitution and congressional enactments in pursuance thereof. Before the Revolution our various colonies, though in many respects so intimately connected, were by the common law deemed foreign to each other, and the courts of one applied to the judgments rendered by the tribunals of the others, the rule then prevailing in England regarding foreign judgments, holding them to be but *prima facie* evidence of debt and not to possess the dignity of a record. Clearly, among a people so closely knit by ties of blood and common interest, such a doctrine must be fraught with inconvenience, and prove a great impediment to commercial intercourse. The logical outcome was a number of statutes, the earliest passed in Massachusetts in 1773, providing that the judgments of the courts of adjacent colonies should be unimpeachable on their merits.[1] When, by the Articles of Confederation, the colonies were united in one nation of States, it was provided:[2] "Full faith and credit shall be given, in each of these States, to the records, acts and judicial proceedings of the courts and magistrates of every other State"; and later, by our present Constitution,[3] it was enacted: "Full faith and credit shall be given in each State to the public acts, records and judi-

---

[1] Hilton v. Guyot, 159 U. S. 113; Bigelow on Estoppel (5th Ed.) p. 266.
[2] Art. 4, Sec. 3.
[3] Art. 4, Sec. 1.

cial proceedings of every other State, and Congress may by general laws prescribe the manner in which such acts, records and proceedings shall be proved, and the effect thereof." In pursuance of the power thus granted the first Congress under the Constitution, sitting in 1790, after prescribing the manner of authentication, enacted that "the said records and judicial proceedings, authenticated as aforesaid, shall have such faith and credit given to them in every court of the United States as they have by law or usage in the courts of the State from whence the said records are or shall be taken."[4] The supplementary act of March, 27, 1804, reënacting these provisions and adding further directions concerning attestation, is made to apply to "the Territories of the United States and the countries subject to the jurisdiction of the United States."

By these constitutional and legislative provisions, all considerations of comity, reciprocity, utility and personal obligation, which render the questions involving foreign judgments so difficult and uncertain, are swept away, and in their place is erected the inflexible and determinate "supreme law of the land." The courts have decided that the record of a judgment rendered by a duly constituted tribunal of a sister State is a *record* in the true sense of the word, to an action on which *nul tiel record* alone is the appropriate general issue;[5] that such a judgment merges the original cause of action,[6] and that it has all the force as evidence or as an estoppel that it would have where given. Even the plea of fraud is not generally available,[7] unless, perhaps, when permitted at home,[8] or when the suit is in equity to restrain proceedings at law.[9] But except so far as they are by the Constitution united for national purposes, the several States of the Union still stand toward one another in the relationship of independent sovereignties; so that, "notwithstanding that provision [Const., Art. 4, Sec. 1] and the statutes passed to enforce it, the jurisdiction of a State court whose judgment is brought

---

[4] Rev. Stat. U. S., Sec. 905.

[5] Mills v. Duryee, 7 Cranch, (U. S.) 481.

[6] Bank of U. S. v. Merchants Bank, 7 Gill. 415.

[7] Christmas v. Russell, 5 Wall. (U. S.) 290.

[8] Hampton v. McConnell, 3 Wheat. (U. S.) 234; Hanley v. Donoghue, 116 U. S. 1, 4; Burras v. Bidwell, 3 Woods (U. S.) 5.

[9] Pearce v. Olney, 20 Conn. 544. Under the modern code practice, such equitable defenses may be interposed in an action at law (Amer. and Eng. Enc. of Law, Tit. Judgments, p. 149 f.).

in question in another State is always open to inquiry. In that respect, every State court is to be regarded as a foreign court."[10]

I.

1. In order that the record of a foreign judgment may be received as competent evidence in our courts, it must be duly authenticated. This is a technical matter into which we shall not enter any further than to say, that it is usual and proper to introduce a copy exemplified under the great seal of the State, or under the seal of the foreign court, in which case, the seal itself must be proved to be genuine by evidence *aliunde*, or the copy may be proved under oath by one who has compared it with the original. The seals of courts of Admiralty, however, will be judicially noticed, they "being the courts of the civilized world."[11] And it is said that the "exemplification will be deemed *prima facie* correct."[12]

Furthermore, though there will be a general presumption in its favor, the record must be fair on its face, and free from uncertainty as to what it professes to decide. Ambiguities will not be removed by argument and inference.[13] In the case first cited (involving a decree of forfeiture rendered by a foreign prize-court), Justice Story said: "If the sentence be ambiguous or indeterminate as to the facts on which it proceeds, or as to the direct grounds of condemnation, the sentence ought not to be held conclusive, or the courts of other countries put to the task of picking out the threads of argument or of reasoning or recital in order to weave them together so as to give force or consistency or validity to the sentence." A patent ambiguity on the face of the record would be fatal,[13a] but where the record is silent, parol evidence is competent to show what points were passed upon,[14] as may also be shown the practice and procedure of the foreign court.[15] Moreover, it ought, as matter of precaution, if not of strict regularity, to appear that the foreign court

---

[10] Fisher *v.* Fielding, 67 Conn. 91-105; Hatch *v.* Spofford, 22 Conn. 485; Thompson *v.* Whitman, 18 Wall. (U. S.) 457, 461; Grover & Baker Mach. Co. *v.* Radcliffe, 137 U. S. 287, 294, 298.

[11] I. Greenl. Evid., Secs. 5, 514; Wharton Conflict of Laws, Sec. 789 *et seq.*; Story Conflict of Laws, Sec. 641.

[12] Woodbridge *v.* Austin, 2 Tyler (Vt.) 364, 366.

[13] Bigelow on Estoppel (5th Ed.), p. 249; Bradstreet *v.* Ins. Co., 3 Sumn. (U. S.) 600; Robinson v. Jones, 8 Mass. 536.

[13a] Bigelow on Estoppel (5th Ed.) 250.

[14] Merchants Bank *v.* Schulenburg, 48 Mich. 102.

[15] Fisher *v.* Fielding, 67 Conn. 91.

had duly acquired jurisdiction, and that regular proceedings were had; for there are cases going so far as to hold that, if it be not shown on the face of the record that all the necessary steps to this end have been complied with, it will not be received even as *prima facie* evidence.[16] It is said that "when the record of a foreign judgment *in rem* is silent in regard to the matters which constitute jurisdiction, jurisdiction will not be presumed,"[17] and it has been held that in order to bind strangers, the grounds of a decision of condemnation in a court of Admiralty must be stated in the record itself.[18]

Finally, we should say, that if it be clear by the record that any of the several essentials to the validity of the foreign judgment or decree hereinafter to be stated do not exist, it will be valueless as evidence and will be treated as a nullity.

2. A judgment or decree rendered in a foreign land has never been awarded the high character of a record. Hence there is no extinguishment or merger[19] of the original cause of action, and the successful plaintiff who desires to reassert his claim in another jurisdiction has the option of relying for his evidence on the record of the former adjudication, or of disregarding that and entering into the merits *de novo*. This has always been the rule in England, and was several times declared by the courts of Texas prior to its annexation to the United States.[20] It is also so held throughout the Union, with the single exception that in Louisiana, under the Code, the original cause of action is regarded as merged in the foreign judgment.[21] This absence of merger is due to the fact that the plaintiff has not by his foreign judgment acquired any higher remedy in our own courts than he had before. The right to issue execution, in the case of domestic judgments, would render

---

[16] Sawyer *v.* Ins. Co., 12 Mass. 291; Bradstreet *v.* Ins. Co., 3 Sumn. (U. S.) 600; Bigelow on Estoppel (5th Ed.) 251.

[17] Bigelow on Estoppel (5th Ed.) 251, citing Com. v. Blood., 97 Mass. 538, and the Griefswald, Swabey 430. Nevertheless, it must be added that the tendency of modern decisions is to treat duly exemplified foreign judgments, bearing nothing to suggest distrust, as being entitled to the *prima facie* presumption that they were given by a duly constituted tribunal acting within its lawful authority.

[18] Dalgleish *v.* Hogson, 7 Bing. 495, 504.

[19] Smith *v.* Nicholls, 5 Bing. N. C. 208; Bank of Australasia *v.* Nias, 16 Q. B. 717.

[20] Frazier *v.* Moore, 11 Texas 755.

[21] N. Y., L. E. & W. R. Co. *v.* McHenry, 17 Fed. Rep. 414; Jones *v.* Jamison, 15 La. Ann. 35.

a second suit on the original demand wholly superfluous and, hence, indicative of bad faith and contrary to public policy; but no such remedy exists in favor of foreign judgments, for here the party is compelled to have recourse to his action, in which the former judgment can, in any event, figure only as evidence."

But if the plaintiff elect so to declare on the merits again, he may nevertheless employ the record of the former judgment as evidence of the strength and extent of his claim, without making any formal allegation in regard to it.[23]

The form of action on the judgment may be either debt, for the liquidated sum adjudged to be due, or *assumpsit*, on the implied promise to satisfy the obligation raised by such adjudication.[24] It is unnecessary to allege in the declaration that the court had jurisdiction, or that it was regularly constituted, or that the proceedings were properly conducted, for all this (provided the record itself be regular), will be presumed, until the contrary is established.[25] And where, in accordance with the form provided in one of our modern Practice Acts, the complainant merely alleges that the judgment was "duly" recovered, this implies that the suit was conducted in due course of law, "which necessarily involves reasonable notice to the defendant of the institution and nature of the action, given (unless this be waived), if he be a non-resident, by personal service within the jurisdiction, and a fair opportunity to be heard before a tribunal of competent jurisdiction," and also that a trial or hearing was had.[26]

3. Having adverted to the main points of procedure which must govern one who seeks to enforce in the courts of one country a demand already passed upon by the courts of another, we come now to consider the defenses by which such an action may be met.

And first, if the plaintiff who has recovered in a foreign court decide to sue a second time on his original cause of action, he waives all advantage of estoppel that might have accrued to him from the prior adjudication, and opens the door for the defend-

---

[22] Smith *v.* Nicholls, 5 Bing. N. C. 208.

[23] N. Y., L. E. & W. R. Co. *v.* McHenry, 17 Fed. Rep. 414.

[24] Henderson *v.* Henderson, 6 Q. B. 288; Grant *v.* Eastern L. R., 13 Q. B. Div. 302; Mellin *v.* Horlick, 31 Fed. Rep. 865.

[25] Gunn *v.* Peakes, 36 Minn. 177; Snell *v.* Faussatt, 1 Wash. C. C. (U. S.) 271; Robertson *v.* Struth, 5 Q. B. 941; Henderson *v.* Henderson, 6 Id. 288; Cowan *v.* Braidwood, 1 M. & Cr. 882, 892-895; 2 Wharton on Evid., Sec. 804 and cases cited.

[26] Fisher *v.* Fielding, 67 Conn. 91.

ant to contest the merits anew." There being no merger, the foreign judgment cannot of course in such case be set up as a bar, as could be done in the case of a domestic judgment," but it would seem that the record may be exhibited as marking the limit of the second recovery," and a plea of judgment recovered and satisfaction thereof will be a good defense to the action." But the pendency in a foreign court of another action for the same cause will not prevent an action here," for that circumstance is not available for a defense even as between our sister States.

But if, in such case, the foreign judgment was in favor of the defendant, he is entitled to plead it in bar, and, if a final adjudication of a competent court having jurisdiction in the cause and not misled by fraud, it will serve as a complete *exceptio rei judicatæ* in his favor." In pleading such a judgment, however, by way of justification or estoppel, it seems that the allegations are governed by a far more stringent rule than that obtaining in respect of declarations, and that it must be made clearly to appear, by express averments, that there existed all matters necessary to confer jurisdiction upon the foreign court, and that

---

[27] Wharton on Evid., Sec. 805.
[28] Wood v. Gamble, 11 Cush. (Mass.) 8.
[29] Smith v. Nicholls, 5 Bing. N. C. 208; dictum of Tindal, C. J. See also The Propeller East, 9 Benedict 76.
[30] Barber v. Lamb, 29 L. J., C. P. 234.
[31] Cox v. Mitchell, 7 C. B., N. S. 55; Russell v. Field, Stewart's Can. Rep. 558.
[32] Phillips v. Hunter, 2 H. Bl. 402, 410; Ricado v. Garcias, 12 Cl. & Fin. 368; Bigelow on Estop. (5th Ed.) 313. The reasonableness of this distinction which awards to a judgment for the defendant the force of an estoppel, but none to a judgment the other way, has been doubted. It is thus defended by a well-known writer: "The distinction, bearing in mind the fact that the doctrine of merger has no application, we conceive to be this: Any party may waive an advantage in his own favor, provided he does not thereby interfere with another's rights. The plaintiff waives such an advantage when he elects to bring a fresh suit upon the original cause of action, and this without injury to the rights of the defendant. He risks losing his case without the power, it would seem, of proving a larger claim than the amount for which the former judgment was rendered. The reason why he could prove no more than the sum recovered in the foreign suit, is that this would be to discredit the foreign judgment upon the merits; and this could not be done against the objection of the defendant, as we have seen. It is quite clear that though the plaintiff waives his rights, he does not endanger those of the defendant." Bigelow on Estop., p. 313. It seems doubtful how far this rule would be affected by the doctrine of reciprocity recently enunciated by the Supreme Court in Hilton v. Guyot, 159 U. S. 113. See *infra*.

the judgment there was a final one upon the identical issue sought to be litigated anew.⁸³

Inasmuch as the foreign judgment is not deemed to give rise to a record or specialty obligation, the appropriate general issue to an action founded upon it is *nil debet*, or *non assumpsit*, as the case may be, and never *nul tiel record*.⁸⁴

4. The statute of limitations of the *forum* may be specially pleaded in bar,⁸⁵ inasmuch as that appertains to the remedy, but a stay of execution granted in the foreign courts will not impair the efficacy of the judgment when employed in litigation here, nor will the pendency of an appeal, even where, by the foreign law, it operates as such a stay; but the domestic court may, if requested, grant a corresponding stay to await the outcome of the proceedings abroad.⁸⁶

5. We shall presently have occasion to discuss those matters which are essential to the validity of a foreign judgment. It would be a mere truism to state that the absence of these may be shown to nullify the force of the judgment in an action. If fraud be set up, the facts must be alleged with great particularity.⁸⁷ And where the jurisdiction of the foreign court is assailed, the pleading must be special, and must carefully negative every circumstance or state of facts by which jurisdiction might, by any possibility, have been rightfully entertained; otherwise it will be declared bad on demurrer.⁸⁸

II.

Hitherto our attention has been directed to foreign judgments solely with regard to matters of procedure, except so far as the question of their force and validity is inseparably involved in that consideration. Such matters, touching the remedy alone, are to be regulated wholly by the *lex fori*.⁸⁹ But

---

⁸³ Taylor on Evid., Sec. 1548; Frayes *v.* Worms, 10 C. B. N. S. 148. But see the language of Earle, C. J., in Barber *v.* Lamb, 29 L. J. C. P. 234.

⁸⁴ Walker *v.* Witter, Doug. Rep. 1; Chitty Pl. 485; Bissel *v.* Briggs, 9 Mass. 462. In Bischoff *v.* Wethered, 9 Wall (U. S.) 812, the plea was *nul tiel record;* but this was unnoticed by the court, the decision proceeding upon another ground.

⁸⁵ Story Conf. of Laws, Sec. 582*a* (8th Ed.); Don *v.* Lippmann, 5 Cl. & Fin. 1, 19–21; McElmoyle *v.* Cohen, 13 Pet. (U. S.) 312.

⁸⁶ See Wharton Conf. of Laws, Sec. 805.

⁸⁷ Ritchie *v.* McMullen, 159 U. S. 235.

⁸⁸ Hill *v.* Mendenhall, 21 Wall. (U. S.) 453; 2 Taylor on Evid., Sec. 1540, and cases cited.

⁸⁹ Story Conf. of Laws, Sec. 556.

turning now to the effect of foreign judgments as adjudications upon the rights of individuals, we find ourselves entering into the province of private international law. It is not our design, however, to make any exhaustive examination of the decisions of foreign tribunals or the opinions of the publicists; we purpose to limit ourselves to a light sketch of what the law of foreign judgments is, as discovered and declared by the courts of this country and of England, and of the grounds upon which it professes to be based.

What, then, is the force of a judgment recovered in a foreign land? And how may it be attacked?

1. It may be stated generally that the courts of England and of this country will not lend their aid to enforce a judgment, whether *in rem* or *in personam*, that was brought about through treachery and fraud. To hold a contrary view would be to force Justice to prostitute herself to the vile purposes of chicanery and corruption. The wise maxim, *Interest reipublicæ ut sit finis litium*, has its limitations, and they are reached when to apply it would be to turn courts into tools of covin, and accomplish rank injustice. So we find the books full of *dicta* to the effect that foreign judgments may be impeached for fraud.[40] Yet it is not so clear of what sort this fraud must be. It has never been doubted that any deception practiced *dehors* the proceedings themselves, by which a party was defrauded of his natural right to a full and fair trial of the merits of the controversy, would render the judgment or sentence a nullity. Examples of such fraud are, corruption of the presiding judge, or bribery of witnesses to disobey a subpœna, or entering judgment through treachery of counsel on the opposite side [41] or through collusion with parties joined with the one injured, or taking judgment by

---

[40] Ochsenbein v. Papelier, L. R. 8 Ch. App. 695, 698; Messina v. Petrochino, L. R. 4 P. C. 144; Bank v. Nias, 16 Q. B. 717, 735; Price v. Dewhurst, 8 Sim. 279; Hilton v. Guyot, 159 U. S. 113; Ritchie v. McMullen, Idem. 235; Fisher v. Fielding, 67 Conn. 91; 2 Taylor on Evid., Sec. 1533; Bigelow on Estop., (5th Ed.) 254; Black on Judgments, Sec. 844; Story on Conflict of Laws, Secs. 592, 597, 608; 2 Wharton on Evid., Sec. 803. In an early Connecticut case, however, involving a sentence of condemnation, passed by a foreign court of Admiralty, the court said: "The court are of opinion that such a sentence cannot thus be called in question, but must remain in full force until avoided in some regular mode, in the country where it passed." Stewart v. Warner, 1 Day (Conn. 1803) 142, 148. But it did not appear that the fraud there set up had affected in any way the decision of the foreign court.

[41] United States v. Flint, U. S. C. C. Cal. 1876. See Hunt v. Blackburn, 128 U. S. 464, 470.

default in breach of an agreement to discontinue suit.⁴² In such cases, there would be no real cause, no real issue, trial or judgment;⁴² but the whole of the proceedings, from start to culmination, would be an utter sham—a mere parody on justice. To reinvestigate this species of fraud is clearly not "to show that the court was mistaken," but to show "that they were *misled*," within the rule laid down in the celebrated opinion of Chief-Justice DeGrey, in the Duchess of Kingston's case.⁴⁴

But of late years there have been in England several express decisions on this subject which seem greatly to extend the doctrine previously advocated by the courts, holding that foreign judgments (and, indeed, it would seem, domestic judgments), may be impeached, if obtained by suppression of evidence and by fraudulent testimony, even though that very matter had been passed upon by the foreign court.⁴⁵ In the case of Aboulof v. Oppenheimer, first cited, (which was a suit on a judgment rendered by a Russian court in an action analogous to our replevin), Lord Justice Brett said:

"I will assume that in the suit in the Russian court the plaintiff's fraud was alleged by the defendants and that they gave evidence in support of the charge. I will assume even that the defendants gave the very same evidence that they propose to adduce in this action; nevertheless, the defendants will not be debarred at the trial of this action from making the same charge of fraud and from adducing the same evidence in support of it. * * * It has been contended that the same issue ought not to be tried in an English court which was tried in the Russian courts; but I agree that the question whether the Russian courts were deceived never could be an issue in an action tried before them."

In the case of Fisher v. Fielding, recently decided by the Supreme Court of Connecticut, this English doctrine is lucidly explained by Judge Baldwin, in the following language:

"In such case [claim of fraud] the merits may be re-tried, not to show that the foreign court came to a wrong conclusion, but that it was fraudulently misled into coming to a wrong conclu-

---

⁴² Ochsenbein v. Papelier, L. R. 8 Ch. App. 695; Pearce v. Olney, 20 Conn. 544; 1 Bigelow on Fraud, 88 n.

⁴³ See Fisher v. Fielding, 67 Conn. 91.

⁴⁴ 2 Smith L. C., 784, 794.

⁴⁵ Aboulof v. Oppenheimer (1882) L. R., 10 Q. B. Div. 295, 305, 308, followed and acted on in Vadala v. Lawes (1890) L. R., 25 Q. B. D. 310, and Crozat v. Brogdon (1894) 2 Q. B. 30.

sion. If the triers are convinced that the foreign judgment should have been rendered on the merits the other way, but still do not find that there was fraud, the defense fails."

These decisions, apparently, introduce a new and important principle into the doctrine of *res judicata* in England, not only in respect of foreign judgments, but in respect of domestic judgments as well. And they have not escaped severe criticism, both in this country and at home.[46] Assuming, for the sake of the argument, that the judgment of a competent foreign tribunal, having the requisite jurisdiction of the cause and of the parties, is to be regarded as conclusive on the merits, it would seem that the doctrine goes very far. Fraud is alleged in an action; evidence is brought forward in support of the allegation and against it; the issue thus raised is considered and passed upon by the court; we fail to perceive why such a decision is not upon the *merits* as fully as would be a decision concerning the validity of an instrument or the existence of a contract. If the court was competent to decide as to whether or not there was a contract, it would be equally competent to determine upon the existence of fraud. The distinction sought to be drawn appears, at first sight at least, to be subtle and metaphysical, rather than practical. In the case of Hilton v. Guyot,[47] the Supreme Court of the United States expressly abstained from passing an opinion concerning the correctness of this view, and it is difficult to see how they could uphold it consistently with the rule hitherto adhered to by that court in regard to domestic judgments.[48] In Vance v. Burbank, just cited, Mr. Chief-Justice Waite said:

"It has been settled that the fraud in respect to which relief will be granted in this class of cases must be such as has been practiced on the unsuccessful party, and prevented him from exhibiting his case fully to the department, so that it may properly be said that there has never been a decision in a real contest about the subject-matter of inquiry. False or forged documents even are not enough, if the disputed matter has actually been presented to or considered by the appropriate tribunal."

---

[46] See Van Fleet on Collateral Attack, Sec. 558; Bigelow on Estop. (5th Ed.), 307; Pigott on Foreign Judgments (2d Ed.), 106 et seq.; 6 Law Quar. Rev., Eng. 460.

[47] 159 U. S. 113.

[48] United States v. Throckmorton, 98 U. S. 61, 64; Vance v. Burbank, 101 U. S. 514, 519; Steel v. Smelting Co., 106 U. S. 447, 453; Moffat v. United States, 112 U. S. 24, 32; Marshall v. Holmes, 141 U. S. 589; see also Green v. Green, 2 Gray (Mass.) 361; Ross v. Wood, 70 N. Y. 8.

According to this view, the test is whether the defense was, or could have been, put in issue at the former trial. If so, relief must be sought in a motion for a new trial, or in some other direct proceeding.

The case of Christmas *v.* Russell, [5 Wall (U. S.) 290] decides that fraud is no defense to an action at law on a judgment of a sister State, on the ground that it will not avail (at law) to impeach a domestic judgment. "It is, however, an equitable bar to its enforcement, just as it is in case of a domestic judgment. A judgment may be good at law, and yet equity deem it against conscience for the plaintiff to stand upon his legal rights. In such a case it is because the judgment is good at law that equitable relief is granted."[49]

We do not understand the case last quoted as approving the doctrine of Aboulofí *v.* Oppenheimer, but, on the contrary, as repudiating it. Defendant had alleged that plaintiffs, well knowing that he was not personally liable for their claim, had nevertheless sued him personally to embarrass him and prevent a fair opportunity to defend, and had thereby sought an unfair advantage over him. The court, however, said:

"In Pearce *v.* Olney,[49a] these principles governed the decision: An injunction was granted on account of a fraud as to a matter which could not have been put in issue in the New York suit. An injunction was refused, on account of a fraud as to a matter which could have been put in issue in the New York suit. In the case at bar, by force of the Practice Act, equitable defenses could be pleaded by way of answer, but the defendant had no equity, because the question of his indebtedness to the plaintiffs, if it was to be contested, should have been put in issue before the English court," thus apparently applying the rule as to sister State judgments to a foreign judgment, and placing the question of fraud raised (if the allegation above referred to was considered as raising such a question), in the same category with other defenses on the "merits."

In England it seems that there is no distinction as respects fraud, between legal and equitable defenses. In a case precisely similar in its facts to Pearce *v.* Olney, the Chancellor said that the rule laid down in the Duchess of Kingston's case applied to courts of law and equity alike, and refused to restrain the action at law on the ground that the legal remedy was full

---

[49] Fisher *v.* Fielding 67 Conn. 91; 1 Bigelow on Fraud, 88 n.
[49a] 20 Conn. 544.

and adequate; and this decision was expressly declared to be uninfluenced by the new procedure permitting equitable defenses in legal actions.[49]

2. If a foreign judgment is to possess any validity before our tribunals, it must have proceeded from a court having competent authority to sit as such, with jurisdiction of the cause, the subject-matter, and the parties.[50]

"In order that a judgment may be relied on as *res judicata*, it must have been one of a legally constituted court. It is of the very root of the idea of the right of the state to settle the disputes of individuals that the machinery employed for the purpose should itself be constituted according to law."[51]

This is true of our domestic judgments; *a fortiori* is it true of judgments given in a foreign land. A party, (at least if he be not the one who sought the foreign jurisdiction), is in no way estopped to dispute the authority of the foreign tribunal, and the validity of its organization and constitution.[52] We have seen, however, that if there be nothing suspicious upon the face of the record, a presumption will be indulged in favor of the legality of the tribunal, and the judgments of a *de facto* court would be respected, for the same reason that gives them validity at home.[53] But no presumption of due constitution will exist where it appears that the court is one of an extraordinary kind, or of special jurisdiction.

The question of jurisdiction, its acquisition and extent, is a subject far too broad and intricate to be discussed with any degree of plenitude in an essay so superficial as this must necessarily be. Viewed from our standpoint, it is a question which has received but an imperfect answer from the courts.

Jurisdiction may be acquired in one of four chief ways: First, by possession of the subject-matter or *res*, entitling the court to pronounce a judgment *in rem;* secondly, by service upon the party defendant within the jurisdiction of the court of actual notice of the action; thirdly, by his voluntary appearance

---

[49] Ochsenbein *v.* Papelier, L. R. 8 Ch. App. 695.

[50] Rose *v.* Himley, 4 Cranch. (U. S.) 241, 269; Story on Confl. of Laws, Sec. 586; Bigelow on Estop., 251.

[51] Bigelow on Estop., 61.

[52] Black on Judgments, Sec. 821; Cucullu *v.* Ins. Co., 16 Am. Dec. 194; Snell *v.* Faussatt, 1 Wash. C. C. (U. S.) 271; The Griefswald, Swabey 430; The Flad Oyen, 1 Ch. Rob. 135; Elliott *v.* Piersol, 1 Pet. (U. S.) 328, 340.

[53] Black on Judgments, Sec. 821; Bank of North Amer. *v.* McCall, 4 Binn. (Pa.) 371.

therein, and fourthly, by constructive notice, through publication or otherwise.[54]

Over all property, whether real or personal, situate within its limits, the jurisdiction and dominion of a State, (except so far as restrictions are *ex comitate* allowed), are exclusive and absolute. It may prescribe the methods of its devolution and transfer, subject it to execution and forfeiture, or in any other manner operate upon it in accordance with its domestic laws, and the title thus conferred, or the changes thus effectuated, will be recognized and respected in every other jurisdiction.[55] On the other hand, any attempt on the part of one sovereignty to bind with its process or decrees property lying within the boundaries of another, would be absolutely nugatory and void. Therefore, a foreign judgment *in rem* or *quasi in rem*, whether it decide the title to a chattel, as in the case of the condemnation of a vessel in a court of admiralty, or the status of an individual, as in the case of a divorce, will be disregarded, if it appear that the subject-matter adjudicated upon was without the territorial limits of the foreign country or without the special jurisdiction of the tribunal that tried the cause.[56]

"The inconveniences of an opposite course would be innumerable, and would subject immovable [and, we add, movable] property to the most distressing conflicts arising from opposing titles, and compel every nation to administer almost all laws except its own in the ordinary administration of justice."[57]

But the court of chancery, provided it have jurisdiction of the parties, may act upon their consciences, (which is a euphemistic expression meaning threatened confinement in the common jail!), and thus indirectly, by a decree purely *in personam*, affect land lying in a foreign country, either to the extent of its entire disposition or with liens and burdens.[58] This has fre-

---

[54] "Considered from an international point of view, jurisdiction, to be rightfully exercised, must be founded either upon the person being within the territory, or upon the thing being within the territory; for otherwise there can be no sovereignty exerted, upon the known maxim. *Extra territoriam jus dicenti impune non paretur*. * * * On the other hand, no sovereignty can extend its process beyond its own territorial limits to subject either persons or property to its judicial decisions." Story on Confl. of Laws, Sec. 559.

[55] Idem, Secs. 550, 555, 557.

[56] Pennoyer *v*. Neff, 95 U. S. 714.

[57] Story Conf. of Laws, Sec. 555.

[58] Idem, Sec. 544.

quently been done in both England and America."⁹ The doctrine, however, should be confined within narrow boundaries, and "must be strictly limited to those cases where the relief decreed can be entirely obtained through the parties' personal obedience; if it went beyond that, the assumption would be not only presumptuous but ineffectual."⁶⁰ And it may be matter of grave doubt how far such decrees would be respected by a court acting under a system of jurisprudence whose genius differed greatly from that of our own.⁶¹

Every sovereign nation, having the sole custody of the lives, liberty and property of all within its dominions, whether citizens or foreigners, may by its laws prescribe through what means their interests shall be brought before its courts for adjudication.⁶² Dispensing with the personal notice, held so dear by the common law, its local policy may provide a purely constructive service, by publication or otherwise, which shall be deemed sufficient notice for all intents and purposes, and thus, without his day in court, and in utter ignorance of the fact that his rights are being assailed, a party may be forever precluded from disputing the subsequent proceedings, because the legislative will has said it shall be so. But this constructive process can never, as regards non-resident foreigners, confer jurisdiction for international purposes. Such proceedings, if not absolutely shocking and contrary to natural justice, can at least find no place in the common jurisprudence of the civilized world. It may then be laid down as a general principle of private international law, that no man, if he be not a citizen, or in some way owing allegiance to the State, will be held bound *in personam* by the judgment of a foreign tribunal in a suit whereof he had no personal notice served upon him, in the jurisdiction, unless he waived the same or voluntarily appeared in the action. This necessarily follows as a corollary from the axiomatic proposition heretofore stated, that within its own territorial limits the authority of every sovereign State is supreme. And so it has been expressly decided by the Supreme Court of the United

---

⁵⁹ Penn *v.* Lord Baltimore, 1 Ves. 444; Massie *v.* Watts, 6 Cranch. (U. S.) 148, 158; Muller *v.* Dows, 94 U. S. 444; Keyser *v.* Rice, 47 Md. 203.

⁶⁰ Westlake's Inter. Law, Art. 65; Story Conf. of Laws, Sec. 545; Wharton Conf. of Laws, Sec. 288, *et seq.*; Bispham's Eq., Sec. 366.

⁶¹ Wharton Conf. of Laws, Secs. 288, 290, 809. That such a decree will be enforced as between England and Ireland, see Houlditch *v.* Donegal, 2 Cl. & F. 470.

⁶² Story on Conf. of Laws, Sec. 541.

States and the Courts of England,[*] and, indeed, would seem self-evident on its face. The effect of such a judgment would be purely local.[*] The question, however, is complicated by other considerations. The courts of England have several times respected constructive service in cases where the party owed a general or qualified allegiance to the sovereignty wherein judgment was rendered against him, such allegiance being deemed to impose an obligation to conform to the determination of the court. Thus, in Douglas v. Forrest,[*] it was said by Lord Chief-Justice Best that "a natural-born subject of any country, quitting that country, but leaving property under the protection of its laws, even during his absence owes obedience to those laws, particularly where those laws enforce a moral obligation;" and, in Becquet v. MacCarthy,[*] Lord Tenterden went even farther and upheld a judgment rendered in the Island of Mauritius against a party who, though once resident there, had departed the jurisdiction before the action was begun, on the ground that process had been served on the Procurator-General who, by the law of the Island, was bound to take care of the interests of such absent party, and that it was to be presumed that the officer did his duty. These cases, however, have been criticized, (if not in effect overruled), in the more recent decisions of Don v. Lippman and Schibsby v. Westenholz;[*] and in the latter case the following conditions were suggested as conferring jurisdiction without personal notice. When the defendant was, at the time of the judgment, a citizen of the foreign country, or resident there and owing a temporary allegiance at the time the suit began, or (possibly) at the time the obligation was contracted, or where he had himself sought the foreign tribunal as plaintiff. The court expressly left open the question whether a party would be bound, who had been forced to come in and defend in order to protect his property, and very much doubted whether the mere existence of property in the foreign country would be sufficient basis of jurisdiction to warrant a judgment *in personam.*[*]

To what extent these suggestions would be adopted by our courts it is impossible to say in the absence of direct adjudica-

---

[*] Bischoff v. Wethered, 9 Wall. (U. S.) 812; Schibsby v. Westenhols, L. R., 6 Q. B. 155.

[*] Story Conf. of Laws, Sec. 546.

[*] 4 Bing., 686, 702.   [*] 2 B. & Ad. 951.

[*] 5 Cl. Fin. 21; L. R., 6 Q. B. 155.

[*] But see Voynet v. Barret, 54 L. J., Q. B. 521.

tion. It seems reasonable at least that a citizen should be held bound by any kind of service authorized by the laws of his country. But in Webster *v.* Reid[69] the court says:

"These suits were not a proceeding *in rem* against the land, but *in personam* against the owners of it. Whether they all resided within the territory or not does not appear, nor is it a matter of any importance. No person is required to answer in a suit on whom process has not been served or whose property has not been attached."

It is sometimes sought to bind a non-resident by an attachment of his property within the jurisdiction. Such proceedings, however, can operate only *in rem*, or *quasi in rem*, upon the property itself, and can confer no jurisdiction of the person which the courts of another sovereignty will respect.[70] Moreover, the "due process of law" of the Fourteenth Amendment requires that all personal judgments rendered in one of our States against non-resident citizens of another shall be preceded by personal service, or its equivalent.[71]

If, however, an individual voluntarily enter within the limits of a foreign sovereignty, he thereby submits himself to the jurisdiction of its courts, and it may be said that he agrees to abide the outcome of any action for damages that may be there instituted against him, and with notice of which he is there personally served. This is true even though his allegiance be of the most temporary character, as that of a mere transient sojourner in the country. The law on the subject has been so clearly laid down in a very recent decision of the Supreme Court of Connecticut that we may be pardoned for quoting from it somewhat at length. The case was one of a citizen of Connecticut temporarily stopping at a hotel in Birmingham while on a business trip in England. Process was served upon him just as he was about to return home. He disregarded it, and judgment went against

---

[69] 11 How. 437, 459. The case cited was one *in personam;* but, when the jurisdiction exercised is one *in rem*, or *quasi in rem*, property within the place of the forum may be subjected to judicial action by construction service of process authorized by statute. Arnot *v.* Griggs, 134 U. S. 316.

[70] Cooper *v.* Reynolds, 10 Wall. (U. S.) 308; Pennoyer *v.* Neff, 95 U. S. 714; The Mecca, 6 P. D. 106; Story on Conf. of Laws, Sec. 549.

[71] Pennoyer *v.* Neff, *supra;* Cooley on Const. Lim., 405. It seems to be taken for granted that our national and state constitutional provisions render substituted service in all cases—even in that of a citizen—ineffectual to bind personally. Cooley on Const. Lim., Sec. 403, *et seq.* But see an interesting and logical discussion in Beard *v.* Beard, 21 Ind. 321.

him in the English court by default. In a suit upon this judgment in Connecticut, the defendant set up a special plea to the jurisdiction of the foreign court, but it was held bad. Judge Baldwin said:

"The fact that the defendant was a foreigner, making but a brief stay in the country, and on the point of leaving it for his own, did not deprive the courts of England of all jurisdiction over him. The Roman maxim, *Actor sequitur forum rei*, if it has any force in English or American jurisprudence, operates as a permission, rather than a command. A man who is absent from his domicile can still be sued there; but he can also be sued wherever he is found, if personally served with legal process within the jurisdiction where the plaintiff seeks his remedy. The action must be brought, indeed, in a court to which the defendant is subject, and subject at the time of suit; but, unless protected by treaty stipulation or official privilege, he is subject to every court within reach of whose process he may enter. The Roman law allowed a non-resident to be sued where he had established a temporary seat of business, and, in some cases, where he had simply contracted a single obligation. The common law, so far as concerns the enforcement of a pecuniary liability, goes farther, and operates alike upon every private individual who may be found, however transiently, within the territory where it is enforced. * * * He [the defendant] put himself under the power of the court, the moment he entered the territory which was subject to its authority. Nor did he put himself under its power simply in the sense that it could issue process and render judgment against him, which would be of force within the limits of the territory. To that extent, its judgments might be valid, though rendered without any personal service, upon a simple attachment of goods, or by publication. But they would be mere expressions of the will of the sovereign, and impose no personal obligation which other sovereigns could recognize or enforce. Judgments rendered against a foreigner who is previously served when personally present stand on a ground wholly different. These, and these only, so far as actions for money damages are concerned, are entitled to full respect in the courts of other countries by the principles of international law. * * * The defendant accepted the forum, when he voluntarily placed himself on English soil, and so came under an implied obligation to respect such legal process as might be served upon him there, to the extent of satisfying any resulting judgment duly rendered for a pecuniary demand.'"[72]

---

[72] Fisher *v.* Fielding, 67 Conn. 91, 104, 108, 109.

But personal service without the jurisdiction can amount to nothing. And if the defendant be shown to have been decoyed into the jurisdiction for the purpose of being there served with process, it may be that a case of fraud is exhibited sufficient to render the whole proceeding void.[13] But an appearance solely for the purpose of safe-guarding property whether already in the hands of the court or liable to seizure on execution, will be considered as a voluntary one.[14]

3. Again, it is agreed that foreign judgments repugnant to natural justice are of no force whatever. And it would seem that the term "natural justice" may have reference to the substantive law of the foreign country,[15] though it would more often denote the method of procedure, and, in this sense. would be more or less merely synonymous with "due process of law"—an expression which implies a reasonable notice to the defendant and a chance to be heard before a competent and impartial tribunal.[16] The line which separates that which is from that which is not natural justice must needs be shadowy and indefinite, and to be determined only in each particular case, in the light of attendant circumstances, and of the general principles of private international law. In Bradstreet v. Neptune Insurance Company[16a] Mr. Justice Story said:

"It is a rule founded on the first principles of natural justice that a party shall have an opportunity to be heard in his defense before his property is condemned, and that charges on which the condemnation is sought shall be specific, determinate and clear. If a seizure is made and condemnation is passed without the allegation of any specific cause of forfeiture or offense, and without any public notice of the proceedings, so that the parties in interest have no opportunity of appearing and making a defense, the sentence is not so much a judicial sentence as an arbitrary sovereign edict. It has none of the elements of a judicial proceeding, and deserves not the respect of any foreign nation. * * * It may be binding upon the subjects of that particular nation, but, upon the eternal principle of justice, it ought to have no binding obligation upon the rights or property of the subjects of other

---

[13] See Black on Judgments, Sec. 909.

[14] Voynet v. Barret, 54 L. J., Q. B. 521; Hilton v. Guyot, 159 U. S. 113.

[15] Henderson v. Henderson, 6 Q. B. 288.

[16] See Price v. Dewhurst, 8 Sim. 279; Shaw v. Gould, L. R., 3 H. L. 55; Bradstreet v. Ins. Co., 3 Sumn. 600: Windsor v. McVeigh, 93 U. S. 274.

[16a] 3 Sumn. (U. S.) 600.

nations; for it tramples under foot all the doctrines of international law, and is but a solemn fraud, if it is clothed with all the forms of a judicial proceeding."

How far our courts would go in upholding judgments rendered by the tribunals of barbarous or semi-barbarous countries is an interesting speculation. An English court has held valid the title acquired by judicial sale of a British ship in the piratical state of Algiers.[77]

In this connection may be noticed judgments rendered abroad on summary proceedings in derogation of the common law, which our courts will not enforce.[78]

4. The local policy, penal or revenue laws and police regulations of another country, are not to be imported and effectuated here through the medium of a foreign judgment.

"Such decrees can have, and ought to have, no extra-territorial significance. They rest upon no principle of universal acceptation, like the obligation of contracts, or the protection of generally recognized private rights."[79]

5. Once more, no action can be based upon a foreign judgment of an interlocutory character, or, indeed, on any that has not the force of *res judicata* in the jurisdiction where rendered. In order that it may be enforced it must have been a final determination of the *rights of the parties*.

"The test of finality and conclusiveness of any judgment," said Lord Justice Lindley, "is to be found in the view taken of it by the tribunals of the country in which it was pronounced, and if a judgment leaves the rights of the parties uninvestigated and

---

[77] The Helena, 4 Ch. Rob. 3. Interesting opinion by Sir William Scott.

[78] Anderson *v.* Haddon, 33 Hun. (N. Y.) 435. In this case it is said that no foreign judgment will be held conclusive, even when the party charged appeared, if it is shown that the cause of action was one not known to the common law, and that the course of procedure did not furnish all the safeguards afforded by it; but in the case of Hilton *v.* Guyot, 159 U. S. 113, where it was urged that the defendant in the foreign action had been deprived of the right of cross-examination, and that various of the common law rules designed to exclude fraudulent and perjured testimony had not been observed, the court say: "It having been shown by the plaintiffs, and hardly denied by the defendants, that the practice followed and the method of examining witnesses were according to the laws of France, we are not prepared to hold that the fact that the procedure in these respects differed from that in our own courts is of itself a sufficient ground for impeaching the foreign judgment."

[79] De Brimont *v.* Penniman, 10 Blatch. (U. S.) 436; The Antelope, 10 Wheat. (U. S.) 66, 123; Ogden *v.* Folliot, 3 Ter. Rep. 726.

undetermined, and avowedly leaves their rights to be determined in some other proceeding, the judgment cannot be treated here as imposing an obligation which our tribunals ought to enforce."[60]

Of course the courts will never give greater effect to a foreign judgment than it would have at home.

And furthermore, a judgment *in personam*, to be enforced in an action, must be for a fixed sum of money, and never such that the obligation to obey it may depend upon the existence or non-existence of a particular state of circumstances. Our courts will never stultify themselves by taking cognizance of a case where the means of enforcing the obligation lie, or may lie, wholly beyond their control.[61]

6. Having considered the necessity of jurisdiction and absence of fraud, and certain other requirements affecting the validity of foreign judgments, we come now to the last, and perhaps the most important, of our inquiries: How far are they conclusive on the merits?

In treating of this interesting subject, it will be convenient to make a customary division of judgments, into those that are *in rem*, and those that are *in personam*.

The distinctive feature of judgments *in rem*, in our jurisprudence, (as distinguished from that of Rome), is that they are binding, not merely *inter partes*, but *inter omnes*, concluding all the world.[62]

Without entering upon a lengthy discussion of the topic, which would be foreign to our purpose, it may be said, generally, that the ground upon which this universal validity rests is, (1) that all persons are deemed to be parties to them; or (2) that the cause was tried between those who had the exclusive interest in the question involved.[63] Examples of cases coming within the first principle are decrees of courts of admiralty, in cases of prize,[64] bottomry, salvage, wages, collision,[65] or foreclosure of liens,[66] sales of wreck and derelict under municipal regulations,[67]

---

[60] Nouvion v. Freeman, L. R., 37 Ch. Div. 244, 255; Burnham v. Webster, 1 Woodb. & N. (U. S.) 172.

[61] Wharton Conf. of Laws, Sec. 804; De Brimont v. Penniman, 10 Blatch. (U. S.) 436.

[62] Bigelow on Estop. (5th Ed.), 45.

[63] Ibid, 45, 46, 224; Croudson v. Leonard, 4 Cranch, (U. S.) 434.

[64] Croudson v. Leonard, *supra;* Williams v. Armroyd, 7 Cranch, (U. S.) 423.

[65] The Propellor East, 9 Bened. 76; Harmer v. Bell, 7 Moore P. C. 267.

[66] Castrique v. Imrie, L. R., 4 H. L. 414.

[67] Grant v. McLachlin, 4 Johns. (N. Y.) 34.

and decrees of probate,[88] while within the latter principle come decrees confirming or dissolving marriage,[89] or establishing pedigree [90] or illegitimacy.[91]

Proceedings in attachment, replevin, and the like, are frequently spoken of as being *in rem;* but, in a strict sense, they are not. "They bind, at most, only the specific parties to the action, including of course their successors in right."[92] "Attachment is simply resorted to in order to take the place of notice or appearance, in other words, merely to give the court jurisdiction; it is a means, and not an end."[93]

It seems to be almost universally held in this country and in England, that the sentence of a foreign court of admiralty, having jurisdiction of the *res*, and in the absence of fraud, condemning a vessel as lawful prize, is conclusive, not only of the change of title, but of all the necessary facts upon which the decision proceeded.[94] The only exception appears to be in New York, where the sentence is held to be conclusive as to the title, but only *prima facie* evidence of the findings upon which it was based.[95] So, also, a sentence of acquittal fixes the fact that the property sought to be condemned is free from all liability to forfeiture.[96] And it makes no difference if an error of law be apparent on the face of the record.[97] But it is only in regard to matters essential to the decree that it is held binding,[98] and it will not

---

[88] Bigelow on Estop. (5th Ed.), 245.

[89] Bigelow on Estop., 243; Story on Conf. of Laws, Sec. 595.

[90] Ennis v. Smith, 14 How. (U. S.) 400.

[91] Blackburn v. Crawfords, 3 Wall. (U. S.) 175; Kearney v. Denn, 15 Idem. 51.

[92] Story on Conf. of Laws (8th Ed.), Sec. 592, note a.

[93] Bigelow on Estop. (5th Ed.), 49; Woodruff v. Taylor, 20 Vt. 65; The Bold Buccleugh, 7 Moore P. C. 267, 282.

[94] Black on Judg., Sec. 815; Bigelow on Estop. (5th Ed.), 221; Hughes v. Cornelius, 2 Show. 232; Bernadi v. Motteux, 2 Doug. 575; Croudson v. Leonard, 4 Cranch, (U. S.) 434; But see The Mary, 9 Cranch, (U. S.) 126, 145, and Brigham v. Fayerweather, 140 Mass. 411, 414.

[95] Vanderheuvel v. U. S. Ins. Co., 2 Johns. Cas. 451; Durant v. Abendroth, 97 N. Y. 132, 141.

[96] McGoun v. Ins. Co., 1 Story (U. S.) 157; The Bennett, 1 Dodson 175; Gelston v. Hoyt, 3 Wheat. (U. S.) 246.

[97] Williams v. Armroyd, 7 Cranch, (U. S.) 423; Castrique v. Imrie, L. R., 4 H. L. 414.

[98] Bernadi v. Motteux, 2 Doug. 574; Fitzsimmons v. Ins. Co., 4 Cranch, (U. S.) 185; Black on Judg., Sec. 817.

be regarded as conclusive, if the grounds of the decision be ambiguously stated, or do not clearly appear."

This doctrine, that such sentences are conclusive as to the necessary findings of fact, frequently comes up in inquiries purely collateral to the judgment itself, especially in suits against marine insurance companies, where it becomes important to know whether the vessel has broken the warranty of neutrality. In such cases, a finding in a foreign decree of condemnation of breach of blockade, for instance, would be conclusive to absolve the insurers from liability.[100]

All other valid judgments *in rem* are binding on all the world as to what is directly adjudicated, but not, it seems, as to the facts on which the decision rests.[101] Thus, in the case of Ennis v. Smith,[102] which was an action by persons claiming to be heirs of General Kosciuszko against the administrator of his estate, the Supreme Court of the United States held that certain decrees of courts in Lithuania, establishing pedigree, were, as judgments *in rem*, evidence against all the world of the matters of pedigree determined.

Decrees of status generally, when not contrary to a nation's policy, ought to be recognized everywhere when the parties interested were *bona fide* domiciled in the country where they were rendered; on the ground that the foreign court had full jurisdiction over the person, and that the cause was tried between those who had the exclusive interest in the litigation.

To treat specifically of the various kinds of judgments *in rem* would be to transcend the scope of this essay. Before leaving the subject, however, it should be said that, were the courts of one country to disregard the judgments of the courts of another, operating *in rem* upon the persons and things within their rightful jurisdiction, not only would great confusion of private interests result, with a consequent injury to commercial relations, but such disregard might possibly give rise to international complications. The pronouncement of a judgment *in rem* is not merely a declaration of justice between individuals; it is also an exercise of sovereign power, which it is the duty of all other sovereignties to respect.

---

[99] Bradstreet v. Ins. Co., 3 Sum. (U. S.) 600.

[100] Croudson v. Leonard, 4 Cranch, (U. S.) 434; Cucullu v. La. Ins. Co., 16 Am. Dec. 199.

[101] See Bigelow on Estop. (5th Ed.), 47; Brigham v. Fayerweather, 140 Mass. 411.

[102] 14 How. (U. S.) 400.

At the time of the Declaration of Independence, it was the established doctrine of the English courts in regard to foreign and colonial judgments *in personam* that, when made the basis of an action for their enforcement, they were to be regarded only as *prima facie* evidence of debt, but that when interposed as a defense, they afforded a complete *exceptio rei judicatæ*.

"It is in one way only," said Chief Justice Eyre, "that the sentence or judgment of a court of a foreign State is examinable in our courts, and that is when the party who claims the benefit of it applies to our courts to enforce it. When it is thus voluntarily submitted to our jurisdiction we treat it, not as obligatory to the extent to which it would be obligatory, perhaps, in the country in which it was pronounced, nor as obligatory to the extent to which by our own law sentences and judgments are obligatory, not as conclusive, but as matter *in pais*, as consideration *prima facie* to raise a promise."[103]

Since that time, the tide of judicial opinion has turned the other way, and it is now firmly held that foreign judgments, though impeachable on other grounds, (which we have already imperfectly considered), are absolutely conclusive on the merits. It is true, that in the important and leading case of Bank of Australasia *v*. Nias,[104] it was a colonial judgment that was involved, and Lord Campbell there expressly based his decision upon the ground that the defendant might have appealed to the Privy Council, and thus have obtained a review, saying out of abundant caution, "how far it would be permitted to a defendant to impeach the competency or the integrity of a *foreign* court, from which there was no appeal, it is unnecessary here to inquire"; but in the later case of Scott *v*. Pilkington,[105] this point of distinction seems entirely to have escaped the court's attention. That was a case involving a judgment rendered in the State of New York, and the Chief-Justice said:

"It was not denied that, since the decision in the case of Bank of Australasia *v*. Nias, we were bound to hold that a judgment of a foreign court, having jurisdiction over the subject-matter, could not be questioned on the ground that the foreign court had mistaken their own law, or had come on the evidence to an erroneous conclusion as to the facts."

---

[103] Phillips *v*. Hunter (1795), 2 H. Bl. 402. It would lead us too far to attempt to trace the vacillating course of the English cases. They are exhaustively collated and reviewed in Hilton *v*. Guyot, 159 U. S. 113, and Bigelow on Estop. (5th Ed.) 256, *et seq*.

[104] 16 Q. B. 717, 734–737.

[105] 2 Best & S. 11.

Not only is this now the settled law of England, but the courts have gone further, and hold that such judgments may not be impeached even when the record clearly shows that the foreign tribunal came to an erroneous conclusion in regard to English law. This was decided in Godard *v.* Gray (1870).[106] In that case, however, it did not appear that the defendant had called the foreign court's attention to what the English law really was, and it is quite possible that, in accordance with the doctrine of a former decision,[107] a manifest and *perverse* disregard of the law of England would still be closely scrutinized.

Naturally enough in the early days, the courts of America were disposed to follow the rule then obtaining in the parent country, and the judgments of foreign lands and of sister colonies were treated as only *prima facie* evidence of debt, before the adoption of the Constitution, and even for some time afterward when those colonies had become States.[108] Thus in Buttrick *v.* Allen (1811),[109] which was an action of *assumpsit* on a judgment from Nova Scotia, the court said:

"There is no doubt that *assumpsit* lies upon a foreign judgment, but the judgment is no more than *prima facie* evidence, and the defendant has all the benefits he would be entitled to in an action upon the original cause."

There are many others of these early cases which express the same opinion, but they are all, or nearly all, decisions concerning the validity of sister State judgments rendered before that question had been settled by the Supreme Court of the United States, or *dicta* concerning the force of foreign judgments thrown out in the course of such decisions.

It would be tedious to enter upon an historical examination of our law in this connection. New York, Maine and Illinois have in recent times declared in favor of the present English doctrine,[110] and within the past year the question has been twice authoritatively pronounced upon from different points of view,

---

[106] L. R., 6 Q. B. 139; see also Castrique *v.* Imrie, L. R., 4 H. L. 414.

[107] Simpson *v.* Fogo (1860), 1 John. & H. 18.

[108] See Hilton *v.* Guyot, 159 U. S. 113; Bigelow on Estop. (5th Ed.), 264.

[109] 8 Mass. 273 (1811).

[110] Lazier *v.* Westcott, 26 N. Y. 146, 150. It should be remarked that the lengthy discussion in this case regarding the conclusiveness of foreign judgments appears to be entirely *obiter*, inasmuch as the only questions raised by the pleas were purely technical, touching the admissibility of the exemplification of the foreign record. Dunstan *v.* Higgins, 138 N. Y. 70, 74; Rankin *v.* Goddard, 54 Me. 28, 55 Me. 389; Baker *v.* Palmer, 83 Ill. 568.

by the Supreme Court of the United States, and once by the Supreme Court of Connecticut.[111]

The first case cited, involved a judgment recovered in France by French citizens against American citizens who had been doing a mercantile business there. The second was an action by two parties plaintiff, one a citizen of Illinois, the other a citizen of Ontario, Canada, against a citizen of Ohio, upon a judgment recovered by the plaintiff against the defendant in the Queen's Bench Division of the High Court of Justice for the Province of Ontario. In both cases the merits of the original controversy were drawn in question by pleas, which were held good in the first instance and bad in the second.

These decisions introduce into our law of foreign judgments a new principle—the principle of reciprocity. The court did not content itself with sifting the American and English precedents and drawing its conclusions from them. The question involved was one, not of municipal, but of international, law, to be solved by the application of principles common to all civilized nations.

"International law in its widest and most comprehensive sense —including not only questions of right between nations, governed by what has been appropriately called the law of nations; but also questions arising under what is usually called private international law, or the conflict of laws, and concerning the rights of persons within the territory and dominion of one nation, by reason of acts, private or public, done within the dominion of another nation—is part of our law, and must be ascertained and administered by the courts of justice as often as such questions are presented in litigation between man and man, duly submitted to their determination. The most certain guide no doubt, for the decision of such questions is a treaty or a statute of this country. But when, as in the case here, there is no written law upon the subject, the duty still rests upon the judicial tribunal of ascertaining and declaring what the law is, wherever it becomes necessary to do so in order to determine the rights of parties to suits regularly brought before them. In doing this, the courts must obtain such aid as they can from judicial decisions, from the works of jurists and commentators, and from the acts and usages of civilized nations."

After an exhaustive examination of all the English and American authorities and of the doctrines adhered to in foreign countries, the court came to the conclusion:

---

[111] Hilton v. Guyot, 159 U. S. 113; Ritchie v. McMullen, Id. 235; Fisher v. Fielding, 67 Conn. 91.

"That there is hardly a civilized nation on either continent, which, by its general law, allows conclusive effect to an executory foreign judgment for the recovery of money. In France, and in a few smaller states—Norway, Portugal, Greece, Monaco and Hayti—the merits of the controversy are reviewed as of course, allowing to the foreign judgment, at the most, no more effect than of being *prima facie* evidence of the claim. In the great majority of countries on the continent of Europe—in Belgium, Holland, Denmark, Sweden, Germany, in many Cantons of Switzerland, in Russia and Poland, in Roumania, in Austria and Hungary, (perhaps in Italy), and in Spain—as well as in Egypt, in Mexico, and in a great part of South America, the judgment rendered in a foreign country is allowed the same effect only as the courts of that country allow to the judgments of the country in which the judgment in question is sought to be executed.

"The reasonable, if not the necessary, conclusion appears to us to be that judgments rendered in France, or in any other foreign country by the laws of which our own judgments are reviewable upon the merits, are not entitled to full credit and conclusive effect when sued upon in this country, but are *prima facie* evidence only of the justice of the plaintiff's claim. In holding such a judgment, for want of reciprocity, not to be conclusive evidence of the merits of the claim, we do not proceed upon any theory of retaliation upon one person by reason of injustice done to another, but upon the broad ground that international law is founded upon mutuality and reciprocity, and that by the principles of international law recognized in most civilized nations, and by the comity of our own country, which it is our judicial duty to know and to declare, the judgment is not entitled to be considered conclusive. * * * By our law, at the time of the adoption of the Constitution, a foreign judgment was considered as *prima facie* evidence, and not conclusive. There is no statute of the United States, and no treaty of the United States with France, or with any other nation, which has changed that law, or has made any provision upon the subject. It is not to be supposed that, if any treaty or statute had been or should be made, it would recognize as conclusive the judgments of any country which did not give like effect to our own judgments. In the absence of statute or treaty it appears to us equally unwarrantable to assume that the comity of the United States requires anything more."[112]

---

[112] Hilton v. Guyot, 159 U. S. 113.

This, then, is the doctrine of the Supreme Court of the United States, and may perhaps be now regarded as the doctrine of our country. It is the very reasonable rule, proposed by Mr. Justice Story, years ago, in his "Conflict of Laws," as likely, "hereafter to work itself firmly into the structure of international jurisprudence,"[113] and it may almost be assumed that it will henceforth, as cases arise, receive the approval of many of our State courts.[114] The fact is not to be overlooked, however, that the decision in Hilton *v.* Guyot was only reached by a majority of one. Mr. Chief-Justice Fuller delivered a very strong dissenting opinion, and Justices Harlan, Brewer and Jackson concurred in this dissent. It is conceived to be not impossible that any two men of equal understanding might well be led to take different sides on the question. In England the credit given to foreign judgments does not rest on comity, but on *obligation*.

"Where a court of competent jurisdiction has adjudicated a certain sum to be due from one person to another, a legal obligation arises to pay that sum, on which an action of debt to enforce the judgment may be maintained. It is in this way that the judgments of foreign and colonial courts are supported and enforced."[115]

These often quoted words of Baron Parke have been disparaged as being an outgrowth of the now exploded "Social Contract" theory, and it has been said that they referred, when spoken, only to matter of technical pleading;[116] but they have repeatedly been reasserted and approved, and are now firmly engrafted upon the English law as expressing the very foundation upon which the validity of foreign judgments is based.[117] It is admitted in Hilton *v.* Guyot that a personal judgment "be-

---

[113] Story Conf. of Laws, Sec. 618.

[114] The case of Fisher *v.* Fielding, involving as it did, an English judgment (like Ritchie *v.* McMullen, 159 U. S. 235), did not require any decision of this kind. If the court were careful in abstaining from any criticism of the doctrine of Hilton *v.* Guyot, they were equally careful to avoid expressing their approval of it. "The effect to be given to a foreign judgment *in personam*, for a money demand, must be determined either by the comity of nations, the rule of absolute reciprocity, or the personal obligation resting on defendant. Whichever test may be adopted, the result will be the same, when a question arises between the courts of England and those of an American State which was once an English colony."

[115] Williams *v.* Jones, 13 Mees. & W. 628, 633.

[116] Hilton *v.* Guyot, 159 U. S. 113, and argument for appellant.

[117] See Godard *v.* Gray, L. R., 6 Q. B. 139, 148.

tween two citizens or residents of the country, and thereby subject to the jurisdiction in which it is rendered, may be held conclusive as between them everywhere. So, if a foreigner invokes the jurisdiction by bringing an action against the citizen, both may be held by a judgment in favor of either. And if a citizen sues a foreigner, and judgment is rendered in favor of the latter, both may be held equally bound."[118] It is only in the case of a judgment "purely executory, rendered in favor of a citizen or resident of the country, in a suit there brought by him against a foreigner" that the principle of reciprocity is to be invoked. Now, assuming that it is the province of courts to do justice between individuals, (having always due regard for local policy), and not to manœuvre governmental affairs, might not this rule of reciprocity defeat the very end for which they exist? Because the courts of another nation refuse to do justice, is that a good and sufficient reason why our courts should follow in their lead? It is the glory of our common law that it recognizes no distinction between the suitors that stand before its altar, but, be they citizens or be they strangers, metes out justice with an even hand. "With us, the law of the land protects all who stand upon it, and whenever a right has been violated, gives a remedy, without regard to the nationality of the offender."[119] "The common law recognizes no distinction whatever as to the effect of foreign judgments, whether they are between citizens, or between foreigners, or between citizens and foreigners. In all cases, they are deemed of equal obligation whoever are the parties."[120]

And if it be contended that the principle of reciprocity is an expedient one to adopt in order to induce such countries as France to change their attitude towards our own judgments, it may not be impertinent to quote the words of Chief-Justice Fuller:

"I cannot yield my assent to the proposition that because by legislation and judicial decision in France that effect is not there given to judgments recovered in this country which, according to our jurisprudence, we think should be given to judgments wherever recovered (subject, of course, to the recognized exceptions); therefore we should pursue the same line of conduct as respects the judgments of French tribunals. The application of the doctrine of *res judicata* does not rest in discretion, and it is

---

[118] Hilton *v.* Guyot, *supra*.
[119] Fisher *v.* Fielding, 67 Conn. 91.
[120] Story on Conf. of Laws, Sec. 610.

for the government, and not for its courts, to adopt the principle of retortion, if deemed under any circumstances desirable or necessary."[121]

And again, of Chief-Justice Taney:

"It is truly said in Story's 'Conflict of Laws,' that, 'In the silence of any positive rule, affirming or denying or restraining the operation of foreign laws, courts of justice presume the tacit adoption of them by their own government, unless they are repugnant to its policy or prejudicial to its interests. It is not the comity of the court, but the comity of the nation, which is administered and ascertained in the same way, and guided by the same reasoning by which all other principles of municipal law are ascertained and guided.'"[122]

It seems not unreasonable to believe that, apart from any "Social Contract" idea, a judgment rendered in a foreign country, after a fair trial according with civilized notions of procedure, does raise an obligation. The maxim, *Judicium redditur in invitum*, is true enough. But all obligations, even express contracts, are enforced *in invitum*, otherwise the intervention of a law suit would be a wholly useless proceeding. Assuredly, when a man enters into business in a foreign land, or even when he resides there for a time, as a sojourner, under the protection of its laws, he impliedly agrees to abide the issue of any litigation into which he may be called, and wherein all things are conducted in conformity with the recognized principles of natural justice. *A fortiori* is this true of one who enters into contractual obligations there, into the very structure of which the *lex loci* must be interwoven. What ground, then, is there for this discrimination, in regard to their legal obligation, between contracts made abroad, and the judgments that may be pronounced upon them?

"In any aspect, it is difficult to see why rights acquired under foreign judgments do not belong to the category of private rights acquired under foreign law. Now, the rule is universal in this country that private rights acquired under the laws of foreign States will be respected and enforced in our courts unless contrary to the policy or prejudicial to the interests of the State where this is sought to be done, and, although the source of this rule may have been the comity characterizing the intercourse between nations, it prevails to-day by its own strength, and the

---

[121] Hilton *v.* Guyot, 159 U. S. 113, 229; dissenting opinion.
[122] Bank of Augusta *v.* Earle, 13 Pet. 519, 589.

right to the application of the law to which the particular transaction is subject is a juridical right."[133]

Foreign laws are generally said to receive recognition only through comity—a term which seems often to signify little more than courtesy to other sovereignties springing from national selfishness. Let it be granted that the State, owing to the infirmities of human nature, must, in its international relations, of necessity be self-regarding; still, in the transactions of individuals, this necessity does not always exist. There is another and a higher view which says that the laws of foreign countries not repugnant to our local policy are recognized in our courts, because, without such recognition, justice between man and man could not be done.[134] The Supreme Court itself must have seen an obligation to obey a foreign judgment, else how could it have consented to confide the sacred rights of American citizens to the rule of absolute reciprocity, which applies as well to despotic military Russia, as to enlightened Great Britain.

On the whole, it appears that the doctrine of England stands upon far loftier principles than the doctrine of the United States. Which of the two will prove superior in practical operation is another question.

There is a further argument for the conclusiveness of foreign judgments, which is based upon the maxims, *Nemo debet bis vexari pro una et eadam causa*, and *Interest reipublicæ ut sit finis litium*. Not only would it be unjust to individuals to permit the reopening of a controversy once fairly tried and settled, after the original evidence may have become unattainable or lost, but the public welfare itself imperatively demands that there shall be some limit set to litigation. A contrary doctrine would injuriously affect the stability of private rights, greatly to the detriment of commercial and business relations, and entail a needlessly heavy burden upon the finances of the commonwealth.

In closing this discussion we cannot do better than quote again from the decision in the case of Fisher *v.* Fielding, so often cited before:

"The maxim, *Interest reipublicæ ut sit finis litium*, is not restricted in its application to controversies or suits originating in the State before whose courts it is invoked. It does not rest on the excellence of any particular system of jurisprudence. It governs wherever the parties come, in the last resort, before a

---

[133] Chief Justice Fuller in Hilton *v.* Guyot, 159 U. S. 113, 229.
[134] See note concluding Ch. II. of Story Conf. of Laws (8th Ed.)

court constituted under an orderly establishment of legal procedure. No one who has been or could have been heard upon a disputed claim, in a cause to which he was duly made a party, pending before a competent judicial tribunal having jurisdiction over him, proceeding in due course of justice, and not misled by the fraud of the other party, should be allowed, after final judgment has been pronounced, to renew the contest in another country. The object of courts is hardly less to put an end to controversies than to decide them justly."[138]

Ernest Knaebel.

---

[138] 67 Conn. 91.

YALE LAW JOURNAL

SUBSCRIPTION PRICE, $2.00 A YEAR　　　　　　　SINGLE COPIES, 35 CENTS

EDITORS:
ROGER S. BALDWIN, *Chairman.*
HUGH T. HALBERT, *Treasurer.*

CHRISTOPHER L. AVERY, JR.　　　GEO. JAY GIBSON,
SAMUEL F. BEARDSLEY.　　　　　JOHN MACGREGOR, JR.
MICHAEL GAVIN, 2D.　　　　　　HENRY W. MERWIN,

Published six times a year, by students of the Yale Law School
P. O. Address, Box 1341, New Haven, Conn.

If a subscriber wishes his copy of the JOURNAL discontinued at the expiration of his subscription, notice to that effect should be sent; otherwise it is assumed that a continuance of the subscription is desired.

A STUDY of the development of civilized society from primeval barbarism is interesting if for no other reason than as emphasizing the power of economic forces. The first law to be recognized by law interpreters and to be declared by law makers was that of self preservation or the law of self-defense. The first idea of this law seems to have been that men were natural enemies, and had no interests in common. This crude conception, however, gave way to the more rational recognition of the mutual benefits arising out of the peaceful intercourse of men. The realization of the dependence and interdependence of individuals was the touchstone which caused the formation of the family, the tribe and the state, and as these organizations assumed various but definite shapes, as their interests grew and the necessity for peace within the organization increased, the rights of man became identified with and subject to the rights of men. Individual reparation might be obtained but only in a manner and by means which would not be detrimental to the rights of others. Tribunals were established where all might set forth their grievances, and obtain redress; interest multiplied and litigation increased but the omnipresent power that enforced the law's decree was the public interest which, as was realized, could be best subserved by orderly submission to superior authority. The unsuccessful litigant, desirous of an appeal to violent measures, was opposed by the rest of the community whose interests lay in peace. So long as men were merely independent individuals and under no social restraint their interests were their own and unshared by others, but as members of a society with their welfare indivisibly connected with the welfare of their neighbors, their interests were mutual, and violence was forced to submit to a curb. That the cause of this result lay in no moral sanction, although morality may have aided in its development, that it was not dependent upon religious influence, although religion may have given its endorsement, is made clear by the fact that those who were forced to submit to peaceable measures were just those who were least susceptible to moral and religious influences. It was not sentiment that controlled society but the power of public interests which demanded and obtained recognition. The development was purely the result of economic conditions sanctioned by economic forces.

* * *

IN discussing international development an application of the principles which underlie the development of man as an individual to man as a member of society seems to be pertinent and inevitable. The position of man as a citizen of a nation may be regarded as similar to the position of a nation as one of the recognized sovereignties of the world. The sovereignty of man was supreme until restricted by an acknowledgment of a superior authority; the sovereignty of nations will be supreme until they in turn are restricted by their acknowledgment of some higher power. The forces which caused the individual to be merged in the nation have been claimed to have been economic; the forces which should cause the nation to become merged in a higher organization would seem to be economic also. The essential characteristics which appear in the development of man as an individual into man as a member of a family were repeated in the development of the family as a separate organization into the family as a member of a tribe, while the same characteristics appeared again in the development of the tribe into a state and of the state into a nation. It was the evolution of a less into a greater; the fusion of many of a lower order into one of a higher order, and there seems to be no reason why this evolution should cease. The forces which were at work then are at work now and the reasons which explained them seem still to be applicable. As individuals recognized that a separate existence was undesirable and as the generation of their relationship towards one another made such separate existence impossible, is it not natural to presume that nations, as they become better acquainted and more nearly identified with their neighbors, will recognize that separate existence in their case also is undesirable, and is it not possible that this development should cause such national individualism to cease? War means destruction of property and interruption of commerce and is opposed therefore to the welfare of nations and of the world. As international interests increase and international commerce grows the dangers resulting from war will become magnified, and since what is best for the majority must eventually triumph it seems as if the forces which caused the individual litigant to submit to a peaceable and impartial hearing might operate upon the individual states also. The peace and welfare of the world might then be emancipated from the willful actions of one nation.

* * *

What then may be said of the application of these principles to the proposed establishment of a permanent international court. Granting that an international organization and a permanent international court under certain circumstances are possible, are we justified in assuming that those circumstances now exist? Has international intercourse so far developed as to warrant the establishment of such a court; have international relations become so intimate and interdependent as to make possible the immediate realization of the poet's dream? The facts do not appear so. Instead of friendly competition we see hostile rivalry; instead of mutual concessions we see mutual selfishness. The position of the nations of the world towards each other to-day is one of watchfulness and suspicion, and there is still an individuality among them which would scarcely admit of the establishment of even a family of nations, still less of a more extended form of organization. The principle of the interdependence of nations is not yet developed and the general understanding seems still to be that each nation is for itself and each nation is against the other. The need or the desirability of amalgamation is not yet recognized.

While believing that international development has not yet so far progressed as to make probable prolonged peace or stability of international unions, the practical adjustment of the Venezuelan difficulty seems to point to the efficiency of the present system of special arbitration and to advocate its continuance, at least until international affairs may warrant, more than they do at present, a change to a more ambitious system. The circumstances indeed surrounding the controversy prove almost conclusively the impracticability of a successful operation of a permanent international court such as is proposed. It was a question of policy whether or not Great Britain should allow the United States to interfere in a dispute which only indirectly concerned her, and this was not a question which could be decided by a third party however justly. It was a question which either party might well have claimed to touch their sovereignty and so to be beyond the jurisdiction of any arbitral tribunal. The sanction which is continually attributed to the proposed count, if established, seems to be based upon the sentiment of public opinion or an indefinite fear of it, a "pious hope" that international comity is sufficiently strong and international honor sufficiently developed to ensure a recognition of the court's jurisdiction and a submission to its decrees. The actual condition, however, of international relations and the spirit which controls them seem hardly to justify such a hope. As recent illustrations of the tendency towards the peaceful settlement of international difficulties we have indeed the Venezuelan dispute, mentioned above, and the submission to arbitration of a dispute between two southern republics which was brought about by the friendly intercession of the United States. But as opposed to this evidence of the increasing fellowship of nations we have a rescission of the provision in the Shimonoseki treaty between Japan and China, which allowed foreigners to engage in manufacturing in China and by this rescission we have a restoration of Chinese exclusion. The recent proclamation of the President of the United States revoking his proclamation of January 26, 1888, by which German vessels were relieved from tonnage dues and other charges in American ports, is surely not to be taken as a sign of international friendship, especially as it is intended to be a retaliation for the alleged unfair treatment of American vessels by Germany. The position of each nation may be individually correct and justifiable, but in weighing it as evidence with other of a similar nature it would surely seem as if the petty and gross jealousies, the suspicions and ambitions which absorb European and perhaps even American politics, gave no great promise of an immediate millennium of peace on earth and the good will of men. A sentimental sanction of such a character seems ephemeral indeed when it is realized that the opposition at the present day of one great power to the decision of a permanent international court might well so further entangle the already snarled strings of international relationships as to render the enforcement of such decision hopeless and not to be expected. The court would then be merely a figure-head, a false idol, a mock symbol of a peace that in reality almost passeth our understanding and a benefit to no one but those whose tender sensibilities can find consolation in the shadow of their desires. The perhaps pardonable enthusiasm which prompts the advocates of the present movement towards a more extended system of international arbitration may be recognized in former treaties and confederations between kindred states and yet these attempts to establish a more perfect union without a corresponding centralization of an adequate superior power have failed whenever put to the test. In the present instance the circumstances seem even less propitious than before, inasmuch as the ties of blood and community of territorial interests would be lacking in any such agreement between nations divided by the sea, by differences of race and of climatic conditions. There is also no immediate and present common danger which would force the half-hearted together, giving them common interests, and there is little or no recognition of that which would be best for the world in general as opposed to the interests of nations individually. Indeed, in this country, which is supposed to be the chief and most powerful advocate of international peace and justice, the victorious party in the last election seems to base its success to no inconsiderable extent upon its advocacy of the principle of Protection, which means a denunciation of the principles of Free Trade, an interruption of a freer action of commerce and consequently a repudiation of what might become a greater bond of union between the nations of the world, a bond far stronger and more real than any artificial symbol of peace which might be invented. Whatever our political beliefs may be it should be clear that the truth or falsity of the theory of Protection does not comprehend the point in issue; it is the existence of these theories and principles, of these conditions and circumstances, that causes hesitation and the belief that the time for the establishment of a permanent international court and for the federation of the world has not yet come. And indeed, it must be a federation which is established before such a court can be of much practical benefit. No mere precatory clause in a treaty, no mere treaty itself or even confederation can be productive of real permanent good except so far as it is evidence of a peaceful disposition. In order to stand the test of the disloyalty and discontent, which is sure sooner or later to arise among the members of an international organization, there must be established an international sovereignty with a positive sanction to sustain it, and to make this possible there must be a greater community of national interests, a higher sense of national duty, and a higher degree of international sympathy. * * *

THE recent election is an encouragement to advocates of democratic government and yet it furnishes much that merits most serious consideration. The experiment, for it must still be considered as such, of uniting so vast a territory as that of the United States under one general government, received indeed a decided endorsement through the result of the popular vote cast in favor of conservatism, but perhaps the greatest encouragement is to be taken from the absolute submission of the defeated party. The conflict of principles even among those who live under the same climatic conditions and with virtually common interests is often sufficiently intense to justify uneasiness, but when to this natural difference of individual opinion is added a difference of latitude and longitude the Civil War is an example of what may under certain circumstances occur in consequence. It seems indeed most doubtful whether the United States, if they were now separate nations, could be united into one great power. It was chiefly due to their gradual growth that their organization was kept intact, and it is to their further development that we must look for a stronger and more perfect union. With a general government sufficiently strong to enforce obedience to its laws, each addition to the number of individual States was a corresponding addition to the strength of the federal sovereignty, and the fact that such an issue as was presented to American citizens in the last election could be decided in accordance with the principles of conservative government and that the result, unfavorable territorially at least to far more than half of the United States, was so peaceably received is proof of the present strength of our nationality. But when we consider the number of States whose interests are thought by the majority of their inhabitants to be antagonistic to the interests of their older and more developed sisters we must realize the difficulties which remain to be overcome before the emblem of our nation can be represented with the feathered wings of rest and security. It is interesting to notice the constitutional provisions which protect sectional interests and yet to perceive the bitterness with which this subject is even now discussed. "The Senate of the United States shall be composed of two Senators from each State, chosen by the Legislature thereof; * * * no Tax or Duty shall be laid on articles exported from any State; * * * the citizens of each State shall be entitled to all Privileges and Immunities of Citizens in the several States." Such are some of the constitutional safeguards against sectional favoritism and yet sectionalism is probably the gravest question in American politics to-day. The fact then that, in the case of such a vexed issue as was submitted to the popular vote in the last election, the result was so satisfactory should be a cause for some congratulation. The United States with its various and diverse interests may become an example to the nations of the world of the possibilities for international organization which may be theirs by right of economic development and evo-

COMMENT.

The case of *Salomon* (pauper) v. *A. Salomon & Co.* (Limited), recently decided by the House of Lords, furnishes an interesting illustration of the extent to which a person may be protected in forming a company to carry on his own private business, selling out to the company and practically operating it as a "one-man" concern.

In 1892 A. Salomon & Co. was incorporated with a capital of $200,000, divided into shares of $5 each. One of the objects for which the company was incorporated was to carry out an agreement which had been entered into by Salomon and a trustee for a company intended to be formed for the acquisition of the business then carried on by Salomon, who had been a leather merchant and boot manufacturer for many years. The business had been prosperous and was solvent at the time of the incorporation. The memorandum of association was subscribed by Salomon, his wife and daughter and four sons each subscribing for one share. Salomon afterwards had 20,000 shares allotted to him and $25,000 of debentures, which were paid for by the purchase money which the company was to pay him for the transfer of the business. Upon the security of the debentures Salomon obtained a loan from one Broderip. No other shares were issued by the company, it having been all along the intention of Salomon to retain the business in his own hands and not allow any outside party in it whatever. Subsequently the debentures were recalled and a new lot issued to Broderip to secure the payment of his loan with interest. Default having been made in the payment of interest upon his debentures, Broderip instituted an action on behalf of himself and Salomon, also a debenture holder, to enforce his security against the assets of the concern. Thereafter a liquidation order was made and a liquidator appointed at the instance of the unsecured creditors of the company. To the suit of Broderip this liquidator, at the suggestion of the presiding judge, set up by way of counterclaim, that the company was formed by Salomon and the debentures were issued in order that he might carry on the business and take all the profits without risk to himself, that the company was the mere nominee and agent of Salomon, and that the company or the liquidator thereof was entitled to be indemnified by Salomon against all the debts owing by the company to the creditors other than Salomon. The judge thought the liquidator entitled to the relief asked for. He was of opinion that the company was only an alias for Salomon; that the intention being that he should take the profits without running the risk of the debts, the company was merely an agent for him and having incurred liabilities at his instance was, like any other agent under such circumstances, entitled to be idemnified by him against them. On appeal this judgment was affirmed by the Court of Appeal, that court being of opinion that the formation of the company, the agreement as to the purchase of Salomon's business and the issue of debentures pursuant to such agreement, were a mere scheme to enable him to carry on business in the name of the company with limited liability, contrary to the true intent and meaning of the Companies Act of 1862, and further to enable him to obtain a preference over other creditors of the company by procuring a first charge on its assets by means of such debentures. The Court of Appeal did not hold that the company was to be regarded as the agent of Salomon. They regarded the relation between them as that of trustee and *cestui que* trust.

The judges of the House of Lords did not agree with the views advanced by either of the courts below. The formalities of law had been in all respects complied with in the formation of the company. The fact that it was incorporated to carry on Salomon's business and that he owned practically all the stock did not make it Salomon's agent; nor did it matter that Salomon's sons were mere "dummies." They owned one share, the law required no more.

The closing words of Lord Watson in distinguishing this case from *Erlanger* v. *The New Sombrero Phosphate Company* (L. R. 3 Ap. Cas. 1218) are worthy of note. He says: "But I am willing to assume that proceedings which are permitted by the Act may be so used by the members of a limited company as to constitute a fraud upon others, to whom they in consequence incur personal liability. In this case the fraud is found to have been committed by the appellant against the creditors of the company but it is clear that if so, though he may have been its originator and the only person who took benefit from it, he could not have done any one of those things which taken together are said to constitute its fraud without the consent of the other shareholders. It seems doubtful whether a liquidator as representing and in the name of the company can sue its members for redress against a fraud which was committed by the company itself and by all its shareholders. However, I do not think it necessary to dwell upon this point, because I am not satisfied that the charge of fraud against the creditors has any foundation is fact. * * * The unpaid creditors of the company whose unfortunate position has been attributed to the fraud of appellant if they had thought fit to avail themselves of a means of protecting their interests which the Act provides, could have informed themselves of the terms of purchase by the company, of the issue of debentures by the appellant, and of the amount of shares held by each member. In my opinion, the statute casts upon them the duty of making inquiry in regard to those matters. Whatever may be the moral duty of a limited company and its shareholders, when the trade of the company is not thriving, the law does not lay any obligation upon them to warn other members of the public who deal with them upon credit that they run the risk of not being paid. * * * In my opinion, a creditor who will not take the trouble to use the means which the statute provides for enabling him to protect himself must bear the consequences of his own negligence."

RECENT CASES.

CONSTITUTIONAL LAW.

Eminent Domain—Taking Private Property without Compensation or Due Process.—Dilworth v. State, 36 S. W. Rep., 274 (Tex.). A statute making it a misdemeanor to build or maintain a fence three miles long without a gate is unconstitutional, for it impliedly creates a public right of way, through these gateways, across the land, without making provision for recompense to the owner or for condemning the property for this public use.

Equal Protection of Laws—License Tax.—In re Yot Sang, 75 Fed. Rep. 983 (Mont.). The Fourteenth Amendment to the Constitution of the United States provides that, "No State shall deny to any person within its jurisdiction the equal protection of the laws," and a Montana statute imposing a license tax of but $15 per quarter upon steam laundries, while levying a tax of $25 per quarter on every laundry business other than that of a steam laundry wherein more than one person is employed or engaged, is a violation of this provision and consequently void.

CONTRACTS.

Claims against Decedent Estate—By Daughter—Implied Contract.—Arnold et al. v. Wise's Adm'r et al., 37 S. W. Rep. 83 (Ky.). Upon the request of her father, the plaintiff and her son left the boarding place provided by her husband, and lived seven years with her father, until his death. Held, that there being no actual contract the facts in the case do not authorize the Court to infer or presume a contract to pay her for her services.

Contract of Sale—Unauthorized Act of Agent—Recision by Purchaser—Placing Vendor in statu quo—Public Policy—Collateral Agreement.—Rackemann v. Riverbank Imp. Co., 44 N. E. Rep. 990 (Mass.). Where an agent employed to sell transcends his authority by promising a purchaser that adjacent lots will not be sold at less than a certain figure, which promise is subsequently broken, the purchaser may effect through equity a recision of the contract, provided the vendor may be put in his original position. And the fact that the purchaser has had possession and enjoyment for nearly a year is immaterial. Such a promise by the agent is construed to be only for a reasonable time and is not contrary to public policy. It is a collateral promise and may be proved by parol.

Destruction of Subject before Completion—Amount of Recovery.—Hayes v. Gross, 40 N. Y. Supp. 1099. Having made a contract for the carpenter work in a building in course of erection, to be paid in installments, and the building being destroyed by fire before the completion of the contract, the contractor is entitled to recover for the work done and the material actually used at contract prices, but not for that on hand.

Landlord and Tenant—Eviction of Tenant by Landlord—What Constitutes.—Silber v. Larkin et al., 68 N. W. Rep. 406 (Wis.). Where a landlord performed acts which interfered with the tenant's possession of the leased premises, and rendered them unfit for occupation and unsuitable for purposes for which they were hired, his action was held to constitute an eviction and the tenant was thereby entitled to damages.

Principal and Agent—Attorney and Client—Power of Attorney to Bind his Client.—Mulligan v. Cannon, 41 N. Y. Supp. 279. In all cases the natural presumption is that credit is given to the principal rather than to the agent. Where an attorney has employed an expert witness, in the absence of proof of an express promise to pay by the attorney or of facts tending to limit his authority such a witness may recover reasonable compensation from the client.

CORPORATIONS.

Distribution of Assets Among Stockholders—Mistake—Recovery of Assets by Corporation.—Grant v. Ross et al., 37 S. W. Rep. 263 (Ky.). Where a corporation declares a dividend under a mistaken belief that it is solvent, and that enough would remain to pay its liabilities, and then makes an assignment, the assignee may reclaim from the stockholders such assets as were thus distributed.

Insolvency—Effect of Preferring Creditors.—Allison v. Bradt Publishing Co., 37 S. W. Rep. 10 (Tenn.). The execution by an insolvent corporation of deeds of trust covering practically all its property and effectually winding up its business and giving preferences to one set of creditors over another is such an overt act of insolvency as to authorize a court of chancery to set them aside; otherwise if corporation continued in business, though actually insolvent.

NEGLIGENCE.

Carriers—Contributory Negligence.—Warfield v. *N. Y., L. E. & W. R. R. Co.*, 40 N. Y. Supp. 785. A person who is crossing a track at a station in order to board a train standing on another track is not obliged to observe the rule requiring a traveler on a highway which crosses a railroad to look and listen for approaching trains before crossing. Also a railroad company must exercise due diligence to warn people of the approach of trains such as by stationing an employee on the end of the train, blowing the whistle or ringing the bell.

Negligence—Who May Recover.—Glenn v. *Winters*, 40 N. Y. Supp. 659. The defendant let a defective coach to a social club for a day's excursion. The plaintiff, a guest of the club, had been invited to join the party and was injured by the overturning of the coach. The defendant was as liable to a guest of the club for a breach of duty in not furnishing a reasonably safe vehicle as to a member of the club itself.

Proximate Cause—Negligence.—Enochs v. *Pittsburgh, C. C. and St. L. Ry. Co.*, 44 N. E. Rep. 658 (Ind.). That a railway company negligently blocks up a street crossing so that a pedestrian, who is in a hurry, is obliged to pass around the train by an unusual route and in the dark, and in so doing sustains serious injury by falling over a misplaced stone, does not render the railway company liable, on the ground of proximate cause.

MISCELLANEOUS.

Australian Ballot Law—Ballots.—Jennings v. *Brown*, 46 Pacific Rep. 77 (Cal.). Voters wrote the party designation "Independent Democrat" upon the ballot in addition to the name of party voted for. Held, that this does not mark the ballot so as to constitute a distinguishing mark and hence does not invalidate the ballot.

Carriers—Fare—Legal Tender—Ejectors of Passenger.—Atlanta Consol. St. Ry. Co. v. *Keeny*, 25 S. E. Rep. 629 (Ga.). Conductor refused to receive a genuine half-dollar of the United States, because he in good faith thought it was a counterfeit. Held, that this does not exempt the company from liability for his ejecting the passenger for not paying fare with another coin.

Cities—Liability for Taxes Illegally Exacted—Payment under Threat of Arrest.—Neumann v. *City of La Crosse*, 68 N. W. Rep. 654 (Wis.).

A city ordinance afterwards declared void imposed a license fee upon those engaged in the sale of fresh meats. Such fees were collected by city's police under threat of arrest for refusal of payment. Evidence tended to prove that the marketmen did not know but what each officer had such warrant at the time of making such threat. Held, that the payment was under duress, and could be recovered.

Discharge in Insolvency—Non-resident Partner.—Chase et al. v. *Henry,* 44 N. E. 988 (Mass.) Where one of three partners, plaintiffs in an action against an insolvent debtor, resides out of the State in which the debtor has been discharged in insolvency, the debt, though barred as to the others, is valid in his favor. (Three judges dissenting).

Habeas Corpus—Verity of Court Records—Collateral Attack.— Whitten v. *Spiegel, Sheriff,* 35 Atlantic Rep. 508 (Conn.). The foreman of a Grand Jury by a clerical mistake, indorsed an indictment against the plaintiff as a true bill although in fact it had been found not to be a true bill. Held, that the records of the Criminal Court are in a collateral proceeding conclusive evidence that the cause was fully within the jurisdiction of the court and no writ of habeas corpus will lie.

Invalid Trust Deed—Estoppel—Equitable Lien—Bona Fide Purchaser—Notice.—Barrett v. *Baker,* 37 S. W. Rep. 130 (Mo.).—A deed of trust executed by the maker of a note on land to which he had no title, but which belonged to the payee, is invalid; but the payee by selling the note is estopped from denying its validity, and a purchaser of the note has an equitable lien against both the payee and purchasers of the land from him with notice. Held, that a purchaser of the land after the note was due and under an abstract of title noting said trust deed, but also containing an attested statement of the payee that he was the legal holder of the note and acknowledged payment thereof and satisfaction of the trust deed, was a bona fide purchaser without notice.

Misuse of Mails—Dunning Letter.—In re Barker, 75 Fed. Rep. 980 (Wis.). A respectful dunning letter in an unsealed envelope bearing the printed words, "Mercantile Protective and Collection Bureau," does not come within the meaning of section 3893, Rev. St., as amended by Act of Congress of Sept. 26, 1888 (25 Stat. 496), prohibiting the sending through the mails of envelopes bearing any language of a defamatory or threatening character, or calculated by its terms or manner of display, and obviously intended to reflect injuriously upon another.

Negotiable Instruments—Alteration.—Light et al. v. *Killinger*, 44 N. E. Rep. 760 (Ind.). The insertion, in pencil in a negotiable note in ink, by an indorsee, of the name of a certain bank after the words, "payable at," is to be taken as a mere memorandum, and is not such a material alteration as would avoid the note.

Neutrality Laws—Military Expedition—Preparation and Transportation of Military Expedition—Evidence.—United States v. *O'Brien et al.*, 75 Fed. Rep. 900. Circuit Court, S. D., N. Y. The defendants were indicted for violating the neutrality laws of the United States by taking part in the preparation and transportation of an alleged hostile military expedition directed against the power of the King of Spain in the Island of Cuba. Of a military expedition there are three distinguishing marks which must concur within the jurisdiction of the United States: Organization, although without military tactics, among men to act together; the presence of arms or weapons which can be used for military purposes, and some command. The owner of a vessel knowing that it is to be used to transport such an expedition, and all persons who knowingly aid in its preparation are guilty of violating the statute. Secrecy and mystery are not conclusive of the illegality of the enterprise.

Nuisance—What is Not—Matters of Taste.—Woodstock Burial Ground Association v. *Hager*, 35 Atlantic Rep. 431 (Vt.). The fact that a lot is "unsightly and needed to be filled in," etc., does not make it a nuisance. The law does not declare that to be a nuisance which is only a matter of taste, or unpleasant to the eye, or even that renders other property less valuable. There must be some substantial or material right invaded.

BOOK NOTICES.

The American Digest Annual, 1896. The West Publishing Company, St. Paul, Minn. Law sheep, 6,343 pages.

The value of the American Digest as an aid to the rapid examination of recent decisions is almost too apparent to require comment by us. It suffices to say that the edition for 1896 is prepared with the same painstaking care as the previous editions, and that the arrangement of the whole subject is as clear and systematic as ever. The latest issue is well bound, has a patent marginal index, and at the end of the book a table of the cases affirmed or overruled by the decisions digested in the body of the work.

Elements of the Law of Contracts. By Edward Avery Harriman, Professor of Law in the Northwestern University Law School. Cloth, 307 pages. Little, Brown & Company, Boston, Mass., 1896.

In this treatise by Mr. Harriman the attempt has been made for the first time, we believe, to explain the rules of law relating to contracts "in accordance with the actual historical development of those rules." That the attempt has been a successful one no one can doubt after reading the book. Another leading feature of the work is the exposition of the principle that contractual obligation may be due to the act of one party or of two. These two varieties the author distinguishes by the terms "unifactoral" and "bifactoral." At the beginning of the book is a brief historical introduction and then the subject is treated in detail, taking up first the formation of a contract and then the facts which affect its validity. It is written in a scholarly style and well-calculated to sustain the high standard which the rest of the "Student's Series" have established.

Marketable Title to Real Estate. By Chapman W. Maupin, of the Washington, D. C., Bar. Law sheep, 820 pages text. Baker, Voorhis & Company, New York, 1896.

An author whose text book serves to lighten the labors of counsel in preparing cases ought certainly to earn the lasting gratitude of the legal profession. No treatise could be better calculated to attain this result than Mr. Maupin's latest work. It treats purely of the rights of vendor and purchaser in respect to the title to the property sold, and of the remedies of the purchaser; "precautionary, where it is anticipated that the title may prove defective, and compensatory, where it has proven to be so." It is primarily a treatise on the law of defective titles, and kindred subjects have been treated of only so far as they serve to illustrate that branch of the law. The author has displayed great skill in his treatment of the subject, and the labor he has expended upon it is shown by the immense amount of information which he has gathered together within the covers of a single book.

MAGAZINE NOTICES.

The Green Bag, November, 1896.

Count Johannes (with portrait),	Irving Browne.
The Vehmic Courts of Westphalia,	George H. Westley.
The Conquest of Maine,	George J. Varney.
The Man with the Iron Mask (verse).	John Albert Macy.
The New York Bar Association (illustrated),	A. Oakey Hall.
Contrasts in Court (verse),	Wendell P. Stafford.
A Curious Case.	
The English Law Courts, X.	
The Game of Politics as a Criminal Conspiracy,	Archibald R. Watson.
London Legal Letter.	
The Lawyer's Easy Chair,	Irving Browne.

Albany Law Journal, 1896.

Oct. 10.	The Plea of *Res Judicata* in Actions for Personal Injuries,	Laiton D. Landburn.
Oct. 17.	The Collegiate Study of Law,	Prof. James F. Colby.
Oct. 24.	The Collegiate Study of Law (concluded),	Prof. James F. Colby.
Oct. 31.	The Danger to the Supreme Court,	George A. Benham.
Nov. 7.	Mandamus—What is the Modern Remedy Bearing this Name,	Guy Carleton Lee.
Nov. 14.	The Time Within which Persons Under a Disability May Bring an Action,	A. S. Norton.
Nov. 21.	The Law of Woman's Suffrage,	James A. Webb.
Nov. 28.	Land in Anglo-Saxon Times,	Guy Carleton Lee.

Central Law Journal, 1896.

Oct. 9.	Legitimate Competition,	William H. Tuttle.
Oct. 16.	Expert Testimony,	Gordon C. Hamilton.
Oct. 23.	The Appointment of their Proxies and Revocation of their Power,	Chapman W. Maupin.
Oct. 30.	Bicycles as Baggage,	Lyne S. Metcalfe, Jr.
Nov. 6.	Limit of Municipal Indebtedness—Aggregate Indebtedness—"Indebtedness" and "Liability,"	Charles E. DeLand.
Nov. 13.	Disbarment for Professional Misconduct Involving Indictable Offense,	Henry Z. Johnson.

Harvard Law Review, November, 1896.

New-Fashioned Receiverships,	D. H. Chamberlain.
The Growth of Trial by Jury in England,	J. E. R. Stephens.
Account of the French Society of Comparative Legislation,	Henri Lévy-Ullman.
Dicey's "Conflict of Laws,"	J. H. Beale, Jr.

December, 1896.

Two Years' Experience of the New York State Board of Law Examiners,	Austen G. Fox.
Keener on Quasi-Contracts, I.,	Everett V. Abbot.
Liability of Massachusetts Stockholders in Foreign Corporations,	William Reed Bigelow.

SUPPLEMENT

CONTAINING

MEMORABILIA ET NOTABILIA.

Hon. J. M. Harlan, one of the Justices of the Supreme Court of the United States, will be the Law School orator at the next Commencement. This announcement will be received with peculiar satisfaction by all students and alumni of the Law Department of Yale.

A reception in honor of Professor James Bradley Thayer of the Harvard Law Faculty, Storrs lecturer for 1896, was given October 26th at the Law School Building.

The Yale *Shingle*, which is the Law School class-book, will be edited this year by N. Candee of the Senior class. It will appear about May 1st.

1881. Hon. Livingston W. Cleaveland was elected Judge of Probate for New Haven in the recent election.

1886. Hon. F. D. Pavey, of the New York Bar, is one of the rising men in legal practice and clean politics.

1887. E. F. Thompson, formerly of Thompson & Curtis, has entered into partnership with G. W. Delamater, F. H. Clark and W. H. Wilkins, for the general practice of law under the firm name of Thompson, Delamater & Clark, with offices at 184 Dearborn street, Chicago.

1888. Howard Wakeman, '88, Orren W. Bates, '91, and Frederick Averill, '95, have been elected to the Connecticut Legislature.

1888. Kojiro Matsugata has been appointed private secretary to his father, Count Matsugata, the new Premier of Japan.

1891. Gregory McPherson died at Delaware Water Gap, Md., on Thursday, October 22, 1896, at the age of 28. His death was due to pneumonia and occurred after an illness of but four days. The funeral was held at his home in Washington, D. C.

1892. John F. Carpenter of Putnam has been appointed Judge Advocate-General of Connecticut by Governor Cooke.

1895. Frank J. Brown was recently elected Justice of the Peace in New Haven.

1895. George W. Cary has formed a partnership with Henry W. Hawley, under the firm name of Hawley & Carey. The offices of the firm are in the Sanford Building, Bridgeport.

1895. Walter P. Judson has opened an office in the Exchange Building, New Haven. He has just been elected to the office of Justice of the Peace on the Republican ticket.

1896. Herbert H. Kellogg has entered the office of Logan, Demond & Harby, 58 William street, New York City.

1896. J. S. Pullman will open an office in Bridgeport.

1896. Frederick C. Taylor, Chairman of the JOURNAL during the past year, has been elected Probate Judge for the District of Stamford.

1896. Edward M. Day is practicing law in Hartford. At the November election the Town of Colchester elected him, by a handsome majority, its Representative in the Connecticut Legislature.

YALE LAW JOURNAL

THE LAW AND PRACTICE OF CONNECTICUT CONCERNING HEARING IN DAMAGES ON DEFAULT, OR DEMURRER OVERRULED.

Necessarily, we in this State are so satisfied with the law and practice pertaining to hearing in damages on default and demurrer overruled, in actions sounding in tort for unliquidated damages, that we forget that such law and practice are peculiar to this State.

Whether the law and practice are founded on logical reasons or not, they have proved in fact very beneficial in their operation. The most frequent instance of their application is in actions for negligence. If we should go into the courts of adjoining States or England, we should find as a rule, actions for negligence tried to a jury, with liberal verdicts for the plaintiff. In this State such actions are generally tried to the court without the aid (or annoyance, as you please) of a jury. As in other States, so here the student will notice that such actions are tried on their merits. In our State the plaintiff is sure to recover a nominal sum, and in a majority of cases fails to recover more than a nominal sum; while in other States the jury is found to sympathize with the plaintiff more than with the defendant.

How did the rule and practice arise in this State?

In order to answer that question it is necessary to state the condition of a case after default, and after a demurrer overruled.

When a defendant has been summoned into court in any jurisdiction—especially so in this State, where, with the summons, there is left with him a copy of the complaint—and he fails to appear, or if appearing, fails to answer to the complaint, he is said to be in "default." His attitude toward the case and court is such that he is regarded as desiring to make no contest over the allegations of the complaint, or over the assumptions of law upon which such allegations are based. Everywhere, as is believed, save in Connecticut, such an attitude on the part of such defendant is regarded by the Court as a conclusive admission of the truth of the well pleaded allegations of the complaint, and as entitling the plaintiff to a judgment for damages measured by the extent of the injury.

In Connecticut also, in such cases of default, the plaintiff is entitled to a judgment of some sort, the nature of which will be discussed after we have brought into view the condition of a cause after a demurrer overruled.

When a defendant has been summoned into Court as above stated and desires to contest the suit, it is obvious that he may dispute the assumptions of law contained in the plaintiff's case, or question his allegations of fact. If he undertakes to dispute the questions of law on which the plaintiff's complaint is based, his method is by demurrer. If he wins the point his demurrer is said to be "sustained." If he loses, the demurrer is said to be "overruled." Thus far he has confined his attack upon the plaintiff's case solely to the questions of law supposed to be involved therein.

Now comes in a very interesting point, which illustrates the length of time over which a peculiar practice may extend. By the very old common law, the defendant in actions at law was restricted to one substantial matter of defense. He could come in and demur to the "declaration." If his demurrer was overruled, final judgment went against him for the narrow and technical reason, that by electing to demur he had exhausted his one opportunity of defense, and so had admitted the allegations of the declaration, and could not afterwards contest them. In other words, upon a demurrer overruled the old common law placed the defendant in a condition of being in default, with reference to the allegations of fact contained in the declaration. In the technical default, the defendant has declined answering the allegations of the declaration or complaint. In the case of a demurrer overruled the defendant by his own choice, according to the principles of the ancient common law, has lost the opportunity of answering the allegations of the complaint.

It is very true that courts almost universally permitted the defendant after demurrer overruled to plead anew with reference to the matters of fact alleged in the complaint, but this was done purely as a matter of privilege to the defendant (Falken *v.* Housatonic R. R. Co., 63 Conn. 262).

"The practice is undoubtedly more liberal in allowing a change of plea in the case of a demurrer overruled, than in allowing amendments to declarations which have been held to be insufficient; but in both cases it is a matter of discretion with the Court" (McAllister *v.* Clark, 33 Conn. 253, in which case the motion to plead anew after demurrer overruled was denied).

Although the statute now makes it peremptory upon the court to permit a defendant to plead anew after demurrer overruled, it still remains optional with the defendant to further plead or not as he chooses. If he does not further plead, then he is regarded as standing before the court with no answer to the allegations of fact in the complaint. His attitude toward the court and case is, for all the purposes of this article, identical with that of a defaulting defendant; in each case the law awards a judgment in favor of the plaintiff against the defendant.

On what ground does the judgment proceed?

Herein lies the mystery. It would seem as matter of logic that the judgment ought to proceed upon the theory that the allegations of the complaint setting up a cause of action were admitted, fully and completely. On what other theory can a court of justice render a judgment in favor of one man against another, except that the one man has maintained or established his cause of action against the other man?

It necessarily results that if the defendant will make no answer to the allegations setting up the cause of action in the complaint, a court may well say that thereby such allegations are established in a very satisfactory manner—in a manner of which the defendant at least, cannot complain.

The general rule of the effect of a default in actions of tort is stated in the "American and English Encyclopedia of Law," volume 5, page 63, as follows:

"A judgment by default in favor of the plaintiff admits the defendant's liability to some damages, but the amount is a matter of proof. The defendant is, therefore, not entitled to *deny the plaintiff's cause of action*, but he may offer evidence in mitigation of damages."

In the case of Lambert *v.* Sanford, 55 Conn. 437, referring to 1 Sutherland on Damages, page 777, it is said:

"It is generally held that on an assessment of damages after default or on an equivalent state of the record, evidence denying the cause of action, or tending to show that no right of action exists, is inadmissible in mitigation of damages. When an action is brought on a contract set out in the declaration, and there is a default on the assessment of damages, no evidence which goes to deny the existence of the contract, or tends to avoid it, is competent; the default admits it as set forth, and concludes the defendant from denying it."

The opinion proceeds as follows:

"In this State in some actions of tort, notably in actions in which negligence is of the gist of the action, evidence in mitigation of damages, which evidence also tends to show the non-existence of some material element of the cause of action, is permitted. But this rule never has been extended to actions upon express contracts set forth in the complaint."

Thus it is seen that in this State courts have arbitrarily drawn a distinction between the effect of a judgment by default or on demurrer overruled, with reference to a cause of action in contract, and one sounding in tort for unliquidated damages.

It may be asked why should the effect of judgments by default in the one class of actions be different from the effect of judgment by default in the other class of actions.

In actions of tort, where the plaintiff obtains against the defendant a valid judgment by default or on demurrer overruled, it is hard, by the rules of logic, to find on what ground such judgment can rest, except it be upon the cause of action stated in the complaint. Necessarily the damages are unliquidated. The defendant has never agreed what the damage was, and the plaintiff desires to show the extent of his injuries, in order to establish the amount of his recovery. If he shall fail to establish any injury the law would presume some damage, because of the conceded violation by the defendant of the plaintiff's rights. When, however, the question of the extent of the plaintiff's injuries is to be tried, it seems anomalous for the court to render judgment, not for the actual damages shown, but for some nominal damages, because, forsooth, the defendant has been able to show that the plaintiff never had any case at all, although he has obtained a valid judgment.

In order to try to understand this matter it is necessary to refer to some of the important cases in which the law and practice of the State of Connecticut on this subject have been established.

The leading case is that of Havens v. Railroad Co., 28 Conn. 69, decided in 1859.

Here the points, so far as I can find, were first established that in a hearing in damages on default, or demurrer overruled, the truth of the allegations of the complaint setting forth the cause of action can be attacked, notwithstanding the judgment; that the judgment arising from the default, or demurrer overruled is, *prima facie*, only a judgment for nominal damages, and that whatever be the basis of such judgment, it does not conclusively settle the truth of the plaintiff's allegations concerning his cause of action.

"Nominal damages mean no damages at all. In the quaint language of an old writer, they are 'a mere peg to hang costs on.' They are such as are to be awarded in a case where there has been a breach of a contract, and no actual damages whatever have been or can be shown" (Stanton *v.* R. R. Co., 59 Conn. 282).

So the judgment by default or demurrer overruled in actions of tort, for nominal damages, in this State is not much of a judgment, though it has some virility, as will be shown later.

The practical effect, however, of Havens *v.* Railroad Co. was to cause these actions in tort to be tried to the court and not to the jury, since in this State, from time immemorial, hearings in damages on default or demurrer overruled could only be to the court, except as modified in a very recent statute, concerning notice of intention to default, which has not materially changed the course of procedure.

The doctrine first established in Havens *v.* R. R. Co. was vigorously contested for many years. Perhaps it receives its best and clearest statement in the case of Batchelder *v.* Bartholomew, 44 Conn. 501:

"From a time early in the history of the jurisprudence of this State, the law has been, that where in an action on a case for the recovery of unliquidated damages, the defendant has suffered a default, that is, has omitted to make any answer, the assessment of damages has been made by the court without the intervention of a jury; also, that by his omission to deny them, the defendant is held to have admitted the truth of all the well-pleaded material allegations in the declaration, and the consequent right of the plaintiff to a judgment for a limited sum, that is for nominal damages and costs, without the introduction of evidence. The defendant standing silent, the law imputes the admission to him, but it does it with this limitation upon its meaning and effect, it does it for this special purpose and no other, and our courts have repeatedly explained that the admission found in a default is not the admission of which the writers on the law of evidence treat. The silent defendant having been subjected to a judgment for nominal damages, from which no proof can relieve him, the default has practically exhausted its effect upon the case; for if the plaintiff is unwilling to accept this judgment evidence is received on his part to raise the damages above, and on the part of the defendant to keep them down to that immovable base of departure, the nominal point, precisely as if a general issue had been pleaded, and although the evidence introduced by the latter has so much force that it would have reduced them to nothing but for the barrier interposed by the default, it cannot avail to deprive the plaintiff of his judgment; in keeping that, the law perceives that he has all that the truth entitles him to, and therefore refuses to hear any objection from him. *Of course the Court might have said that if the defendant thus defaults he shall not hereafter be heard in proof or argument upon any other than the single question as to the extent of the injury inflicted*, but it has contented itself with saying that if he stands silent the law will pronounce judgment upon him for nominal damages; *in either form, the rule, like all other rules of practice, is arbitrary in its nature, but in neither is there any inconsistency or want of logic.* If in our courts the admission in a default had ever been used in the broadest sense of which the word is capable, then, of course, any limitation thereafter put upon it would have been an inconsistency, but from the earliest use, the narrower meaning went with it" (citing no case or authority prior to Havens *v.* Railroad Co.).

It will be observed that the rule of Connecticut is correctly asserted to be a rule of practice, and arbitrary in its nature; but when the court says that there is neither inconsistency or want of logic in the rule, the inquiry may be properly made, how a judgment by default conclusively establishes the truth of the allegations of the cause of action in an action of contract, and does not so conclusively establish them in an action of tort?

The practice under the rule of Connecticut was, at the outset, somewhat uncertain. Should the plaintiff in these actions of tort introduce his whole case in chief, the same as if there had been no default, or should he confine himself to the extent of the injury? In some counties the practice was one way, and in some the other, and some lawyers in the same county tried their cases in one way, and some in the other.

In Daniels *v.* Saybrook, 34 Conn. 377, the court apparently decided the question: holding that the effect of a judgment by default or upon demurrer overruled, was such as to confer upon the plaintiff, *prima facie*, the right to his full damages, and requiring him upon the hearing to show in the first place only the amount of such damages; making it, however, only a question of the burden of proof, and throwing upon the defendant the burden of proving that the plaintiff had no cause of action, in case such was the real defense of the defendant.

This case was decided in 1867, yet notwithstanding the decision the practice continued more or less uncertain until the decision of Crane *v.* Eastern Transportation Line, 48 Conn. 361, decided in October, 1880. It is now well settled in this State that the Connecticut rule and practice on these hearings in damages, after a judgment by default, or demurrer overruled, are that the plaintiff is *prima facie* entitled to recover his full damages, and on such hearings, offers in chief only evidence as to the extent of his injury, while the defendant is at liberty to show that the plaintiff never had any cause of action at all; the burden of proof in this respect being upon him.

In other words, we have established in Connecticut a most peculiar form of judgment by default or demurrer overruled in actions of tort for unliquidated damages. *Prima facie*, and in a peculiar way, such judgment establishes the truth of the allegations of the complaint concerning the cause of action. In point of fact, it probably establishes nothing of the kind. In point of logic the inquiry must arise, "How can a judgment *prima facie* establish anything?" The general conception of a judgment is that it is conclusive, or is nothing.

It was contended at one time, that the allegations of the complaint, after default, or demurrer overruled, might be regarded as *prima facie* evidence of the facts therein asserted, so that if the defendant failed to negative such allegations in his defense, such allegations might be regarded as sufficient proof of such facts. The Supreme Court, however, says that such is not the law; that the allegations of the complaint in such cases are not to be taken as evidence in any manner: they probably are true, for purposes of the burden of proof, but such probability vanishes when the defendant attempts, however unsuccessfully, to disprove them (Nolan *v.* R. R. Co., 53 Conn. 461; Crogan *v.* Schiele, 53 Conn. 186).

While the practical effect of the Connecticut rule and practice with reference to the judgment by default or demurrer overruled, is beneficial, I cannot subscribe to the assertion that it is entirely logical and consistent with other established rules and maxims.

It is a case of a *prima facie*, probably correct judgment, which the defendant, however, is allowed to prove the plaintiff was never entitled to obtain, but which, even then, the defendant may not be able to wholly set aside, but must suffer, for an amount which is now expressed by the phrase "nominal damages."

In its final form, if the plaintiff is successful, it is the ordinary judgment by default for the plaintiff to recover damages measured by the extent of his injuries.

In its final form, if the defendant is successful, it is a judgment for the plaintiff to recover "nominal damages," not because the plaintiff has proved a violation of his rights and shown no injury, for in such cases the defendant has not violated the plaintiff's right, and the plaintiff has usually suffered considerable damage. It is not a judgment against the defendant, because he has not filed an answer to the allegations of fact in the complaint, for he may "default" after filing such answer, and be dealt with as is usual in cases of default (Lennon *v.* Rawitzer, 57 Conn. 583).

I have never been able to satisfactorily define the rules of law and practice of this State, on this subject, in any other manner than to say that they are arbitrary and constitute a system of judicial procedure peculiar to this State, in actions in tort for unliquidated damages.

A curious illustration of the rule is found in Martin *v.* New York and New England Railroad Company, 62 Conn. 331; an action against a railroad company for communicating fire from its locomotive engine to adjoining property. In this case it is held that the liability of a railroad company in such case is statutory and does not depend upon the existence of negligence.

The complaint alleged that fire was communicated to the plaintiff's property by a locomotive engine of the defendant, and that the property was destroyed by fire. The defendant suffered a default, and the case was heard in damages. Held, that the plaintiff was, *prima facie*, entitled to recover her actual loss from the fire, to the full extent proved, but the defendant, to reduce the damages to a nominal sum, might show that the fire was not communicated by its locomotive; in other words, the default did not conclusively admit the vital allegations of the complaint, that the fire came from the locomotive engine of the defendant, and this in a statutory action, where negligence of the defendant need not be alleged or proved.

Obviously the extent to which the rule will be applied in Connecticut is as yet unknown.

It would seem as if in actions of slander and libel the defendant could default or demur, and on a hearing in damages on such default or demurrer overruled, could show that he never uttered the slanderous words, or published the libellous matter.

For some years the General Assembly has made it a condition precedent to suits brought against municipal and other corporations that notice of the time and place of the injury must be given by the plaintiff within a limited time, to the defendant.

In an action against the City of New London the complaint alleged the giving of sufficient notice. The case was defaulted. On the trial of the case the defendant offered in evidence the notice which in fact had been given, and which was defective; a fact which would have entitled the defendant to a judgment in its favor, if the case had been tried, whether to court or jury.

What was the effect of the default upon the sufficient allegation of the complaint concerning notice?

A result was reached by which the plaintiff was entitled to a judgment for nominal damages by virtue of the default, and the defendant could attack the allegations of notice in the complaint, notwithstanding his default with reference to it. As this decision was in 1893, it is well to quote from it:

"This makes it necessary to consider very briefly what matters, in cases like the one at bar, under our practice, may be contested by the defendant upon a hearing in damages, after default, or demurrer overruled, for the purpose of keeping the damages down to a nominal sum. As a general proposition, it must now be regarded as conclusively settled that the defendant in such cases, and for such purposes, may contest his liability for any damages whatsoever; may show if he can, that the plaintiff is entitled to nominal damages only, because in reality, and but for the default or demurrer, he is entitled to none; may offer evidence in effect tending to prove such non-liability, as if no demurrer had been introduced, or default had been suffered, although such fact as a basis for nominal damages had been conclusively admitted. * * * For the purposes indicated and after default suffered or demurrer overruled, the defendant has been permitted to show that an assault by servants of a railroad company was justifiable, and so was in law no assault" (apparently rendering pleadings or notice of special defense wholly unnecessary) " * * * that a claimed trespass was in law no trespass, because the acts were done under a contract with the plaintiff, which amounted to a license."

Now a license surely may not ordinarily be offered in evidence by the defendant except by way of special defense, but apparently it is permissible on a hearing in damages.

It seems to me that it would have been more logical, and more consistent, if the Supreme Court had ruled that the default or demurrer overruled admitted nothing with reference to the merits of the case, and left the burden of proof with the plaintiff to make out his claim for substantial damages.

I think also that the early case of Lamphear v. Buckingham, 33 Conn. 237, is not in harmony with the later decisions. That was a case of an administrator suing a railroad company (operated by Buckingham and others, trustees) for the loss of the life of the intestate, through the negligence of the railroad company. If the case for negligence was made out the statute fixed the sum to be recovered, as not less than one thousand dollars nor more than five thousand dollars.

On a hearing in damages on demurrer overruled the Court found that the railroad company was not guilty of any negligence, and fixed fifty dollars as the "nominal damages." The Supreme Court decided that the judgment for nominal damages on the demurrer overruled, was at least one thousand dollars.

Thus in this case the judgment for nominal damages assessed at fifty dollars, became in fact a judgment for substantial damages of one thousand dollars, in the teeth of the conclusive finding that the defendant was guilty of no negligence, and that the plaintiff had no case except from the demurrer overruled.

It is not to be understood that we are criticising any decision rendered by the Supreme Court as at present constituted. The law and practice on this subject were settled thirty-five years ago in Havens v. R. R. Co., 28 Conn. All that has occurred since has been simply but a development of the doctrine therein announced. The General Assembly alone can alter the rule of law in this State, which has been so long established.

The rule has worked admirably. In Connecticut, actions of negligence against corporations, private or municipal, against horse, steam or electric railway companies, and private individuals, have been tried to the court in one of the two peculiar methods above described. Nominal damages have been any where from one dollar to one hundred dollars, depending upon some process of judicial reasoning not capable of exact description or analysis. The judgment carries with it also plaintiff's costs.

The result has been a confidence on the part of such corporations and individuals that they would be fairly dealt with in actions of this character, and that their property would not be imperilled by the uncertainty of jury trials. There can be no question about the superiority of a trial by the court instead of by the jury in actions of this character, if the attainment of justice is to be regarded.

So, also, the General Assembly has sustained the peculiar law and practice of the State which I have attempted to describe. Efforts have been made in the General Assembly to cause this whole system to be overthrown, yet such efforts have always come to nothing.

It may be confidently asserted that the rule and practice will rather be extended than contracted.

In establishing the law and practice in this State in hearings in damages on default or demurrer overruled in actions in tort for unliquidated damages, our Supreme Court has accomplished very beneficial results by the use of something closely akin to a "legal fiction."

There is nothing strange in this regard. The use of "fiction" in the English courts has been frequent and salutary.

Moreover Connecticut always has been and still is a State noted for invention.

John W. Alling.

THE PROMOTION OF UNIFORM LEGISLATION.

Of the five objects for the promotion of which the American Bar Association was organized in 1878, one is "the Promotion of Uniform Legislation." Various papers were read before that body, at its annual meetings, demonstrating the annoyance, confusion, and waste arising from variant and conflicting laws in the different States on matters of common interest, and where no good reason seemed to exist for any difference.

It was even claimed by some that this difference occasioned unnecessary insecurity in contracts, and had a tendency to hinder the freedom of interstate trade.

In July, 1888, the State Bar Association of Tennessee passed a resolution instructing its delegates to present the recommendations of its president, in his address with reference to uniformity of laws in the several States, to the American, and National Bar Associations. The recommendations of the President, Mr. L. B. McFarland, were, in effect, in favor of a conference of Commissioners on Uniform Laws from the different States.

At the meeting of the American Bar Association, which was held in Chicago in 1889, Mr. Collier of Tennessee, presented a resolution authorizing the President of the Association to appoint a committee, consisting of one from each State, to meet in convention for the promotion of uniformity of legislation. A committee for that purpose was appointed.

In the meantime in the Winter of 1888, a bill drafted by Mr. Albert E. Henschell of New York City, present Secretary of the Commission of that State, was introduced in the Legislature of that State, for the appointment of a "Commission for the Promotion of Uniformity of Legislation in the United States."

After three years of resolute effort on the part of Mr. Henschell, aided by Mr. William Allen Butler, Professor Theodore Dwight, Professor Austin Abbott, Surrogate Rollins, Henry E. Howland, Noah Davis, William Dorsheimer, John Cadwallader and other prominent New York lawyers, the following statute was passed in 1890:

"Section 1. Within thirty days of the passage of this Act the Governor shall appoint, by and with the consent of the Senate, three commissioners, who are hereby constituted a board of commissioners, by the name and style of 'Commissioners for the Promotion of Uniformity of Legislation in the United States.' It shall be the duty of said board to examine the subjects of marriage and divorce, insolvency, the form of notarial certificates, and other subjects; to ascertain the best means to effect an assimilation and uniformity in the laws of the States, and especially to consider whether it would be wise and practicable for the State of New York to invite the other States of the Union to send representatives to a convention to draft uniform laws to be submitted for the approval and adoption of the several States, and devise and recommend such other course of action as shall best accomplish the purpose of this Act."

Members of the New York Commission, appointed by Governor Hill, met the committee of the American Bar Association, at its annual meeting in 1890, and that committee reported the action of the State of New York, and recommended that the association should thereafter simply assist in the creation and work of State commissions throughout the Union. The American Bar Association, by its committee and local councils, has lent efficient aid ever since.

The first general meeting of the commissioners of seven States was held at Saratoga in August, 1892, at the time of the meeting of the American Bar Association, and their subsequent meetings have been held in connection with the annual meetings of that association. In 1893 the movement had grown from seven States to nearly twenty, and at the sixth conference in 1896 twenty-nine States were represented.

Up to 1896 the work of the Commissioners on Uniform Laws was confined to the preparation of forms for the execution and acknowledgment of written instruments, laws regulating the use of seals or their substitutes, laws legalizing extra-territorial wills, laws abolishing days of grace, and those establishing a uniform standard of weights and measures.

In 1896 the Committee on Commercial Law, instructed to that effect by the conference of 1895, caused to be drafted an Americanized form of the British Act on Bills and Notes, passed in England in 1882. This was done by Mr. John J. Crawford of the New York City Bar, who published the first draft, with notes and references, and along with the English Act. This draft was sent to all the Commissioners on Uniform Laws, and to many of the authors and experts on that subject, inviting criticisms and suggestions. After receiving such criticisms and suggestions, the Committee on Commercial Law went over the Act now entitled "A General Act relating to Negotiable Instruments," carefully with its author, and the bill, as so revised, was presented to the conference in 1896. The conference spent several days in its consideration, making some slight changes in its phraseology, and recommended the Act as so prepared and perfected for adoption in the several States.

The author, and some of the revisers, of the English Act, have expressed the highest commendation of the work of Mr. Crawford, and in no way more so than in saying that those features of their Act which were recommended by the drafters and first revisers, and rejected by the over-conservative Parliament —such as the abolition of Days of Grace—had been adopted by Mr. Crawford.

If the size of the proposed act—almost reaching the limits of a small code—should intimidate those conservative members, of the most conservative of professions, to whom the very name of "code" is an abomination, it may be proper to suggest, that none of the ordinary objections to a "code" apply in this case.

Separate complete codes of different States might tend to make permanent local differences, but a short code, on a special branch of commercial law, adopted by the States generally, would have precisely the opposite effect.

The production of a single mind, however learned and skillful, may well be regarded with distrust, but the product of scores of lawyers of Great Britain, best qualified to know the law on the subject, tested by fourteen years of successful experience, and revised by commissioners from thirty States in this country, aided by the experts, who have written on the topic, may surely inspire the confidence that the work is thoroughly done.

Then, too, while the bill is simple, and intelligible in its expression, great care is taken to preserve the use of words which have had repeated legal constructions and become recognized terms in the Law Merchant.

The reception of the Act will be a fair test of the interesting question as to how far forth the Legislatures will adopt the work of the Commissioners. Its importance, in this point of view, may justify some additional remarks upon it. A more useful, or thoroughly prepared statute on Commercial Law would be difficult to find. All the fundamental principles, and essential definitions of the law on commercial paper, the law, in short, of some ten thousand reported cases, is, in substance, condensed into thirty-six pages. The disputed points, and variant laws, whose discussion occupies so large a share of two and three volumed treatises on the subject, are decided and harmonized. This decision and harmony is not the dictum, or opinion of one man, or one body of men, or one State, or one country. The English Bill, originally drafted by Judge Chalmers, passed by the committees of both Houses of Parliament, adopted by all of its self-governing colonies, has had the test of fourteen years' experience, and the testimony is all one way as to its worth and efficiency.

Lord Chancellor Herschell, in 1894, says of it:

"There is, I believe, a common agreement that the code embodying the law of 'Negotiable Instruments' has been of great utility. It has given rise to very few questions requiring decisions by the courts, and it has put beyond controversy not a few that were in doubt. * * * A similar code for the United States will be, I think, a boon for the commercial community of both countries."

Of this Act, the report of the Master, Treasurer and Assistants of the Edinburgh Merchant Company, given in a late number of the *Scots Law Times*, says, speaking of the desirability of a Commercial Code for Great Britain:

"Already without any serious difficulty, the laws of Bills of Exchange, Partnership, and Sale of Goods, have been digested and stated clearly in comparatively short statutes for Scotland, as for the rest of the realm. The first mentioned Act states in a hundred sections, what had previously to be collected from twenty-five hundred English and several hundred Scottish decisions. It is certainly not beyond the understanding of the commercial men, and it has lessened disputes, and litigations as to bills. Much of the diminished litigation is due, beyond doubt, to the settled law being stated clearly, and to moot points being settled by force of statute."

There is much more reason for semi-codification of this sort in this country than in Great Britain.

In England there is one court of final resort. In the United States, over fifty courts are of this character. It is the same obvious reason that largely induces codes of the whole law, on the Continent of Europe, viz., the inconvenience of the existence of different systems of law and decisions in a single nation.

That is, there is on the Continent and in this country the advantage of unification, as well as codification. Nor is there any *real* opposition, between codified law (if a statute on a special branch of commercial law can fairly be denominated a code) and case law.

"The true opposition is between codified law, and scattered statute law. Case law is a necessary complement to all, but the case law, which grows out of a well-ordered code, is, in itself, harmonious, and symmetrical, while case law, grafted on a multitude of statutes, cannot possibly be consistent or compendious" (from a paper read at Lincoln's Inn Hall, May 17, 1896, by Ernest J. Schuster, Esq., on "The German Civil Code," published in the *Journal of the Society of Comparative Legislation*, Vol. I., No. 1, page 210.

How much "scattered statute law" we have already, on the statute books of the different States on the subject of Negotiable Paper is denoted by the fact that the general statement of the differences occupies more than a dozen pages in the first volume of Mr. Stimson's "American Statute Law," published in 1886.

Mr. Schuster, while arguing strongly the advantages of codes in general, does not regard the law in Great Britain as ripe for general codification. He urges that it should be systematized, to prepare it for general codification.

But while the trend of the more recent discussion on this subject among lawyers and jurists is to "go slowly" in the direction of general codification, there appears to be hardly any difference of opinion, either among jurists or representative business men, on both sides of the Atlantic, as to the necessity of a commercial code.

This statement, or rather outline, of the progress so far made by the Board of Commissioners on Uniform Laws, has from the nature of the case been the story of preparation rather than of achievement. Until a fair majority, and that fairly representing all portions of the Union, had joined the Conference, it was impossible to take action, except upon the simplest matters of most obvious importance. For the very object of mutual comparison, and deliberation assumed, and required that substantially all parties, to be affected by Uniform Legislation, should be represented in the convention.

What has so far been accomplished has been chiefly to create an opportunity for concerted action for uniformity, and an opportunity to test the readiness, or the reverse, with which that action will be accepted by the various States.

I have already suggested the peculiar advantage the Conference has, at this time, in following the action of the mother country in the scientific and systematic definition and the putting into statutory shape of branches of commercial law.

The composition of the Boards of Commissioners from the

different States is perhaps not unfavorable to practical efficiency. While it has the great advantage of having among its members law professors and judges of the highest courts, the bulk of the conference is composed of practicing and practical lawyers, whose every day business not only necessitates a familiar knowledge of the laws of their own States but of their working also, which is quite as important. They work without compensation, only necessary expenses being paid to any members, and some States not even providing for expenses. This is a serious drawback, and will prove more and more so, as the conferences are necessarily longer, and the labors of the members more complex.

It is doubtless a compliment to the *esprit de corps* of the profession, to assume that a hundred or more lawyers should be willing, for the sole purpose of bettering the statutes of their own and sister States, by rendering them more uniform, to give to the task several weeks of each year, and some of them a much longer period. Probably, the commissioners, as a body, could well afford to forego the compliment, if at least enough compensation was provided, so that clerical and expert work could be adequately paid for.

While, so far as I am aware, no discussion, much less any action, has ever been taken by the Commissioners in conference, as to any future plan of work, or what particular fields to enter upon, or what method to pursue towards the promotion of uniformity in general, some conditions already indicate the true methods of amelioration in some important matters. On some subjects it is probable that a few general rules adopted by each State would render more elaborate unification unnecessary. For instance, in the matter of insolvency, if all preferences were abolished and the rights of extra-territorial assignees and attaching creditors defined alike, most of the present evils of variance in that important part of the law would be greatly modified, if not wholly avoided.

Another broad and useful field of investigation, is the adoption of statutes modifying or neutralizing the difficulties arising from variant statutes, without trying to make them uniform. Of such is the short statute on Wills, recommended by the Conference, and before the existence of the Conference passed in a number of States—the provision that a will valid where made should be good everywhere, so far as the formalities of execution are concerned.

As against the objection to the project of promoting uniformity, because there may often be local reasons for a divergence from the general law in other States, still operating, but not now easily traceable, it is curious to observe how often on examination it is found that the divergence never had any real "*raison d'etre.*" An interesting example of this arose, from a suggestion of the Secretary of the Conference of Commissioners —an author equally accomplished in the fields of law and of literature—Mr. F. J. Stimson of Boston, in his most instructive address before the American Academy of Political and Social Science on "Uniform State Legislation." In speaking of the fact that estates go generally to the parents, in the absence of children, under the statutes of distribution, while in the State of Connecticut, and he might have added seven other States, it goes to brothers and sisters, before going to the parents, he adds, "I doubt not that there is an historical reason for that fact." But I have been utterly unable to find any reason assigned, except that "estates can never ascend" according to the common law, and this logic comes to a sudden stop as soon as it answers its purpose for brothers and sisters, for the parents come, next in order, and the descending argument fails to work. And, of course, the common law rule, above referred to, had no more "historical" weight, in the eight States than in the others.

It is said that in the prodigious fecundity of legislation in this country, any attainable uniformity would soon disappear, in amendments, and alterations of the "uniform" statutes. But the experience of the codes in this country, and Europe, is the other way, and an appreciation of the advantages of uniformity may be assumed to have some effect in deterring from reckless changes in statutes passed for the special purpose of reaching uniformity.

Of the many questions that naturally arise in connection with the general subject of "Uniform State Laws"—looking over the whole field suggested by the terms "Legislative Uniformity"; *e. g.*, the conflict between federal, and State decisions, outside of statutory differences—to what topics the action of the Commissioners is practically, or theoretically limited—how far Congressional statutes can aid, or supplement the voluntary action of the States, if the recommendations of the Commissioners are adopted on all these, and kindred topics, the Conference has so far done nothing—not even debating, or considering them. They have simply gone to work, in an exceedingly practical way, so far, to attempt to remedy some of the most obviously harmful, and needless differences in instruments of conveyance, and commerce, and have appointed for investigation, and report, the following committees; viz., on Commercial Law, Wills, Marriage and Divorce, Deeds and other Conveyances, Certificates of Depositions and Notarial Certificates, Weights and Measures, Uniformity of State Action as to Presidential Electors, Uniform Hours of Labor in Factories, Insolvency, Insurance, Trading Corporations, Descent and Distribution, and on Congressional action as to Uniformity. On the whole it can hardly be doubted that in the attempt to promote uniformity of law the experimental way, substantially adopted by the Conference of Commissioners, is likely to prove the most workable.

When a given subject is brought before the Conference by the report of a committee, to whom that subject has been referred, the special knowledge of each commission of the laws of its own State, not only affords a comparison, and basis of action, otherwise unattainable, but also develops best the recommendations most likely to be universally adopted.

If the matter of promoting uniformity is worth going into at all it should largely enlist the interest of business men and lawyers. How far the Boards of Trade and other business organizations will give their aid and above all how far the members of the bar in their State and county organizations will give support to the movement, remains to be seen. Without the coöperation of both, but little can be accomplished. With their aid, there is no reason why some permanent good should not result. If the movement leads to a more adequate study of comparative legislation, and a tendency to assimilate the legislation of the various States, its work will not be without some good effect toward the unification of the law.

But whatever degree of success the present movement may attain it may be true that, after all, above the question of convenience and annoyance—of facility of trade, and certainty of contract, or any questions of property right, is to be placed the salutary effect of unity in law upon National unity itself. Of the four great promoters of National unity—religion, language, custom and law—the last is certainly not the least in importance.

The limits of a single article, devoted to nothing else, would not suffice to discuss the great theme of so many of the writers on the Philosophy of History—the subtle, pervading, and profound influence of the laws of a nation on its life and character. What Mulford says of the freedom of a nation, as affected by its laws, is equally true of its unity: "Freedom does not gain much, when it is held as an ideal conception, and is left to the pages of scholars or the rhymes of poets, or the voices of orators. These are not laws, and the condition of any advance in freedom, is its operation in laws, and its organization in rights" (The *Nation*, page 120). As the laws are the expression of the life and character of the nation which enacts them, so the life and character of the nation are developed, shaped and moulded by the laws it enacts. As the National Constitution and National laws express the unity of the people of the United States, so do they in turn, powerfully tend to preserve, and promote the sentiment of unity. It goes without saying that the voluntary unification of the laws of the various Commonwealths composing the Union, would exert the same influence quite as powerfully.

The "common law" itself, is a constant and beneficent influence towards unity, and would be far more so than it is if we had one instead of nearly fifty courts of final resort, but when by conflicting decisions and variant statutes, that unity is weakened and impaired, then may we not believe that the voluntary attempts of the Commonwealths to restore and preserve that unity may have a higher significance than mere utility; that it may well be interpreted to denote the attachment of States and people to that Union they have created whose first object, as expressed in the preamble of the Constitution, is "*to establish Justice.*" On the other hand is it not certain that the realization of a common freedom, the organization of common rights, the development of a common civilization and their expression in common laws, make a bond of unity stronger even than the mighty bonds of territory, race or commerce?

Surely in these days, when so many centrifugal and disrupting forces in society are at work, the importance of a healthy public sentiment that shall desire, and seek to obtain, statutory unity rather than diversity, in matters of common interest to all, and to that end frames the general rules of equity and law, if not in one mould, at least on the same essential principles and rules of action, can hardly be overestimated.

Lyman D. Brewster.

PERSONAL TRADE-NAMES.

"A trade-name is a name which by use and reputation has acquired the property of indicating that a certain trade or occupation is carried on by a particular person. The name may be that of a person, place or thing, or it may be what is called a 'fancy name,' or word invented for the occasion and having no sense at all." Trade names are treated in most text-books under the general subject of trade-marks, which are defined as "a distinctive mark, device or emblem which a manufacturer stamps, prints or otherwise affixes to the goods he produces, so that they may be identified in the market and their origin be vouched for."[1] This difference between the two must be noted, that whereas the trade-mark is stamped, printed or otherwise affixed to the goods to act as a passport accompanying the goods and vouching for them, and the trade-name may be so used, the latter has the additional and more general use of a *name* under which business is conducted. It may be that of an individual, firm or corporation not engaged in manufacture of goods at all, but engaged in mercantile trade, wholesale or retail, handling no goods of their own make; a banking institution, publishing house or, in general, anyone engaged in trade or business, and to whom a recognized and distinctive name is valuable.

In general it may be said that when a person bearing a particular name or having adopted a particular distinguishing mark or device, is engaged in business and uses such name or device to distinguish himself and his wares from all other parties engaged in a similar business, and such name or device becomes recognized as such, the law recognizes in him a valuable right in such name or device and will protect him in its exclusive use. Thus broadly stated, the principle has not always been recognized, but like many another thing, has been slowly worked out by the courts, and I cannot do better on this point than to quote at length from the opinion in Singer Manufacturing Co. *v.* Wilson.[2] "All actions of this sort must be founded on false representation. Originally I apprehend, the right to bring an action in respect of the improper use of a trade-mark arose out of the

---

[1] Defs., Black's Law Dictionary.
[2] 2 Ch D. 453.

common-law right to bring an action for false representation, which, of course, must be a false representation made fraudulently. It differed from an ordinary action for false representation in that an action for false representation is generally brought by the person to whom it is made; but in the case of an improper use of a trade-mark the common-law courts noticed that the false representation which is made by putting another man's trade-mark on the goods which the wrong-doer sells, is calculated to do an injury, not only to the person to whom the false or fraudulent representation is made, but to the manufacturers whose trade-mark is imitated, and, therefore, the common-law courts held that such a manufacturer has a right of action for the improper use of his trade-mark. Then the common-law courts extended that doctrine one step further in the case of Sykes *v.* Sykes.[3] There it was held that although the representation was perfectly true as between the original vendor and the original purchaser, in this sense, that the original purchaser knew perfectly well who was the real manufacturer of the goods, and therefore was not deceived into believing he had bought goods manufactured by another person, yet if the trademark were put on the goods for the purpose of enabling that purchaser, when he came to resell the goods, to deceive any one of the public into thinking he was purchasing the goods of the manufacturer to whom the trade-mark properly belonged, then that was equally a deception, a selling of goods with a false representation, which would give the original user of the trademark a right of action. Then in Millington *v.* Fox[4] the Court of Chancery extended the doctrine still further. To give an action at common law, the thing must have been done fraudulently, it must have been intended to deceive. But the courts of equity said, if you have purchased goods with another man's trade-mark upon them, although you have done it perfectly honestly, not knowing that it was another's trade-mark, or if you have manufactured goods for somebody else, who has ordered you to manufacture them with a certain trade-mark upon them, perfectly honestly, and not knowing you were doing anything wrong in putting that trade-mark upon them, yet nevertheless you cannot be allowed to put the goods into the market with that trade-mark upon them, because the effect of it will be that the goods will pass from hand to hand as being goods manufactured by the person whose trade-mark it is, and therefore you shall

---

[3] 3 B. & C. 541.
[4] 3 M. & C. 338.

be restrained from doing that. The courts of equity having taken that step trade-marks began to be considered as property, and no doubt there is, in a certain sense, a property in a trade-mark and equally in a trade-name, because a trade-name may be used and is very commonly used, as a trade-mark properly so-called, that is a mark put upon the goods themselves."

Misrepresentation or deceit, therefore, is the basis for the relief sought for violation of a trade-mark or name, whether it be an action at law for damages, or in equity by means of injunction against future injuries from a continued use. In the case of a trade-mark or a mere fanciful name, this is not difficult to prove, since it is a mere arbitrary device, sign or symbol, originated by the party using it. It is in a real sense *property* and its use by any other person can only be to gain the advantage to be had from the reputation of the goods or business of the first maker or trader, since presumptively there is no merit in the trade-mark itself, aside from the goods it is intended to distinguish. Given, therefore, identity or close similarity of trade-marks, and you have made out your case for the relief sought.

The case is different, however, with a personal trade-name. It is in no sense an arbitrary sign or symbol and generally the person using it has had no choice in its selection, as applied to him. As a heritage of birth man comes into life with a surname already destined to his use, and the use of the family name is a natural right.[5] It becomes valuable to him just in proportion as he makes it so, and yet it is apparent that no man has an exclusive property right in his name, even in a particular business, as against others bearing the same name. As against one not bearing the name, a trade-name can undoubtedly be protected upon the same showing as in case of a trade-mark and upon the same principle of property right. But against one bearing the same name, the action must be sustained not on the ground of any property in the words used, but because the words are used for the purpose of passing off the goods of the maker or trader as the goods of another and thus perpetrating a fraud upon the original party. It becomes then not a question of trade-mark at all but what "Browne on Trade-Marks" styles "Unfair Competition in Trade,"[6] and is grounded in fraud upon the plaintiff, and, also, upon the public, as will more fully appear.

It may be considered an elementary principle that every man

---

[5] Higgins *v.* Higgins, 144 N. Y. 462.
[6] Browne on Trade-Marks, § 43; 26 Am. and Eng. Enc. of Law, 434.

is entitled to the use of his own name in his own business; and it makes no difference how many Smiths are making and selling "Smith's Soap" or "Smith's Hats," if my name be Smith I have a right to engage in a similar business and sell my wares under the same name—provided I resort to no artifice or other means calculated to deceive purchasers into believing they are purchasing the goods of one of the other makers; that is, no deception other than that which may exist out of the confusion caused by similarity of name. For "in absence of fraud or deceit, where two parties have the same surname, equity will not enjoin defendant from using his name in pursuit of his lawful business, even though such use by defendant results in injury to plaintiff; since there cannot under such circumstances be a trade-mark in the surname which will prevent defendant from its use.'" It was thus held in Meneely *v.* Meneely above cited, a leading case in this country, wherein certain sons of one Meneely deceased succeeded to their father's name and business in the operation of a bell foundry at Troy, N. Y., which had obtained a high reputation for its products. Another son started the same business in the same place using his own name, and the brothers, succeeding to the use of the father's business, sought to restrain the use of the name. The court, however, said:

"The Court will not absolutely restrain the defendant Meneely from the use of his own name in any way or form, but simply from using it in such a way as to deceive the public and injure plaintiffs. The manner of using the name is all that would be enjoined, not the simple use of it, for every man has the absolute right to use his own name in his own business, even though he may thereby interfere with, or injure the business of another person bearing the same name, provided he does not resort to any artifice or contrivance for the purpose of producing the impression that the establishments are identical, or do anything calculated to mislead. A person cannot make a trademark of his own name and thus obtain a monopoly of it, which will debar other persons of the same name from using their own names in their own business."

And in Croft *v.* Day,[2] where two persons bearing name of Day and Martin respectively, began the manufacture of shoe blacking and polish under the firm name of "Day & Martin,"

---

[1] High on Injunctions, § 697. See also, Massam *v.* Thorley's Cattle Food Co., 6 Ch. D. 574; Meneely *v.* Meneely, 25 Barb. 79; Higgins *v.* Higgins, *supra.*
[2] 7 Beav. 84.

whereas there had been a previous firm bearing the same name, of established reputation for the quality of their output, whose business was being carried on by the administrator of Day's estate, the Court used the following language:

"It is a person's right to be protected against fraud, and fraud may be practiced against him by means of a name, though the person practicing it, may have a perfect right to the use of that name, provided he does not accompany the use of it with such other circumstances as to effect a fraud on others. * * * Relief is granted not on the basis of an exclusive right in plaintiff to the name 'Day & Martin,' but on the fact that defendants are using those names in connection with certain circumstances and in a manner calculated to mislead the public and to enable defendants to obtain at expense of Day's estate a benefit to themselves to which they are not in fair and honest dealing entitled. They have the right to carry on the business of blacking manufacturers honestly and fairly; they have a right to use of their own names; but they must not use them in such manner or way as to deceive and defraud the public and obtain for themselves at expense of plaintiff an undue and improper advantage."

And in this case relief was granted not against the use of the name but against further imitation by defendants of bottles, labels, etc., used by plaintiff, and to same effect are cases cited below.[9]

It must be observed that it is not the mere tendency to deceive, nor the probability to effect an injury, that governs the relief in such cases, as is the case in a trade-mark no matter how innocent its use, but the intentional employment of other means *calculated to deceive.* And that even though there is a strong probability that the public will be excessively misled by the similarity of names, or that the original user of the name will be injured in his business, yet in absence of such means of deception relief will not be granted. But it must be a true use of the name; the person whose name is used must be a real party to the business. Thus where one Devlin was doing business as "Devlin & Co.," whereas he had no partner or other party interested with him in the business, an injunction was allowed against the use of the "& Co." at the instance of another Devlin

---

[9] Sykes *v.* Sykes, 3 B. & C. 541; Holloway *v.* Holloway, 13 Beav. 209; Gilmore *v.* Hunnewell, 122 Mass. 139; Britannia Co. *v.* Parker, 39 Conn. 450; Cohn *v.* Kahn, 8 Ohio Bull. 154; Turton *v.* Turton, 42 Ch. Div. 128.

& Co., where there was a true partnership.[10] But this rule does not apply to cases of partnership names where the name originally was properly used, for the name may be, and often is, used a long time after parties have deceased or lost their interest in the business. In such case it is merely an equivalent to the statement that certain parties have succeeded to and are continuing the business of the old firm. So the sale of one's interest in a co-partnership together with the good-will of the business, carries with it all advantages that may pertain to the firm name, and such retiring partner will not afterward be permitted to renew the business under such a name as will imply that he is the successor to the old firm.[11]

As a person may use his own name in his own business, so a person may permit a corporation to use his name in its own title and such corporation will not be enjoined at instance of another, if the name is used in such manner as not to lead the public to believe that they are dealing with such other or are buying the article manufactured by it under the same name, no fraud or deceit being shown.[12] And where a corporation with the consent of its stockholders has embodied one or more of their names in the corporate name, the right to use the name so adopted will continue during the existence of the corporation. The person so giving the use of his name parts with the right to its personal use in the same or similar business, during the life of the corporation. Thus in Holmes, Booth & Hayden v. Holmes, Booth & Atwood Co., cited, where Messrs. Holmes and Booth retired from the first company and organized the second company for the purpose of engaging in the same line of business in competition with the first company, the Court held that when they gave their names to the first company they gave it the right to the exclusive use of its name, so far as they were concerned, so long as it might survive, and the Court enjoined them from the use of their own names in the competitive business, when it was shown that great confusion would result and the plaintiff corporation be seriously injured in its business.

But there cannot be said to be the same merit in a corporate name as in an individual's, since the corporation has no name

---

[10] Devlin v. Devlin, 69 N. Y. 212.

[11] Leather Cloth Co. v. Am. Leather Cloth Co., 11 H. L. Cas. 523; Clinton v. Douglass, 5 Jur., N. S. 887; High on Inj., §1080; Hazard v. Caswell, 57 How. Pr. 1.

[12] Massam v. Thorley's Cattle Food Co., 6 Ch. D. 574; Holmes, Booth & Hayden v. Holmes, Booth & Atwood Co., 37 Conn. 97.

until christened by its incorporators. The name chosen may be valuable as indicating the men back of it, but in the end it is a mere fanciful name—a chosen name. A company therefore employing a name—even of one or more of its stockholders—similar to name of a corporation or co-partnership previously in existence will receive less consideration from the courts than an individual under similar circumstances and in some States recent statutes prohibiting the selection of a name similar to any name theretofore in use, have been enacted.[13]

There remains one class of cases to be mentioned where the long-continued use of a personal name in connection with a given article has caused the name to attach to the article as descriptive of it. This is the case frequently with patented articles where during the monopoly given by law the article comes to be called and generally known as "Blank's Patent." "Thus in Cheavin v. Walker,[14] the defendant manufactured and sold a water filter under the name of "Cheavin's patent filter," it being, in fact, the same article made by plaintiff, but on which the patent had expired, and the Court held that defendant had the right to make same and to sell them as "Cheavin's patent filter," provided he resorted to no means to cause the public to believe they were purchasing Cheavin's own product. Likewise in Singer Mfg. Co. v. Wilson,[15] where the Singer sewing machine had acquired a great reputation during the life of certain patents, it was held after their expiration that defendant was entitled to manufacture the same machine and to advertise his machines for sale as "Singer" machines, his advertisements always stating that the machines he sold were manufactured by him and in no manner indicating them to be the product of the Singer Mfg. Co.

A few words only as to the remedy—and here the practice varies immaterially from that in trade-mark cases in general. As previously stated, it may be an action for damages at law, or by injunction with an accounting for profits. In the action at law, actual injury must be shown, but to support an injunction it is only necessary to show that an injury is threatened and that it will follow as a natural consequence of the acts complained of. The complainant must not sleep upon his rights, or long continued use with the knowledge of complainant, especially where defendant has been permitted to spend time, labor and money in

---

[13] 92 Ohio Laws 320, Act of Apr. 27, 1896.
[14] 5 Ch. Div. 850.
[15] 2 Ch. Div. 434.

building up a business, may be read into an acquiescence on the part of complainant in its use. And a less lapse of time will be a defense against an accounting for profits.[16] As to the degree of similarity necessary to warrant relief, the rule is well stated that "if the similarity would not probably deceive the ordinary mass of purchasers, an injunction will not be granted. It is not those who give the matter no attention, for they cannot be said to be misled. The similarity must be such as is calculated to mislead those in the use of ordinary caution. We must assume that consumers and dealers of a commodity have ordinary intelligence, and adopt ordinary precaution against imposition and fraud."[17] This principle will also be found running through all the cases heretofore cited and, in other words, must be such similarity as is "calculated to deceive" and so to gain an unjust advantage over the rightful user of the name.

Francis W. Treadway.

---

[16] Menendez v. Holt, 128 U. S. 523; McLean v. Fleming, 96 U. S. 258; High on Inj., §1100-1101.

[17] Blackwell v. Wright, 73 N. C. 313.

PARTY FEELING IN 1796 AND 1896.

TOWNSEND PRIZE ORATION.*

De Toqueville has defined party association as the inalienable right of men to advance or defend their political beliefs. Political parties have arisen as the means of enforcing independent thought. In all free governments, dating from the Athenian and Roman Republics the popular will has been expressed by party action. In America the spirit of party is the motive power of the machinery of government. Bold and resourceful it has moulded in no small degree the construction of the Constitution and influenced the development of our legal institutions.

Washington's endeavor was to consider the nation as a single party and thereby prevent discord and jealousy. But the adoption of the Constitution disclosed an opposition between national and state sovereignty; a tendency toward a strong centralized government and a conflicting tendency to maintain the majesty of the communities. This contest, which for years has overshadowed all others in our history, was not confined to the interpretation of the Constitution, but affected current legislation and foreign policy. When Hamilton sought to establish a national credit by his system of assumption, he was met with protests that his measures infringed the sovereignty of the States. Because they believed the Union was becoming too strong, the opponents of centralization opposed the founding of a National Bank and the enforcement of the Excise Tax.

A question of foreign politics was destined to arouse the clashing elements to organized action and separate the people into distinct political parties. The enthusiasm which welcomed the supposed advent of French Liberty had been widespread. But when the Revolutionists mistook License for Liberty, when they abandoned all principles of Justice and Humanity and would entangle us in a foreign war, a wave of reaction turned sympathy into disgust. The "bloody work of redemption" did not lessen the enthusiasm of those whose cry had been "Popular Liberty," who had formed Jacobin Clubs and deified Robes-

---

* Delivered June, 1896.

pierre and Danton. Moreover, England's hostile action upon the frontier, her restrictions upon our trade, incurred popular hatred and increased the sympathy for France.

When Washington declared a policy of neutrality, party lines were drawn. The spirit of opposition crystallized in organization. Jefferson founded the Republican party whose policy was to protect the rights of the States, aid France and oppose the Federal Administration. The Agricultural interests of the South were arrayed against the Commercialism of the North. The popular sympathy for the Atheism and Anarchy of the French Revolution was resisted by the unbending Puritanism of New England.

In the ensuing campaign of 1796, partisanship spread among the people and infected Congressional legislation. In the debates upon the Jay Treaty the Republicans charged the Administration with betrayal of American liberties to British interests. It was retorted that the Republicans were lead by French agents and were seeking the national destruction in a war with England. By a close party vote the treaty was ratified and a probable war averted. Canvassing continued to the meeting of the electors. Persons and principles were assailed with equal acrimony. Adams was described as a champion of ranks and titles and kings. Jefferson was denounced as a traitor who had encouraged the French agents to insult the President and defy the laws. The clergy warned the people against the Republican tendencies towards Atheism and Jacobinism. Secret political clubs were formed for the purpose of inventing and circulating party scandal and creating disorder. Not even Washington was spared. The Republican press published him as "Debaucher of his Nation's Liberties," and Congress insulted him at the delivery of his annual message. The most menacing feature was the existence and approval of foreign intrigue. Adet, the French Minister, attempted to win votes for Jefferson by picturing the horrors of a war with France and then announcing that his country would cease diplomatic relations until the result of the election was known.

Saddened by this apparent forgetfulness of the nation, Washington arose to stay this party zeal. Bidding his country farewell, he exclaimed, "I solemnly warn you against the baneful effects of party strife. It is a fire not to be quenched and demands vigilance to prevent its bursting forth in consuming fury."

It is almost incredible that this infant nation, exhausted by a seven years' war, its government barely established and its very existence threatened by two powerful nations, should have divided itself into hostile factions; that party spirit should have weakened the administration of the government and obstructed the development of a national life. This intensity of party feeling was of great significance. Its explanation is only to be found in a consideration of the economic condition of America and of the political philosophy of the times. The Reformation had revolutionized the accepted theory of the antecedent state of man by substituting freedom for slavery. All Europe was shaken with the strife between the Divine Right of Kings and the Divine Right of the People. Its culmination was the French Revolution. Under such conditions America was colonized. The philosophy of toleration was the mental outfit of the colonists and America was a fertile soil to sow the doctrines of Milton and Locke. Democracy was a physical and economic result. Unlimited land abolished such distinctions as landlord and tenant. There was but one class. Equality of property, equality of family, equality of labor—these were the elements that made America an ideal democracy. Liberty was enjoyed to it utmost limit. The colonists were free from religious restraint from the fear of strong neighbors, from the warring of classes.

With the development of the country such an ideal state could not continue. As population grew the amount of free land was reduced and rents were increased. There was no longer equality of property and labor. Society became more complicated. The antagonism between equality and liberty was evident. By this social differentiation the American democracy was first tested. The conflicts between the opposing interests caused the fundamental divisions of the political parties of 1796. The issue was between Liberty and Order. Fresh in the minds of the people was the liberation of England by Hampden and Cromwell, the colonial defiance of the mother country and the fierce struggle for independence. Inspired by such thoughts it was but natural that the common people should embrace the extreme principles of liberty, sympathize with France and identify themselves with the party of Jefferson. In the refusal of the Administration to aid France they saw a surrender of their rights to English interests. Accustomed to the maximum of liberty they opposed the centralization of government as an eventual restriction upon their individual freedom.

What has been called the natural aristocracy of America abhorred these ultra-democratic views. They had acquired wealth, education and power. The French Revolution had taught them that absolute equality and absolute liberty meant division of wealth and insecurity of life and property. The landed proprietors had no desire to ruin their fortunes in a war with England. Their influence was for a strong national government, that laws might be enforced, property protected and trade developed. It was also a consequence that the men of culture and refinement who had raised themselves above the common level should distrust the infallibility of the multitude and the theory of unlimited government by the people.

The Republicans believed in the final wisdom of the people, in leaving things to their natural course. The Federalists insisted upon the maintenance of Order and the respect for Authority.

While the issues of this first act in the drama of American politics have long since been extinct, the tendencies then set in motion have influenced all subsequent legislation. They serve as chains in the transition of parties. They bind the Republican party of 1796 to the Democratic party of to-day, the Federalist to the modern Republican party.

The development of party spirit may best be studied by a consideration of our present political situation. It would be a difficult task to distinguish the respective principles and doctrines of our two great political parties. Both have histories; both have leaders and war cries. Yet what principles of governmental policy divide them? Their positions upon questions of Free Trade and Protection are merely relative. Reform in the Civil Service receives the support of the best men in either party. Each faction acting upon similar principles has made similar successes and blunders in financial legislation and foreign policy.

Our parties exist because the events of 1796 endowed their predecessors with the sinews of party loyalty and party discipline. Their spirit has become effective through far-reaching and powerful organization. The power of control is centered in a select few who frame all political issues, declare all party policies, name all candidates. The frequency of elections, the increase of ignorant voters, the ease of naturalization, are all forces which increase the power and importance of these expert politicians. The vital policies of the past have been realized or abandoned.

The object of parties of to-day is their own existence and for that reason modern legislation has been partisan in the extreme.

Territories have been admitted to statehood, not because of their fitness but to strengthen the power of the dominant party. The extravagant granting of pensions is an instance of party popularity at the expense of the public treasury. Foreign affairs are discussed in a warlike tone in order to win the patriotic approval of the people. The gross corruption and inefficiency which investigation has revealed in the affairs of our cities are but the results of the extension of party government to municipalities.

It is not intended to condemn political parties or disparage their existence. Our form of government demands their continuance. Their evils arise when they are controlled by men whose title to authority is neither character nor statesmanship; when party action is but the impulse of popular prejudice.

What issues the impending presidential campaign will produce it is impossible to predict. The hardships and distress of the past few years have brought into prominence certain tendencies which are most harmful to our institutions. Not the least dangerous has been the growth of Sectionalism. It was upon this principle that the members from the Silver States obstructed all legislations, although they might ruin a nation already staggering with financial disaster. The present tariff bill involving the gravest principles of economic policy was the result of efforts to secure selfish ends, regardless of the welfare of the whole people,

The election of Populist Governors in our Southern and Western States, the popularity of schemes for fiat money, Government control of railways, are all indications of the communistic belief that the State can create wealth and regulate prosperity.

Of still graver importance is the vague desire for unregulated liberty which was expressed in the sympathy among the laboring class for the Homestead rioters and their resentment of Federal interference in the Chicago strike. These signs of discontent present real dangers which sometime must be met. Should they assume the character of political issues, the intensity of party feeling would surpass that of 1796. What was then a struggle of political equality would now become a struggle of industrial equality. The forces of Order would again oppose those of Liberty although Liberty might approach Anarchy.

The manifestations of party feeling of these two eras, has lead to the conclusion that the parties of 1796 were more truly great. They were impelled by principles rather than by their consequences. They were distinguished by higher motives and broader doctrines. Their action was more sincere and resolute. Their aim was not mere office. "Bosses" would not have been tolerated nor would they have peaceably submitted to a "machine." Yet they were but parties. Like those of to-day they had their passions and hatreds and greed. They weakened the Government at a critical point and laid it open to foreign intrigue and corruption. The comparison teaches us that the evils of party spirit arise when it prevents the growth of an honest public sentiment, when the integrity of the state is impaired, when public policies are considered not in the "light of truth but for the agitation of the people," when party is elevated above country.

The great significance of the comparison is brought home to us by the fact that while the tendencies and principles and issues of 1796 are dead the spirit of party remains. The lesson is that whether the motive is principle or patronage, parties should be considered as the agents of public opinion. When they extend beyond this sphere, lose their animating principles, and exist for their own welfare, party loyalty is at the expense of public interest. There is no magic in the words Republican and Democrat. When parties outlive their usefulness, it is time for the intelligence of the community to sacrifice party allegiance, break party shackles, and promote good government by independent action.

John Loomer Hall.

YALE LAW JOURNAL

SUBSCRIPTION PRICE, $2.00 A YEAR   SINGLE COPIES, 35 CENTS

EDITORS:

ROGER S. BALDWIN, *Chairman.*
HUGH T. HALBERT, *Treasurer.*

CHRISTOPHER L. AVERY, JR.   GEO. JAY GIBSON,
SAMUEL F. BEARDSLEY.   JOHN MACGREGOR, JR.
MICHAEL GAVIN, 2D.   HENRY W. MERWIN,

Published six times a year, by students of the Yale Law School
P. O. Address, Box 1341, New Haven, Conn.

If a subscriber wishes his copy of the JOURNAL discontinued at the expiration of his subscription, notice to that effect should be sent; otherwise it is assumed that a continuance of the subscription is desired.

AT a recent meeting of the New York State Bar Association complaint was made of "an already existing and still growing evil, the great bulk and consequent increasing uncertainty of the law." The existence of the evil will not be disputed but the remedy is neither easy of suggestion nor of application. At the meeting mentioned above it was proposed that general rules concerning the writing and publication of judicial opinions should be adopted by judges of the Appellate Courts. This suggestion if acted upon would seem to lead to valuable and practical results, but to the further remedial suggestions offered at the same meeting some objections may be presented. It was proposed to restrict the verbosity of judicial decisions in general and to prevent entirely the delivery of opinions by the court in those cases which involve merely the application of well settled principles of law. Were this as easily accomplished as proposed the practice would still seem to be of doubtful value. The duty of courts of law is primarily to settle disputes and to settle them justly, but a further and by no means unimportant duty is to make such settlements as satisfactory as possible to all parties concerned. The defeated litigant can never perhaps be thoroughly convinced of his error, yet a dismissal of his cause with simply the citation of a decision of which he is probably already cognizant would do little but increase his dissatisfaction with the results of his suit, while questioning the integrity of his lawyer who had failed to see the application of a case when, in the opinion of the court, its application was so obvious as to require no comment.

But apart from this view of the subject it would seem that in most cases the application of previous decisions would not be so clear as to make comment and explanation unnecessary. The principle may be clear and easy of expression, yet its application may be most difficult and involved; the decision of a stated case may be most definite and yet an interpretation of the law therein contained may well tax the ingenuity of even judicial minds. In such cases the litigant parties are entitled to hear the reasons which led the court to adopt its view of the application of the law and as most cases involve such application and interpretation the proposed change if suitably modified would lose much if not all of its significance.

It was further proposed at the same meeting that opinions should be handed down as the opinions of the court as such, and not as the works of individual judges. It is claimed that this plan if adopted would shorten the opinions, would place responsibility upon all the judges, and would provide against dissenting opinions. This suggestion would seem to make doubtful the attainment of the promised result and at the same time to be open to the gravest objections. Opinions in their new capacity would embody the reasoning of all the judges instead of merely the one who under the present system is its author, while the conclusion would be reached through various and varying processes, according to the disagreement of the judges as to the proper grounds upon which to base their decision. The decision would be the decision of the court, the reasoning would be a *potpourri* of legal applications and interpretations, terminating it is true, in one common conclusion, but wanting in the two requisite virtues of brevity and clearness, the attainment of which was the very object in view. Farther than this the weakening of individual responsibility for the doubtful strength of a court acting as a whole is also a matter for question. The author of an opinion is individually responsible for the law therein contained, but under the proposed system this responsibility would be abolished. Dissenting opinions, which now serve to place the minority judges in a true light and which have often materially aided in the logical growth of the law, would, under the new system, totally disappear, and a bare majority of the court would have even a greater influence than is now their privilege. Finally, the loss of valuable opinions and the loss of the authority of the authors' names would seem to negative any benefits which might be derived from the above suggestions. The law as we have it to-day is often found best interpreted in the opinions of our judges and the weight and authority of the opinions are often enhanced by the eminence and reputation of their authors. If this source of legal literature is cut off the science and the art of law will be left with only text books and magazine articles, while these, especially in this country, are only too often mere digests of the law without even suggestions as to causes and effects. The evil of verbose and prolix judicial opinions may be a crying one, but its remedy would seem to lie more in individual discretion than in such radical action as proposed.

* * *

REFERENCE to arbitration in all disputes of whatever nature will not become possible nor indeed will the principle itself be seriously entertained or relied upon by nations until, either by changes supplementing the rules of international law at present existing, or by treaty, the rules of law are developed so as to render the rights of parties under given conditions capable of being clearly ascertained, and the remedies to be applied certain and such as under all the circumstances will work substantial justice between the governments concerned. In controversies concerning land some period of limitation ought to be fixed upon whereby the adverse possession of territory for a certain length of time should be deemed conclusive evidence as to title, thus placing territorial disputes between nations in a position to be dealt with upon a basis analogous to that upon which private titles to real estate are now adjusted. It is unreasonable to demand or expect that an independent state will consent to refer questions affecting the rights and citizenship of its own subjects, who have been for many years in peaceable possession of a tract of territory in good faith believing they had a right to occupy it, to any tribunal, however eminent, whose decision might be conclusively determined by the contents of some docuument exhumed from among the refuse of former centuries. The Venezuela Boundary Treaty was of course designed to fit a particular instance and its provisions will have no weight in another case except possibly the authority of precedents. The reported stipulation, however, that exclusive political control of a district for fifty years as well as the actual settlement thereof shall be sufficient to make title by prescription is, under the circumstances, an exceedingly fair and equitable settlement of an otherwise difficult point, and deserves to be acquiesced in and followed by other nations in cases which may arise in future. The interests of society demand that a period be fixed upon after which no evidence of adverse title will be heard. It will be then possible to submit territorial claims to arbitration, knowing that the decision is to be based upon the fact of settlement and actual occupancy and not upon the theoretical interpretation of uncertain documents from the past. In these days of bitter commercial competition between states, and headlong eagerness to embark upon "land grabbing" schemes without pretense of right or shadow of excuse, the rules of law must be definite and the remedy certain and reasonable if arbitration treaties are to be of any avail in averting the ultimate appeal to force.

* * *

THE arbitration treaty, which has been signed by the diplomatic agents of the United States and Great Britain, if newspaper reports are correct, expresses the desire to consolidate the relations of international amity now existing between the two countries and to provide for the perpetuation of these relations in the future. This is not an attempt to establish a permanent international court but to provide for the establishment of special courts as the need for them is felt. In brief, the treaty provides for the peaceable settlement of those questions which would naturally seem to be capable of peaceable settlement without such a treaty, and interposes a barrier which, if unbroken, will serve to delay an immediate recourse to arms in those cases where a peaceable settlement is not possible. The courts created under this treaty, when deciding non-territorial claims, will consist of one neutral judge, assisted by quasi-judges whose chief duties, however, will be to represent the interests of their respective countries by whom they will be appointed, while territorial questions will come before a court composed entirely of quasi-judges of the above description. War is still recognized to be the supreme arbitrator in certain cases, although in those cases where it is not so recognized there would be little reason to fear it even under the present system. By the treaty there is an official establishment of a peace which is already established, an official postponement of a war which in all probability could not be definitely postponed should its causes arise.

Whether or not international intercourse has sufficiently developed to insure the success of such a treaty is a matter for the future to prove. In the meantime, however, and at the present time, it seems as if our efforts should be directed towards the development of trade and commerce between nations instead of merely endeavoring to find new expressions for a peace which by our evident apprehension we show to be of doubtful stability and of an illusionary and uncertain character. International unions, it may be said, will only then be placed upon a safe ground when they are based upon economic conditions which demand and sanction them and not alone upon the perhaps more attractive but less practical ground of peace and good will. The influence of the arbitration treaty for good has perhaps in the main been already accomplished in furnishing evidence, which indeed should not be despised, of an apparent desire on the part of the two governments for peace; its influence for evil is unknown and can only be foreshadowed by the different motives which have been attributed to its creation, the balancing of international accounts which it seems to have caused, and its possibly detrimental effect upon diplomacy. Indeed, during this exchange of courtesies the two countries seem to be strictly adhering to the old adage, "In time of peace prepare for war," and those who are skeptical as regards universal and perpetual peace under existing conditions are found to be indulging in the thought that "mere names do not alter facts and no amount of legislation can make a reality out of a fiction." The value of the treaty would certainly seem to be sentimental rather than practical and it only remains for us to hope in regard to it that sentiment may play a more important part in international affairs in the future than it has in the past.

On the other hand, the treaty is certainly evidence of the friendly relations now existing between the two countries and expresses the desire that these relations may continue. It may be that the objections urged against it are more technical than real, however well they may seem to be founded on reason and history. The main object is the prevention of war and possibly the delay for which this treaty provides will have a salutary effect upon the minds of the people should the peace now prevailing be ever endangered. The same object, however, might perhaps be attained and with less cause for objection by the mere adoption of a resolution recently offered in the Senate which declares that "the United States favor the principle and practice of international arbitration for the settlement of all questions in difference between them and any other nation, which they may fail to adjust by treaty or diplomatic negotiations," and invites "all civilized nations to make a corresponding and reciprocal declaration to the end that wars between nations may cease and that a universal reign of peace may be inaugurated and perpetually maintained." The practicability of adopting this resolution instead of ratifying the pending treaty of arbitration is a matter for the Senate to decide, but it seems as if such action might be safer and easier and perhaps as efficient as an adoption of the more elaborate and pretentious plan under discussion. The final sanction, other than war, of all international contracts or quasi contracts, whether they take the shape of treaties or resolutions, must be national integrity and honor, and as the main object is an avoidance of war so long as it is avoided honorably, it seems as though a resolution, all things considered, might be as salutary in its results as a treaty, although it may be thought that a treaty would appeal more strongly to the sense of national honor than a mere resolution. There can be no difference of opinion as to the end in view; it is only the means which are debatable, and those means should be chosen which will afford the greatest efficiency with the least danger and complexity.

* * *

THE frequent attempts to set aside wills upon the ground of undue influence or lack of testamentary capacity, emphasize the importance of the passage of a bill which has been proposed in Connecticut. The bill provides that a person may deposit his sealed will in the Probate Court, whereupon notice of such deposit shall be published, and any one desiring to contest the will upon the ground of a lack of testamentary capacity or undue influence must do so before the death of the maker of the will. The advantages of such a law are obvious. Under the present practice appeals from probate are necessarily protracted, and in the majority of cases the appellant does not improve his condition. Other cases on the docket are delayed for weeks and often for months. The dead man is abused by foe and kin, and the details of his entire life are related, with particular emphasis upon his eccentricities and misdeeds, and are published throughout the community. The public, who have heretofore regarded the man with the highest respect, are asked to heap abuse upon his head. Family secrets are disinterred and the surviving members of the family blush with shame. The testator cannot speak and explain his conduct, so his nearest relatives, who oftentimes have been his worst enemies, try to set aside the last formal declaration in which he has provided for those who were his true friends. Under the proposed law these contests would largely disappear. Unfriendly relatives would seldom attempt to establish a lack of testamentary capacity, and the temptation to use undue influence upon weak-minded men would be lessened. Should contests arise, they would be decided promptly and the great expense incident to the present practice would cease. That such a law would be approved by the courts seems certain; that it would be welcomed by the bar is apparent to those who realize that a lawyer has other duties than fighting cases for the purpose of consuming large estates; that it would command public sanction can scarcely be doubted. It is to be hoped that the Legislature will pass the bill.

COMMENT.

The recent decision of the Supreme Court of the United States in *Fallbrook Irrigation District* v. *Bradley*, upholding the validity of the California irrigation laws and sustaining the decisions of the Supreme Court of that State as announced in *Turlock Irrig. Dist.* v. *Williams*, 76 Cal. 360; *Central Irrig. Dist.* v. *De Lappe*, 79 Cal. 351; *Board of Directors* v. *Tregea*, 88 Cal. 334, and *re* Madera Irrig. Dist. Bonds, 92 Cal. 297, is of great interest, involving as it does, the existence of these water companies by which some four million acres of land have already been reclaimed and rendered productive and whose bonds have been purchased by innocent investors, whose security would be valueless if the enactments of California and legislation of a similar character in other States providing for the organization of such corporations had been declared unconstitutional. In view of the vast interests to be jeopardized by an adverse holding the fairness of the decision cannot be questioned, and we avoid comment thereon. There are, however, some points in the opinion of Mr. Justice Peckham to which we call attention.

This case arose upon an application for an injunction, brought by one Maria Bradley in the United States Circuit Court to restrain the collector of the Fallbrook Irrigation District from executing a deed conveying her land under a sale, made pursuant to the provisions of the irrigation law of California, known as the "Wright Act." The grounds upon which the relief was sought were that the act in question was in violation of the Constitution of the United States and also of the Constitution of the State of California. Upon the latter question the Supreme Court agreed with the opinions rendered by the state court in *Turlock Irrig. Dist.* v. *Williams; Central Irrig. Dist.* v. *De Lappe*, and cases referred to above. The real point in the decision was that the act did not infringe upon that clause of the Fourteenth Amendment of the Federal Constitution which provides that no person shall be deprived of life, liberty or property without "due process of law," since the landowner has an opportunity to be heard both as to whether his land would be benefitted by the irrigation proposed and also upon the question of the valuation and assessment of as much as might be included in the district. The court held, moreover, that the use of water for the irrigation of land in the manner provided could not be considered otherwise than as a public use; nor is it material to this view that in some cases the only effect might be to render more productive lands already capable of cultivation. See *Wurts* v. *Hoagland*, 114 U. S. 606; *Spencer* v. *Merchant*, 125 U. S. 353; *Head* v. *Amoskeag Mfg. Co.*, 113 U. S. 9; *Hagar* v. *Reclamation Dist. No. 108*, 111 U. S. 701; *Davidson* v. *New Orleans*, 96 U. S. 97, and California cases above referred to.

In concluding his opinion Mr. Justice Peckham said that the imposition of an *ad valorem* tax upon the land to be benefitted in a case of this nature, whether such tax might or might not be contrary to the fundamental law of a State, violates no provision of the Federal Constitution. The remedy for abuse in case the burden rests unequally is to be pursued in the State courts, for, in the language of Mr. Justice Field, in *Mobile* v. *Kimball*, the Supreme Court of the United States "is not the harbor in which the people of a city or county can find a refuge from ill-advised, unequal and oppressive State legislation."

In *Anglo-California Bank* v. *Secretary of Treasury*, 76 Fed. Rep. 742, the Circuit Court of Appeals discusses the effect of the passage of a new tariff law upon goods imported and placed under bond under a prior law. Certain steel rails had been so treated, the warehouse entries being liquidated under the tariff law of March 3, 1883. They remained in the warehouse over three years and became liable to be abandoned to the Government under Rev. Stat., section 2971, which provides that goods left in bond more than three years shall be regarded as abandoned to the Government and sold; the sale was, however, postponed several times by the Secretary of the Treasury at the request of the importer, until finally the Wilson Bill was passed. The importer then offered to withdraw the rails upon paying the duties imposed by the latter act, but the court held that they must pay the duties imposed by the act of 1883, affirming 71 Fed. 505. Its views were that since the act of July 28, 1866, the word "abandonment," as used in section 2971, does not mean an absolute abandonment, so as to vest the title in the Government, but a vesting of absolute authority in the Government, when goods have remained in the warehouse more than three years, to sell them in order to pay the duties and charges thereon and to pay the balance to the owner, or an authority to allow the owner to withdraw the goods on such payment, and that as no rule of the Secretary of the Treasury can annul or amend revenue laws the Government's right of sale was an accrued right and within the saving clauses of the McKinley and Wilson Acts. It declined to follow *Abbott* v. *U. S.*, 20 Ct. Cl. 280, where the court held that where goods were imported and the duties paid before the passage of the act of 1883, but not removed from the warehouse until after the passage and more than three years from the entry, the difference in the amount of the duties should be refunded. In *in re* Schmid, 54 Fed. 145, the goods had been in bond less than three years.

By the decision of the Circuit Court for the District of Connecticut in the case of *in re* Hirsch, 74 Fed. Rep. 928, the right of an Internal Revenue Collector to refuse to produce in the State courts, in a prosecution for the illegal sale of liquor, papers or records which are not private in their nature, but are on file in the Revenue Collector's office for the inspection of the public, is denied. For this refusal Hirsch was sentenced for contempt of court, whereupon he petitioned the Circuit Court for a writ of habeas corpus. The justification offered by the petitioner for this refusal was an alleged rule or regulation of the Commissioner of Internal Revenue "prohibiting the Collectors to produce in State courts any papers or documents relating to the business of the taxpayer, upon prosecutions for violations of State laws in regard to the sale of intoxicating liquor, against those who have paid a special tax." Judge Shipman held that, since the power to compel the production of this class of testimony is the same in both State and Federal courts, it is not a question of power generally, and this kind of evidence has no special immunity peculiar to itself, since the returns are not privileged, and the inconvenience caused the officers is part of their duties. The petition was therefore dismissed.

RECENT CASES.

CORPORATIONS.

Street Railroads—Refusal to Give Transfer—Action for Penalty.—Meyers v. *Brooklyn Heights R. R. Co.*, 41 N. Y. Sup. 798. The law will not enforce a penalty for refusal to give a transfer to "any passenger desiring to make one continuous trip" between two points on a street railway system, where it appears the passenger was riding solely for the purpose of demanding the transfer and recovering the penalty on refusal. He is not, within the term of the statute, a passenger seeking to make one continuous trip on the connecting lines of the system.

Street Railroads—Contributory Negligence—Failure to Look Back.—Rooks v. *Houston, W. S. & P. F. R. Co.*, 41 N. Y. Sup. 824. If a person, while riding a bicycle along and upon a cable car track, is struck by an overtaking car he is guilty of no contributory negligence from the mere fact of his failure to look back for such car. The law imposes no such duty upon a person.

Street Railway Companies—Improvements of Streets—Contracts.—Borough of Shamokin v. *Shamokin St. Ry. Co.*, 35 Atl. Rep. 862 (Pa. St.). A street railway company was required by the terms of its grant to lay its tracks on the grade of the streets thus used, and to share with the municipality the expense of "repairing or macadamizing" any of these streets. The company received notice that the municipality had decided to pave a street with asphalt; also that its tracks therein were not placed on the proper grade. The company paid no attention and the municipality, by itself, changed the grade of the tracks and paved the entire street. Held, that the company is liable to the municipality for the cost of altering the tracks and also for the preliminary work of paving the street, but not for the actual laying of the asphalt.

Carriers of Passengers—Steamboats—Liability as Innkeeper.—Adams v. *New Jersey Steamboat Co.*, 45 N. E. 369 (N. J.). Money for traveling expenses was stolen from a cabin passenger on a steamboat without negligence either on his part or that of the carrier. "The relations that exist between a steamboat and its stateroom passengers differ in no essential respect from those that exist between an inn-keeper and his guests." For cases holding steamboat company not liable as inn-keeper see *Steamboat "Crystal Palace"* v. *Vanderpool,* 16 B. Mon. 302; *Clark* v. *Burns,* 118 Mass. 275.

Railroad Companies—Receivers—Supply Claims—Diversion—Equity —Reasonable Time.—Southern Ry. Co. v. *Carnegie Steel Co., Limited,* 76 Fed. Rep. 492 (Va.). When renewable notes of a railroad company were taken in payment for current supplies, and after renewal, but before maturity, the company went into the hands of a receiver, it was held that such notes for current supplies, contracted within a reasonable time before the receivership, and, by the principles governing the administration of the assets of a railroad by receivers, payable from the surplus earnings, have a priority over claims for improvements, interest, or dividends, and equity will give supply creditors, as against mortgage creditors, the right to recover money thus spent. The case of *Bound* v. *Railway Co.,* 8 U. S. App. 472; 7 C. C. A. 322, and 58 Fed. Rep. 473, was distinguished in that the appellant, by taking notes for eight months was held to have assented to the use of the earnings for the payment of interest. Similar decision in *Southern Ry.* v. *American Brake Co. et al.,* 76 Fed. Rep. 502, and in *Southern Ry. Co.* v. *Tillett,* 76 Fed. Rep. 507, in a claim for necessary repairs.

Municipal Corporations—Public Improvements—Enactment of Ordinances—Evidence of Fraud.—Morse et al. v. *City of Wesport et al.,* 37 S. W. Rep. 932 (Mo.). The fact that a city council orders a large number of streets to be macadamized and curbed at the expense of the abutting property owners in anticipation of a new legislative enactment forbidding cities to pass such ordinances, except upon petition of a majority of the resident real estate owners, held by a majority of the court not, in itself, proof of fraud.

INSURANCE.

Marine Insurance—Substitution—Construction of Contract.—New Haven Steamboat Co. v. *Providence Washington Ins. Co.,* 41 N. Y. Supp. 1042. An insurance policy was issued on plaintiff's steamer *C. H. Northam,* the policy providing that the insurance should cover any other steamer that should take her place, notice of such substitution to be given. Soon after the steamer

Continental was substituted for the *Northam*, and notice thereof duly given. Several weeks later the *Northam* resumed running, the *Continental* being laid off, and was injured in a collision. Plaintiff claimed indemnity for the loss, but the insurance company repudiated liability, and action was brought on the policy to recover insurance. Held, on a close decision, two of the five judges dissenting, that, in the absence of specific notice of the resubstitution of the original steamer the policy still attached to the *Continental*, and did not reattach to the *Northam* from the mere fact of her having resumed her place.

Chattels of a Wife—Delivery to Husband and Investment—Insurance Rights of Creditors.—Eggleston v. *Slusher et al.*, 69 N. W. Rep. 310. A wife received moneys from relatives and delivered the same to her husband, who invested them in property in his own name. A portion was destroyed by fire and the insurance policy on it was assigned by the husband to the wife, ostensibly to repay her for a loan of the money; at this time the husband was insolvent. It was not proved that the delivery by the wife to the husband was considered as a loan nor that there was any agreement for its repayment. In a suit against the husband by creditors, held, that the money passed to the husband according to the law when he received it; that the subsequent assignment of the policy lacked consideration, and that the equities of the creditors would prevail over those of the wife.

Eminent Domain—Public Use.—Bridal Veil Lumbering Co. v. *Johnson*, 46 Pac. Rep. 790 (Or.). A lumbering company, incorporated also to construct a railroad for the benefit and use of the general public in transportation of passengers and freight, will be entitled to the exercise of the power of eminent domain, to complete their road which has already been extended for a few miles; although the part already in operation extends through a thinly settled and mountainous region, with no villages or other railroad at its terminals.

AGENCY.

Principal and Agent—Ratification of Unauthorized Act—Warehousemen—Lien of Storage—Replevin.—Knight et al. v. *Beckwith Commercial Co.*, 46 Pac. Rep. 1094 (Wy.). Company's agent made an unauthorized agreement to store plaintiff's goods without charge. The company retained possession of the goods for storage fees without notifying party that it repudiated said agreement. Held, that the company did not have a warehouseman's lien for storage.

Real Estate Agent—Commission.—Moses v. *Helmke*, 41 N. Y. Supp. 557. A real estate broker is entitled to his commission provided he arranged for a sale satisfactory to his principal, although his principal later refused to consummate the sale and sold the property to other parties.

MISCELLANEOUS.

Monopolies—Combination of Patent Owners.—National Harrow Co. v. *Hench*, 76 Fed. Rep. 667, Circuit Court, E. D. Penn. A combination of patent owners, by which each manufacturer assigns to a corporation organized for the purpose the legal title to his patents and receives back an exclusive license to make and sell only the same style of articles as before, all parties being bound to sell at the same prices and on the same terms, is as much a monopoly as any other such combination.

Chinese Labor—What Constitutes.—United States v. *Sun*, 79 Fed. Rep. 450. That a Chinaman, member of a trading firm in which he had an interest, lived with some of the partners at their store and did housework for them, makes him a domestic servant and not a "laborer" for hire, and hence not liable to deportation under registration and deportation acts of 1892 and 1893.

Federal Jurisdiction—State Taxation of National Bank Stock—Injunction.—Third Nat. Bank of Pittsburg v. *Mylin, Auditor-General et al.*, 76 Fed. Rep. 385. Where a tax is sought to be levied against a national bank by State officers claiming under a State statute which is violative of the Fourteenth Amendment and of Sec. 5219 of the Revised Statutes of United States, a Federal court has jurisdiction to issue an injunction against such officers enforcing such tax.

Federal Courts—Following State Decisions.—Ryan v. *Staples*, 76 Fed. Rep. 721, Circuit Court of Appeals (Col.). A single decision by the highest court of a State declaring a judgment void and based on the principles of the common law and not on the construction of any statute, does not establish a rule of property binding on a Federal court in a case where the rights of a third party claiming property under such judgment became vested before the decision was made.

Res Judicata—Application—Limits.—Fuller v. Metropolitan Life Ins. Co. of New York, 35 Atl. Rep. 766 (Conn.) Considerations of public policy do not justify the extension of the rule of *res judicata* to make a fact adjudicated in an action between two persons in their individual capacity, *res judicata* in subsequent actions brought by one, as assignee of a chose in action between the other and a third person, which plaintiff has purchased of such third person after his right therein has become fixed, and since the rendering of judgment in the first action. The parties in both actions must be identical in the same right or capacity, or their privies claiming under them.

Constitutionality—Scandalous Publications—Freedom of the Press.— State v. Van Wye, 37 S. W. Rep. 938 (Mo.). A legislative enactment providing that anyone who published or disseminated a newspaper, the contents of which were licentious, scandalous and immoral, should be deemed guilty of a felony, does not conflict with the Constitution of the State which guarantees liberty of speech and of the press.

Rewards—Arrest of Fugitive from Justice—Right of Claimant.— Coffey v. Commonwealth, 37 S. W. Rep. 575 (Ky.). A person who in good faith and in accordance with the provisions of the statutes apprehends and delivers over a fugitive from justice is entitled to a reward offered by the Governor notwithstanding the prisoner was apprehended before the reward was offered.

Contributory Negligence—Icy Sidewalks.—Manross v. Oil City, 35 Atl. Rep. 959 (Penn.). The fact that the plaintiff knew that a sidewalk had ice upon it and attempted to cross is not contributory negligence sufficient to withdraw the case from the jury.

Bequest—Satisfaction of Debt—Interest.—Adams v. Adams, 35 Atl. Rep. 827 (N. J. Eq.). Where the legatees of a will do not, within the statutory period of time, demand payment of their unpaid legacies but wait until after the death of the executrix and life tenant of the estate, held that the heirs, the remainder men, are not liable for interest on the legacies since this dilatoriness of the legatees operates as a waiver by them of their interest.

Frauds on the Revenue.—United States v. One Hundred and Thirty-two Packages of Spirituous Liquors and Wines et al., Circuit Court of Appeals, Eighth Circuit, 76 Fed. Rep. 364. Under the United States revenue statutes all packages containing spirituous liquors must be marked with the proper name or brand known to the trade and the term package includes every receptacle into which liquor is placed.

Trustees—Commissions in Two Capacities.—In re Spaulding's Estate, 41 N. Y. Supp. 1022. Where a will naming certain persons as executors also gives them the residuary estate in trust for the purpose of separating, from the body of the same, funds sufficient to yield an annuity for the testator's widow, such executors are entitled to commissions for services in the capacity of trustees as well as in that of executors.

Expert Witnesses—Opinion Evidence.—People v. Youngs, 45 N. E. Rep. 460. No error is committed in allowing an expert to declare upon the sanity of the accused after he had made an examination and before stating all the grounds for his opinions.

BOOK NOTICES.

A Treatise on the Law of Circumstantial Evidence. By Arthur P. Will of the Chicago Bar. Law sheep, 500 pp. text. T. & J. W. Johnson & Co., Philadelphia, 1896.

Mr. Will's work will be of the greatest benefit to the criminal lawyer, although it contains also much matter of great assistance to the general practitioner. It is an admirable combination of the theory and the practice of the law of circumstantial evidence, beginning as it does with the rules of logic which govern the production and effect of this sort of evidence, and closing with an exceedingly interesting collection of cases in which those rules have had a practical application. The best feature of the book, we think, is the clear and logical way in which the question of the relative value of direct and circumstantial evidence, and the whole subject of the *corpus delicti* are handled. The volume is unique in that it has brought the subject up to almost the moment of publication, many of the cases reported having been decided within the past year.

The Law of Evidence in Civil Cases. By Burr W. Jones of the Wisconsin Bar. Law Sheep, 3 vols., 16 mo., 1,998 pp. text. The Bancroft-Whitney Co., San Francisco, Cal., 1896.

This is one of the most convenient and practical books we have ever examined. It has been arranged with special reference to rapid examination of the different branches of the subject, the heading of each section clearly indicating its contents, and the authorities cited in each paragraph being placed immediately after the paragraph. In the case of disputed points there is a complete list of references on either side, and the reasons for the author's opinion are logically stated. An original feature is found in the fact that citations to the leading articles in the various law journals are placed side by side with those to the reports and text books. The type is clear and legible and the division into three volumes and the small size of each volume make the book very easy to carry about for ready reference. As a practical working text-book it leaves little to be desired.

The General Digest, American and English. Law sheep, 1,708 pages. The Lawyers' Co-operative Publishing Company, Rochester, N. Y., 1896.

"Good wine needs no bush." The "General Digest" in former years has so conclusively proved its merit and value that it does not require further praise from us. It is a sufficient guaranty of its excellence that the practical work of producing this issue has been done by the same hands and under the same skillful supervision as in former years. The paragraphs are clear and concise and are so arranged that those referring to any required subject are easily and quickly found. In a supplement which accompanies the volume are contained the cases which have not been officially reported.

Commentaries on American Law. By James Kent. Law sheep, 4 vols., 718, 1,061, 787 and 673 pages text. Little, Brown & Company, Boston, Mass., 1896.

By far the most valuable edition of this "masterpiece of Chancellor Kent's" is the present one, the fourteenth, produced under the editorship of Mr. John M. Gould, Ph.D. The notes and citations of Judge Holmes, the editor of the twelfth edition, have been altered wherever there has been a change in the meantime in the legal principle involved, and an addition of some nine thousand cases has been made to the former list. Considering the development and advance which has taken place in American law since the first quarter of the century, when Chancellor Kent first delivered the lectures which form the basis of his Commentaries, it is an arduous task indeed to so annotate the work as to make it fully harmonize with the present state of the law. This labor Mr. Gould has shown himself fully able to undertake and to complete with marked success. His notes are copious when dealing with doubtful or disputed points, yet so clearly and logically arranged are they that the principle stated is never lost or rendered obscure in a multitude of conflicting cases, as is often the case in text-books which deal with so important and fundamental legal subjects. In the words of the editor, Kent's Commentaries "will doubtless continue to rank as the first of American legal classics so long as the present order shall prevail." Be the future what it may, for the present these Commentaries owe their usefulness in no small degree to Mr. Gould's careful work as an annotator.

Illustrative Cases in Torts. By James Paige, LL.M. Cloth, 776 pages. T. & J. W. Johnson & Company, Philadelphia, Penn., 1896.

The above collection of cases forms one of the so-called "Pattee," series of illustrative cases. There are upwards of one hundred and fifty decisions, selected with great care, and serving to illustrate the leading points of the whole subject of torts. Most of them contain the opinions of the judges of this country and the book is thus expressly valuable to the American lawyer. The cases are printed in large, legible type, with a succinct statement of the principle involved at the head of each, and are arranged in proper order and sequence to be of the greatest assistance to one pursuing a systematic study of the subject.

MAGAZINE NOTICES.

The Green Bag, December, 1896.

John Marshall (illustrated), . . .	Sallie E. Marshall Hardy.
Forgiveness (verse), ...	Davenant.
New Abridgment of the Laws of England (with portrait).	
An Assassin's Plea, ...	Irving Browne.
A Blackstone Christmas Eve.	
London Legal Letter.	
The Lawyer's Easy Chair, ...	Irving Browne.

American Law Review, September and October, 1896.

International Law (Annual Address before the American Bar Association). . . .	The Rt. Hon. Lord Russell.
Government by Lawyers, . . .	Seymour D. Thompson.
Constitutional Changes which are Foreshadowed, .	Walter Clark.
Judge and Jury, ...	Hon. H. Teichmueller.
Can Contracts to Pay in Specific Coin (Gold) be Enforced?	N. M. Thygeson.

November and December, 1896.

The Reorganization of Railway and other Corporations,	Moorfield Story.
The Blending of Law and Equity, . . .	Texas Bar Committee.
Necessity of Alleging what you Intend to Prove in Negligence Cases, ...	Seymour D. Thompson.
The Fellow-Servant Doctrine, ...	Speed Mosby.
The "Sugar Bounty" Cases, . . .	Joseph Whelesa.
Parol Evidence in Respect to Writings Under the Statute of Frauds, ...	Irving Browne.

Albany Law Journal, 1896–7.

Dec. 5.	Inconsistent Defenses Under the Code,	John C. Kleber.
Dec. 12.	The Liability of a Forwarder of Collections for Acts of his Correspondents, .	William A. Way.
Dec. 19.	Elevator Injuries to Trespassers and Licensees,	James A. Webb.
Dec. 26.	A Prohibitive Tax on Litigation, .	Willis E. Heaton.
Jan. 2.	Some Hints on Speaking.	
Jan. 9.	Verdicts by Less than a Unanimous Jury,	Charles L. Gray.
Jan. 16.	How Great Law Offices Work, . .	Benjamin F. Tracy.

Central Law Journal, 1896-7.

Nov. 20.	Can the Liability of a Carrier of Passengers be Limited by Contract?	George Lawyer.
Nov. 27.	Are Judgments Quasi-Negotiable?	Roscoe Pond.
Dec. 4.	The Dog in Law,	W. C. Rodgers.
Dec. 11.	Can Judgments be Sold under Attachment or Execution?	John C. Kleber.
Dec. 18.	Service of Process on Corporations,	Seymour D. Thompson.
Dec. 25.	Index Digest of Vol. 42.	
Jan. 1.	Parol Evidence to Add a Warranty to a Written Sale,	Irving Browne.
Jan. 8.	Scope of a Lis Pendens,	S. S. Merrill.
Jan. 15.	The Effect of Municipal Ordinances upon Civil Liability Between Private Parties,	James L. Hopkins.

SUPPLEMENT

CONTAINING

MEMORABILIA ET NOTABILIA.

[Graduates are requested to contribute to this column and address their communications to YALE LAW JOURNAL, box 1341, New Haven, Conn.]

Hon. Frederic R. Coudert, LL.D., of the New York Bar, will be the Wm. L. Storrs Lecturer for 1897.

* * *

Among the Yale Kent Club lecturers for this year will be I. H. Bromley, Esq., of the New York *Tribune*.

* * *

It is probable that Geo. M. Sharp, Esq., of the Baltimore Bar, will deliver one of his courses of lectures on Insurance, during the Winter term.

* * *

Professor Baldwin represented the New Haven Colony Historical Society at the meeting of the American Historical Association held at Columbia University, New York City, on December 30th.

* * *

At a meeting of the Kent Club held January 11th the following officers were elected for the Winter term: President, R. C. Stoll, '97; Vice-President, E. W. Beattie, '99; Secretary, C. A. Fuller, '99; Assistant Treasurer, H. M. Burke, '97; Executive Committee, T. H. Cobbs, '97, A. A. Alling, '99, and E. W. Beattie, '99; First Critic, W. F. Alcorn, '97; Second Critic, M. F. Hatcher, '97.

* * *

The Townsend Club has recently been organized by members of the Senior class and the Wurts Moot Court Club and Beers Debating Club by the Juniors.

* * *

The Senior class have voted to wear caps and gowns during Commencement.

1872. Henry C. Baldwin died of nervous prostration at Waterbury on January 15th. Mr. Baldwin was born in Naugatuck in 1842. He was the Greenback candidate for Governor of Connecticut, and later an active supporter of the Democratic party.

1878. Kazuo Hatoyama has recently been elected Speaker of the House of Commons of the Imperial Parliament of Japan. From 1881 until 1889 Mr. Hatoyama was Professor of International and Roman Law in the University of Tokio, and at varied intervals has been Dean of the University Law School, Director of the Bureau of Law in the Department of Foreign Affairs, and a member of the Higher Civil Service Commission. In 1889 he resigned all these positions, entered active practice and became one of the leaders of the Japanese bar. In 1894 he was elected to the House of Commons from one of the districts of Tokio, and has since been regarded as the leader of his party. Mr. Hatoyama is also a Railroad Commissioner, a member of the Council of State for the Doctorate Degrees, and President of the Tokio College of Law and Politics.

1879. Edward D. Robbins has recently been elected Vice-President of the New England Railroad Co. He was a member of the temporary Board of Directors which purchased the company before it came under the control of the New York, New Haven and Hartford Railroad Co., and has been its counsel for several years.

1881. Charles P. Woodbury died of pneumonia at Norwalk on December 30th. Mr. Woodbury was Assistant Clerk of the Connecticut House of Representatives in 1882 and Clerk of the Senate in 1883, and at the time of his death was connected with the Connecticut Building and Loan Association.

1883. Charles Kleiner has been elected President of the New Haven Social Science Club.

1885. Hon. John G. Tod has been chosen Judge of the Civil District Court of Houston, Texas. Since 1892 he has been County Judge of Harris County, Texas.

Charles F. Watts is City Solicitor of Toledo, Ohio.

1890. Edwin F. Bugbee of Willimantic, has formed a law partnership with John L. Hunter, State's Attorney for Windham County, Connecticut.

Leonard T. Waldron has entered the office of Hatch & Wickes, 100 Broadway, New York City.

1891. Benjamin H. Charles, Jr., has opened an office in the Union Trust Building, St. Louis, Mo.

John A. Hoober is lecturer on patents in the Dickinson Law School, Carlisle, Penn., and has an office in the Security Title and Trust Building, York, Penn.

Robert J. Lewis is City Solicitor of York, Penn.

Frederick A. Scott has been elected Clerk of the Connecticut House of Representatives.

1892. William J. Neary is a member of the Connecticut Legislature.

Francis W. Treadway, a former editor of the JOURNAL, was married January 5th to Miss Esther S. Frisbie, niece of Mr. and Mrs. S. W. Sessions of Cleveland, O.

Lebbens R. Wilfley has an office in the Union Trust Building, St. Louis, Mo.

1893. Alfred W. Carter is Judge of the First Circuit Court of Hawaii. His office is in Honolulu, H. I.

James St. C. McCall has an office on East Market street, York, Penn.

1894. Albert A. Moore, Jr., is practicing in Oakland, Cal.

Pierpont Fuller is with Rogers, Cuthbert & Ellis, Denver, Col.

Arnold W. Sherman is with Logan, Demond & Harby, 58 William street, New York City.

1895. Robert Adair has an office at 208 Equitable Building, Wilmington, Del.

Joseph Anderson, Jr., is temporary Prosecuting Attorney of the City Court of Waterbury.

Frederick L. Averill has been appointed Clerk of the Judiciary Committee of the Connecticut Legislature.

The engagement is announced of Albert H. Barclay to Miss Laura Whitney Williams of Rochester, N. Y.

John E. Bishop is with George W. Taussig, 178 and 180 Laclede Building, St. Louis, Mo.

Thomas H. Breeze, a former editor of the JOURNAL, is with Van Ness & Redman, Mills Building, San Francisco, Cal.

Frank J. Brown, a former editor of the JOURNAL, is principal of the Elementary Department of the New Haven night school.

W. B. Brown and Bennie A. Younker have formed a law partnership with offices in Des Moines, Iowa.

William C. Hungerford is in charge of the Hartford office of Mitchell, Hungerford & Bartlett.

Eugene Kreamer is practicing law in California, Mo.

F. M. Peasley has an office in the Bohl Building, Waterbury. He was the Republican candidate for Judge of Probate in the recent election.

Dexter E. Tilley is in the office of Judge Charles L. Long, Springfield, Mass.

Alfred C. Woolner, a former editor of the JOURNAL, is in the office of Tracy, Boardman & Platt, New York City.

1896. Robert S. Alexander has entered the office of Judge Hough in Danbury.

Raymond H. Arnot has entered the office of one of the leading law firms in Rochester, N. Y.

Andrew T. Bierkan is a Notary Public and is associated with Dillon & Douglass, New Haven.

Thomas H. Cox is with Arvine & Hubbard, 42 Church street, New Haven.

John J. Cuneo has opened an office in South Norwalk.

Edward M. Day has been appointed on the Judiciary Committee of the Connecticut Legislature. His office is at 333 Main street, Hartford.

Winthrop H. Duncan is with Stickney, Spencer & Ordway, New York City.

Benjamin B. Holston has purchased the office and fixtures of an established law firm in Nashville, Ill.

James A. Howarth, Jr., and Frederick C. Taylor were admitted to the Connecticut Bar in December.

James S. Jenkins has entered the office of Hart & Keeler in Stamford.

George B. B. Lamb is practicing law in Brooklyn, N. Y. He has recently had a severe illness but is recovering.

Patrick J. McMahon has been elected Justice of the Peace in Waterbury.

Edward H. McVey has formed a law partnership with his father, under the name of McVey & McVey, in Des Moines, Iowa.

Robin Macdonald is studying for the degree of M. L. at the University of Pennsylvania. Address, 20 Green street, Philadelphia.

Wilbur G. Manchester has entered the office of S. E. Harmon, Winsted.

Frederick S. Martyn has opened an office at 44 Pine street (room 902), New York City.

John A. Matthewman is with his father, Charles B. Matthewman, 42 Church Street, New Haven.

Daniel C. Morrissey is counsel for D. C. Morrissey & Co., mortgages and real estate loans, Champagne, Ill.

John S. Pullman has opened an office at room 42 Sanford Building, Bridgeport.

Walter B. Riley has opened an office in Champagne, Ill.

Carl F. Stahl is with David Strouse, 823 Chapel street, New Haven.

Edward L. Steele has entered the office of his father on Main street, Hartford.

Robert C. F. Stoddard is with Stoddard, Goodhart & Graves, 82 Church street, New Haven.

Charles B. Waller has entered the office of his brother, Tracy Waller, in New London.

YALE LAW JOURNAL

SOME RECENT DEVELOPMENTS OF THE LAW OF PATENTS.

The Supreme Court of the United States, in the closing years of its ordinary appellate jurisdiction, has settled several hitherto vexed questions of patent law, and has shed new light upon others. It is doubtful whether any other like period in the history of this law has been distinguished by so many important decisions. It would seem as though the Supreme Court had discussed and disposed of the questions presented, having in mind that the principles and rules enunciated must serve as permanent guides for the new Circuit Courts of Appeal.

It has become the fashion, among the patent bar, to contend that these decisions have revolutionized rather than developed the former practice and law. This tendency has been especially noticeable since, under the operation of the Evarts Act, the Circuit Courts of Appeal have become the tribunals of last resort.

It is true that the Supreme Court has made some material modifications in the generally accepted theories as to certain phases of patent law. Thus, by a strict interpretation of the statute, it has been decided that the term of a United States patent is limited by the duration of a foreign patent for the same invention (Bate Refrigerating Co. *v.* Sulzberger, 157 U.S. 1). Subsequent to the jurisdiction act of 1887 and prior to *In re* Hohorst, 150 U. S. 659, it had been generally supposed that suits for infringement of patents against citizens of the United States could only be brought within the district where defendant resided. It now appears to be the prevailing opinion in view of *In re* Hohorst, *supra* and *In re* Keasbey & Mattison Co., 160 U. S. 221, that such suits may be brought in any district in which the defendant may be found. It is hardly necessary to suggest the strategic importance of this decision in many cases.

This doctrine, and the rule that the burden of proof is upon a complainant, in a suit for infringement, to allege and prove actual or constructive notice of the patent (Dunlop *v.* Schofield, 152 U. S. 244; Coupe *v.* Royer, 155 U. S. 584) are contrary to the general practice formerly prevailing in the lower courts, and are not easily reconcilable with some of the earlier decisions of the Supreme Court.

The Supreme Court has also definitely determined the relations of the Federal Government to owners of patents. It is now settled that while the Federal Government is liable under its contract for the use of a patented invention, it is not liable in tort, and an officer of the United States exercising his official functions in the use of Government property, cannot be restrained by injunction against infringement (U. S. *v.* Berdan Fire-arms Co., 156 U. S. 552; Belknap *v.* Schild, 161 U. S. 10; Kirk *v.* U. S., 163 U. S. 49).

In actions at law it has sharply drawn the distinction between the respective functions of court and jury in cases of infringement (Coupe *v.* Royer, 165 U. S. 565; Black Diamond Co. *v.* Excelsior Co., 156 U. S. 611; Market-street Cable Co. *v.* Rowley, 155 U. S. 621), and has held that the statutes of limitation of the various States are applicable thereto (Campbell *v.* Haverhill, 155 U. S. 610). It has approved the practice of taking advantage on demurrer of invalidity apparent on the face of a patent (Richards *v.* Chase Elevator Co., 158 U. S. 300) has laid down the rule that the decision of the Patent Office upon questions of priority is conclusive thereafter between the parties, unless the contrary is established by indisputable evidence (Morgan *v.* Daniels, 153 U. S. 120), and has strictly enforced the doctrine of estoppel in the determination of the rights of employers in patents taken out by employees (Lane *v.* Locke, 150 U. S. 193; Gill *v.* U. S., 160 U. S. 426).

In the Singer Sewing Machine case the relations between the public and the owner of a patent at the date of its expiration, are exhaustively discussed. The court there holds that a generic name passes to the public simultaneously with the dedication resulting from the expiration of the patent (Singer Mfg. Co. *v.* June Mfg. Co., 163 U. S. 169.

Upon the vexed question of damages, it has declared the unsatisfactory doctrine, that while at law a plaintiff is entitled to recover what he has lost even though it exceed defendant's profits, a defendant in equity is liable to account only for such profits as are found to have actually accrued to him from the use of the patented invention (Belknap *v.* Schild, 161 U. S. 10; Keystone Mfg. Co. *v.* Adams, 151 U. S. 139; Coupe *v.* Royer, 155 U. S. 565, 583).

The question as to what constitutes invention is necessarily left to be determined upon the facts in the particular case. A valuable modification of the tests formerly employed is found in Potts *v.* Craeger, 155 U. S. 597, where, *inter alia*, it is held that a double use may involve invention provided the second use is in an art remote from the former art.

The cases which have been most extensively discussed are Miller *v.* Eagle Mfg. Co., 151 U. S. 189; Risdon *v.* Medart, 158 U. S. 68, and Morgan *v.* Albany Co., 152 U. S. 425.

In Miller *v.* Eagle Mfg. Co., the inventor claimed two different functions or operations of a spring in separate patents. The Supreme Court found that the operation covered by the second patent was necessarily included in that of the earlier one, and might have been claimed therein, and that the two functions were identical. It held that where matters covered by a second patent were thus inseparably involved in matters embraced in a former patent, issued to the same inventor, the second patent was void. The use of the term "inseparably involved" gave rise to much contention among the patent bar. It has been strenuously claimed that a generic description of an invention and a specific description of a definite combination of elements embodying the invention in a particular form with or without improvements thereon, were so inseparably involved that they could not be the subjects of separate patents. It is to be borne in mind, however, that in Miller *v.* Eagle Co., the devices of the two patents were identical in construction and operation, and the second patent was for a function necessarily exercised in the first patent. If the words "inseparably involved" be limited to such identity, and the other language used by the court be confined to the case there presented, it will not be found that it lays down any rule inconsistent with the previous decisions of the court. It seems now to be recognized by the Circuit Courts that the term is to be limited to cases where the second patent claims a function necessarily performed by the device of the first patent. If the claims of the two patents specify different parts of a combination or if one omits one or more of the elements contained in the other, they are not "inseparably involved" (Walker on Patents, 3d edition, §180a; Thomson-Houston Elect.

Co. v. Winchester Ave. Ry. Co., 71 Fed. 205; *Id. v.* Elmira & H. Ry. Co., 71 Fed. 405; Deering v. Winona Co., 155 U. S. 286; Fassett v. Ewart Mfg. Co., 62 Fed. 407; McBride v. Kingman, 72 Fed. 908).

"The test of identity is whether both when properly 'construed in the light of the description define essentially the same thing. When the claims of both cover and control essentially the same subject matter both are for the same invention and the later patent is void" (Thomson-Houston El. Co. v. Elmira & H. Ry. Co., *supra*).

In this connection may also be considered the case of Risdon v. Medart, 158 U. S. 68. There the court stated that as a general rule neither a process not involving chemical or other elemental change but consisting solely in the operation of a machine, nor the function of a machine, was patentable. Here again, when the patent for the machine covers the invention by which the process is necessarily carried on, there is but one invention and but one patent therefor. The application of this principle, however, is attended with great difficulty. As Mr. Walker says in his work on patents: "This question of the patentability of processes which consist entirely of mechanical transactions, but which may be performed by hand, or by any of several different mechanisms or machines, is the most important unsettled question known to the patent laws of the United States." Walker on Patents, § 3a.

The distinction between a process and a function had already been previously repeatedly announced and applied in the second Circuit (Risdon v. Medart, *supra;* see, also, Blakesley Novelty Co. v. Conn. Webb Co., 78 Fed.; Travers v. Gem Hammock and Fly Net Co., 75 O. G. 678; Wells Glass Co. v. Henderson, 67 Fed. 935).

If, however, there is such a change in the method or arrangement of operations as involves invention and produces a new and useful result, and if it covers only means or methods of producing such result irrespective of the effect of mechanism, the process may be the subject of a separate patent (Risdon v. Medart, *supra;* Schwarzwalder v. N. Y. Filter Co., 66 Fed. 157).

In Morgan Envelope Co. v. Albany Paper Co., 132 U. S. 425, the Supreme Court passed on the comparatively modern doctrine of contributory infringement. There the plaintiff sold patented fixtures for delivering toilet paper to such persons only as dealt in and used its toilet paper. Defendants having obtained such patented fixtures from the original purchasers from the patentee, fitted them with paper of their own manufacture and also sold their paper to others with the intention that such paper should be used in plaintiff's fixtures. The Supreme Court affirmed the principle already announced by the lower courts "that the manufacture and sale of a single element of a combination with intent that it shall be united to the other elements and so complete the combination is an infringement." But it held that this doctrine had no application to cases where the element made by the alleged infringer was not separately patented and was of a perishable nature to be delivered by the combination and used periodically when put in actual use.

In the further consideration of the development of or limitations upon this doctrine two questions have arisen:

Is the alleged infringement reconstruction or repairs?

May the owner of the patent lawfully impose a limitation upon a purchaser as to the use to which such combination is to be put?

As to the first question the Court of Appeals in the Eighth Circuit in Shickle Harrison & Howard Iron Co. *v.* St. Louis Car-Coupler Co., 77 Fed. 739, holds that the fact that the alleged infringing article is an important element of the patented combination and only capable of use in connection with the other elements thereof is not conclusive against the right to replace, but that when it is liable to break or wear out long before the rest of the combination, and other parts are equally or more important and the invention is not confined to the part broken, anyone may furnish to original purchasers a new article to replace the worn out or broken one, but could not sell to other persons or for other purposes.

The same rule is applied by the Court of Appeals in the Second Circuit in Thomson-Houston Co. *v.* Kelsey El. Ry. Spec. Co., 75 Fed. 1009, where the defendant, by public advertisement, had offered to sell to the public generally one element of a patented combination. There the defendant was permitted to sell said elements to replace those broken or worn out, or to substitute its manufacture for those sold by complainant, but was enjoined against the reconstruction of those not so sold. See also Thomson-Houston Electric Co. *v.* Ohio Brass Co., 78 Fed. 139.

In Heaton *v.* Peninsular Button Fastener Co. *v.* Eureka Specialty Co., 77 Fed 288, the parties sought to take advantage of the principles enunciated in the decision in Morgan Envelope Co. *v.* Albany Paper Co., *supra.* The complainant sold a patented machine for affixing buttons to shoes, upon the condition that it should only be used in connection with the unpatented staples made by it. The defendants manufactured staples adapted only for use in said machines and induced purchasers of said machines to buy their staples in violation of said restriction. The court below dismissed the bill on demurrer on the theory that it would be contrary to public policy to enforce said restriction. The Court of Appeals held that the rules as to contributory infringement already considered were applicable to the facts as charged in the bill and reversed the decree.

On the other hand in Keeler *v.* Standard Folding Bed Co., 157 U. S. 659, the Supreme Court has held, three Justices dissenting, that the purchaser of a car-load of beds from the owner of the territorial right for the State of Michigan, for the express purpose of selling them in Massachusetts, had the right to sell them anywhere within the United States, even within territory already assigned to another party. In the forcible dissenting opinion of Mr. Justice Brown it is pointed out that the effect of this decision is to place it in the power of a patentee to sell licenses to make and sell for every State in the Union except his own, and to then establish a rival factory and undersell and ruin his licensees.

These cases show something of the present status and tendency of the law of patents in the United States. The charge of departure from principles heretofore established previously referred to, appear to be due to a strict application by the Supreme Court of the rules of law and statutory construction to questions of jurisdiction, practice and evidence at the expense in some instances of the doctrine of *stare decisis.*

But in its disposition of the fundamental questions of invention, infringements and the respective rights and obligations of patentees and the public, the Supreme Court has consistently applied and developed the earlier decisions.

It is impossible to predict the influence which the Supreme Court is hereafter to exert upon the law relating to inventors. This will largely depend upon the extent to which the Circuit Courts of Appeals may certify to it, or it may deem it advisable by certiorari to pass upon, new questions concerning which there may be a division of opinion in the various circuits.

It is a matter for congratulation that the structure of the patent law of to-day rests on such a firm foundation and has been so harmoniously built up that the additions of the future must be in the line of development subordinate to the existing plan. *William K. Townsend.*

THE PRESUMPTION OF INNOCENCE IN CRIMINAL CASES.[*]

In the case of Coffin v. United States,[1] decided in March, 1895, the Supreme Court of the United States had an opportunity to clear up the confusion and ambiguity that hang over the common talk about the presumption of innocence in criminal cases. The opportunity was sadly misimproved. It is quite time that the opinion in this case should be subjected to a critical examination. This is all the more desirable because the tendency of it is to encourage that feeble administration of our criminal law which is doing so much in these days to render it ineffectual.

It will be desirable, in order fully to understand the matter, to enter upon some preliminary explanations. England, our mother country, had formerly an extremely harsh body of criminal law. Fitzjames Stephen, forty years ago, declared that "the English judges of the eighteenth century administered what, without any exception, was the most cruelly severe penal code that ever existed."[2] Blackstone tells us that, in his time there were one hundred and sixty capital offences without benefit of clergy, for "actions which men are daily liable to commit!"[3]

In Henry the Eighth's reign of thirty-eight years it is said that eighty thousand persons were executed in England as common malefactors. In ten years of James the First's reign, from 1609 to 1618, inclusive, nearly fifteen hundred persons were hanged in the city of London, and in the County of Middlesex alone, including the considerable number (thirty-two in Middlesex) who died by the *peine forte et dure*.[4] In the sixteenth century, in treason and felony, no witness was allowed for accused persons; in the seventeenth century the witnesses that were received for them were not allowed to be sworn; and no counsel was permitted to help them in trying their case on the

---

[*] This paper contains the substance of one of the Storrs Lectures of 1896.
[1] 156 U. S. 432.
[2] Jurid. Soc. Papers, i. 468.
[3] Com., IV. 18.
[4] Jeaffreson's Middlesex County Records, Vol. 2, xvi-xxi.

facts, until in the eighteenth century, "by the connivance of the court," and, finally, by statute, in 1834. The judges were removable by the Crown until the English Revolution, and notwithstanding the maxim that *they* were to act as counsel for the accused, they were greatly in the habit of considering everything favorably to the Crown. Torture was practiced in some cases. It may be remarked, in passing, that torture was recognized even in New England in the seventeenth century. In the colonial laws of Massachusetts we read: "No man shall be forced by torture to confess any crime against himself or any other, unless it be in some capital case, where he is first fully convicted by clear and sufficient evidence to be guilty; after which if the case be of that nature that it is very apparent there be other conspirators or confederates with him, then he may be tortured, yet not with such tortures as are barbarous or inhumane."[5]

But all this cruelty was accompanied and relieved by humane maxims, rules of procedure, and practical adjustments of one sort and another, which tended to make it endurable.[6] There was the jury system, which protected accused persons through the sympathies of their fellow-citizens. There was the common law system of evidence which saved them, in an increasing degree, from being tried on prejudice. There was the maxim, running back into the earliest Year Books, that no person should be twice put in jeopardy of life or limb. And there was the principle that it were better that a guilty person should be un-

---

[5] Laws of 1660 (Whitmore's Edition), 187; Anc. Charters and Laws of Mass., 180. The year of this enactment is not given. What is called "The Laws of 1660," is a compilation of that year.

[6] It may be added that our administration of the criminal law to-day, in a period when the substantive law is merciful, is sadly enfeebled by a continuance of some rules and practices which should have disappeared with the cruel laws that they were designed to mitigate. I may refer to the refusal of new trials to the government in some classes of cases, to the absurd extreme to which the rule about confessions in evidence is sometimes pressed, to the strained interpretation of the prohibition of *ex post facto* laws, to the continuation of technicalities of criminal procedure and practice which have lost their reason for existence and to a superstitious rigor in enforcing these, which still shows itself. In following English precedents in such matters, we forget to supplement them by that saving good sense which appears in the swiftness and vigor of the English administration of criminal law. If we follow English practices we should remember that they are all meant to go together. Excellent criticisms of this sort may be found in the dissenting opinion of Peckham, J., speaking for himself and Justices Brewer and White, in Crain *v.* U. S., 162 U. S. 625, 646, 650. He justly characterizes the result arrived at in the opinion of the court as "most deplorable."

punished than that an innocent one should be condemned—a doctrine laid down in the Digest,[7] where it is attributed to the Emperor Trajan.

That maxim, by the way, has had a singular history. First found in the Digest, it appears in the Year Books of Edward the First, twelve centuries later, in substantially the same form above quoted.[8] In the fifteenth century we find Fortescue saying: "Truly I would rather that twenty guilty men should escape through pity than that one just man should be unjustly condemned."[9] Two centuries later we have Sir Matthew Hale saying that "It is better that five guilty persons should escape unpunished than that one innocent person should die."[10] A little later we find one of the victims of Titus Oates's perjury saying to the judges with pardonable exaggeration that, "It is better a thousand guilty men should escape than one innocent man should die."[11] A century later Blackstone tells us that, "It is better that ten guilty persons should escape than that one innocent person should suffer."[12] Early in the present century, in a series of Irish cases, we find it repeatedly said that "It is better that ninety-nine guilty persons should escape than that one innocent man should be punished."[13] Finally, in an article upon the trial of Dr. Webster, in 1851,[14] Professor Joel Parker, formerly Chief-Justice of New Hampshire, is found, as Paley before him, and Fitzjames Stephen since, stoutly controverting the statement of Blackstone, that ten guilty persons should escape rather than one innocent person suffer; but prepared to admit that it is better that one should escape than that an innocent person should suffer. And thus we may return to the moderation of the early proposition in the *corpus juris*. Obviously these phrases are not to be taken literally. They all mean the same thing, differing simply in emphasis—namely, that it is better to run risks in the way of letting the guilty go, than of convicting the innocent.

Another of those practical adjustments favorable to the accused person which enabled our English ancestors to endure the horrors of their substantive criminal law, was the doctrine of

---
[7] 48, 19, 5.
[8] Y. B. 30 and 31 Edw. I., 538.
[9] De Laud. c. 27.
[10] P. C. II., 289.
[11] Lord Stafford's Case, 7 How. St. Tr. 1529 (1690).
[12] Com. IV., 358.
[13] *E. g.*, in Killen and McCann's Case, 28 St. Tr. 1013 (1803).
[14] 72 N. A. Rev. 200–202.

benefit of clergy: originally the benefit in certain capital cases, if the accused were an ecclesiastic, of being turned over to the spiritual arm, and not hanged, for the ecclesiastics never hanged. The test of an ecclesiastic was that he could read, and so the Bishop sent in a representative to try the accused with his "neck verse." As Smith in the sixteenth century, in his "Commonwealth of England," tells us: "In many felonies, as in theft of oxen, sheep, money or other such things, which be no open robberies by the highway side, nor assaulting one by night in his house, putting him that is there in fear, such is the favor of our law, that for the first fault the felon shall be admitted to his clergy, for which purpose the Bishop must send one with authority under his seal to be judge in that matter at every jail delivery. If the condemned man demandeth to be admitted to his book, the judge commonly giveth him a psalter, and turneth to what place he will. The prisoner readeth so well as he can (God knoweth, sometimes very slenderly): then he [the judge] asketh of the Bishop's commissary, *legit ut clericus?* The commissary may say *legit*, or *non legit*; for these be words formal, and our men of law be very precise in their words formal. If he say *legit*, the judge proceedeth no further to sentence of death; if he say *non*, the judge forthwith, or the next day, proceedeth to sentence."[15] This came to be the general test in what continued to be called the benefit of clergy—the power to read, and these imaginary ecclesiastics, were discharged with little or no punishment. One who had claimed this privilege, and had it, was branded on the brawn of his thumb, so that if he appeared again he might be known; for he could have it only once.

We also had benefit of clergy, on this side of the water. It was allowed in the case of the soldiers who were convicted of manslaughter at the Boston Massacre. Benefit of clergy, in England, was abolished in 1827. For centuries it mitigated, substantially, the severity of the English criminal law.

Always, of course, there was operating in favor of the accused the sound maxim of general jurisprudence that the plaintiff or, rather, the party who seeks to move the court, must make out a reason for his request. This rule is sometimes expressed in the form of a presumption, *presumitur pro neganti;* or, having regard to the Latin terms for plaintiff and defendant, *actor* and *reus,—presumitur pro reo.* That is a maxim of policy and practical sense; it is not founded on any notion that defendants generally are free from blame. It is a maxim or principle that

---

[15] Smith's Com., Eng. Bk. II. c. 27. This book was written in 1565.

saves the defendant by the mere inertia of the court, if the plaintiff does not make out his case. This maxim, in this bare form, and without the familiar additional clause as to the greater force of persuasion in criminal cases, always operated for the accused. It is probably true that in the form last given it has sometimes been mistranslated, and given a special application to criminal cases, as if *reus* necessarily meant a person charged with crime, and not merely, as it truly does, a defendant in any sort of a case. The operation and exact scope of this maxim, both in civil and criminal cases, was very neatly expressed by the General Court (the Legislature) of Massachusetts so long ago as 1657, as follows: "Whereas, in all civil cases depending in suit, the plaintiff affirmeth that the defendant hath done him wrong and accordingly presents his case for judgment and satisfaction —it behoveth the court and jury to see that the affirmation be proved by sufficient evidence, else the case must be found for the defendant; and so it is also in a criminal case, for, in the eye of the law every man is honest and innocent, unless it be proved legally to the contrary."[16]

In this country and in recent times, much emphasis in criminal cases has been put on the presumption of innocence. Always and everywhere great emphasis was placed on the rule that in criminal cases there can be no conviction unless guilt is established with very great clearness—as we say nowadays, beyond reasonable doubt. In civil cases it is enough if the mere balance of probability is with the plaintiff, but in criminal cases there must be a clear, heavy, emphatic preponderance.

Now, what does the presumption of innocence mean? Does it mean anything more than a particular application of that general rule of sense and convenience, running through all the law, that men in general are taken, *prima facie—i. e.*, in the absence of evidence to the contrary, to be good, honest, free from blame, presumed to do their duty in every situation in life; so that no one need go forward, whether in pleading or proof, to show as regards himself or another, that the fact is so, but every one shall have it presumed in his favor? If it does, what is its meaning?

Let us trace the use of this maxim. In recent years, in this country, at the hands of heated counsel and of some judges, it has been given an extraordinary stretch. One may read, for instance, in a late American book on Evidence, the following statement: "The presumption of innocence is not a mere

[16] Records of Massachusetts, III., 434-435.

phrase without meaning; it is in the nature of evidence for the defendant; it is as irresistible as the heavens till overcome; it hovers over the prisoner as a guardian angel throughout the trial; it goes with every part and parcel of the evidence."[17] That "purple patch" is not marked as being quoted from anybody; but in reality, I believe, it was an impassioned utterance of Rufus Choate, one of the most eloquent and successful advocates of his time.[18] Such a passage as that, gravely woven into the text of a legal treatise may show the extent to which the presumption of innocence has been overdone in our hysterical American fashion of defending accused persons. But let us observe it in its earlier history. In Bracton, say in 1260, we find it in the most general form—*de quolibet homine presumitur quod sit bonus homo donec probetur in contrarium.*[19] In a great and famous continental work on Presumptions by Menochius,[20] three centuries later, we have the simple phrase: "*Illa presumptio qua dicimus quemlibet presumi innocentem,*" and that is all the emphasis he gives it. In the middle of the next century, the General Court of Massachusetts, in a passage partly quoted before, said, simply and precisely, "It behoveth both court and jury to see that the affirmation be proved by sufficient evidence, else the case must be found for the defendant, and so also it is in a criminal case; for in the eyes of the law every man is honest and innocent unless it be proved legally to the contrary. In criminal prosecutions the presumption is in favor of the defendant, for thus far it is to be hoped of all mankind, that they are not guilty in any such instances, and the penalty enhances the presumption."[21]

Very little is said about it before this century, and these quotations fairly illustrate the slight emphasis given it, and the part it plays. In looking through the arguments of Erskine and Curran and other great lawyers famous for their defence of accused persons, and through the charges of the court given to juries—in the last century and the early part of this, we shall find very little, indeed almost nothing, about the presumption of innocence. But a great deal will be found, a very great emphasis is placed, upon the rule that a party must be proved guilty by a very great weight of evidence. That is the important thing.

---

[17] Bradner, Evidence, 460.
[18] Lawson, Pres. Ev. 433 n.
[19] Bracton, 193.
[20] 955, col. 1, 16.
[21] *Ubi supra.*

And I think it will be found that, in English practice, down to our time, the presumption of innocence—except as a synonym for the general principle incorporated in that total phrase which expresses the rule about a reasonable doubt, namely, that the accused must be *proved* guilty, and that beyond a reasonable doubt—plays a very small part indeed.

Take, for example, two famous English cases of this century. In Despard's case[22] the Attorney-General in his opening argument said: "I am, however, gentlemen, ready to admit what no doubt the counsel for the prisoner would be glad to have brought forward to your attention, that the great depravity which is required to conceive and to execute a crime of such extensive mischief, so far from operating to create any prejudice against the prisoner, ought rather to give him a fairer claim to the utmost benefit of that indulgent and salutary principle of our law, which holds every man to be innocent till he is proved to be guilty; and, therefore, he will unquestionably be entitled to that which I am sure he will experience at your hands, that the charge should be well watched, that the evidence should be well sifted, and that your minds should be most satisfactorily convinced of his guilt, before you think of pronouncing a verdict against him." Serjeant Best (afterwards Chief-Justice Best), for the defence (col. 437) said: "Gentlemen, having made these observations, I am persuaded it will be unnecessary for me to desire you to do all that men can do to divest yourselves of that prejudice which you feel against a man in his situation; to do all that which the Attorney-General has emphatically and distinctly told you to do—that which the law of this country has told you to do—that, without which there can be no liberty existing in this country—that is, to presume him innocent till guilt is established in evidence; for, until his guilt be made out, not merely by vague and unconfirmed stories told by suspicious witnesses, but by that species of evidence which is required by juries in cases of this sort, it is your bounden duty to presume him innocent." And, again, at the end of his argument (col. 458, 460): "This case is not to be made out by conjecture, you are not to condemn unless all idea of innocence be completely extinguished by the weight of the evidence that has been produced upon the cause. * * * Remember the maxim of the Attorney-General, that 'in proportion as the crime is enormous so ought the proof to be clear.'"

At the trial of William Palmer for poisoning in 1856, the

---
[22] 28 St. Tr. 345, 363 (1803).

counsel have nothing to say of the presumption of innocence. And this is what Lord Campbell says in his charge:[23] "Gentlemen, I must begin by conjuring you to banish from your minds all that you may have heard before the prisoner was placed in that dock. * * * I must not only warn you against being influenced by what you have before heard, but I must also warn you not to be influenced by anything but by the evidence which has been laid before you with respect to the particular charge for which the prisoner is now arraigned. * * * By the practice in foreign countries it is allowed to raise a probability of the prisoner having committed the crime with which he is charged by proving that he has committed other offences—by showing that he is an immoral man, and that he is not unlikely therefore, to have committed the offence with which he is charged. That is not the case in this country. You must presume that a man is innocent until his guilt is established, and his guilt can only be established by evidence directly criminating him on the charge for which he is tried. * * * Unless by the evidence for the prosecution a clear conviction has been brought to your minds of the guilt of the prisoner, it is your duty to acquit him. You are not to convict him on suspicion, even on strong suspicion. There must be a strong conviction in your minds that he is guilty of this offence, and if you have any reasonable doubt you will give him the benefit of that doubt."

That is the simple, intelligible, plain way in which the presumption of innocence is dealt with in important cases in England. The prisoner is, indeed carefully protected, but his bulwark is not found in any emphatic or strained application of the phrase or the fact of a presumption of innocence.

A Scotch case in 1817[24] should now be mentioned. We shall see hereafter the use made of it in Coffin v. U. S. One Andrew McKinley was indicted for administering false oaths. There was a question as to the true interpretation of the oaths, and the counsel for the accused insisted upon his right to have a favorable construction put on them. He said (col. 283): "In all criminal cases everything must be strictly interpreted in favor of the accused and against the prosecutor," and other similar things. The Advocate Depute, replied (col. 334): "A great deal was said about the presumption in favor of the innocence of the panel. This is a common topic of declamation,[25]

---

[23] Palmer's Trial, 166.
[24] McKinley's Case, 33 St. Tr. 275.
[25] The reader will observe that this is said of Scotland and not of England.

but I never could understand the presumption of the innocence of a panel. The *onus probandi* lies on the prosecutor, and he must make out his case, but I see no occasion for a presumption of any sort, but what arises from a want of contrary proof. And I know no such doctrine in any work on the criminal law of Scotland." The defence (col. 438-439) declared that "this was the very first time in a criminal case," that the existence of a presumption of innocence had been denied, and referred to the "very obvious and common-place rule of law that in all trials for crimes there is a presumption in favor of innocence which runs through the whole proceedings and is applied to the indictment, to the proof, to the verdict." In deciding the question then under discussion in favor of the prosecution, Lord Pitmilly said (col. 518) that if anything were doubtful about the construction of the oaths "the presumption must be in favor of innocence. * * * We are not to presume guilt because the prosecutor alleges guilt * * * and until guilt is established, we must hold the presumption to be in favor of innocence." Lord Justice Clerk said (col. 538), that if the oath were doubtful he was bound "to let the doubt lean in favor of the accused." None of the other judges commented on this subject except the single dissenting judge, Lord Gillies. He said (col. 506) in an emphatic passage that, to be sure, he himself suspected that the oath was as bad as it was contended, "But," he went on, "the presumption in favor of innocence is not to be redargued by mere suspicion. * * * The public prosecutor treats this too lightly. He seems to think that the law entertains no such presumption of innocence. I cannot listen to this. I conceive that this presumption is to be found in every code of law which has reason and religion and humanity for a foundation. It is a maxim which ought to be inscribed in indelible characters in the heart of every judge and juryman, and I was happy to hear from Lord Hermand that he is inclined to give full effect to it.[26] To overturn this there should be legal evidence of guilt, carrying home a degree of conviction short only of certainty."

It will be noticed, as I said, that this is a Scotch case, and Lord Gillies a dissenting judge. The Scotch law is not the common law, and in Scotch courts the Continental refinements about presumptions are far more familiar than in England. The handling of the matter in this case is indeed very simple,

---

[26] All that Lord Hermand is reported as saying on this matter is (col. 499) that "Where there is a possibility of a favorable construction for the panel, it ever will receive effect from me."

and not at all strained, but the case is not an authority in English law, or at all indicative of any emphasis, even in the Scottish courts, in recognizing the presumption of innocence.

The English conception of the presumption of innocence has been expressed by a writer peculiarly learned in the criminal law, who had devoted much time to the study and exposition of it, and, as a judge, was long engaged in administering it. Fitzjames Stephen, in the second edition of his "General View of the Criminal Law of England," published in 1890, when the author had been eleven years a judge of the Queen's Bench Division, says (p. 183): "I may mention the general presumption of innocence which, though by no means confined to the criminal law, pervades the whole of its administration. * * * [Here he quotes from his "Digest of Evidence" the Article which is given below.] This is otherwise stated by saying that the prisoner is entitled to the benefit of every reasonable doubt. The word 'reasonable' is indefinite, but a rule is not worthless because it is vague. Its real meaning, and I think its practical operation, is that it is an emphatic caution against haste in coming to a conclusion adverse to a prisoner. It may be stated otherwise, but not, I think, more definitely, by saying that before a man is convicted of a crime every supposition not in itself improbable, which is consistent with his innocence ought to be negatived." In his "Digest of Evidence," Article 94, under the title "Presumption of Innocence," he presents as its definition, this: "If the commission of a crime is directly in issue in any proceeding criminal or civil, it must be proved beyond reasonable doubt. The burden of proving that any person has been guilty of a crime or wrongful act is on the person who asserts it."[17]

This mode of stating or indicating the substance of the presumption of innocence as applied in criminal proceedings, is more or less found in our own decisions. Obviously, it is in a very compact form; and it seems plain that such a statement adds something to the mere presumption of innocence, for that, pure and simple, says nothing as to the quantity of evidence or strength of persuasion needed to convict. But as it is stated above, the rule includes two things: First, the presumption; and second, a supplementary proposition as to the weight of evi-

---

[17] This article has a second paragraph which runs thus: "The burden of proving that any person has been guilty of a crime or wrongful act is on the person who asserts it, whether the commission of such act is or is not directly in issue in the action." The doctrine here expressed is probably not the law in most parts of this country.

dence which is required to overcome it; the whole doctrine when drawn out being, first, that a person who is charged with crime must be *proved* guilty; that, according to the ordinary rule of procedure and of legal reasoning, *presumitur pro reo, i. e., neganti*, so that the accused stands innocent until he is proved guilty; and, second, that this proof of guilt must displace all reasonable doubt.

As regards the simple, just, unambiguous rule, which, in requiring proof, thus emphasizes the weight of evidence and the strength of persuasion necessary to make it out in a criminal case, this rule, thus appearing to Stephen to embody and to be identified with the presumption of innocence as applied to criminal cases, is a very ancient one. We read in the *Corpus Juris*, as far back as the fourth century, a direction which is attributed to several Emperors in succession: "Let all accusers understand that in bringing up a matter for judgment it must be supported by fit witnesses, *vel apertissimis documentis vel indiciis ad probationem indubitatis et luci clarioribus*"[28] This passage was cited for the accused in a Scotch criminal case of piracy in 1705,[29] and scraps of it lingered long in our own books; as when Coke in his Third Institute, 76, in speaking of treasons, says: "There should be a substantial proof in a cause so criminal where *probationes oportent esse luce clariores*"; and again, of treason and felony,[30] that the reason for not allowing counsel to the accused is that, "the testimonies and proofs of offence ought to be so clear and manifest as there can be no defence of it." and still again, he speaks of the rule of law *quod in criminalibus probationes debent esse luce clariores.*"[31]

This rule in England was the one constantly pressed; while, as I have said, little or no mention was made in terms of a presumption of innocence. This was the chief rule urged in behalf of accused persons by the great advocates in the last century and later, in such cases as those of Lord George Gordon, Hardy, Horne Tooke and others. MacNally, in his "Treatise on Evidence in Criminal Cases," at the beginning of this century, saying little of a presumption of innocence, remarks: "It may also at this day be considered as a rule of law that if the jury entertain a reasonable doubt they should deliver the prisoner."

---

[28] Cod. IV. 19, 25.
[29] Captain Green's Case, 14 St. Tr. 1199, 1245.
[30] *Ib.* 29, 137.
[31] *Ib* 210.

There is no need to trace it further, for no one doubts that in one form or another this has always continued to be a great and recognized rule. It has, in our inherited system, a peculiarly important function, that of warning our untrained tribunal, the jury, against being misled by suspicion, conjecture and mere appearances. In saying that the accused person shall be *proved* guilty, it says also that he shall not be presumed guilty; that he shall be convicted only upon legal evidence, not tried upon prejudice; that he shall not be made the victim of the circumstances of suspicion which surround him, the effect of which it is always so difficult to shake off, circumstances which, if there were no emphatic rule of law upon the subject would be sure to operate heavily against him; the circumstances, *e. g.*, that after an investigation by the grand jury he has been indicted, imprisoned, seated in the prisoner's dock, carried away handcuffed, isolated, watched, made an object of distrust to all that behold him. He shall be convicted, this rule says, not upon any mere presumption, any taking matters for granted on the strength of these circumstances of suspicion; but he shall be *proved* guilty by legal evidence, and by legal evidence which is peculiarly clear and strong—clear beyond a reasonable doubt. The whole matter is summed up and neatly put by Chief-Justice Shaw in Webster's case:[12] "The burden of proof is upon the prosecutor. All the presumptions of law independent of evidence are in favor of innocence, and every person is presumed to be innocent until he is proved guilty. If upon such proof there is reasonable doubt remaining, the accused is entitled to the benefit of it by an acquittal." We observe, then, in this form of statement that the general rule of policy and sense, that all persons shall be assumed, in the absence of evidence, to be free from blame, appears in the criminal law, on grounds of fairness and abundant caution, in an emphatic form, as the presumption of innocence, and it is there coupled with a separate special rule as to the weight of evidence necessary to make out guilt.

As to the real nature of the rule about a presumption of innocence, an important intimation is contained in Chief-Justice Shaw's phrase that, "All the presumptions of law *independent of evidence* are in favor of innocence." That appears to be accurate and exact. The presumption is "independent of evidence," being the same in all cases, and in all operating indiscriminately, in the same way, and with equal force. On what is it founded? On the fact that men in general do not commit crime? On

---
[12] 5 Cush. 295, 320.

what is the presumption of sanity founded? On the fact that men in general are sane? Perhaps so, as a legislative reason, so to speak, or one of the reasons. But the rule itself is a different thing from the grounds of it, and when we speak of the presumption of innocence or of sanity we are talking of a legal rule of presumption, a legal position, and not of the facts which are the basis of it.

It is important to observe this, because, by a loose habit of speech, the presumption is occasionally said to be, itself, evidence, and juries are told to put it in the scale and weigh it. Greenleaf, in a single phrase, in the first volume of his treatise on Evidence, section thirty-four, a phrase copied occasionally into cases and text-books, has said: "This legal presumption of innocence is to be regarded by the jury in every case as matter of evidence, to the benefit of which the party is entitled."[22] This statement is condemned by the editor of the last edition of Greenleaf's book; and in Taylor on Evidence, the great English handbook, which followed Greenleaf's text closely, this passage is omitted, and always has been omitted. In the latter part of Greenleaf's Evidence, Volume III., which deals specifically with criminal cases, it does not appear. It is denied also by Chamberlayne, the careful editor of the works on Evidence of Best and Taylor.

What can such a statement as this mean—that the presumption is to be regarded as evidence? Is it meant that on grounds of natural presumption or inference, innocence is ordinarily found in criminal cases? As to that, if one would see the true operation of natural inference, and natural presumption in crimi-

---

[22] Compare the remarks of Clifford, J., in Lilienthal's Tobacco v. U. S., 97 U. S., 237, 267, where an opinion marked by very loose thinking is paraphrasing some unsupported expressions of Wharton on Evidence. It is easy to be misled by the figure of speech about turning the scale. When Greenleaf (Ev. iii. s. 29), in commenting on the difference between criminal and civil cases as to the quantity of evidence required, after saying that in the latter it is enough if the evidence preponderates, adds that "in criminal trials, the party accused is entitled to the benefit of the legal presumption in favor of innocence, which in doubtful cases is always sufficient to turn the scale in his favor;" and that it is a rule of criminal law that the guilt of the accused must be fully proved, and then goes on to give the rule about reasonable doubt — it seems fairly clear that he is not thinking of the presumption of innocence itself, as placed in the scale, but rather of the rule requiring evidence beyond a reasonable doubt, as being placed there; and, of course, that is not so much putting evidence into one scale as saying what evidence shall be put into the other. It is *this rule* that "turns the scale," and in this way.

nal cases, and would appreciate how entirely artificial, how purely a matter of policy the whole rule is which bids a jury on the trial to assume innocence, let him turn his attention to the action of courts at other stages than the trial. In State *v.* Mills, 2 Dev. 421 (1830), as illustrating another point then under discussion, the court (Ruffin, J.) said: "After bill found, a defendant is presumed to be guilty to most, if not to all purposes, except that of a fair and impartial trial before a petit jury. This presumption is so strong, that, in the case of a capital felony the party cannot be let to bail." In *Ex parte* Ryan, 44 Cal. 555 (1872), a party indicted for attempting to murder a policeman had been held, in the lower court on $15,000 bail. On an application to reduce the bail the court (Wallace, C. J.), refused, saying: "I am bound to assume guilt for the purposes of this proceeding, for certainly I have no means of determining his innocence, to say nothing of the principle of law that, except for the purposes of a fair and impartial trial before a petit jury, the presumption of guilt arises against the prisoner on finding the indictment." In the case of In the matter of Henry Alexander, 59 Mo. 598 (1875), the question was, in a capital case, after repeated trials and disagreements of the jury, whether bail should be allowed. The Constitution of Missouri, it was held, allowed bail, except "when the proof was evident or the presumption great." In allowing it in this case the court (Wagner, J.), said: "The indictment furnishes a strong presumption of guilt. * * * Hence, in all such cases, there must be facts and circumstances which counteract or overcome this presumption, before bail will ever be admissible." The same doctrine was held in State *v.* Madison County Court (Mo., Dec., 1896), 37 S. W. Rep. 1126, in which the court (Burgess, J.) quotes with approval the language of the Supreme Court of California in People *v.* Tinker, 19 Cal. 539, that "It [the indictment] creates a presumption of guilt for all purposes except the trial before the petit jury." These cases are the true ones to illustrate the operation of natural presumption and natural inference. Yet, at the trial all such natural probabilities are held off; the board is swept clear of these, and the accused, while kept well guarded, a prisoner, is yet to be treated as if no incriminating fact existed. His record, by a dead lift of legal policy, is now presented as clean and white. Whatever of wrong or guilt is to be inscribed on it must be the result of legal evidence now presented to the jury.

The effect of the presumption of innocence, so far from being that of furnishing to the jury evidence—*i. e.*, probative matter, the basis of an inference—is rather the contrary. It takes possession of this fact, innocence, as not now needing evidence, as already established *prima facie*, and says: "Take that for granted. Let him who denies it, go forward with his evidence." In criminal cases if the jury were not thus called off from the field of natural inference, if they were allowed to range there wherever mere reason and human experience would carry them, the whole purpose of the presumption of innocence would be balked. For of the men who are actually brought up for trial, probably the large majority are guilty. In inquiring lately of a prosecuting officer for the statistics about this, he replied that out of every one hundred persons indicted for crime in his jurisdiction, twenty were tried and acquitted, twenty pleaded guilty, and sixty were tried and convicted. Now the presumption of innocence forbids the consideration of such probabilities as are here suggested and says simply this: "It is the right of this man to be convicted upon legal evidence applicable specifically to him. Start then with the assumption that he is innocent, and adhere to it till he is proved guilty. He is indeed under grave suspicion, and it is your duty to test and fairly to weigh all the evidence against him as well as for him. But he is not to suffer in your minds from these suspicions or this necessity of holding him confined and trying him; he is to be affected by nothing but such evidence as the law allows you to act upon. For the purposes of this trial you must take him to be an innocent man, unless and until the government establishes his guilt."

It may be asked, if then a presumption be not evidence, how can you know when it is overcome? That depends on the nature of the case. It is the office of a presumption, as such, to fix the duty of going on with argument or evidence, on a given question; and is only that. As to how much evidence is to be produced, that is another matter. In criminal cases the rule is fixed that the evidence must negative all reasonable doubt; nothing else will make a case which the defendant need meet. Sometimes the presumption calls only for evidence enough to put the question really into the case, to make it really a question; sometimes for a full *prima facie* case. But in no case is there a weighing, a comparison of probative quality, as between evidence on one side and a presumption on the other.[a]

[a] See an article on Presumptions and the Law of Evidence, 3 Harv. Law Review, 141, 165. The author may be allowed, perhaps, to say that a revision of this article will appear later in the year, in the concluding part of his "Preliminary Treatise on Evidence at the Common Law" (Little, Brown & Co.)

While then it is true that a presumption may count as evidence, and be a substitute for evidence, in the sense that it will make a *prima facie* case for him in whose favor it operates, and while it is true that the facts on which a presumption is grounded may count as evidence, the presumption itself; *i. e.*, the legal rule, conclusion, or position cannot be evidence. This question was neatly and accurately dealt with by the court in Lisbon *v.* Lyman, 49 N. H. 553 (1870). On an issue as to the emancipation of a minor, the jury were instructed "that there was a presumption that children under twenty-one are not emancipated; that the presumption was not conclusive, and the fact might be shown by proof to be otherwise; but that in deciding what the fact was, the jury would take this presumption into account, as one element of evidence, and weigh it in connection with all the testimony." Doe, J., for the court, said: "The burden was on the plaintiff to prove that when the town was divided, the last dwelling place of Volney was in the defendant's territory. The plaintiff claimed, that Volney, though a minor, had, by emancipation, acquired a right to have a home of his own, free from the control of his father. The emancipation of Volney was set up as an affirmative and essential part of the plaintiff's case; and in that view it was necessary for the plaintiff to prove it. Without any evidence, or with evidence equally balanced, on that point, emancipation would not be proved. The burden of proof was on the plaintiff, and this burden was not sustained unless the plaintiff proved it by a preponderance of all the evidence introduced on the subject. But it was not necessary for the plaintiff to produce anything more than the slightest preponderance; or to produce a preponderance of anything but evidence. * * * A legal presumption is a rule of law—a reasonable principle, or an arbitrary dogma—declared by the court. There may be a difficulty in weighing such a rule of law as evidence of a fact, or in weighing law on one side against fact on the other. And if the weight of a rule of law as evidence of a fact, or as counterbalancing the evidence of a fact, can be comprehended, there are objections to such a use of it. * * * A legal presumption is not evidence. * * * The presumption against the freedom of minors was not an element of evidence; could not be weighed as evidence, and it does not appear that any use could rightfully be made of it in the case. It was put into the scale with the defendant's evidence, where it would be likely to mislead the jury, and give the defendant a material advantage to which he was not entitled.'"[36]

Upon the whole, then, it seems to be true that the presumption of innocence, as applied in criminal cases, is a form of expression which requires to be supplemented by the rule as to the weight of evidence; that it is merely one form of

---

[36] For a different, and, as I must think, a mistaken exposition of the subject, see Barber's Appeal, 63 Conn. 393, 403, 406 (1893). In a probate appeal involving the question of testamentary capacity, after a verdict against the will, it appeared that the charge of the judge below was objected to by the proponents as "confusing and contradictory." Among other things the judge had said to the jury: "If when the whole matter is before you on the evidence given on both sides, it is left uncertain whether or not the testator was of sound mind, then * * * the will should not be sustained. In the course of the trial the balance of evidence may fluctuate from one side to the other, but the burden of proof remains where it was at the outset, upon the advocates of the will, and, unless at the close of the trial the balance is with the advocates of the will, unless the beam of the scale tips down on the side of the advocates of the will, they must fail." The Supreme Court (Fenn, J.) reversed the judgment below, and in the course of a difficult and unsatisfactory exposition of the meaning and application of the term "burden of proof," the opinion says; "The law presumes every person to be so [of sound mind] until the contrary is shown, and this presumption is of probative force in favor of the proponents of the will. * * * In short * * * on the whole case the question would be whether the evidence of the contestants sufficiently preponderated over the rebutting and special evidence of the proponents, including the evidence of the attesting witnesses, to overcome the presumption of sanity which constituted the proponent's *prima facie* case. In other words, leaving the presumption of sanity out of the case, was there more evidence of insanity than of sanity? So that, putting it again into the case there would still be as much. Then and then only would the scales of justice, to which the court below in the case before us referred, be so adjusted, according to law, that it would be correct to say 'unless at the close of the trial the balance is with the advocates of the will they must fail; it is not sufficient that the scales stand evenly balanced.'" The opinion does not give its reasons for the statement that the presumption has a probative quality, and can be "weighed in the scale," and the case does not necessarily involve the point above discussed; so that it is quite possible that the above exposition does not carry with it the authority of all the judges of the court. For the true basis and operation of this presumption see Davis *v.* U. S., 160 U. S. 469, 486 (1895): "If that presumption [of sanity] were not indulged the government would always be under the necessity of adducing affirmative evidence of the sanity of an accused. But a requirement of that character would seriously delay and embarrass the enforcement of the laws against crime, and in most cases be unnecessary. Consequently the law presumes that everyone charged with crime is sane, and thus supplies in the first instance the required proof of capacity to commit crime. It authorizes the jury to assume at the outset that the accused is criminally responsible for his acts." Harlan, J., for the Court.

phrase for what is included in the statement that an accused person is not to be prejudiced at his trial by having been charged with crime and held in custody, or by any mere suspicions, however grave; but is only to be held guilty when the government has established his guilt by legal evidence and beyond all reasonable doubt; that the presumption of innocence is often used as synonymous with this whole twofold rule, thus drawn out; that it is a convenient and familiar phrase, and probably a useful one, when carefully explained; but that it has not played any conspicuous part in the development of our criminal law except as expressed in the fuller statement given above. It may be added that the phrase presumption of innocence if used to a jury, peculiarly needs to be carefully explained, because of the very great ambiguity connected with the terms "presumption," "burden of proof" and "evidence," and the way in which these abused expressions reflect their own ambiguities upon each other.

Let me return now to the case of Coffin v. U. S.[26] It will be necessary to consider it in some detail. It came up from the Circuit Court of the United States for Indiana, and was a proceeding against officials of a National Bank who were convicted below of wilfully misapplying funds of the bank, and of other related offenses. A great number of exceptions were taken to the charge given by the court to the jury. All but two of these were overruled. The principal exception was against the refusal of the judge to charge as he was requested on the subject of the presumption of innocence."[27] He had been asked to charge that, "the law presumes that persons charged with crime are innocent until they are proved by competent evidence to be guilty. To the benefit of this presumption the defendants are all entitled, and this presumption stands as their sufficient protection unless it has been removed by evidence proving their guilt beyond a reasonable doubt." The judge refused to give this charge, but instructed the jury that they could not find the defendants guilty unless satisfied of their guilt beyond a reasonable doubt, and he said: "If you can reconcile the evidence with any reasonable hypothesis consistent with the defendant's innocence, it is your duty to do so. In that case find defendant not guilty. And if, after weighing all the proofs, and looking only to the

---

[26] 156 U. S. 432.

[27] The action of the trial Judge is described in the opinion of the upper court thus: "Whilst the court refused to instruct as to the presumption of innocence, it instructed fully as to reasonable doubt." This statement is not quite exact, as will be indicated later.

proofs, you impartially and honestly entertain the belief that the defendant may be innocent of the offences charged against him, he is entitled to the benefit of that doubt, and you should acquit him." In various forms the judge went on to explain what "a reasonable doubt" is, and to make very clear the duty of the jury as to the weight of evidence which they were bound to require before they could find guilt.

The Supreme Court held that there was error in refusing the charge which was desired on the presumption of innocence; and, while recognizing that no particular form of words was necessary, in dealing with this presumption, they held that the error was not made good by anything found in the rest of the charge. The opinion of the court was given by Mr. Justice White, and was not accompanied by any expression of dissent. It declares that the principle that there is a presumption of innocence is "axiomatic and elementary, and its enforcement lies at the foundation of the administration of our criminal law." Many citations are given to show that there is a presumption of innocence. The doctrine that guilt can only be found by the clearest evidence is quoted from various writers, and this principle is referred to as being, in the language of the court, one of the "results of this maxim" of the presumption of innocence, but no reason is given for this view other than what will be stated hereafter. The language of Lord Gillies, the dissenting judge in the Scotch case already referred to, McKinley's case, is cited at length, as showing, in the phrase of the opinion, "how fully the presumption of innocence had been evolved as a principle and applied at common law"; but it is not remarked that this is a dissenting opinion, and that the case is a Scotch case, and not one at common law. The opinion then goes on to inquire whether the charge did substantially embody a statement of the presumption of innocence. It is declared that the authorities upon what is a sufficient statement of this presumption are "few and unsatisfactory." Referring to cases in Texas, Indiana, Ohio, Alabama and California, on one side and the other of the question, to an anonymous article in the Criminal Law Magazine, and to Stephen's statement of the presumption of innocence, and the remarks of Mr. Chamberlayne, the editor of Best, the opinion goes on to say that it is necessary to consider "the distinction between the presumption of innocence and reasonable doubt, as if it were an original question." The question is then put as being "whether the two are equivalents of each other?" and it is proposed to "ascertain with accuracy in what each consists." It may be remarked, at this point, that this form of putting the question, imputes a very fatuous confusion of ideas to those who hold that the rule requiring proof of guilt beyond a reasonable doubt embodies in it all that the presumption of innocence really means. They would hardly agree that they are arguing that the presumption of innocence and reasonable doubt are "equivalents of each other"; or that the exploit of the opinion as it is described in a later case[38] in saying, "The court drew a distinction between the presumption of innocence as one of the instruments of proof, contributing to bring about that state of case from which reasonable doubt arises, and a condition of mind called reasonable doubt produced by the evidence,"—that this feat was either one that required much pains to accomplish or one that particularly concerned their own contention.

Having thus started on this interesting and important inquiry the opinion proceeds: "The presumption of innocence is a conclusion drawn by the law in favor of the citizen, by virtue whereof when brought to trial on a criminal charge he must be acquitted unless he is proven to be guilty. In other words, this presumption is an instrument of proof created by the law in favor of one accused whereby his innocence is established until sufficient evidence is introduced to overcome the proof which the law has created. This presumption, on the one hand, supplemented by any other evidence he may adduce, and the evidence against him on the other, constitute the elements from which the legal conclusion of his guilt or innocence is to be drawn." The court then quotes the passage from Greenleaf on Evidence,[39] upon which I have commented; a passage from Wills on Circumstantial Evidence, stating that there is such a presumption and that it prevails "until destroyed by such an overpowering amount of legal evidence of guilt as is calculated to produce the opposite belief"; another from Best on Presumptions, simply saying that it is *presumptio juris;* another from an anonymous article in the Criminal Law Magazine,[40] stating that the presumption is "in the nature of evidence in his favor, and a knowledge of it should be communicated to the jury," etc. The opinion then goes on, "The fact that the presumption of innocence is recognized as a presumption of law, and is char-

---

[38] Cochran v. U. S., 157 U. S., 286, 299.
[39] Grlf. Ev. I. s. 34.
[40] Which appears to have been an advance chapter of Thompson on Trials. The passage is found in that work, s. 2461.

acterized by the civilians as *presumptio juris*, demonstrates that it is evidence in favor of the accused; for in all systems of law legal presumptions are treated as evidence giving rise to resulting proof to the full extent of their legal efficacy. Concluding then that the presumption of innocence is evidence in favor of the accused, introduced by the law in his behalf, let us consider what is reasonable doubt." We are then told that reasonable doubt is "the condition of mind produced by the proof resulting from the evidence in the cause. It is the result of proof, not the proof itself; whereas the presumption of innocence is one of the instruments of proof going to bring about the proof from which reasonable doubt arises; thus one is a cause, the other an effect. To say that the one is the equivalent of the other is therefore to say that legal evidence can be excluded from the jury, and that such exclusion may be cured by instructing them correctly in regard to the method by which they are required to reach their conclusion upon the proof actually before them. In other words, that the exclusion of an important element of proof can be justified by correctly instructing as to the proof admitted." Farther on, the opinion says: "It is clear that the failure to instruct them [the jury] in regard to what that is [the presumption of innocence], excluded from their minds a portion of the proof created by the law, and which they were bound to consider." And it is added that the judge below in limiting the attention of the jury " 'to the proofs and the proofs only' confined them to those matters which were admitted to their consideration by the court, and among these elements of proof the court expressly refused to include the presumption of innocence to which the accused was entitled, and which the court was bound to extend him."

The following remarks are also thrown in near the end of the discussion: "The evolution of the principle of the presumption of innocence, and its resultant, the doctrine of reasonable doubt, makes more apparent the correctness of these views, and indicates the necessity of enforcing the one in order that the other may continue to exist. While Rome and the Mediævalists taught that wherever doubt existed in a criminal case acquittal must follow, the expounders of the common law in their devotion to human liberty and individual rights traced this doctrine of doubt to its true origin, the presumption of innocence, and rested it upon this enduring basis." It would be instructive to know the ground for this statement as to "the expounders of the common law," and the establishing of this "enduring basis." Unless the phrase refers to an occasional loose *dictum* of a law writer or judge in this country, or to an occasional ill-considered judicial opinion here, I know of no ground for these remarks.

Such was the decision, in Coffin *v.* U. S., so far as relates to the point now under consideration, and such was the general course of the exposition. It proceeds, in a word, on the ground that the lower court refused to recognize the presumption of innocence, and thus kept from the jury a piece of evidence in behalf of the accused to which he was entitled. The immediate result of the decision was that it helped to delay the punishment of persons well deserving it, as appeared when the case came back again after another trial, and all of "very numerous grounds of error" urged by these defendants were overruled.[41] It is interesting to observe that, at the new trial, the charge, so far as quoted, dealt with the matters now under consideration in this form (p. 681): "The burden of proving Haughey and the defendants guilty as charged rests upon the government, and the burden does not shift from it. Haughey and the defendants are presumed to be innocent until their guilt in manner and form * * * is proved beyond a reasonable doubt. To justify you in returning a verdict of guilty, the evidence should be of such a character as to overcome this presumption of innocence and to satisfy each one of you of the guilt of Haughey and the defendants as charged, to the exclusion of every reasonable doubt." This instruction seems to have raised no question. Except as leaving to the jury without explanation two phrases full of ambiguity, namely, "presumption of innocence" and "evidence * * * to overcome" it, it seems not to differ materially from the former charge. Can it reasonably be supposed that on such a charge anybody would imagine the presumption to be a piece of evidence, to be placed in the scales and weighed against other evidence? Such a charge is only in form an acceptance of the exposition in the former opinion of the Supreme Court; it is mere lip service.[42]

That opinion, however, has had an effect outside of the particular case. Its somewhat wider range than common of reference and allusion, has caused the imputing to it of an amount of learning and careful research to which, when scrutinized, it can lay no claim; and, to be quite just, it does not, in fact, lay claim to it. But it does lay claim to exactness of discrimination, to a

---

[41] Coffin *v.* U. S., 162 U. S. 664 (May, 1896).
[42] See also Agnew *v.* U. S., 17 S. C. R. 234, 241 (January, 1897).

searching and fundamental examination of the nature of the questions involved, and to the character of a leading and, in a degree, a final discussion of a peculiarly vexed and difficult subject. This claim must be disputed. What has been said in the earlier pages of this paper will serve to show grounds for denying the truth of the chief historical suggestions of the opinion, and the validity of some of its fundamental conceptions. Instead of settling anything outside of the particular controversy, it leaves matters worse off than before. Its work of mischief may be seen in the use of it in such later cases as Cochran *v.* U. S.,[43] U. S. *v.* Davis'[44] Agnew *v.* U. S.[45] (I do not now speak of the actual point decided in either of these cases), and No. Ca. *v.* Gosnell.[46] The difficulty with the case is not with the actual decision—namely, that on the point in question a new trial was granted; that could easily be agreed to, without any serious difference as to the principal matters. The trouble is with the exposition and the reasons. The absence, therefore, of dissent in this case may have very little significance.[47]

It may readily be admitted, as the event shows, that it would have been practically wiser on the part of the judge below to have given the charge as requested and to have accompanied it

---

[43] 157 U. S. 286 (March 25, 1895).
[44] 160 U. S. 469.
[45] 17 S. C. R. 234.
[46] 74 Fed. Rep. 734 (W. D. No. Ca., June, 1896).
[47] That the exposition and the reasoning in Coffin *v.* U. S., 156 U. S. 432, count for little in the mind of the court, may be seen in Allen *v.* U. S., 164 U. S. 492, 500 (Dec. 1896). Error was assigned in a refusal to charge that "where there is a probability of innocence, there is a reasonable doubt of guilt." In overruling the exception, the court (Brown, J.) after remarking that in the Coffin case a refusal to charge on the presumption of innocence was held not to be met by a charge that a conviction could not be had unless guilt were shown beyond a reasonable doubt, added: "In the case under consideration, however, the court had already charged the jury that they could not find the defendant guilty unless they were satisfied from the testimony that the crime was established beyond a reasonable doubt; that this meant: 'First, that a party starts into a trial, though accused by the grand jury with the crime of murder, or any other crime, with the presumption of innocence in his favor. That stays with him until it is driven out of the case by the testimony. It is driven out of the case when the evidence shows beyond a reasonable doubt that the crime as charged has been committed, or that a crime has been committed. Whenever the proof shows beyond a reasonable doubt the existence of a crime, then the presumption of innocence disappears from the case. That exists up to the time that it is driven out in that way by proof to that extent.' The court having thus charged upon the subject of the presumption of innocence could not be required to repeat the charge in a separate instruction at the request of the defendant." Compare Agnew *v.* U. S., *ubi supra.*

with such explanations as would clear away ambiguity and would prevent the jury from misapplying the statements. And, farther than that, it may be true, as a general proposition, that the right should be maintained to have the presumption of innocence, specifically and by name, drawn to the attention of the jury. If so, it should also be required that it be definitely and accurately explained, so that it be not misused as if in itself it constituted a piece of probative matter to be weighed against other evidence; and again, so that it be not used in a way to prevent the jury from allowing all evidence against the accused to have its full natural effect, all through the case, as it is put in. Certainly such a specific declaration and explanation as to the presumption of innocence would draw pointed attention to those dangers of injury to the accused from mere suspicion, prejudice or distrust, and to those other grounds of policy on which it rests, which make these judicial warnings so important.

Now what, exactly, was it that the judge below said on this subject? He said something which, although quoted, is not commented upon, or, as it would seem, duly appreciated by the court, viz: "If, therefore, you can reconcile the evidence with any reasonable hypothesis consistent with the defendants' innocence, it is your duty to do so, and in that case find the defendants not guilty. And if, after weighing all the proofs, and looking only to the proofs, you impartially and honestly entertain the belief that the defendants may be innocent of the offense charged against them, they are entitled to the benefit of that doubt, and you should acquit them." This language required the jury, in considering the evidence, to put upon it the construction most favorable to the defendants' innocence. In effect it said to the jury. "So long and so far as you reasonably can, hold them innocent, assume them innocent, or, if you please, presume them innocent, for these forms of phrase mean the same thing. Let nothing but legal evidence count against them, look to the proofs and the proofs only, and let not the evidence or any amount of evidence count against them, so long as you can continue as reasonable men to think them innocent."

When the judge below had said that, in addition to further elaborate and confessedly adequate instructions as to the rule which requires a weight of evidence beyond reasonable doubt, I think that it cannot truly be said, as the opinion does say, that "the court refused to instruct as to the presumption of innocence"; and, again, that "among these elements of proof the court expressly refused to include the presumption of innocence." What the judge below did was, in reality, to refuse to instruct in the particular form requested; and that sort of refusal is not necessarily fatal; for, as the court in the Coffin case justly says, "It is well settled that there is no error in refusing to charge precisely as requested, provided the instruction actually given fairly covers and includes the instruction asked." The whole question is, then, whether the instruction below fairly covers the instruction asked. The instruction asked was this: "The law presumes that persons charged with crimes are innocent until they are proven by competent evidence to be guilty. To the benefit of this presumption the defendants are all entitled, and this presumption stands as their sufficient protection, unless it has been removed by evidence proving their guilt beyond a reasonable doubt." I think that this charge was, in effect, given when the jury were told that they were to reconcile the evidence with the supposition of the defendant's innocence if it was reasonably possible; to consider nothing but the evidence and only to find the defendants guilty when the evidence proved it beyond a reasonable doubt.

It will be noticed that the charge requested did not ask for any explanation of the presumption of innocence, nor did the charge given make any explanation of it. As the request for a charge did not say that the presumption of innocence was in itself evidence, so the charge given did not deny that it was evidence. Why the jury should presume innocence was not stated in the request for a charge, and in the charge as actually given it was not stated why the jury should construe the evidence favorably to the accused so long as it was reasonably possible to do so. It was not necessary to do it, in either case, for in both cases it was *a rule* that was being laid down to the jury, and the grounds of the rule were not necessarily to be stated. In so far as evidence, in any proper sense of the word, was concerned, no question was made about it, in the talk about the presumption. If it be thought true that the fact that men in general are innocent is the evidential ground for the rule mentioned in the request, or in the charge, it was nothing to the purpose to go into that; for it is merely the legislative reason for laying down such a rule. In so far as the facts on which the rule rests were themselves to be regarded as evidence or a basis for inference in the case, the request draws no attention to them, and the mere omission to charge on them is no legitimate ground of exception—according to a familiar rule on that subject. Moreover, in so far as the fact that men in general are innocent is a ground of inference for the jury it is one to be taken notice of by court, counsel and jury without proof, and without anybody's moving them thereto. Certainly there was no refusal of any request to call the attention of the jury to the fact that men in general are innocent; the refusal was one to charge on the presumption of innocence in the form above stated, and that form offered no suggestion whatever as to what the true import of the phrase is. The accused then had no cause of complaint that any request of his counsel was refused.

But now we come to the kernel of the matter, the exposition in the opinion of the meaning of that phrase. Let us look at that. It is said that the presumption of innocence is a conclusion drawn by the law by virtue of which, on a trial, the accused must be acquitted unless proved guilty. This, it will be observed, states the presumption as being a legal "conclusion" requiring exactly what was fully set forth by the trial judge. Then we are told that the presumption is an instrument of proof created by law in favor of the accused whereby his innocence is established until sufficient evidence is introduced to overcome the proof which the law has created. Here the presumption becomes an instrument of proof establishing innocence, and is itself proof, created by the law. This presumption, it is said again, supplemented by any other evidence the accused may produce, on the one hand, and the evidence against him on the other, constitute the elements from which the legal conclusion of guilt or innocence is to be drawn. Here the presumption, our "conclusion drawn by the law," our "instrument of proof," our "proof created by law," becomes evidence; *i. e.*, probative matter, to be added to the evidence of the accused, and balanced against the evidence of the government. How the presumption can be weighed and estimated as evidence we are not told.

After some quotations the opinion then says that the fact that the presumption of innocence is a *presumptio juris*, demonstrates that it is evidence in favor of the accused; for, it is added, in all systems of law, legal presumptions are treated as evidence giving rise to resulting proof, to the full extent of their legal efficacy. No authority is given for that statement, and no explanation of what it means; but it is added, "Concluding then that the presumption of innocence is evidence in favor of the accused, introduced by the law in his behalf," etc., etc.; and then later, it "is one of the instruments of proof, going to bring about the proof from which reasonable doubt arises."

Again, the exclusion of it is called excluding "legal evidence," excluding "an important element of proof," excluding "a portion of the proof created by law."

To sum it up, the substance of all this is, as I have said before, that the presumption of innocence *is a piece of evidence, a part of the proof—i. e.*, a thing to be weighed as having probative quality. And the grounds for saying it are: (1) The authority of the phrase in Greenleaf's Evidence, to which I have referred; (2) A similar phrase in an article in the Criminal Law Magazine, that it "is in the nature of evidence"; to which are added (3) a statement in another text-book (Wills' Circumstantial Evidence) that the presumption must prevail till destroyed by such an overpowering amount of legal evidence of guilt as is calculated to produce the opposite belief; and (4) a statement in Best on Presumptions that it is *presumptio juris*. This is the authority, and it is slight indeed. And the opinion adds a strange, unsupported assertion that the recognition of the presumption of innocence as a presumption of law (*presumptio juris*) demonstrates it to be evidence, and that in all systems of law legal presumptions of law are treated as evidence. It is easy to make such an assertion and to leave the matter there. But as one who has long and attentively studied the subject of presumptions, I can only say that I know of nothing to support it in any sense which tends to sustain the reasoning of the opinion.

What appears to be true may be stated thus:

1. A presumption operates to relieve the party in whose favor it works from going forward in argument or evidence.

2. It serves therefore the purposes of a *prima facie* case, and in that sense it is, temporarily, the substitute or equivalent for evidence.

3. It serves this purpose until the adversary has gone forward with his evidence. How much evidence shall be required from the adversary to meet the presumption, or, as it is variously expressed, to overcome it or destroy it, is determined by no fixed rule. It may be merely enough to make it reasonable to require the other side to answer; it may be enough to make out a full *prima facie* case, and it may be a great weight of evidence, excluding all reasonable doubt.

4. A mere presumption involves no rule as to the weight of evidence necessary to meet it. When a presumption is called a strong one, like the presumption of legitimacy, it means that it is accompanied by another rule relating to the weight of evidence to be brought in by him against whom it operates.

5. A presumption itself contributes no evidence, and has no probative quality. It is sometimes said that the presumption will tip the scale when the evidence is balanced. But, in truth, nothing tips the scale but evidence, and a presumption—being a legal rule or a legal conclusion—is not evidence. It may represent and spring from certain evidential facts; and these facts may be put in the scale. But that is not putting in the presumption itself. A presumption may be called "an instrument of proof," in the sense that it determines from whom the evidence shall come, and it may be called something "in the nature of evidence," for the same reason; or it may be called a substitute for evidence, and even "evidence"—in the sense that it counts at the outset, for evidence enough to make a *prima facie* case. But the moment these conceptions give way to the perfectly distinct notion of evidence proper—*i. e.*, probative matter, which may be a basis of inference, something capable of being weighed in the scales of reason and compared and estimated with other matter of the probative sort—so that we get to treating the presumption of innocence or any other presumption, as being evidence in this its true sense, then we have wandered into the region of shadows and phantoms.

James Bradley Thayer

THE HAWAIIAN JUDICIARY.

The Hawaiian Islands have been prominently before the American public for several years on account of their proposed annexation to the United States. But they had long previously been objects of interest to a large portion of the American people, not only on account of the excellence of their climate, the beauty and grandeur of their scenery, and their close commercial relations with the United States, but also and more especially because of their strategic position at the cross-roads of the Pacific, and because they have been a favorite field of American missionary effort. They now furnish the one conspicuous example of a nation graduated from the field of missions as substantially raised from a state of barbarism to one of Christian civilization; moreover, they furnish the only example of a colony thoroughly American in spirit on foreign soil. At some future time they may be known, to the student at least, as a contributor of an interesting and instructive chapter in the history of constitutional government and the history of civilization. Unlike most aboriginal races of other islands and the new continents, whose lands have been seized by foreign powers and upon whom foreign governments and laws have been forced, the Hawaiian people not only have always maintained their independence and have since 1840 enjoyed a constitutional government having treaty and diplomatic relations with the great nations of the earth, but they also present a complete history of a growth from absolute government by a despot to constitutional government by the people.

This history is in some respects a parallel of English history. For instance, in the islands to the southwest inhabited by other branches of the Polynesian race and from some of which the Hawaiians originally came, there existed the mark or community system of tenure and government similar to that which existed among the Anglo-Saxons before their emigration to England; and the Hawaiians themselves after their immigration to these islands passed through various stages of the feudal system much as did the early English. So, too, the evolution of the various departments of government in Hawaii is very suggestive of English history,—the gathering of counselors about the king, the gradual enlargement of their advisory functions into legislative powers resulting in the formation of the upper branch of the legislative body; and the gradual separation of the legislative and judicial powers of this body resulting finally in the exercise of the latter by a distinct set of persons, the judiciary.

Of course Hawaiian constitutional development since the discovery of the islands has been rapid and has been due chiefly to foreign influence. It has, nevertheless, been a growth, the natural consequence of the adoption of foreign ideas by the natives, and the working together of foreign residents and natives as one people, not the result of forced foreign influence from within or without. And, strange to say, the movement towards the establishment of individual rights and representative government was from the kings and high chiefs rather than from the petty chiefs or common people, such was the wisdom and magnanimity of the former during the Kamehameha dynasty (1782-1872). Those kings and chiefs were wise enough to seek and follow the advice and ideas of the better class of foreigners and to see that the welfare and independence of their nation could be maintained only by keeping pace with advancing civilization. They were magnanimous enough to sacrifice their own powers and rights for the good of their people. After the extinction of the Kamehamehas, the tendency of the crown was backward, and the so-called revolutions during the reigns of Kalakaua and his sister, Liliuokalani, terminating in the abolition of the monarchy, were but resistances of the better classes of whites and natives against the attempts of those sovereigns to resume the absolute powers their predecessors had so wisely and generously surrendered.

Hawaii is now a completely organized republic, the product of the past. In this brief paper an attempt will be made to outline the evolution and present organization and working of only one of its departments—the Judiciary.

The Hawaiians migrated to these islands probably about the end of the fifth century. From that time they were divided into a number of separate kingdoms until the close of the eighteenth century, when, after four centuries of almost constant warfare, they were united under one government. This was the achievement of the great Kamehameha I. During this period there grew up a feudal system of government and land tenures. The king was lord paramount and owned the country. The chiefs were mesne lords, and the common people, tenants paravail. Each subject held land of his immediate superior in return for military and other services and the payment of taxes or rent. Under this system all functions of government, executive, legislative and judicial, were united in the same persons and each function was exercised not consciously as different in kind from the others but merely as a portion of the general power possessed by a lord over his own. There was no distinct judiciary and yet judicial forms were to some extent observed.

The usual method of obtaining redress was for injured parties or their friends to retaliate, as in cases of assault or murder. The offender might, however, escape by fleeing to a city of refuge, as under the old Jewish law. In case of theft the injured party might go to the thief's house, if known, and take what he could find—the thief, though the stronger of the two, being restrained by public sentiment from offering resistance. This practice of taking the law into one's own hands calls to mind the remedies by distraint, recaption and abatement of nuisances among civilized nations. If the wrong-doer was of higher rank than the injured party or if he belonged to a different chief, the usual course was to apply for justice to the king or to the chief upon whose land the accused resided. Then, sitting cross-legged before the judge, each party presented his own case, without witnesses, lawyer or jury. An appeal from the judgment lay to any superior chief or to the king. Thus there was in a certain sense a series of courts, local, superior and supreme, held by the petty chiefs, the high chiefs and the king respectively. The personal and official characters of the judge were not distinguished. There was no distinction between public and private wrongs. The penalty or relief might be the restoration of property, the specific enforcement of a right, the imposition of a fine, banishment, torture, death, or other punishment, in the discretion of the judge, or the offender might be granted immunity from punishment by the exercise of the pardoning power by the judge.

There were also ecclesiastical tribunals. These had jurisdiction to some extent over civil wrongs as well as over religious matters. Their trials were by ordeal—fire and water. One form of water ordeal was this. A calabash of water was placed before the suspected person. The priest offered a prayer. The accused was required to hold his hands, with fingers spread out, over the calabash. If the water shook, the accused was guilty, otherwise he was innocent. (The conscience of the accused, if guilty, may have caused his hands to shake and thus produce a tremulous appearance in the water.) A form of ordeal by fire was as follows. Three *kukui* nuts (candle-nuts) were broken. One was thrown upon a fire. While it burned, the priest uttered a prayer. So with the other nuts. If the wrong-doer, who probably had learned, by proclamation, that the trial was to take place, appeared and confessed before the last nut was consumed, he was simply fined. Otherwise proclamation was made that the offender would be prayed to death. Then, doubtless overcome by superstitious fears, he would pine away and die. It will be noticed that the ascertainment of the truth was left to the guilty conscience of the accused, and the presumption was in favor of innocence, the Hawaiian ordeals differing thus from most forms of ordeal found among other races.

An idea of the nature of the cases that were likely to arise may be obtained from the character of the laws. These were either customary or declared by the king and proclaimed by heralds. The taboos, both religious and social, formed the most complex and oppressive body. Next in number but first in importance came the laws of real property upon which the whole system of government was based, including the laws of tenure, taxation, fishing rights and water rights, the last being so important as to give their name to laws in general. Laws relating to personal security were few, the violations of which were considered more as torts than as crimes. There was little occasion for the law of contracts, for estates in real property were transferred by favor of the king or chiefs rather than by contract; and personal property, of which there was little, was exchanged only by barter, in which case the bargain was not binding until delivery of the goods and expression of satisfaction by both parties and then it became irrevocable. Domestic relations were little regulated by law; parents might do as they pleased with their children, and marriage and divorce rested upon the consent of the parties or their relatives.

Under the wise and strong rule of Kamehameha I. (1782-1819), the central government was greatly strengthened, but with a view to the best interests of all, not merely the gratification of a despotic ambition; the laws were made more uniform throughout the islands and were rigidly enforced; peace prevailed everywhere; the oppression of the chiefs was checked; the person and property of the common man became comparatively secure; and the King gathered about him the ablest and best chiefs as a council of advisors—the embryo of a future

House of Nobles and Supreme Court. During this reign many foreign vessels touched at the islands and as a result largely of the influences, good and bad, thus brought to bear upon the natives, they lost faith in their idolatrous religion and on the death of Kamehameha abolished it as a state religion, thereby terminating all ecclesistical jurisdiction. Religious matters continued, however, to be subjects of civil jurisdiction, chiefly for the suppression of the idolatry that remained among the people.

During the next twenty years (1820-1840) the good forces set in motion by Kamehameha I. continued to operate. Christianity was introduced the year after his death and schools were established. Under their new religion and learning, the chiefs became more considerate of the rights of the common people, and the common people grew to realize more fully that they had rights; all became more tolerant in their religious views; a few written laws were published; there developed a conception of judicial as distinguished from other functions of government; trials were conducted with greater formality and in capital cases even the jury was introduced. In 1839 a course of lectures on the science of government was delivered to the chiefs at their request. In that year were issued the Edict of Toleration and the Declaration of Rights, Hawaii's *Magna Charta*, and in the following year (1840) the first constitution was promulgated.

These documents guaranteed religious liberty and removed religious matters from civil jurisdiction as civil matters had twenty years before been removed from ecclesiastical jurisdiction. They also guaranteed personal and property rights. Before the reign of Kamehameha I., tenants might be removed at will, and, although they were usually allowed to hold for life, there was no assurance that upon their death their descendants would be allowed to hold in their places; and upon the death of a king his successor generally made a redistribution of lands. By 1840, however, it had become pretty well established by custom that a tenant or his descendants should not be removed except for cause. This custom was made positive law by the Declaration of Rights; and between 1845 and 1855 in pursuance of appropriate legislation and upon proof of claims before a special court, all lands occupied by the king, chiefs and common people were secured to them respectively in fee simple. Titles and laws of real property, the recording system included, have ever since been substantially the same as in the United States.

The constitution also outlined a system of government. We have seen that Kamehameha I. gathered about him a council of the ablest chiefs. With these he consulted more or less in matters of state, whether of an executive, legislative or judicial nature. Owing to certain weaknesses of his son and successor, he appointed by will a Premier, to have power coördinate with that of the king, each to have a veto on the acts of the other, as was the case with the early Roman consuls. These two acted during the next twenty years as the king alone had previously acted, and the council of advisors grew in power. The different functions of government had become more clearly distinguished, although still exercised by the same persons. Under the constitution, the council of chiefs became the upper house (Nobles, since evolved into a Senate,) of the legislative body, and the king, premier and four of the chiefs became the Supreme Court. The governors of the various islands, who were high chiefs, continued as before to exercise the jurisdiction of superior courts, by custom and inference rather than by the express provisions of the constitution. There were also local or district courts.

The provisions of the constitution were meager and the courts were left for seven years more to evolve, with little aid from statutes. They were now recognized as a distinct department of government, though not held by distinct persons, but their procedure and powers were uncertain. The distinction between torts and crimes came gradually to be recognized, at first not by trying the wrong-doer in two separate actions, one civil and the other criminal, when the wrong was both public and private, but by dividing the fine or damages between the government and the injured party. Finally, however, the actions themselves were distinguished and tried separately, first in foreign cases and then in Hawaiian. For the policy of the courts was to apply in each case as far as possible the law to which the offender had been accustomed. This meant in most foreign cases the law of the United States or England so far as it was known. Similarly, the distinction came gradually to be recognized between law cases,—civil and criminal, and chamber cases,—equity, admiralty, probate and bankruptcy. So, as to the jury. After this became established it was frequently employed in all sorts of cases, and sometimes upon questions of law as well as of fact, but gradually, partly by usage, partly by statute, it came to be confined to questions of fact and almost exclusively to law cases. Complaints and answers came to be more formal and to be written, and demurrers and special pleas were finally allowed. The judges still possessed much discretionary power. They might punish offenses not defined by law and impose a great variety of penalties, and continued to exercise occasionally even the pardoning power. As foreign cases increased with the growing foreign population, the need of judges learned in foreign law became more pressing and finally the Governors, who as we have seen acted as superior judges, appointed foreign judges to sit as their substitutes in foreign cases. These judges issued rules of pleading and practice. Then came the comprehensive Act of 1847, embodying the results of the experiences of the preceding seven years.

This Act, besides setting forth the organization and jurisdiction of the courts, and rules of pleading and practice, provided that the judges should be independent of the executive department. But this was understood to mean, not that judicial and executive, to say nothing of legislative, functions should not be exercised by the same persons, but that the functions themselves when exercised should be kept separate and distinct, and be exercised independently. For instance, the King in his executive capacity was not to interfere with a judicial act of a Governor. The Governors continued to try many cases. The King, Premier and four Nobles continued to constitute the Supreme Court. The new constitution of 1852, however, practically completed the separation of the various departments. It provided that legislative and judicial functions should not be united in any individual or body. Nevertheless, under other constitutional provisions the upper house has ever since been a court of impeachment, though no case of impeachment has ever been tried in these islands; and jurisdiction over election cases remained in the legislative branch of the government until 1894, when by the constitution of the Republic it was turned wholly over to the courts,—the separation of judicial and legislative functions in this respect following the English practice and being carried further than in the United States. The constitution of 1852 also practically completed the separation of judicial and executive functions. It abolished the Supreme Court consisting of King, Premier and four Nobles. We have seen that the Governors acted as superior judges, and that they had already appointed foreign judges to act for them in foreign cases. Two such judges had been appointed at the capital. These with a third judge, a Hawaiian, became under the Act of 1847, the superior court not only for the island on which the capital was situated, but for all the islands, and for Hawaiian as well as foreign cases. It had both original and appellate jurisdiction.

On account of the learning and ability of its members, it became in effect the supreme court, and in 1852, it was made the Supreme Court in name as well as in reality. The judges of this court might sit singly or together and were severally to "go circuit" and sit with the local circuit judges. An appeal lay from one of the judges to the full court. In practice all the judges sat together, except on circuit, until 1869. After that they sat singly and appeals were taken to the full court. It was unsatisfactory to appeal to a court of only three members, one of whom had rendered the decision appealed from, and so in 1886 the number was increased to five. This, however, was not much more satisfactory, and in 1888 the number was reduced to three again, and the evil was remedied in 1892 by making the Supreme Court almost purely an appellate court, original cases being left to the Circuit and District Courts.

As shown above, prior to the Act of 1847, the courts possessed much discretionary power in both civil and criminal matters, but in practice followed the common law more and more. That Act expressly provided that in civil matters the courts might adopt the reasonings and analogies of the common law and of the civil law, when deemed founded in justice and not in conflict with Hawaiian laws and usages. Under this authority the courts in fact followed the common law, when applicable,—deliberately departing from it on probably not more than a dozen points in forty-five years and then only where it had grown obsolete or had been repealed by statute in most other common law countries. Finally, in 1892, it was provided by statute that in civil matters the common law, as ascertained by English and American decisions, should be the common law of these islands except as otherwise established by Hawaiian law, judicial precedent or national usage. As to criminal matters, a penal code was enacted in 1850, since which date penal offenses have been wholly statutory,—with penalties practically confined to fines and imprisonment.

Having thus traced in outline the evolution of the Hawaiian Judiciary, let us now look at it as it exists to-day.

The Hawaiian Judiciary comprises the three sets of courts usually found elsewhere—a supreme court, superior courts of record, and local courts. They are called the Supreme Court, the Circuit Courts, five in number, and the District Courts, twenty-nine in number. They are held or presided over by Justices, Judges and Magistrates, respectively, as they are called for convenience.

The District Magistrates, sitting without a jury, have criminal jurisdiction of misdemeanors, that is, in general, of offenses the penalty for which is imprisonment for not over two years, and civil jurisdiction in cases involving values up to three hundred dollars except cases of slander, libel, malicious prosecution, false imprisonment, seduction, breach of promise of marriage, and cases involving title to real estate. The jurisdiction for purposes of arrest, to compel the attendance of witnesses and for some other purposes, extends over the entire circuit within which the district is situated. If an offense is committed in one district and the accused is arrested in another, he may at his option and with the consent of the prosecuting officer, be tried in the district in which he was arrested. If the offense is not of a serious nature and there is no reason to suspect that the accused will attempt to elude justice, he may be merely summoned to appear, as in civil cases, without being arrested, unless an arrest is expressly requested by the complaining party. The civil jurisdiction is exclusive up to fifty dollars and concurrent with that of the Circuit Courts from fifty to three hundred dollars. A general appeal lies in all cases, civil and criminal, to the Circuit Court of the circuit in which the district is situated, or an appeal solely on points of law may be taken either to the Circuit Court or to the Supreme Court.

The Circuit Courts sit at regular terms with or without a jury, as the case may be, for the trial of most original law cases not begun in the District Courts and all appealed cases brought to them from the District Courts. Their jurisdiction for purposes of arrest, to compel the attendance of witnesses, and for some other purposes, extends over the entire Republic. Twelve terms, not exceeding four weeks each, are held each year, that is, one each month,—four in the first circuit and two in each of the others. Thus no two terms are held at the same time and the attorneys, most of whom reside at the capital, may conveniently attend any or all of the terms. The Circuit Judges sit without a jury in chambers throughout the year, chiefly in equity, admiralty, probate and bankruptcy cases. Divorce cases are regarded as law cases and are tried by the court at regular term, though without a jury. Exceptions lie from the Circuit Courts in law cases on points of law, and a general appeal lies from a Circuit Judge in chambers, to the Supreme Court.

The Supreme Court consists of a Chief-Justice and two Associate Justices. It holds four terms of three weeks each annually, one the last month of each quarter. It hears appeals on points of law from the District Courts, exceptions on points of law from the Circuit Courts, and general appeals from the Circuit Judges. Writs of error also lie to the lower courts but are seldom resorted to as exceptions and appeals are found more convenient and satisfactory methods of bringing cases to the Supreme Court. The Supreme Court has original jurisdiction over cases against the government, election cases, and the issuance of certain writs, such as *habeas corpus*, prohibition, *mandamus* and *certiorari*, though the use of these by the Supreme Court is confined chiefly to the aid of its appellate jurisdiction. If a Justice is absent or disqualified in any particular case, his place for that case may be filled by a Circuit Judge or a member of the bar, and no party may be compelled to have his appeal disposed of by a court of less than three persons. There is or was formerly in Connecticut a somewhat similar provision for the substitution of Superior Court Judges for Supreme Court Judges in certain contingencies. We have also a provision that if a point not raised or argued by counsel shall be deemed material by the Court, a decision shall not be rendered upon that point until an opportunity has been given counsel to argue it. The Justices wear gowns, thus following the practice of the English Justices and those of the Supreme Courts of the United States and of the State of New York. These gowns are of black silk and patterned after those of the Justices of the United States Supreme Court. The Supreme Court and the First Circuit Court sit only at the capital and occupy, with clerk's offices and library, the second floor of a capacious and architecturally beautiful building known as the Court House.

There is a Clerk of the Judiciary Department, under whom are three Deputy Clerks, for the first circuit and one for each of the other circuits. There are also stenographers and interpreters, the latter often playing very prominent parts in trials on account of the large number of different races of which our population is composed, Hawaiians, Portuguese, Japanese, Chinese and others, besides Americans, English and Germans. The executive officers of the courts are a Marshal of the Republic, Sheriffs of the several circuits, Deputy Sheriffs of the several districts, and police officers and constables. Methods of service of process and enforcement of judgments and decrees, as well as the prison system, are for the most part similar to those generally prevailing in the United States. Prisoners are obliged to work, mostly on the public roads. The pardoning power is vested in the President, with the advice of the Cabinet and a Council of State.

The Justices and Judges are appointed by the President with the approval of the Senate; the Magistrates by the President with the approval of the Cabinet. They have never been subjected to popular elections. The Justices hold office during good behavior, that is, for life; the Judges for six years; the Magistrates for two years. The Justices and Judges may be removed only by impeachment, or, upon a recommendation of the Executive Council (President and Cabinet), by a two-thirds vote of all the elective members of the Legislature (Senators and Representatives) sitting together and after notice to the Justice or Judge and an opportunity given him to be heard. The Chief-Justice receives $6,000 a year; each of the Associate Justices, $5,000; their salaries cannot be diminished during their term of office; the Circuit Judges receive, some, $3,000, others $4,000 each; the Magistrates from $300 to $2,500 each. In all these respects—appointment, tenure and salaries—we follow the Federal and English systems rather than those of the great majority of the States. As a consequence of this as well as of public opinion, the influence of the bar and the good sense of the appointing power, the Hawaiian Judiciary has always maintained a much higher standard than could have been possible under a system of popular elections, short terms and small salaries, such as exists in many of the States. As a rule the best and ablest men who would accept office have been appointed, and these when appointed have always shown themselves independent. Even during the reigns of the last two sovereigns when scandalous conduct was at times so prevalent in the executive and legislative branches of the government, the Supreme Court remained unimpaired and was looked to by the people as their one impregnable bulwark. These sovereigns, much as they desired to subject the judiciary to their control, dared not make the attempt until the final act of the last sovereign, which proved futile and cost her her throne.

The Justices of the Supreme Court are all of American descent. The Chief-Justice and First Associate Justice are graduates of Yale College; the former has also received the honorary degree of Doctor of Laws from Yale University; the latter graduated also from the Yale Law School. The Second Associate Justice is a graduate of Harvard College and the Boston Law School. The Circuit Judges comprise one Portuguese, one Hawaiian and three Americans, one of whom is a graduate of the Yale Law School. The District Magistrates are mostly Hawaiians, but some of them are Americans or English.

Our jury system has some peculiar features. As above

stated, the Circuit Courts alone sit with a jury and then almost exclusively in law cases, occasionally upon certain issues of fact in probate and bankruptcy cases and never in equity, admiralty or divorce cases. We have the racial and mixed jury system. Criminal actions against persons of foreign descent (whether naturalized or alien) and civil actions between foreigners are tried by foreign juries. Similarly, criminal actions against Hawaiians (whether of the whole or mixed blood) and civil actions between Hawaiians are tried by Hawaiian juries. Civil actions between Hawaiians and foreigners are tried by juries composed of six Hawaiians and six foreigners. Compare this with the jury *de mediatate linguæ* of English history. The jury numbers twelve, but an agreement of nine is sufficient for a verdict. This is the rule in all cases, civil and criminal, and has been for fifty years. It was the rule previously in all but capital cases. It has worked most satisfactorily. The jury may be waived in all civil cases and in practice is waived in a majority of such cases. The constitution of the Republic (1894) authorized the Legislature to provide for a waiver of jury in all criminal cases also, except capital cases. This was designed chiefly to obviate the expense of jury trials in minor cases, especially those appealed from the District Courts, and appropriate legislation has since been enacted permitting a waiver of jury in such cases. Until recently the relations between judge and jury were much the same as they are in the Federal and English courts; but in 1892 a statute was passed, similar to statutes passed in many of the United States, prohibiting the judges from commenting upon the weight of the evidence or the credibility of the witnesses. This, however, does not prevent the setting aside of a verdict as against the evidence and the granting of a new trial, or the directing of a verdict or the entry of a judgment *non obstante veredicto* in a proper case. The doctrine of "scintilla of evidence" has never obtained here. And judgments *non obstante* have always been granted here for the defendant as well as for the plaintiff and upon the evidence as well as upon the pleadings, if the material facts were undisputed. As a rule our juries have performed their duties well and our annals are comparatively free from the classes of verdicts, especially in criminal cases, which have so often in the United States tended to bring the jury system into disrepute. Such verdicts however, were somewhat frequent at times during the last two reigns, when race prejudices were aroused.

The grand jury has never existed in these islands. In criminal cases triable originally before a jury, the accused is first brought before a District Magistrate or a Circuit Judge (in practice generally the former) for examination, and, upon probable cause found, he is committed for trial in the Circuit Court. The Attorney-General then prepares an indictment, which is found a true bill or not as the case may be by the judge of that court.

The same judges sit in both law and equity, as well as in admiralty, probate and bankruptcy cases, but they do so as distinct courts, each with its peculiar procedure. Some features of the code pleading and practice have been introduced, but there has not been that complete fusion of law and equity that is found in some of the American States. Hawaiian procedure is based chiefly upon the English common law and equity procedure, but with the omission of all useless forms and fictions. It is characterized by simplicity and directness. This is indeed true of the whole course of the administration of justice in these islands. Trials, whether in civil or criminal cases, with or without a jury, are as a rule short and to the point—the lawyers attending strictly to business. Few delays are sought or allowed in either original or appealed cases. The Supreme Court, which, as above stated, sits three weeks the last month of each quarter, generally hears all cases put upon its calendar up to the end of the term, unless counsel mutually agree upon a continuance, and decides all or most of the cases so heard and files the decisions, before the next term. The Hawaiian bar is composed of two classes of lawyers, those admitted to practice in all the courts and those admitted to practice in the District Courts only. The former are mostly foreigners, chiefly Americans; the latter mostly Hawaiians. The English distinction between barristers and attorneys does not exist. Nor is there that degree of specialization that is possible in large cities. The Supreme Court, which hears most applications for admission, insists upon a high standard of legal learning as well as satisfactory proof of good moral character. The members of the bar are for the most part men of ability, high character and public spirit, and have always shown deep concern in the proper administration of the various branches of government, often sacrificing lucrative practice for longer or shorter periods to serve the public interests, as occasion demanded, especially in the executive and legislative departments.

As to the laws administered by the courts, these are in general such as might be looked for in the United States, with such differences in detail as are found in the different States of the Union. There is first the constitution, consisting chiefly of what may be called a "bill of rights" and an outline of the organization of the three departments of government, in this respect resembling the Federal Constitution with its amendments rather than the prolix or quasi-code constitutions of many of the States. Hawaii being one independent State has not the two sets of constitutions, state and federal, and consequently each of the three departments of government has in general the powers and duties of the corresponding branch of both State and Federal Government in the United States. The courts may declare laws unconstitutional, following in this respect the American rule rather than that of the European states which have written constitutions, such as France and Switzerland, where the Legislature decides for itself upon the constitutionality of the laws it enacts. Next come the treaties with foreign nations. Differing from the practice in the United States the Hawaiian courts have always held treaties to be of superior force to statutes, thus rendering it impossible for the legislative branch of government to break faith with other nations. In connection with this it may be added that the Hawaiian courts in the administration of private international law have always favored principles of comity rather than of selfishness or retaliation. And in matters of extradition, even in the absence of treaty provisions upon the subject, alleged criminals are delivered up, upon the production of proper papers and *prima facie* proof of guilt. Next come the statutes. No complete codification has been attempted, except that criminal offenses are wholly statutory. These, consisting of treason, felonies and misdemeanors, are embodied in a penal code and various statutes since passed, and are practically the same as exist generally in the United States. There is also a civil code. This relates chiefly to subordinate bureaus and offices in the executive department and the jurisdiction and practice of the courts, and also contains statutes of frauds, limitations, wills, descent, and some other provisions. Of course, numerous statutes upon all sorts of subjects have been passed at the regular biennial sessions of the legislature. Next comes the case law. This is found in both Hawaiian and foreign reports, and about the same weight is given to Hawaiian and foreign precedents respectively as is given by the courts of one American State to their own former decisions and those of the courts of other states or England respectively. The Hawaiian reports, comprising ten volumes, cover just fifty years. At present a volume is published about once in two years. These Hawaiian decisions resemble the decisions found in the reports of the American States both in the nature of the cases decided and in the law and authorities followed. Both American and English decisions are cited. The Supreme Court library contains about five thousand volumes of reports, text books, digests and statutes. In several instances in America, peculiar weight is given by the courts of a newer State to the decisions rendered in some older State from which many of the inhabitants of the former have come or from which it has borrowed much of its statutory law. Perhaps Hawaii cannot be said to have a parent state in this respect; and yet, from the fact that many of its leading people, including some of its ablest lawyers and judges, have come from Massachusetts or have received much of their education there—coupled with the fact of the high character of Massachusetts' law itself—the law of that State, both statutory and judicial, naturally has been followed in Hawaii more than that of any other one State. The American colony in Hawaii is, indeed, more largely of New England than of Western origin, but as New Englanders cannot long live in a new country without becoming infused with the so-called Western spirit of unconventionality and enterprise, the prevailing character of the people and institutions of Hawaii is not sectional but broadly and thoroughly American.

W. F. Frear.

YALE LAW JOURNAL

SUBSCRIPTION PRICE, $2.00 A YEAR   SINGLE COPIES, 35 CENTS

EDITORS:

ROGER S. BALDWIN, *Chairman.*
HUGH T. HALBERT, *Treasurer.*

CHRISTOPHER L. AVERY, JR.	GEO. JAY GIBSON,
SAMUEL F. BEARDSLEY.	JOHN MACGREGOR, JR.
MICHAEL GAVIN, 2D.	HENRY W. MERWIN,

Published six times a year, by students of the Yale Law School
P. O. Address, Box 1341, New Haven, Conn.

If a subscriber wishes his copy of the JOURNAL discontinued at the expiration of his subscription, notice to that effect should be sent; otherwise it is assumed that a continuance of the subscription is desired.

THE marriage laws of the State of New York have long offered a field for speculation and criticism. The reduction of the marriage relation to a civil contract is well established and is the result of the modern tendency to separate Church and State. The law in New York, however, which allows the status of a man and woman to be changed by the mere expression of such intention has perhaps gone farthest in the secularization of the marriage contract. A bill was lately submitted to the New York State Board of Health which although not restrictive in character is nevertheless regulative of the present system. The bill provides for a license in ceremonial marriages and for its return by the officiating clergyman to the local Board of Health within thirty days under a penalty of two hundred and fifty dollars. A further requirement is made of residents who go outside of New York to avoid its marriage laws, that they file a certificate of a marriage consummated in another State. But the bill is evidently aimed directly at common law marriages for it is further stipulated that certificates of such agreements must be filed with the State Board of Health and that a failure to comply with this provision shall render these marriages null and void.

The effect of such a law would be far-reaching and salutary. The importance of the marriage relation to our moral and civil welfare would well warrant its reasonable regulation by the State and the entrance upon such a relation should certainly be made a matter of State record. A provision which makes nec.

essary a license for a ceremonial marriage is perhaps of minor importance, as evidence of such marriages is generally obtainable, but the requirement of a certificate of common law marriages could avoid at least some of the dangers attending this form of contract which is only too often of a posthumous character. The agreement between the parties is the essential element in every contract—the meeting of their minds upon a common resolve—and it is this which constitutes marriage if marriage between the parties is otherwise lawful. It is the agreement itself rather than any symbol of it which should determine the relation. The danger of this doctrine however, does not lie so much in the ease with which such marriages are consummated as in the ease with which the fact of such marriages are afterwards simulated by those who are interested in proving their consummation. The present law not only makes secret marriages possible but also offers opportunity for the fraudulent assertion of marriages which were never intended. These results, dangerous to the morality and integrity of the community and disturbing to the distribution of property after the death of the owner, are defects which the proposed bill seeks to remedy.

* * *

IN one notable particular the present Executive enters upon his administration with a great advantage over his predecessors. We refer to the placing of nearly all of the administrative offices of the Government under the operation of the Civil Service Law, thus relieving the President of what must formerly have been a great burden. That the chief officer of our Nation should be compelled to devote the largest part of the first months of his term to settling rival claims for petty offices is inconsistent with efficient government, and the country is to be congratulated that the practice has been discontinued. This is only one instance of the enormous gain effected by the civil service system, both in the efficiency of the Government and in the destruction of much that is corrupting in politics. The fact that there are now not more than 10,000 public offices unaffected by the operation of the Civil Service Law is indicative of the extent to which this reform has been applied. *The Nation*, in calling attention to this far-reaching influence, very suggestively remarks, "To appreciate what all this means one must remember that it is only fourteen years this Winter since the Civil Service Act was passed as a harmless concession to the reformers."

The friends of this reform, however, have much to fear from the efforts of spoilsmen to get control of and corrupt the machinery of the merit system. Strong efforts have very recently been made in New York to weaken the influence of the civil service movement by transferring the examinations from the management of the Civil Service Commissions to the heads of the various State and Municipal departments, which would practically amount to a return to the very practices that the reform was calculated to remedy. In the face of such attempts to undo the wholesome influences of the civil service movement, the decision of the Appellate Division of the Supreme Court of New York, lately rendered, reaffirming Judge Keogh's decision as to the meaning and force of the constitutional requirement of appointments by merit to the civil service of the State, is very welcome news and deals a hard blow to spoils politicians.

*

ONE of the last acts of the outgoing Administration was the vetoing of an Immigration Bill which provided for the restriction of immigration into the United States. One of the first acts of the incoming Administration was the recommendation in the inaugural address of an improvement in our naturalization and immigration laws. Yet the two acts were perfectly consistent and should result in beneficial legislation. The Immigration Bill was vetoed because of the uncertainty and inefficiency of the restrictions which at the present, in view of our industrial condition, seemed neither expedient nor wise. The recommendation on the other hand was made for legislation which should be suited to our present dangers and demands. With changed conditions the laws of citizenship and inhabitancy must change also and the need or policy of a century ago is little likely to be that of the present. The country is more developed than was formerly the case and yet the development is not so great that we should shut our doors entirely against those who may assist us. On the other hand the character of our citizenship is such that restriction of some sort should be placed upon it, and the discordant and objectionable elements eliminated and restrained as far as possible. Legislation on the subject should be with reference to all interests, and must be so to avoid the dangers which lie in the advocacy of measures tending towards either extreme.

COMMENT.

The case of *Heaton-Peninsular Button-Fastener Co.* v. *Eureka Specialty Co.*, 77 Fed. Rep. 288 (C. C. of A.) presents a new and novel aspect of the right of a patentee to sell his articles with restrictions on their use. Complainants manufactured certain machines for fastening buttons to shoes with metallic fasteners and sold them on condition that they should be used only with fasteners manufactured by them, title to revert upon breach of condition. The result was that complainants acquired the monopoly of the manufacture and sale of an unpatented article (the fastener itself), as their machine had superseded all others of the kind. Defendants manufactured and sold to the users of these machines fasteners intended to be used therein.

The court held that the buyers, as regards their right to use the machines, were mere licensees, and any use contrary to the condition would be not only a breach of contract but also an infringement (*Rubber Co.* v. *Goodyear*, 9 Wall. 788-90), and therefore it must follow that defendants were contributory infringers, as they were intentional aiders and abettors of the buyers. The same principle is here involved as in the intentional making and selling a necessary element of a combination patent (*Wallace* v. *Holmes*, 9 Blatchf. 65). But the real distinction between this case and that of *Morgan Envelope Co.* v. *Albany Perforated Wrapping Paper Co.*, 152 U. S. 425, where the sale of rolls of paper (unpatented) adapted and intended to be used with complainants' mechanism for delivering them was held not to be an infringement, is that here an express contract of restriction was made.

The court also held that the condition was not void either as in restraint of trade or against public policy. That a monopoly of an unpatented article so created was only an incidental and therefore a legitimate result of complainants' lawful use of their monopoly of a patent; its life and extent would depend entirely on the merits of the patent. This case is essentially different from the telephone cases—*State* v. *Bell Tel. Co.*, 23 Fed. 539, and *State* v. *Del. & A. Tel. & Tel. Co.*, 47 Fed. 633, *Id.* 50 Fed. 677— where similar restrictions were held void, as telephone companies are charged with public duties and subject to regulation by law.

The question whether electric light companies are contemplated under the term "manufacturing industries," where such industries are exempted from municipal taxation by the State Legislature was considered by the Court of Appeals of Maryland in the case of the *Frederick City Electric Light and Power Co.* v. *Mayer, etc., of Frederick City, et al.*, 36 Atl. Rep. 362. On February 4, 1891, the Mayor and Aldermen of Frederick passed an ordinance providing that the machinery and apparatus of all manufacturing industries established within the corporate limits of the city within a certain period from the passage of the ordinance should be exempt from taxation for a number of years. Whether an electric company could properly be said to "manufacture" electricity is immaterial. An ordinary, non-scientific citizen, such as the mayor and aldermen presumably were, in speaking of the advantages of his town would mention that it was lighted by electricity, but would scarcely include an electric plant among its "manufacturing industries." It could not be seriously contended that an electric plant connected with a private residence or a hotel should be exempt from taxation as a "manufacturing industry." The purpose of the ordinance was declared to be to encourage manufacturing industries to locate in the town, and there was no need of the advantage of exemption from taxation to induce an electric light company to locate in a place the size of Frederick. Where there is a reasonable doubt as to whether a certain concern was intended to be exempted from taxation, the doubt must be resolved in favor of the taxing power (60 Md. 280). The case of *People* v. *Wemple*, 129 N. Y. 543, 29 N. E. 808, held such concerns to be within the exemption of "manufacturing corporations;" but O'Brien, J., said, "the policy of the law must be considered, and should have great weight," and the legislature subsequently declared that they should not thereafter be deemed to be within the exemption. The case of *Com.* v. *Northern Electric Light & Power Co.*, 145 Pa. 105, 22 Atl. 839, was also decided by the same principle.

The force of the much discussed South Carolina Dispensary Act has been so largely destroyed by the recent decision of the Supreme court, in the case of *Scott* v. *Donald*, that the statute is now practically a nullity. The case is an important one, as it raises a constitutional question, the difficulty of which is shown by the frequent and numerous dissenting opinions in the many cases where similar questions have been considered. In the present case Mr. Justice Brown renders a strong dissenting opinion.

The case was brought to recover damages for the action of the defendant, a state constable, of South Carolina, in seizing, in accordance with the Dispensary Act, several packages of wines and liquors belonging to the plaintiff and at the time of seizure in possession of a railway company which had brought the packages within the state. In reviewing the judgment of the United States Circuit Court, the Supreme Court holds that a state cannot prevent the private importation of spirituous liquors from another state, so long as it continues to recognize them as articles of lawful consumption and commerce. The ground upon which the court condemns those provisions of the statute affecting the plaintiff, is that they constitute an interference with interstate commerce. It is important to notice that the statute does not prohibit either the importation, manufacture or sale of intoxicating liquors; it merely turns these operations over to the state. Therefore the Supreme Court insists that such liquors must be regarded as the subject of foreign and interstate commerce, and that it is the duty of the Federal courts to afford such commerce the same measure of protection as is given to other articles of trade. By permitting only the state to import, "those citizens who wish to use foreign wines and liquors are deprived of the exercise of their own judgment and taste in the selection of commodities."

The main ground upon which the defense sought to justify the statute was as an inspection act, and the act does, indeed, contain provisions looking to the ascertainment of the purity of liquors, but they do not redeem it from the charge of being an obstruction to commerce. In disposing of this point, the court upholds *Minnesota* v. *Barber*, 136 U. S. 313, and a large list of other cases involving questions of interstate commerce.

Mr. Justice Brown, in his dissenting opinion, considers the rulings in *Minnesota* v. *Barber* as having no considerable bearing upon the question; and contends that inasmuch as public sentiment favors some restriction of the sale of ardent spirits, the question of whether such restriction shall take the form of a license upon dealers, the total prohibition of the manufacture, or the assumption by the state government of the power to supply liquors, is a matter exclusively for the state to determine.

RECENT CASES.

CARRIERS.

Railroad—Fellow Servant—Personal Injuries—Negligence.—*Oregon Short Line Railway Co.* v. *Frost's Adm'x,* 44 U. S. App. 606. In an action for damages for the death of a trainman killed in a collision, it appeared that the accident was due to the negligence of a telegraph operator at a local station; and the question arose whether or not the operator was the fellow-servant of the company's employees who were in charge of the train. It was held, following *Slater* v. *Jewett,* 85 N. Y. 61, 72, that the operator was a fellow-servant, inasmuch as his duty was so closely connected with the work of the trainmen in the movement of the train. *No. Pacific Ry.* v. *Charles,* 7 U. S. App. 359, 371, which the dissenting judge adhered to, was distinguished by the fact that there the allegation of the complaint and the admission of the answer placed the operator practically in the position of a train-despatcher, ordering the movement of trains, and not in that of a local operator through whom the orders of a superior were to be delivered, and that the question of the present case was not involved.

Street Railroads—Tender of Fare—Reasonableness.—*Barker* v. *Central Park, N. & E. R. R. Co.,* 45 N. E. Rep. 550 (N. Y.). The tender of a five-dollar bill in payment of a five-cent fare is unreasonable as a matter of law; it is not a question for the jury in the absence of any custom of making such a tender or of any rule of car company requiring conductors to make change in such an amount. But see *Barrett* v. *Railway Co.,* 81 Cal. 296, where a tender of a five-dollar gold piece was held reasonable, though possibly for local reasons, it being the smallest gold coin in general circulation.

EVIDENCE.

Dying Declarations—Attendant Circumstances—Evidence to Impeach—Proof of Conversation.—*Carver* v. *United States,* 17 Sup. Ct. Rep. 228. "Evidence that the deceased, who was a Catholic, had received the last rites of the church is admissible as tending to show that she must have known that she was 'in articulo mortis,' and to lend an additional sanctity to her statements. And where the whole or a part of a conversation has been put in evidence by one party, the other party is entitled to explain, vary or contradict it." Also defendant should be allowed to show that the deceased made statements in apparent contradiction to her dying declaration.

Statute of Frauds—Evidence—Usage and Custom.—Salomon v. *McRae,* 47 Pac. Rep. 409 (Col.). The fact that a bill of goods is marked "O. K.," followed by the agent's name, is not a sufficient memorandum, within the Statute of Frauds, to bind the agent on a contract of guaranty for all goods sold on credit. Evidence of a usage or custom is inadmissible to show that the letters used implied a guaranty of payment.

FEDERAL JURISDICTION.

Federal Jurisdiction—Creditors' Bill—State Judgment.—First Nat. Bank of Chicago v. *Steinway et al.,* 77 Fed. Rep. 661. A creditors' bill was filed by the plaintiff against the defendant, a citizen of another State, to reach equitable assets, the amount in question being sufficient to sustain the jurisdiction of the federal court. The bill was demurred to, on the ground that it was not maintainable, because based upon a judgment rendered by a State court, and because statutory remedies were available in the State courts. The court, in overruling these demurrers, held that "the equity jurisdiction of the circuit court of the United States cannot be taken away or diminished by State legislation."

Federal Courts—Jurisdictional Amount—Recoupment.—Pickham v. *Wheeler-Bliss Mfg. Co.,* 77 Fed. Rep. 663. When in an action in a Circuit Court to recover an alleged balance due of over $2,000, the amount in question is reduced by counter-claims to less than that sum, the court does not lose jurisdiction, if the plaintiff had no knowledge of such set-off before bringing the suit.

Criminal Law—Federal Jurisdiction—Larceny in Post Office.—77 Fed. 170, D.C. (Ind.).—*U. S.* v. *Saunders.* Felony in building used in part as post-office, does not come under federal jurisdiction unless felony is attempted to be committed within the part so used. Failure to so distinguish held ground for demurrer in *U. S.* v. *Campbell,* 16 Fed. 233. Indictment stating that the money stolen belonged to U. S. held sufficient. *U. S.* v. *Williams,* 57 Fed. 201.

REAL PROPERTY.

Estates—Life Tenant—Oil Lease.—Marshall v. *Mellon et al.*, 36 Atl. 201 (Pa.). Oil is a mineral (*Frink* v. *Haldeman*, 53 Pa. St. 229); also gas (*Blakeley* v. *Marshall*, 174 Pa. St. 425, 18 Atl 725); and so a part of the realty. A life-tenant, therefore, has no authority to lease lands, never theretofore used for the purpose, with right to tenant to extract oil and gas.

Homestead—What Constitutes—Intention to Occupy.—King v. *Wright*, 38 S. W. Rep. 530. No title is conveyed by a sale of land under an execution, levied before a house was built on said land, since the owner, owning no other real estate, had had for several years the intention to build upon same, and hence the land bore the homestead character.

Double Taxation—Taxing Landlord on Rental.—Kennard v. *City of Manchester*, 36 Atl. Rep. 553 (N. H.). Taxing a landlord on capital estimated sufficient to produce an income equal to the net rental, the tenant also paying a tax on the property itself as a part of the rental, is in effect a double tax on the property and illegal.

MISCELLANEOUS.

Mandamus to Canvassers of Election.—Baker v. *Board of State Canvassers*, 69 N. W. Rep. 656 (Mich.). A writ of mandamus will not be granted to compel a board of canvassers of an election to give certain candidates credit for votes cast for them which have been rejected because irregular, it appearing that neither the election of any of the candidates nor the relative position of the candidates' party on the official ballot of the next general election would be affected thereby. The writ is a discretionary one and will not issue to compel an idle ceremony.

Injunctions Against State Officers.—Scott et al. v. *Donald*, 17 Supreme Court Rep. 262. When one brings an action for compensation or injunction against State officers acting under color of an unconstitutional statute and committing acts of wrong and injury to the property of the plaintiff, such an action is not in violation of the 11th amendment of the Constitution of the U. S.

Conflict of Statute with State Constitution—Decision of State Court—Prepared Case—"Nichols Law"—Validity—Taxation of Express Companies.—Sanford v. *Poe, Ohio State Auditor, et al., Fargo* v. *Same,*

Platt v. *Same, Seward* v. *Same*, 17 Sup. Ct. Rep. 305. A State has the right to tax the property of an express company within the State upon the basis of the value of the whole capital of the company as laid down in the " Nichols Law," and although a decision that the statute did not conflict with the State constitution was given by the highest court of the State in a test case, involving no actual controversy, said decision will be accepted as conclusive by the Supreme Court of the United States. Four Justices dissented.

Parol Contract—Consideration of Adoption—Trusts—Will Cannot Defeat Contractual Rights.—*Heath* v. *Heath et al.*, 42 N. Y. Sup. 1087. A parol contract, made by decedent, to adopt the plaintiff and to leave to her at his decease his entire property, subject only to dower right of widow, is valid, placing a binding trust on the property, and cannot be defeated by a will contrary to its provisions.

Malicious Prosecutions—Termination of Criminal Proceedings—Failure to Prosecute.—*Hinds* v. *Parker*, 42 N. Y. Sup. 955. Where one committed to await the action of the grand jury is discharged on habeas corpus and institutes an action for malicious prosecution two days after release, no further steps being taken in the criminal proceedings, such release is not a termination of the criminal proceedings sufficient to support the action for malicious prosecution.

Corporations—Approval of Certificate Sunday Meetings.—*Agudath Hakehiloth*, 42 N. Y. Sup. 985. The certificate of incorporation of a membership corporation, arranging for annual meetings to be held on Sunday, was refused approval, as being against the public interest.

Great Lakes—Submerged Land—Title—Conveyance—Legislature.—*People* v. *Kirk et al.*, 45 N. E. Rep. 830. Dominion and title of lands beneath the waters of the Great Lakes are in the States within whose boundaries such lands are located—the States holding them in trust for the people, who have the right of navigation and fishing in the waters submerging them. And a State acting through its Legislature may convey such lands to private individuals provided it does not thereby impair the above common rights of the people in the lakes. Such an act, though unwise, is within the power of the legislature—redress must be had to the ballot, rather than to the courts.

Insurance—Change of Interest—Mortgage.—Lampasas Hotel and Park Co. v. *Phœnix Ins. Co.*, 38 S. W. Rep. 361 (Texas). A policy insuring a building against fire contained a condition that the policy should be void "if any change other than by the death of the insured take place in the interest, title, or possession of the subject of the insurance." After obtaining this policy the insured executed a mortgage on the property insured. Fire occurring, the insurer claimed that the insured had forfeited the policy by executing a mortgage on the property since the issuance of the policy, such mortgage working "a change of interest" within the meaning of the condition; but the court held otherwise, following the construction put by the New York Court of Appeals (*Walradt* v. *Ins. Co.*, 136 N. Y. 375) upon the words "change of interest," to the effect that such words "are substantially synonymous with the words 'change of title,' and neither event occurs until the sale upon the execution."

Patents—Invention—Coating Photographic Paper—Analogous Use.—Eastman Co. v. *Getz et al.*, 77 Fed. Rep. 412. An alteration of a machine for making photographic films by coating the paper with an emulsion, which simply increases the distance between the coating roll and the driven, smooth-faced rolls, with the object of giving the gelatine longer time for drying and settling, is not an invention. The adaptation of a machine for coating glass and emery paper to coating paper with a solution of gelatine, is merely an analogous use and not an invention, it appearing that such changes would reasonably occur to a skilled mechanic employed to adapt the old machine to its new use.

Naval Officer—Duty on State Nautical School Ship—Secretary of the Navy—Accepting Pay from the State.—United States v. *Barnette*, 17 Sup. Ct. Rep. 286. A naval officer assigned by the order of the Secretary of the navy to duty as executive on a nautical school ship loaned a State by the general government, is entitled to sea-pay while the vessel was at the dock, where he lived on board and performed the same duties as when cruising at sea. The fact that such duty is called "shore duty" in the secretary's order makes no difference. His right to sea-pay is not affected by the fact that he also receives pay from the State.

BOOK NOTICES.

Handbook of the Law of Private Corporations. By Wm. L. Clark, Jr. Law sheep. 652 pp. text. The West Publishing Co., St. Paul, Minn. 1897.

It is manifestly impossible to confine within the limits of a single volume the ever-increasing mass of legal lore in respect to private corporations. Mr. Clark has wisely not attempted this. His treatise is really a digest and needs to be supplemented by some more exhaustive work to be truly efficient. The strong points of his work are its logical arrangement, the completeness with which it deals with many as yet unsettled points, and the fact that it represents the law as it is, not as it has been.

A Practical Treatise on the Law of Receivers. By Charles Fisk Beach, Jr., of the New York Bar. Second edition by Wm. A. Alderson, of the St. Louis Bar. Law sheep. 885 pp. text. Baker, Voorhis and Company, New York. 1897.

The first edition of this work ten years ago took its place at once as an authority upon this peculiarly American subject. The book has been entirely rewritten by Mr. Alderson, who has enlarged it and added the leading cases decided in the meantime. We predict for it increased success.

Digest of Insurance Cases. Vol. IX. By John A. Finch, of the Indianapolis Bar. Half law sheep. 332 pp. text. The Bowen-Merrill Company, Indianapolis and Kansas City. 1897.

The ninth volume of the *Insurance Digest* is larger and more complete than former volumes. It contains all the cases decided in the Federal and State Courts up to October 31, 1896, and references to the leading articles in many law journals. It is carefully indexed and well arranged.

MAGAZINE NOTICES.

The Green Bag, February, 1897.

    Joseph Story (with portrait).
    Wills of Famous Americans.
    Oaths, ... R. Vashon Rogers.
    Love and Law (verse), ... John Albert Macy.
    Mysterious Finding of Lost Papers, . . T. W. Albertson.
    Place aux Dames.
    Curiously Caught Criminals.

March, 1897.

    Daniel Cady (with portrait).
    Beyond a Reasonable Doubt, ... Chas. E. Grinnell.
    An Indian Deed.
    Presidential Lawyers.
    The Death Penalty in the United States.

Central Law Journal. Leading Articles.

    Jan. 29. Recent Phases of Contract Law. I.—The Right of a Third Party to Sue for a Breach of Contract, ... John D. Lawson.
    Feb. 5. Liens of Attorneys, . . Morton John Stevenson.
    Feb. 12. Relief in Equity for Mistakes of Law in Written Instruments, . . . C. A. Bucknam.
    Feb. 19. The Police Power, . . . Lewis Hochheimer.
    Feb. 26. Mental Anguish in Telegraph Cases, . Oscar H. Ecke.

The Albany Law Journal, 1897.

    Jan. 30. Survival of Causes of Action, . . Harold D. Alexander.
    Feb. 6. Legal Authors of Familiar Quotations, Law Times (London).
    Feb. 13. Inter-State Rendition in its Constitutional Aspects, ... Ben S. Dean.
    Feb. 27. Has the Physician Ever the Right to Terminate Life? . . . *Medico-Legal Journal.*
    March 6. Are Public Corporations Subject to Garnishment or Creditors' Suit, . . Morton J. Stevenson.

American Law Review, January and February, 1897.

    Coke and Bacon: The Conservative Lawyer, and the Law Reformer.
    Contracts of Foreign Corporations.
    A New Departure in French Marriage Law.
    The Fallacy of Compromise and Arbitration.
    Bracton—A Study in Historical Jurisprudence.
    The Cuban Insurrection and American Neutrality..
    Under What Circumstances a Servant Accepts the Risk of His Employment.
    The Law as a Profession for Young Men.

SUPPLEMENT
CONTAINING
MEMORABILIA ET NOTABILIA.

[Graduates are requested to contribute to this column and address their communications to YALE LAW JOURNAL, box 1341, New Haven, Conn.]

Dean Wayland has been elected President of the Associated Charities of New Haven.

* * *

The Senior Class has voted, for the first time, that those who have a college degree shall wear appropriate hoods attached to their gowns at the next commencement.

* * *

The first lecture in the Kent Club course was delivered by Isaac H. Bromley, Yale '53, in College street Hall, on Thursday evening, February 18th, the subject being "The Fall of the Second Empire."

* * *

1866. Hon. Wm. E. Simonds delivered a lecture entitled, "In the Woods," at the annual meeting of the Connecticut Board of Agriculture, at Danbury, Conn., on December 16th.

1867. Morris Goodhart died at his residence in New York City, February 6th. Mr. Goodhart was born in Amsterdam, Holland, in 1838, coming to America with his parents in 1846. Two years after graduation, he was admitted to the bar in New York City, where he acquired a large practice. In 1884 he was chosen President of the Hebrew Mutual Benefit Society, and in 1896 President of the Hebrew Sheltering Guardian Society, and he has also held many high positions in the B'nai B'rith organization, the greatest of the Hebrew organizations. In 1871 Mr. Goodhart married a daughter of the late Judge Joachimsen of New York.

1873. Hobart L. Hotchkiss has formed a law partnership with Harry L. Asher, under the firm-name of Hotchkiss & Asher, with offices in the Exchange Building, New Haven, James S. Green, 1895, who has been for two years with Hotchkiss & Wright, of New Haven, will be managing clerk of the new firm.

Professor Woolsey has been elected President of the Graduates Club of New Haven.

1874. James Bishop has been chosen Judge of the New Haven City Court to succeed Judge J. C. Cable, '73.

1875. Hon. John P. Studley has been elected Judge of the Common Pleas Court of New Haven county, Connecticut.

1875. Hon. George M. Sharp was elected Vice-President of the Maryland Alumni Association at their second annual banquet, held at the Hotel Stafford, Baltimore, Md., February 16, 1897.

Prof. Geo. D. Watrous is Chairman of the Citizen's Committee appointed to revise the charter of New Haven. Prof. Geo. E. Beers is also a member of the same committee.

1876. Theodore S. Woolsey has an article in the March *Forum*, entitled "Some Comments on the Treaty."

1880. Henry W. Lamb was married to Mrs. Emily Hotchkiss in New Haven, February 18th.

1883. Carter H. Harrison has been nominated for Mayor of Chicago by the Democratic and Populist Parties.

1885. John P. Kellogg of Waterbury, Conn., has been chosen assistant State's attorney for the Waterbury district of the Superior Court.

1889. James A. Wilson died in Bridgeport, February 12th. He had been, since graduation, a member of the firm of Nobbs & Wilson in Bridgeport.

1889. Prof. Geo. E. Beers acted as one of the judges in the final debate to choose the speakers for the coming intercollegiate debate with Harvard. The finals were held March 2, 1897. Messrs. Kilker, '97, Gorham, '99, and Pleasant, '99, spoke as representatives of the Kent Club selected one week earlier.

1891. Charles H. Sherrill, ex-'91, has formed a law partnership with Woolsey Carmalt, Yale '83, formerly Assistant Corporation Counsel of New York City, and Benoni Lockwood, Jr., under the firm-name of Carmalt, Sherrill and Lockwood, with offices at 35 Nassau street, New York.

Joseph E. Morgan, ex-'96, is in the office of the Excelsior Coke and Gas Company of Topeka, Kan.

1892. John F. Carpenter has been appointed Clerk of Bills in the Connecticut House of Representatives.

Edward Van Ingen, ex-'93, was married on January 21st, to Miss Mae Bell, daughter of Mr. and Mrs. E. T. Bell, of Paterson, N. J.

1893. James K. Blake has been appointed a member of the New Haven Board of Health.

1893. John Hone, Jr., has resigned his position with the law-firm of Carter & Ledyard, and has opened an office at 62 Nassau street, New York City.

A. Maxcy Hiller, '97, has been elected President of the Board of Directors of the New Haven Public Library.

1893. Jas. D. Dewell, Jr., has been appointed one of the harbor commissioners for New Haven.

1893. R. U. Tyler has been made a partner in the law firm of Warner & Wilcox, at Middletown, Conn., the firm-name now being Warner, Wilcox and Tyler.

1893. Samuel A. Davis has been elected Associate Judge of the City Court of Danbury, Conn., for two years.

1893. George H. Huddy, Jr., has opened an office at 48 Weybosset street, Providence, R. I.

1894. Percy Finlay is now a member of the firm of Finlay & Finlay. Offices in Equitable Building, Memphis, Tenn.

1894. John W. Larkin has been appointed City Clerk at Derby, Conn.

1894. Jas. F. Torrance has been elected Judge of Probate at Derby, Conn.

1894. Harold R. Durant is in the office of Lucien F. Burpee, at Waterbury, Conn.

1894. G. Fauvel Gouraud, has produced a volume of verses entitled "Ballads of Coster-Land," published by the Herald Square Publishing Co., of New York. Mr. Gouraud is practicing law in New York City.

1895. Frank E. Donnelly has opened an office at Rooms 11-15, Laning Building, Wilkesbarré, Penn.

1895. Edward L. Seery has opened an office in the Apothecaries' Hall Building, at Waterbury, Conn.

1895. Joseph S. Peery has been elected District Attorney for Weber County, Utah.

1895. M. L. Geo. C. Breckenridge is in the office of Daniel Daly, 38 Park Row, New York City.

1895. Frederick Keeler has opened an office in the Bishop Block, Bridgeport, Conn.

Tokichi Masao of the D. C. L. class will return to Japan this fall and take examinations for appointment to the foreign service.

Ex-'95. The engagement of Wm. R. Begg has been announced to Miss Spencer of Hartford.

1895, M. L. Jas. J. Sheridan is with the firm of Bulkley, Gray & More, Home Insurance Building, Chicago.

1896. Edward A. McClintock has opened an office at room No. 39 Court Square Theatre building, 15 Elm street, Springfield, Mass.

YALE LAW JOURNAL

VOL. VI APRIL, 1897 No. 5

INJUNCTION IN THE FEDERAL COURTS.

The jurisdiction of the National courts to issue the writ of injunction is not peculiar or exceptional. Within the classes of cases of which they may take cognizance those courts grant or refuse that kind of relief by the same rules and principles which from time immemorial have prevailed in the English Chancery and in the equity courts of those States of the Union which derived their jurisprudence from the mother country. Equity as a system, more perhaps than the Common Law, has been enlarged and modified to meet the changing conditions of business and civilization, and it is only natural that there should have been instances in which jurisdiction has been exercised in excess of rightful power, but when error of that kind has occurred it has been promptly corrected, either by direct appeal or by force of contemporary and more authoritative decision, and it is safe to say that no essential departure from recognized principles has become abiding or permanent. Steam power, electricity, railroads, telegraphs, corporate organizations, labor unions, trusts and other agencies and schemes of modern enterprise have vastly extended the field and multiplied the occasions for the exercise of equity powers including the power to enjoin, but the character of the jurisdiction and the principles which govern its exercise have been changed or enlarged no more than the provisions and underlying principles of the National Constitution and the powers of government thereby established have been modified or increased by the admission of new States into the Union. No decision of the Supreme Court, or of any United States Circuit Court of Appeals, touching the subject of injunction, can be said to be founded on or to involve any new doctrine, or any application of established principle which was new save in the circumstances and conditions brought under consideration, and with two or three exceptions the same is true of the recent Circuit Court decisions, which have been made the subject the country over of discussion and criticism. Brief references to the more notable of these cases will not be out of place.

In the Ann Arbor case, in the United States Circuit Court at Toledo, the Pennsylvania Company and other railroad companies and their employes were enjoined against refusing to receive the cars of a boycotted connecting line, and Mr. Arthur, the chief executive of the Brotherhood of Locomotive Engineers, was forbidden to issue or to continue in force any rule or order of the brotherhood which should require any of the employés of the respondent companies to refuse to receive, handle and deliver cars of freight in course of transportation from one State to another over the boycotted road. An engineer who, without quitting his locomotive, refused to attach to his train cars from the Ann Arbor road, was declared guilty of contempt of court and adjudged to pay a fine.[1]

Serious objection, so far as known, has been made in no respectable quarter to anything actually decided in that case by either the circuit or district judge. Each of them delivered an opinion in which the right of employés individually or collectively to quit work or employment, unhindered by injunction, is distinctly recognized, but in the opinion of the district judge are *dicta* to the effect that it may be proper for a court of equity under peculiar circumstances of danger and hardship to the public, or in dealing with a conspiracy to boycott, to prevent an employé from quitting the service in which he is engaged. As an example of public danger which would justify the writ it is suggested that the engineer and fireman might be enjoined against abandoning a train part way on its route at a place where passengers and property would be imperiled. The suggestion seems impracticable. If the probability of such conduct could be known in time to apply for an injunction, the answer of the court would be: Discharge the men before they start, and if you cannot find trustworthy substitutes take off your train. There might be some danger, however, in such a course, if the law were as declared some years ago by a Judge of the Superior Court at Indianapolis, where, strikers having taken possession of a street railway in such manner as to make the running of cars impossible, the Judge, on motion of a citizen, declared the failure of the company to keep its lines running to be such a dereliction of duty to the public as to call for the appointment of

---

[1] Toledo, A. A. & N. M. Ry. Co *v.* Pennsylvania Co., 54 F. R. 730, 746.

a receiver to discharge that duty. In the Southern District of California, upon the petition of a railway company against its own employés, alleging that though remaining in the employment of the company they "refused and still refuse" to move any train with a Pullman car attached, an injunction was granted "requiring the defendants to perform all their regular and accustomed duties so long as they remain in the employment of the complainant company."[2] If not wrong that order is very near the line of error. The company being at liberty to discharge all who refused to do their accustomed duties and to employ others to take their places, why should equity interfere —especially to order the performance of personal service?

The *dicta* of the Ann Arbor case soon ripened into a decision by the United States Circuit Court for the Eastern District of Wisconsin, reported in Farmers Loan and Trust Co. *v.* Northern Pac. R. Co., 60 F. R. 803. By the injunction granted in that case the employés of receivers in charge of the Northern Pacific Railroad, besides being forbidden to do specified acts of depredation and direct interference with the operation of the road, were restrained "from combining and conspiring to quit * * * and from so quitting the service of the said receivers, with or without notice, as to cripple the property or to prevent or hinder the operation of said railroad." That injunction in so far as it undertook to restrain men from quitting the employment of the receivers was annulled by the decision of the United States Circuit Court of Appeals for the Seventh Circuit, in Arthur *v.* Oaks, 24 U. S. App, 239, 11 C. C. A. 209. In the opinion there reported, written by Mr. Justice Harlan of the Supreme Court, it is said: "It would be an invasion of one's natural liberty to compel him to work for or to remain in the personal service of another. One who is placed under such constraint is in a condition of involuntary servitude—a condition which the supreme law of the land declares shall not exist within the United States, or in any place subject to their jurisdiction. * * * The rule, we think, is without exception that equity will not compel the actual, affirmative performance by an employé of merely personal services, any more than it will compel an employer to retain in his personal service one who, no matter for what cause, is not acceptable to him for service of that character. If the quitting in the one case or the discharging in the other is in violation of the contract between the parties, the one injured by the breach has his action for damages. * * * The exercise

---
[2] Sou. Cal. Ry. Co *v.* Rutherford, 62 F. R. 796.

by employés of their right to quit in consequence of a proposed reduction of wages could not be made to depend upon considerations of hardship or inconvenience to those interested in the trust property or to the public. The fact that employés of railroads may quit under circumstances that would show bad faith upon their part or a reckless disregard of their contract, or of the convenience and interests of both employer and the public, does not justify a departure from the general rule that equity will not compel the actual, affirmative performance of merely personal services, or (which is the same thing) require employés against their will to remain in the personal service of their employer."

These utterances, it may be remarked in passing, made it natural and probable, not to say logically necessary, that Justice Harlan should have dissented, as he did, from the recent opinion of the Supreme Court in Robertson *v.* Baldwin, where it was held that, notwithstanding the Thirteenth Amendment to the Constitution, a seaman, who in violation of his contract of service had deserted a vessel, "engaged in a purely private business," could be arrested and remanded against his will to the service of the master.

The opinion in Arthur *v.* Oaks had not been handed down, but what it would be was known to me, when the injunction of July 2, 1894, was ordered against the officers of the American Railway Union and others engaged in riotous interference with interstate commerce and the carrying of the mails upon the railroads entering Chicago, and accordingly, though the application then made was for a writ quite as broad as that against the employés of the receivers of the Northern Pacific, the order proposed was so modified as to impose upon employés, individually or collectively, no restriction against quitting service, or striking, if done without direct and active interference with the operations of the roads engaged in interstate commerce and in carrying the mails. The injunction was disregarded, and when the officers of the Railway Union were arraigned for contempt the jurisdiction of the court to issue the injunction was denied. For an understanding of the many questions raised in the course of the discussion of that case reference must be made to the opinions delivered in the Circuit Court[3] and in the Supreme Court of the United States.[4] The opinion in the Circuit Court was designed to show that the jurisdiction exercised was justifi-

---

[3] U. S. *v.* Debs, 64 F. R. 724.
[4] 158 U. S. 564.

able both upon general equitable principles and by the Act of Congress of July 2, 1890, known as the Anti-Trust Law. For reasons stated the decision was based upon the statute, though if the hearing had been in a court of last resort the broad equity ground would have been preferred, as it was by the Supreme Court, though that court was careful to say that it must not be understood that they dissented from the conclusions of the Circuit Court in reference to the scope of the Act of Congress, and that they, in fact, concurred in those conclusions is demonstrated by a statement to that effect in the dissenting opinion of Mr. Justice White in United States *v.* Trans-Missouri Freight Association, decided a short while ago—the dissenting criticism being that in its last decision the Supreme Court had given the statute a wider and an unwarranted scope. In the contempt case it was held, or, perhaps it would be more accurate to say, it was assumed, that the contracts, combinations and conspiracies which under the statute might be enjoined were such as would be deemed to be unlawful irrespective of the act; but by this decision the Supreme Court goes much further, holding that every contract, combination or conspiracy, which in fact is in restraint of interstate commerce, being expressly declared unlawful, is thereby brought within the scope of the act. The distinction manifestly is one of very great significance.

The officers of the American Railway Union, when arraigned for contempt, demanded but were denied a trial by jury, and having been found guilty by the court, after a protracted and formal hearing, were sent to jail, one for six months and the others each for three months, and though such had always been the practice, and from the nature of an equity court there could have been no right to a jury trial, this denial of a demand for such trial was made the excuse or pretense for an attempt, not wholly unsuccessful, to excite public sentiment against the power of the courts, both of law and equity, to punish contempts of their authority, though the power, as every intelligent man must know, is essential to the usefulness of a court, and has been exercised, as occasion required, since the Government was founded. As late as April, 1894, a juror in the Federal Court at Indianapolis, detected in an effort to be bribed, was summarily declared guilty of contempt of court and sent to State prison for fifteen months; but that incident excited no fear that the Constitution was being undermined or the liberties of the people endangered. It is hard to believe that any one in his sober senses thinks the imprisonment of Debs a dangerous precedent; yet at the instigation of Grand Masters and Grand Chiefs of various well-known and reputable organizations, claiming to represent 800,000 railroad employés, in whose behalf they especially urged that in prosecutions for contempt there should be a right of trial by jury, a number of bills on the subject were introduced in the last Congress, one of which was passed by the Senate embracing that provision, together with others which are not essentially objectionable. It is not unreasonable that in a case of contempt committed out of the presence of the court there should be a formal procedure upon affidavit showing the facts supposed to constitute the contempt, to which the defendant should be allowed to make answer, and that the trial should be upon evidence adduced in open court. If the practice in such cases in any court has ever been essentially different the fact was not disclosed in the Senate debate. The bill undertook to put no limit upon the amount of fine or imprisonment in such cases, but contained a provision for an appeal, which the writer thinks ought to be allowed in cases of all sorts when the matter is of importance and especially when personal liberty is involved. It might well be provided, too, that for a contempt infamous punishment should not be inflicted. Such punishment can be appropriate only to infamous crimes. But the privilege of trial by jury is inconsistent with the purpose of the power to punish in such cases and could only result in crippling and demoralizing the courts in the daily administration of justice. In a court of law, if a juror or panel of jurors should refuse to attend, it would be necessary that other jurors be summoned to try them for the contempt, and what if they, too, should refuse to come? And what if the marshal and his deputies should refuse to serve the writs of the court? An equity court has no jury and, unless it is to be supplied with a new and incongruous piece of machinery to be kept on hand, or summoned when needed, solely for the trial of contempts as they may occur, will have to send its contempt cases to a court of law, to be tried when in the course of business in that court they shall be reached, suspending meanwhile its own procedure.

It is well to observe, moreover, that if the trial by jury were allowed, a strike like that of 1894 at Chicago would have no better chance of success. Now that the jurisdiction of the courts in such cases is beyond question, an injunction would certainly issue as before and if not heeded the President, if true to his trust, would send the army as before to compel submission, and that accomplished it would be a matter of comparatively small importance whether there should be trials for contempt, or whether, if had, they should be by the court or by jury. The question involves no more the rights and liberties of laboring men than of other citizens. Nobody in his right mind believes that there has been usurpation of power by the courts, or that the power exercised is the source or beginning of peril to individual or collective rights. Out of all that has been done by the courts since the Government was founded there can be deduced no sound reason for depriving them of their accustomed and well-understood power to enforce respect and order in their presence, and to compel obedience to their writs and commands wherever lawfully sent.

W. A. Woods.

WHEN MAY A RAILROAD COMPANY MAKE GUARANTIES?

The question of a railroad company's power to make guaranties usually arises upon collateral undertakings of this character, written upon the bonds and coupons of another company, in whose success the guarantor has an interest. The underlying principles which control the power are common in theory to private corporations in general. But the volume of railroad securities is now so great, and their sale so large an element in the activities of investment, that our discussion need not go beyond this class of corporations.

The transportation companies are closely allied in business—the overwhelming tendency of the day is to consolidate lines by merger, or lease, or traffic contract. A receiver of an extensive railroad system in the West informed the writer of this article last Summer that although he had the care of more than a thousand miles of road, reaching into eight or ten large cities the principal corporation in his care had no interest of ownership in a terminal station at any one of the large cities. They were all controlled by lease or traffic contract. The property under his care was originally owned by ten or more corporations. This single example, which has exceptional features in the matter of terminals, is not, on the whole altogether strange in the history of modern railroad companies. As railroads have been largely built upon bonds, and as the bonds are constantly maturing, and are usually renewed in some form or another, it is to be expected that new parties will be interested in their renewal, and so it is every day's experience, that the investing public is asked to purchase bonds of a railroad company which are guaranteed for principal and interest by another corporation.

Two suggestions are worthy of early consideration in examining the subject: First, the contract of guaranty of negotiable securities, unless restricted in its terms, is held to be a contract by the guarantor with the owners of the guaranty. Second, the general power of guarantying the contracts of one company by another is held to a less strict limitation in the case of bonds and coupons than of some other contracts. The reason for this distinction in favor of negotiable bonds and coupons is, that railroad bonds, payable to bearer, are held both in this country and England to pass, like bills and notes, free from equities existing between the original holders. Authorities to this point the student will find collected at considerable length in Jones on R. R. Securities, Secs. 197 and 198.

The language of Judge Nelson, in White *v.* R. R. Co., 21 How. 575, expresses in forcible phraseology, the common result of intelligent tribunals in this matter. The Supreme Court of Indiana in R. R. Co. *v.* Cleneay, 13 Ind. 161, says: "Though not exactly governed by the law merchant, these bonds are entitled to the privileges of commercial paper." The negotiability of coupons payable to bearer is even more pronounced than of the bonds themselves. They are held to possess all the attributes of negotiable paper. The purchaser acquires title by delivery, and the promise to bearer is a promise to him directly. The title passes from hand to hand by mere delivery, and the transfer of possession is presumably the transfer of title.[1]

Upon general principles of law a railroad company has no power to guaranty the contracts of another company, unless such power is expressly conferred by law, or is incidental to its corporate character. A leading case in England on this subject is Coleman *v.* R. R. Co., 10 Beav. 1. In that case the railroad company thought it could increase its traffic and profits by the aid of a steam packet company to be formed and whose vessels should run from its railroad terminus to the northern parts of Europe, and they attempted to guaranty five per cent dividends to the stockholders of the packet company. A shareholder in the railroad company sought an injunction, and Lord Langdale, Master of the Rolls, held that no such contract was within the power of the railroad company. His opinion as to the importance of preserving the property of railroad companies may seem strange to some readers to-day: "If there is one thing more desirable than another, after providing for the safety of all persons traveling on railroads, it is this, that the property of a railroad company shall be itself safe; that a railroad investment shall not be considered a wild speculation exposing those engaged in it to all sorts of risk, whether they intended it or not. Considering the vast property which is now invested in railroad companies, and how easily it is transferable, perhaps one of the best things that could happen would be that the

---

[1] See Mercer County *v.* Hackett, 1st Wal. 83. Ketchum *v.* Duncan, 96 U. S. 659. Haven *v.* R. R. Co., 109 Mass. 88.

investment should be of such a safe nature that prudent persons might, without improper hazards, invest their moneys in it. Quite sure I am that nothing of that kind can be approached, if railroad companies shall be at liberty to pledge their funds in support of speculations not authorized by their legal powers, and might possibly, to say the least, lead to extraordinary losses on the part of the company." This case has been approved by the United States Supreme Court in Pearce *v.* R. R. Co., 21 How. 441, and in Pa. Co. *v.* R. R. Co., 118 U. S. 290. The case of Madison Plank Road Co. *v.* Watertown Co., 7 Wis. 59, held that the railroad company's guaranty of a loan to the Plank Road Company, which was in continuation of the railroad company line, was in excess of the powers of the railroad company. This case has also been favorably quoted by the Supreme Court of the United States.[2]

That the legislative power may be expressed in a private charter or by general law is conceded by all the cases.

The General Statutes of Connecticut restrict the issue of guarantees by railroad companies and of course, by implication, thereby recognize the right as one to be exercised under proper circumstances and within the statutory limits.

The rule of presumption of legality or illegality has been several times adjudicated. The leading case is R. R. Co. *v.* Howard, 7th Wal. 392. The opinion says: "Private corporations may borrow money or become parties to negotiable paper in the transaction of their legitimate business, unless expressly prohibited; and, unless the contrary is shown, the legal presumption is, that their acts in that behalf were done in the regular course of their authorized business."

The instances in which a railroad company has an implied power to make such guaranties are commonly found where the company has acted upon a consideration for its own benefit and under the general powers of making beneficial contracts within the lines of its corporate purposes, which is an incident to all corporate business. Thus a guaranty of this kind is held to be good where the guarantor owned all the capital stock of the principal debtor; where the debtor's road was an essential part of the general system of the guarantor, or was held by the guarantor under lease; where the guarantor had advanced the money in its own interest, and not against legislative prohibition, to build the road of the debtor company, and the bonds were used to reimburse them for the money advanced; where

---

[2] See also Transp. Co. *v.* P. P. Co., 139 U. S. 478.

the bonds of the debtor company were owned by the guarantor, and were by it negotiated for the purpose of giving additional credit to the instrument, and where the consideration of the negotiation of guaranty was actually received by the guarantor and appropriated to its own use. Cases supporting these propositions are many. We give a few of the principal ones.[8]

Our Connecticut Courts define these incidental powers as those which are necessary to the use of a corporation's granted powers. Thus the power to make notes for debts, or to evidence the consideration of a mortgage of real estate properly purchased, are incidental; the one to the business methods of the day, and the other to the right of purchasing land. On the other hand, the same courts hold that making accommodation paper for another's benefit is *ultra vires*. The Connecticut courts include as within the chartered powers of a corporation those acts which may be exercised within the "fair intent and purposes of their creation."

The principle of estoppel has been by some eminent tribunals, held to defeat the defense of *ultra vires*, when made by a company against a *bona fide* holder of securities for value. In the case already cited in the 7th of Wallace the Court says: "Corporations as much as individuals are bound to good faith and fair dealing, and the rule is well settled that they cannot, by their acts, representations or silence, involve others in onerous engagements, and then turn around and disavow their acts, and defeat the just expectations which their own conduct has superinduced."

In the case of Arnott v. R. R. Co., already cited, and approved by later cases in New York, the Court of Appeals held that, even if a guaranty were originally an act *ultra vires*, when it is transferred for a valuable consideration the defense cannot be maintained.

The case of Credit Co. v. Howe Machine Co., 54 Conn. 357, is an important one to our discussion. The defendant, a manufacturing company, was limited by its charter, in its use of mercantile paper, to the convenient prosecution of its business. The Treasurer of the company, who was the proper officer to

---

[8] Zabriskie v. R. R. Co., 23 How. 381. Todd v. Ken. U. Co., 57 Fed. Rep. 47. Marbury v. Ken. U. Co., 62 Fed. Rep. 350. Arnott v. Erie R. R. Co., 67 N. Y. 321. Rogers Works v. Southern R. R. Assoc., 34 Fed. Rep. 278. Low v. R. R. Co., 9 Am. R. R. 366. Olcott v. R. R., 27 N. Y. 546. Smith v. Johnson, 3 H. & N. 222. R. R. Co. v. Fletcher, 24 A. & E. R. R. cases 24.

make acceptances, accepted accommodation drafts made for the benefit of a former president. The court estopped the defendant from setting up the claim of *ultra vires*. If railroad bonds and coupons are to have the same protection, in the hands of *bona fide* holders for value, as notes and bills, the doctrine of this case would prevent the companies from setting up the defense. In drawing a distinction between the notice that a party dealing with a corporation is bound to take of the extent of its corporate power, and of the circumstances under which the power is exercised, the opinion says that parties may be required to take notice of the former, but to require them to take notice of the latter would frequently result in gross injustice.

It has been claimed that the obligation of a guarantor is to be strictly confined to the precise terms of his guaranty, and this principle has been asserted in a number of strong cases. But it should not be forgotten that the converse of this proposition has been held by equally good authority—to wit, that a guaranty is to be construed as strongly against a guarantor as its terms will admit. The case of Douglas *v.* Reynolds, 7 Peters 113, has been recognized as a leading case upon the point, and followed by as many as eight cases in the Supreme Court of the United States.

In Bank *v.* Savings Bank, 21 Wal. 294, there was a written guaranty against shipment of cattle to the extent of $10,000. It appeared upon the trial that the only cattle shipped were a lot of hogs, and the guarantor claimed strict privileges, and that the terms of the guaranty didn't apply to hogs. But the Court dismissed the defense, and said: "Like all other contracts it must receive the construction which is most proper and natural under the circumstances, so as to attain the object which the parties to it had in making it." And the same court in Davis *v.* Wells, 104 U. S. 159, uses significant language when it says that "the contract of guaranty is to be liberally construed to advance commercial intercourse."

Questions sometimes arise as to the nature of these guaranties. When the guaranty is attached to the bond and the bond makes reference to a mortgage which has peculiar provisions about foreclosure and limitations upon the maker's liability other than as owner of the property, the claim is set up that the guaranty is one of collectibility under the terms of the mortgage and not of payment. It may be fairly said that, if the word "payment" is used, a court will be reluctant to reduce the contract from the well-known and important commercial contract of guaranty of payment to the inferior and uncommercial contract of collectibility. Because the bonds and especially the coupons are protected by the law merchant, there is justifiable inclination on the part of courts to hold guarantors, in actions by *bona fide* holders for value, to the responsibilities of the ordinary guaranty of payment.

In the case of Security Co. *v.* Lombard Co., 73 Fed. Rep. 537, Judge Caldwell sustains the legal conclusion of the Master in Chancery, and fixes the obligation of a guaranty of payment as a direct and absolute thing upon default by the maker, but subordinates the right to enforce the guaranty to a period of two years after default, as specified in the guaranty.

There is a recent case (Louisville Co. *v.* Ohio Valley Co., 69 Fed. Rep. 431) in which a number of the questions considered in this article are passed upon. The negotiability of the guaranty is sustained in face of a statute which made assignable obligations subject to equities. The guaranty in this case was set aside because not authorized by the stockholders. The directors authorized the execution of the guaranty, and the stockholders promptly disavowed the action of the directors. The court held that there was no recital in the bond or other circumstance in the case which estopped the stockholders from setting up the invalidity of the guaranty. The statute provided for railroad guaranties of the bond of other roads, and that they should be made, at the instance of the stockholders, by the board of directors. It was claimed in the argument that other statutes gave the corporation, by implication, authority to make these guaranties. The court held that the principal statute was exclusive in its effect, and that no other methods could be pursued by the corporation. Many authorities are cited to that point. The case is distinguished from the Zabriskie case, 23 Howard, already alluded to. It also approves Justice Swayne's language in Merchants Bank *v.* State Bank, 10 Wal. 604, as to estoppel, but points out the fact that the question of *ultra vires* did not and could not arise in the case.

Henry C. Robinson.

THE LAW OF ICY SIDEWALKS IN NEW YORK STATE.

The tendency in modern times of the inhabitants of our country to congregate in our great cities has enormously increased the population of our different municipalities, and this, in conjunction with the severe and changeable winter weather in the State of New York, and the consequent slippery and snowy condition of our sidewalks during several months of each year, has given rise to almost numberless litigations against our cities for injuries caused by falling on ice-coated and snow-covered sidewalks, and the law bearing upon this subject from a state of uncertainty has become fixed and certain.

It has been the common belief among the laity, that any person falling on an icy or snowy sidewalk, irrespective of its condition as to repair, or how long the snow and ice have remained on the sidewalk, can recover from the city in whose limits is situated the sidewalk on which he has fallen. It has been very commonly believed that our cities are sort of accident insurance companies to protect everyone against injuries occasioned by such accidents. The decisions of our courts have, however, very properly held otherwise, and it is the purpose of this article to recite briefly the present condition of the law of the Empire State bearing on this interesting question; a question which may become of importance to some of my readers.

Primarily it is the duty of every municipality to keep its streets, which includes the sidewalks, in a safe condition, suitable for the public use, and the city must exercise active vigilance in seeing that its streets are thus kept in the proper condition.

One of the earliest cases in our Court of Appeals on this question is that of Todd *v.* the City of Troy, reported in 61 N. Y. at page 506. Judge Earl in his opinion says: "It was the duty of the city under its charter to keep the streets in repair and in suitable condition for public travel, and any person suffering damage or injury, without any fault on his part, from a neglect of this duty, has a cause of action against the city." However, before any municipality can be held liable it must be shown that it had notice of the bad condition of the walk. This notice may be either actual or constructive. By actual notice is meant that some officer of the city had received notice of the condition of the walk. Judge Earl in his opinion in the case above referred to, says: "By constructive notice is meant such notice as the law imputes from the circumstances of the case. * * * They [the municipal authorities] cannot fold their arms and shut their eyes, and say they have no notice. After a street has been out of repair so that the defect has become known and notorious to those traveling the street, and there has been every opportunity for the municipality, through its agents charged with that duty, to learn of its existence and repair it, the law imputes to it notice and charges it with negligence."

One case, however, has held that notice to a policeman is not necessarily notice to the city because he was not deemed a proper officer of the municipality to acquire such notice. Another case, however, that of Twogood v. the Mayor, etc., of New York, 102 N. Y. 216, holds that in an action for negligence in not causing an accumulation of ice to be removed from a sidewalk, the fact that a patrolman, who was on duty, had reported to the Inspector each day for several days prior to the injury complained of, that the snow and ice had not been removed from the sidewalk in question, and where it was the custom for these reports to be forwarded to police headquarters and from there to the office of the corporation counsel, was sufficient to charge the city with notice.

Although the city is required to use active diligence in keeping its sidewalks in proper repair so far as actual defects in their construction are concerned, it is incumbent upon it to exercise only what the law terms reasonable diligence to remove from its sidewalks ice which has formed during the existence of cold weather from natural causes.

In the case of Kaveney v. the City of Troy, reported in 108 N. Y., page 571, the Court said: The city is not bound to the exercise of unreasonable, persistent and extraordinary diligence during freezing weather to remove ice formed from natural causes; it is simply bound to keep sidewalks reasonably clean and safe."

In Corbett v. the City of Troy, 53 Hun. 228, the evidence shows that a city hydrant was so constructed that water escaped therefrom and ran across the street, freezing upon the sidewalk and forming a layer of ice. Some snow fell the day before the accident, completely covering the formation of ice. The plaintiff in this action could not see the ice because of the recent fall of snow. There was testimony tending to show that the ice had existed for some weeks prior to the accident, but this was disputed; but since the hydrant was shown to have been leaking, although the accumulation of ice may not have existed for a sufficient length of time to prove constructive notice to the city, the jury would have been justified in finding negligence on the part of the city in allowing the water to escape from the hydrant. The Court says in this case that it was not one where the ice was formed from what is known as natural causes, such as the freezing of rain or sleet, and the formation of the ice being the natural result of the escape of the water, the city might justly be found guilty of negligence.

The neglect of municipal duty must be very clear in order to hold the city liable for injuries caused by snow and ice.[1] A city is not liable in damages for any injuries which are the results of the slippery condition of a sidewalk produced solely by ice which is of recent formation.[2]

It is, however, liable to any one using the sidewalk for injuries occasioned by an accumulation of ice which has been of long duration, provided no recent change in the temperature has caused the formation of a new coating of ice over the old accumulation, and which may have been the direct cause of the injury. Something more must always exist than the slippery condition of the sidewalk to allow a person to recover from a municipality.

The practitioner in New York State is oftentimes taken by surprise in the trial of an action for damages resulting from a fall on a slippery sidewalk. He brings an action on the statement of his client, and perhaps after careful examination of other witnesses, by whom he is assured that the accumulation of ice and snow has been of long duration, but on the trial he is met by the testimony of the Chief of the Weather Bureau, who with his records is able to give proof which cannot be rebutted, that during the day on which the accident happened the temperature has risen and fallen to such an extent that an entirely new coating of ice must have been formed during the very day of the accident. In such a case the courts say that there are two causes contributing to the accident; one the accumulation of ice and snow, which has been of sufficient duration to charge the municipality with constructive, if not actual notice, and

---

[1] Pomfrey *v.* Saratoga Springs, 104 N. Y. page 459.
[2] Kinney *v.* the City of Troy, 108 N. Y. 567.

render the city liable for damages; the other, the recent coating of ice, for which the city is not liable, and in such a case the jury cannot be allowed to speculate as to which of the two conditions was the approximate cause of the injuries, and so the plaintiff should be non-suited.[8]

In the case above referred to, for two years prior to the accident there had been a bank of earth adjoining the sidewalk, and the rain and frost had forced upon the sidewalk sand, gravel and stone until the flagging was entirely covered, the deposit sloping about one inch to the foot from the outer edge of the walk to the curb. Snow and ice had also for a long time accumulated upon this slope. The night before the plaintiff fell there was a rainfall, the rain freezing as it fell, forming a new coating of ice, and rendering all of the streets in the city slippery and travel dangerous. It was held that in the absence of evidence showing that the slope of the walk, or the old snow and ice, was a concurrent cause without which the accident would not have happened, the plaintiff could not recover and that it was an error to submit the question to the jury to speculate upon, and that there was nothing in the case pointing to the slope as a concurrent cause, beyond the bare fact that it existed, and so nothing to redeem the inference from the domain of mere guess and speculation.

The court also held that the rule is well settled in New York "that the defect, even when a concurrent cause, must be such that without its operation the accident would not have happened"; that where there is any other cause for which no one is responsible, "the plaintiff must fail if his evidence does not show that the damage is produced by the former cause," and that "he must fail also, if it is just as probable that the injury came from one cause as the other, because he is bound to make out his case by a preponderance of evidence and the jury must not be left to a mere conjecture or to act upon bare possibility. In this case that rule is violated. The plaintiff slipped upon the ice. That by itself was a sufficient, certain and operating cause of the fall. No other explanation is needed to account for what happened. It is possible that the slope of the walk had something to do with it. It is equally possible that it did not. There is not a particle of proof that it did. To affirm it is a pure guess and an absolute speculation. Are we to send it to the jury for them to imagine how it might have happened? The great balance of probability is that the ice was the efficient cause. There

---

[8] Taylor v. the City of Yonkers, 105 N. Y., 202.

is no probability not wholly speculative that the slope was also such. * * * No knowledge or intelligence can determine or ascertain that the slope had any part or share in the injury, and to send the question to the jury is simply to let them guess at it, and then upon that guess to sustain a verdict for damages."

The court said in this same case that it was willing to hold cities and villages to a reasonable performance of their duty, but was not willing to make them insurers by founding their liability upon mere possibilities.

The question of contributory negligence frequently arises in this class of negligence cases. The fact, however, that an embankment of snow and ice is visible to the plaintiff and that he does not see fit to walk elsewhere than on the sidewalk, is not of itself such negligence on the part of the plaintiff that he could not recover.

In the case of Pomfrey v. the Village of Saratoga Springs, 104 N. Y. 459, the defendant requested the court to charge the jury, "That if the obstruction was visible and apparent to any passerby, the plaintiff was guilty of negligence in attempting to cross it," and also that "if the defect complained of was such as would be seen by any ordinary person passing along the street, it was negligence for the plaintiff to attempt to pass over the defect, but she should have gone around the same." This the court refused to do and the Court of Appeals held that it would not have been proper for the court to have charged as a matter of law that it was negligence for the plaintiff, in the circumstances, to endeavor to pass over the embankment, and a refusal to so charge was not error.

So it is not negligence for a person to walk upon an icy sidewalk without rubbers. As no one is bound to anticipate that the sidewalks are in a dangerous condition, those using them have the right to assume that they are in proper and safe condition, and also the right to use them in the usual manner.

It is noteworthy that the Pennsylvania courts hold a much stricter doctrine on this point, and deem it the duty of a person approaching a sidewalk which he sees to be icy, to go out into the street, or even around the block, to avoid it.

Loran L. Lewis, Jr.

SOME QUESTIONS RELATING TO THE MEASURE OF DAMAGES IN STREET OPENING PROCEEDINGS IN NEW YORK CITY.

The statutory proceedings for acquiring private property for street purposes in New York City have given rise to a number of interesting theories as to the proper method of ascertaining the damages.

The city never becomes the owner in fee simple absolute by proceedings to acquire land for streets. It acquires merely a limited fee for street purposes subject to the easements in the abutting owners.[1] The city's title is not corporate or municipal property, but is held by it in trust for the public use of all the people of the State, and is under the unqualified control of the Legislature.[2]

Section 956 of the Consolidation Act as amended by the laws of 1893 states that the city's title is "In trust, nevertheless, that the same be appropriated and kept open for and as part of a public street, avenue, square, park or place forever in like manner as the other public streets, avenues, squares and places in the said city are and of right ought to be."

The damages awarded for land taken and the costs of the proceeding are generally paid by assessments upon the property deemed to be benefited. These awards and assessments are determined by three commissioners appointed in the proceeding by the Supreme Court. The statute directs that "compensation and recompense" shall be made to the owners whose land is taken, and that the commissioners shall ascertain "the loss and damage" caused by the taking, and the "benefit and advantage" to the land remaining after the taking.[3]

It should be noticed that the statute in every case speaks of "compensation and recompense" for the "loss and damage" to the "owners."

Whenever these sections have been before the courts for construction it has been held in every instance that the measure of

---

[1] Story against the New York Elevated Railroad Company, 90 N. Y. 155-156.
[2] People v. Kerr, 27 N. Y. 188.
[3] Consolidation Act, §§ 963, 970, 978.

compensation to be awarded to the claimant is, where his interest in the whole of the parcel of land owned by him is taken, its market value; and where his interest in a part of his land is taken and his interest in a part is left, the difference between the market value of his interest in the whole parcel before the taking and the market value of his interest in the part remaining after the taking, disregarding, however, any benefit to the part remaining by reason of the proposed improvement.

Judge Dillon, in his work on Municipal Corporations, Section 624, discussing the rule as to the measure of damages in proceedings to take private property for public uses, referring to the property owner, says: "He is entitled to the fair and full market or pecuniary value of the property at the time it is appropriated and no more. This statement of the rule excludes from consideration all such elements as that the owner does not desire to sell, or that the property is endeared to him by association, and the like. * * * The amount to which the owner is entitled is not simply the value of the property at forced sale, but such sum as the property is worth in the market, if persons desiring to purchase were found who were willing to pay its just and full value, and no more."

In the Matter of the New York, West Shore and Buffalo Railway Company (35 Hun. 633) the court in opinion said:

"In the opinion of the Legislature full payment, *at the market value of the property taken*, answers the constitutional provision requiring a just compensation to be paid to the owner of property taken for the public use. The courts have uniformly concurred in such construction and uphold the validity of statutes limiting damages to the market value of the estate seized."

The rule as to the measure of damages is comparatively simple when the whole of a claimant's parcel of land is taken, and even where part only of his land is taken and part left the problem would not be such a difficult one if the commissioners were obliged to report only the excess of damage over benefit, or benefit over damage, as was once the practice in these proceedings; but in 1839 a statute was passed requiring "commissioners in all cases to report fully and separately to the court the amount of loss and damage and of benefit and advantage to each and every owner," etc.[4] This presents many difficulties. On the one hand commissioners must avoid paying for damages that are not suffered. On the other hand they must avoid offsetting any of the benefits of the improvement in making their estimate

[4] Cons. Act, sec. 975.

of damage, as there is to be an assessment for benefit, and the owner of property partly taken and partly left must not be obliged to pay twice for the improvement—once in having a part of the benefit offset against his damage, and, in addition to that, an assessment for the same benefit that has been already charged to him. There is involved a good deal of abstract reasoning. In practice the damage and benefit are coincident, and in many cases, as where a street is widened a few feet, to separate damage to the whole parcel and benefit to the part remaining involves supposing what has never existed in fact.

Real estate experts through being asked on cross-examination their reasons for their opinions are accustomed to apply rules more or less inflexible, and express their opinions of the amount of damage in given cases to the fractional part of a cent. But while it may be necessary that they should adopt certain rules to govern their estimates in most of the cases, only to be modified where some unusual element caused by the peculiar shape or situation of the property or the uses to which it may be applied should be taken into account, the bare fact that they can thus appear to be consistent in their answers is not enough to justify their rules, unless the rules themselves can be shown to be fairly deduced from observed facts.

Owing to the fact that the courts do not set aside the reports of commissioners on account of the introduction of immaterial, irrelevant or incompetent evidence, there is a paucity of judicial decisions which indicate the correct rules to follow.

Perhaps one of the most far-reaching and important errors into which commissions have been led is that involved in adopting the so-called Hoffman rule,[5] and it is very necessary for a clear idea of the assessment of damages in street-opening proceedings that this rule and the principle upon which it is based should be clearly understood. The general principle upon which it is based is that the value of all land is to be estimated with reference to some strip of land upon which it is to be deemed as having a front, and that land near the front is more valuable than land in the same parcel lying further from the front if it is to be valued with reference to the same frontage. It was formulated for the purpose of adjusting the interests of two owners, one owning the front and one the rear of a standard city lot, 25 by 100 feet, their ownership being in fee simple absolute, upon uniting the two parts in one ownership.

---

[5] The Hoffman rule is explained by Murray Hoffman in his work on the laws relating to the City and County of New York, Vol. 2, p. 844.

Thus, it appears that if we take the value of the whole parcel of 25 by 100 feet as $1,000, then that portion of the lot within 10 feet of the street line, being 25 feet front by 10 feet deep, is worth 160, or 16 per cent of the whole; that portion of the lot within 25 feet of the street line, being 25 feet front by 25 feet deep, is worth $375, or 37½ per cent of the whole; the half of the lot nearest the street, being 25 feet front by 50 feet deep, is worth $670, or 67 per cent of the whole; that portion of the lot lying more than 75 feet from the street line, being the rear, 25 by 25 feet, is worth $125, or 12½ per cent of the whole, and that portion of the lot lying more than 90 feet from the street line, being 25 by 10 deep is worth but $40, or 4 per cent of the whole.

The attempt has persistently been made by claimants to awards in proceedings to widen streets to show that the Hoffman rule was applicable in their cases, and that they were entitled to front values, calculated according to the Hoffman rule, where the fronts of their lots were taken; for instance, if a street was to be widened 10 feet, a lot originally 25 by 100 feet on the old street, which would be reduced to a lot 25 by 90 feet on the new street, was to be deemed as damaged 16 per cent of the value of the whole lot by reason of the taking of this strip of 10 feet from the front.

They contend that the general rule of the measure of damage, as so often laid down by the courts, namely, the difference between the value of the whole before the taking and the value of the part remaining after the taking, disregarding the benefit caused by the improvement, is only to be called in for the purpose of estimating those damages over and above the value, spoken of as consequential damages, and that the owner of land taken for a public improvement is entitled first and always to the full value of the land taken, disregarding entirely its connection with any other land and the purpose for which it is taken, and that his land not taken is to be assessed for benefit, and, he having been paid his damages on the theory that the part of his lot remaining has been deprived of its old front, the part remaining can be assessed in accordance with the same theory the amount which its owner should pay in view of its receiving a new front.

The answer to this contention is, in the first place, that even though the rule may be a proper one to use for the purpose for which it was originally framed, that purpose was to adjust the interests of two owners in fee simple absolute in the case where the owner of the front land stood between the owner of the rear land and any means of access to his lot, and the two parts are to be united into one ownership, and that this is not the condition of affairs upon the taking of a front strip for street purposes, because the city does not take the fee simple absolute, shutting off the original owner of the whole parcel from any front at all on the new proposed street, but takes in the land a qualified fee in trust to maintain the same as a public street, subject to the easements of right of way, light and air in favor of the owner of the abutting property and of the whole public, and that at no time is that portion of the lot remaining, after the taking of such strip for the purposes of a street, deprived of a front, and that, consequently, damages should not be assessed on the theory that such lot has been deprived of a front.

Furthermore, it must be always remembered that when part of a parcel of land is taken, the question before the commissioners is not the value of the land, but the market value of the owner's interest in the land, and the damage caused to that interest by reducing the size of his plot.

The statute does not say he is entitled to the value of his land taken, considering it as separated entirely from the part remaining; in other words, what it would be worth if the title to it were vested in a separate owner and unconnected with the part remaining. The statute says he is to receive compensation and recompense for the damages which his property rights suffer.

In former times the public did not take even a qualified fee, but only an easement, for the street purposes, and this is still the case in the country, and, I believe, in many of the cities of New York State. The public in such case is called upon to pay to the persons who are deprived of their rights in the property only damages; it does not pay for the property; it gives compensation and recompense for the damages caused by the taking of the rights in the property which it must take for the public purpose.

But we have a direct and controlling judicial decision upon the application of the Hoffman rule in such a way as has been above described, namely, in the Matter of Opening College Place, decided by Judge Beach at the Special Term of the Supreme Court in April, 1894. This was a most important proceeding, involving more than $1,500,000 in awards.

College place was widened on its west side 25 feet; the east side of the old street was not disturbed. The commissioners presented their report to the court, in the first instance having made up their awards and assessments in accordance with the

Hoffman rule, as above described. As they gave awards on the theory that they took front property, and that the parcels remaining were deprived of a frontage, they laid their assessments on the same theory and assumed that the parcels remaining gained by the improvement a new frontage on a wider and extended thoroughfare, which caused the assessments on the west side, where the parcels were deemed to get the benefit of an entirely new front, to be much greater than the assessments on the east side, where the benefit was only the widened street. Judge Lawrence, before whom the report was presented for confirmation, declined to confirm it, on the ground that an erroneous principle must have been adopted by the commissioners which would lead to their making such a difference between the assessments imposed on the property on the east side and the property situated on the west side of College place.

The report then went back to the commissioners for correction, and they continued to apply the Hoffman rule, but in the opposite way; instead of considering the parcels remaining to be deprived of a frontage by reason of the taking of the front part of the lots for the widened street, they considered that the parts remaining still retained their frontage, and that the measure of damage was the difference between the value of the College place lot before the improvement and the value of a lot on College place of the size of the parcel left after the improvement, making the comparison between lots fronting on the same thoroughfare in order to avoid taking into consideration the benefit from the new widened thoroughfare. Thus the owner of a 100-foot lot, 25 feet of which was taken, instead of getting $37\frac{1}{2}$ per cent of the whole value of his 100-foot lot as damages, on the theory that he was deprived of a front, received but $12\frac{1}{2}$ per cent of the value of his original 100-foot lot, on the theory that he was not deprived of a front, and his parcels remaining, instead of being assessed more than the lot across the street, on the theory that it was given a new front, was assessed the same amount as the lot across the street, on the theory that the benefit of the improvement was the same in both cases; namely, such benefit as comes from a widened street in place of a narrow street.

When the report thus corrected was again presented to the court for confirmation, it was duly confirmed. Judge Beach, in his opinion, after stating that the assessments on the east and west sides of the street had been equalized to conform with the suggestions contained in the opinion of the court, said: "In changing the principle of assessment after the first report was returned for revision they necessarily changed the awards. * * * The present report seems founded upon the principle that the damage to any lot is the difference in value between it as it now is and the value of what remains after the improvement, exclusive of any increase in value therefrom, and the benefit is the enhanced value of the decreased lot, because of its fronting upon a street of increased width with an outlet instead of upon a narrow street without an outlet. I think this rule is correct."

Although a large amount of money was involved in this proceeding no appeal was taken from the decision of the court as thus expressed.

The same question presented in the College place widening case was presented to the General Term in the Matter of Widening Riverside Avenue,[6] and decided the same way.

It will be noticed that the net results in the two reports in the College place proceeding are practically the same. To most of the owners it made no difference which theory was adopted. The reduced assessment in the second report was offset by an equally reduced award. But in many cases where streets situated in the upper portion of the city are opened through large unimproved tracts, it makes a very great difference. Commissioners are not permitted to assess property for benefit more than one-half its value as found by the Tax Commissioners for purposes of taxation;[7] and in the case of unimproved property the Tax Commissioners place the so-called tax value usually at about 25 but sometimes as low as 10 per cent of its actual value. Consequently, it is often a difficult task to lay an assessment for benefit where the awards are made on a vastly different valuation of property from that which limits the amount of the assessment, without enlarging the area of assessment to the point of doing gross injustice, and hence the theory which gives the lowest award is very much in the interest of those who pay the costs.

That the claimant is to be paid for only the damage which is suffered is shown in another line of cases, where the claimant's rights in the property are encumbered or restricted.

It is frequently the case that the rights of the owner of the fee in a piece of property which, if unencumbered, would be worth a large sum of money, are of hardly more than nominal value because of some encumbrance or restriction. As Judge

---

[6] 64 State Rep. 366.
[7] Cons. Act, Sec. 975.

Magruder said in an Illinois case[8] "where the owner of land is restricted by the statute or by the provisions of the instrument under which he holds his title, or in any other binding way, to a particular use of it so that he cannot lawfully apply it to any other use, the measure of his compensation, where the land is taken by condemnation, will be its value to him for the special use to which he is so restricted. Thus, *In re* Albany Street in New York City, 11 Wendell, page 149, the ground taken for a street was a cemetery, and it appeared that it could not be used for any other purpose by the corporation of Trinity Church than for burying the dead. It was there held that it was the damage sustained by the church which the commissioners were to ascertain, and that the true rule of determining such damage was to appraise the property at its then present value to the owner, considering the extent of his interest and the qualified rights which might be exercised over it. To the same effect is Stebbins *v.* Metropolitan Board of Works, 6 Q. B., page 37, where a part of a graveyard was condemned for a street and where the owner held it subject to a restriction 'which it was not practically possible for him to remove.'" And a nominal award in this last case was upheld, although the land taken became of immense value as soon as title was vested in the public relieved of the restriction.[9]

It is frequently the case that a piece of land taken for street purposes is encumbered by easements of right-of-way created by private contract. The Court of Appeals has held[10] that the owner of the naked fee of a strip of land encumbered by easements which permit the abutting owners to use the strip for street purposes, where such owner of the fee is not an abutting owner, is entitled to only a nominal award for his interest in such strip of land. But in another leading case[11] where a municipality sought to condemn the fee in the bed of an existing street owned by the abutting owners it was held that the ownership of the fee of the land in a street by an abutting owner vests him with the right to defend against and enjoin a user for an encroachment upon the street by any legislative or municipal authority for purposes inconsistent with those uses to which streets should be or have ordinarily been subjected, unless provision for just compensation is made; and that where this fee is taken by legislative

---

[8] 119 Illinois, page 529 (Railroad Company *v.* Catholic Bishop).
[9] See also B. R. & M. R. R. Co. *v.* Barnard, 9 Hun. 104.
[10] Matter of Adams, 141 N. Y. page 297.
[11] City of Buffalo *v.* Pratt, 131 N. Y. 293.

authority, the owner is entitled not merely to nominal damages, but to such substantial damages as may be ascertained by measuring the effect upon the value of his remaining property of the loss of the fee of the street. It is to be noted that the measure of damage in this case is the depreciation in value of the abutting property which is not taken by reason of the taking of the fee in an existing street, and that the damage is not at all to be measured by what might be the value of the land in this street, if it were not a street, but freed from street easements.

Again in the Matter of One Hundred and Sixteenth Street [12] the court unanimously concurred in Judge Ingraham's opinion, which states that the commissioners cannot properly award damages to an owner of an easement of right-of-way and use for street purposes over a strip of land taken for a street, the reason being that his easement is not taken and destroyed, and that he therefore is not damaged. Judge Ingraham, in his opinion, said:

"The New York Hospital was the owner of the fee of the land taken, and was entitled to be paid its value in this proceeding. * * * It is the property owned by the New York Hospital that is to be valued, and if such property is subject to any easement either in favor of the public or of an individual the award should be for the value of the property subject to such easement, as such easement is not in this proceeding taken or appropriated."

The principle upon which all these cases seem to rest is that the owner is entitled to compensation only for the market value of his holding in its encumbered or restricted condition, and where nothing of value is taken or destroyed, no damages are recoverable.

Experts seem to differ in their opinions as to the value of similarly situated lots of different depths. When they were accustomed to apply the Hoffman rule they were obliged, in order to be consistent, to express the opinion that a lot 25 feet front and 100 feet deep was worth less per square foot than a lot similarly situated 25 feet front and only 75 feet deep, and that a lot 125 feet in depth was worth still less per square foot, and that, generally speaking, the deeper a lot was the less valuable was it per square foot, and that the shallower it was the greater value did it have per square foot.

Notwithstanding the general agreement of experts on this rule I was led to investigate the matter as a fact. I considered

---
[12] 1 App. Div. Rep. 436.

that auction sales of lots lying next to each other, where the rear line of the tract was not parallel to the front line, and where, in consequence, the lots were of different depths, made on the same day, under the same conditions, to different vendees, would furnish a fair criterion. In every case that I investigated I found that where the difference in the depths of the parcels varied from 40 to 125 feet, the parcels sold for very nearly the same price per square foot whether they were shallow parcels or deep parcels, the variation in the price per square foot being only the usual variation observed at every auction sale where lots similarly situated and lying next to each other are sold to different vendees; and that no rule could be deduced from these sales showing that shallow lots were more valuable per square foot than deep lots. Of course the location and the uses to which the property could most profitably be put would have a great deal to do with the depth which a parcel might have without a proportional decrease in its value per square foot.

Some experts who formerly testified according to the Hoffman rule, and persisted in asserting that a lot 25 feet front and 25 feet in depth was worth more per square foot than a lot 50, 75 or 100 feet in depth, of the same frontage, now that they have stopped using that rule, maintain that a lot less than 75 feet in depth on a residence street is of less value per square foot than a lot of the same frontage and between 75 and 125 feet in depth. Others maintain that until a lot has been reduced to a depth less than 50 feet, it does not by reason of its reduced size become of less proportional value. Others again hold that a lot 125 feet in depth does not get a proportional increase in value over what it would be worth if it were only 100 feet in depth.

These are questions which must be taken up and considered in each particular case.

Where there are improvements on the land it is a favorite contention that the measure of damages is the market value of the owner's title to the bare land without improvements, plus the *cost* of the improvements, less the depreciation in the value of the improvements by reason of deterioration. There is no authority for proving damages in this way except that this method has often been pursued by commissions. Of course, under some circumstances, this method does not lead to a different result than would be arrived at if the strictly legal method of presenting proof were pursued. For instance, if the improvements on a lot, the whole of which is taken, add to the market value of the real estate the full cost of the improvements, the market value of the entire real estate would be the value of the owner's interest in the land unimproved, plus the cost of the improvements. But in very many cases the market value of the real estate is much less than the value of the property if vacant, plus the cost of the buildings and other improvements, less deterioration by reason of wear and tear and the elements. Particularly is this frequently the case in the upper part of the city where pieces of land have erections on them that were put up for an entirely different use than that for which a reasonable man would use the property at the present time. For instance, near Casanova Station on Hunt's Point, the so-called Whitlock Mansion was, before the war, erected at an expense of $300,000, but this same mansion, with ninety acres of land, was sold for something like $80,000 only a few years ago. Then there may have occurred after the erection of the improvements some change in the surroundings which seriously affects their value. For instance, the grade of One Hundred and Forty-ninth street, near the Harlem Railroad tracks, was changed, and the owners of the buildings fronting on the street recovered thousands of dollars as damages from the city; but when One Hundred and Forty-ninth street was subsequently widened the builders called to testify as to the value or cost of reproduction of these same buildings, for which damages on account of the change of grade had already been awarded, made no allowance for such damages but gave the cost of reproduction as the value of these buildings, regardless of the injury done them by the change of grade. Of course, less conspicuous examples of the truth of the general proposition that the cost of its construction, or the cost of reproducing a building, has nothing to do with its market value, will readily occur to every one.

An important reason why testimony should not be offered in this way is that it does not give counsel an opportunity to cross-examine witnesses. The real estate expert is called to testify to the value of the land alone, and can be cross-examined upon that. The builder is called to testify as to the cost of reproducing the improvements, or, as it is sometimes expressed, the value of the improvements separate from the land. The builder can only be cross-examined as to the quantity of material he thinks is necessary for the construction of such a building and the price of the materials and labor involved. He knows nothing of the value of the building as it exists on a definite parcel of land and taken in connection with it, and is not offered as a real estate expert. There has, therefore, been no testimony offered as to the market value of the whole property as it stands before condemnation. It is only by an inference, and that, too, an inference that is not a proper one to draw, that the commissioners can deduce from the testimony offered the amount to which the owner is entitled as his damages, and counsel is not afforded any opportunity to cross-examine witnesses on the real question which it is competent for the commissioners to investigate. This is a very serious matter, particularly so where the commissioners are laymen and not familiar with the legal measure of damages.

The attempt, therefore, to prove the value of improved property in this way is as improper as it is unwarranted by any authority. To pursue this method is to treat the building as personalty, as separated from and not as part of the land, for obviously the builder is testifying to what would be the value of the building placed on the most advantageous site for a building of its kind and character. It is not proper to consider the building as separated from the land. The statutes authorizing street opening proceedings contemplate the taking of real estate only, and the city cannot condemn personal property.[13] The investigation must be confined strictly to the value of the real estate, the owner's estate in the land including the improvements.

Of course a builder's testimony may be proper if a proper foundation is laid for it. If, for instance, a real estate expert states on cross-examination that he based his opinion on what a builder had told him as to the cost of reproducing the building, it might be deemed proper to offer a builder's testimony to show that the witness was wrongly informed.

In a railroad case [14] the court says: "The cost of structures put upon the land was not competent, and such evidence was properly rejected. The value of the land and structures thereon was alone to be determined; the cost is not a rule of damages."

In the Matter of Opening One Hundred and Thirty-ninth street, on the motion to confirm the report, O'Brien, J., said: "Objections are made to the confirmation of the report of the Commissioners, as follows:

"*First*—That the Commissioners failed to make any award for the fruit trees of Mrs. Riddock.

"The trees are a part of the freehold and should be valued as such. There was no error on the part of the Commissioners in failing to make a specific award for the trees."

---

[13] In the Matter of N. Y. C. & H. R. R.R. Co., 36 Hun. 306.
[14] Matter of the N. Y., W. S. & B. Ry. Co., 37 Hun. 318.

In Evans v. Keystone Gas Company[15] Gray, J., in his opinion, said: "This action was brought to recover damages of the defendant for the injury caused to shade trees belonging to the plaintiff, by the escape of natural gas from a main or pipe laid along the street bounding his premises. * * * The witness was asked to state the value of the trees in question. * * * The argument now is that the evidence was incompetent on the question of the damage. That is true, and the rule in such a case as this is the difference between the value of the land before and after the injury."

In a recently reported case[16] a railroad proposed to cut through a farm, leaving 46 acres on one side of its tracks and 167 acres on the other side. One of the witnesses said on re-direct examination, that he made up the $9,000 of depreciation to which he had testified as follows: "I have several items: First, the loss in the quantity of production I put at sixty dollars; on account of the drainage, etc., I think sixty dollars per year. I put twelve hundred dollars on interest at five per cent to produce that amount. The driving and crossing with stock I put at fifty cents per day, amounting to one hundred and eighty-two dollars and fifty cents for one year; for all time, three thousand six hundred and fifty dollars. I find another element, the crossing and re-crossing with teams to work the land on the south side. Third—I put the last item at one thousand three hundred and sixty dollars. Fourth—From fire there is some damage; I put that at sixty-two dollars per year, and for all time, twelve hundred and forty dollars."

In this case the award was reversed on the ground that "the opinion of the witness should have been limited to the market value of the farm after the completion of the road, taking into consideration all the incidental injuries to the remaining lands, if any."

It is often attempted to prove damages in street openings in the same way.

Another way of applying the same theory is to divide a parcel of land into lots and to claim damages for each individual lot, the result being to largely increase the apparent damages.

The correctness of this method is very frequently seriously argued. But as Judge Learned in a railroad condemnation case said:[17] "It is very plain that to make a map of a tract of land

---

[15] 148 N. Y. 112.
[16] Matter of N. Y., W. S. & B. Ry. Co., 29 Hun. 609.
[17] Matter of N. Y., L. & W. R. R. Co., 27 Hun. 151.

and lay out streets thereon does not add in the least to its value, any more than it would to mark out churches and school-houses on the lots themselves."

It is often suggested to commissioners by claimants that because the owner of the fee has carved out of it a leasehold estate, the sum of the damages to the tenant and the landlord amounts to more than the full value of the property. The authorities, however, are clear that full payment at the market value answers the constitutional provision regarding a just compensation to be paid to the owners, and that, when payment has been made for all that the property is worth, nothing more can be demanded. The value of the leasehold is to be carved out of the full award for the damage to which the owner in fee would be entitled if he had not parted with an interest in the property.[18]

The above are only a few of the many ways in which it has been sought to apply a general rule of damage, which sounds plain enough when stated, but still gives opportunity for much ingenious theorizing. Some of them, like the application of the Hoffman rule, have been successfully urged upon commissioners and have gone unchallenged for years. Others are coming up now for the first time. In most of the cases the foundation for the inequitable claim is some statute. Concerning street openings in New York City it is particularly true, what is, in general, true of all branches of the law, that legislation is enacted with too little intelligent consideration and with too great facility. Each year's flood of new statutes creates new uncertainties and renders more difficult the task of him who seeks to know the law.

Henry deForest Baldwin.

---

[18] In the Matter of the N. Y., W. S. & Buffalo R. R., 35 Hun. 633; Matter of Newton, 45 State Reporter 18; Matter of Dept. of Pub. Parks, 53 Hun. 280-298.

YALE LAW JOURNAL

SUBSCRIPTION PRICE, $2.00 A YEAR SINGLE COPIES, 35 CENTS

EDITORS:

ROGER S. BALDWIN, *Chairman.*
HUGH T. HALBERT, *Treasurer.*

CHRISTOPHER L. AVERY, JR.   GEO. JAY GIBSON,
SAMUEL F. BEARDSLEY.   JOHN MACGREGOR, JR.
MICHAEL GAVIN, 2D.   HENRY W. MERWIN.

Published six times a year, by students of the Yale Law School
P. O. Address, Box 1341, New Haven, Conn.

If a subscriber wishes his copy of the JOURNAL discontinued at the expiration of his subscription, notice to that effect should be sent; otherwise it is assumed that a continuance of the subscription is desired.

THE case of United States *v.* The Trans-Missouri Freight Association, lately decided by the United States Supreme Court, is peculiarly interesting as emphasizing the importance of certainty of expression in the statute law, and as defining the relative duties of our courts and legislatures. The heart of the dispute seems to be the interests of the public, and involved in those interests we find freedom of individual trade and freedom of individual contract. Both should be preserved, and yet each seems to be in apparent conflict with the other. In one sense at least contracts of trade are contracts in restraint of trade and the difficulty lies in determining where the line shall be drawn. At early common law the question was debated, how far individuals might contract their freedom of trade away; now the debate has developed into one concerning the power of corporations to restrict the free exercise of their right to contract. The change in the complexion of the question denotes merely a change of society and social development. It was once asked what interest a tradesman in London could have in what another might do in Newcastle. The answer was given by a later period of society, when commerce and trade were more highly organized and developed. It is now asked what concern it may be of the public whether its business is conducted by a few large corporations or by many unorganized individuals.

The common law has been developed until now all contracts in unreasonable restraint of trade are held to be void and this has been accepted as the true doctrine both in England and in this country. But the Act of Congress, passed in 1890, and commonly known as the Anti-Trust Law, has in terms changed the common law rule and has prohibited all contracts in restraint of trade, whether those contracts be reasonable or unreasonable or whether the restraint be great or slight. The construction of this law by the courts became necessary and the intention of those who passed it became relevant. It was found, however, that the intention was expressed in legal terms and while by some it was claimed that these terms should be given their legal significance, by others a doubt was entertained whether the legal significance was generally understood, and even if understood and intended by the Judiciary Committee, whether the intention of that committee might be taken as the intention of the House and Senate collectively. On the one hand it is said that law makers must be presumed to have intended to make a law which would be reasonable and would have reasonable results, and the dissenting opinion in the case above cited, after tracing the history of the meaning of the words, "restraint of trade," concludes that technically and legally they are now equivalent to the words, "unreasonable restraint of trade." On the other hand it is contended that the duty of a court is not to make laws or even to amend them, and if the use of reasonable means of interpretation does not render the spirit of the law certain, that then its letter should be followed. In the one case the consideration of results predominates, in the other the consideration of the means to be employed. Indeed if you adopt the principle that words which have a technical as well as a popular meaning should be construed to have that meaning which under the circumstances it can be presumed that they were intended to have, you are even then brought face to face with the circumstances surrounding the passage of the law, and the evident uncertainty of the legislative mind, equalled only by the uncertainty of its expression, renders certainty impossible.

The difference seems apparently to be one of legal technicality, and to be open to different views. The proximate cause of the difficulty, however, should not be attributed to an abstruseness of legal science or to an exaggerated acuteness of the legal profession. The real cause presents an uncertain intention quite as much as an uncertain expression and the responsibility for this uncertainty rests with the legislative and not with the judicial department of our government. The duty of law making is entrusted to Congress; the duty of law interpreting is left to the Supreme Court. But a law must exist before it may be interpreted and there must be an intention before one may be found. The tendency on the part of legislatures to throw upon our courts the duty of legislation as well as interpretation is singularly illustrated in this Anti-Trust Law. Disagreeing among themselves our Representatives seem to have depended upon the Supreme Court not only to refrain from reading the rule of reason out of the statute but in effect to read into it a rule of reason which was not there before. Instead of clearing up the doubt as to their intention the Legislature cast this imperfect foundling upon the country and expected the Supreme Court to father and bring it up in the way that it should go. That court, however, was established for no such purpose, and should cease to be regarded as the unwilling guardian of laws which are disowned by those who are responsible for their creation. It may be true that our Judiciary is better fitted than our more immediate Representatives to legislate for the best interests of the country, but to admit this is to admit the failure of the Republican form of Government.

* * *

THE thought occurs, however, that the embarrassment from which we seem now to be suffering may not wholly be due to uncertainty of intention or even of expression but to the uncertainty inherent in the subject itself. The difference of opinion found in our Supreme Court is not confined to that body or to the Legislature. The whole country, if not the world, shares in their disagreement, and the question seems to be one which no statute of Congress or no decree of court may finally determine. The position of corporations and trusts in the society of to-day is as strongly advocated by some as denounced by others and the variation of opinion seems sometimes at least to be partly due to the varied character of conditions. The cause of the difficulty seems to be economic development and the settlement should be brought about by economic forces. Questions of similar importance have come up before, have met with similar treatment and their determination by the Supreme Court has been received with equal dissatisfaction by a large portion of the public. The Dred Scott decision might be cited for one and the more recent Income Tax decision for another. No question of economics was definitely settled by either of those decisions, nor was their indefiniteness due to the disagreement of the court or to the closeness of the vote which determined them. The questions to be decided were not those to which legal principles might conclusively be applied, for the questions themselves were economic and involved principles of a higher order. The question lately submitted to the Supreme Court may be of a similar character and require submission to the jury of economic development before a definite and final result may be obtained.

* * *

THERE seems to be a growing tendency on the part of lawmakers throughout the country to legislate unfavorably to combinations of capital of every kind. This tendency has been especially noticeable in the West, as would naturally be expected from the local growth of populistic ideas, but it is by no means confined to that locality, and a striking instance of such legislation has recently occurred in Connecticut. The fire insurance companies of the State have been greatly concerned over the passage, by the lower House of the Legislature, of a bill prohibiting combinations of fire-insurance companies to establish rates. Two things are worthy of remark in connection with this measure, (1) that it is the first attempt at legislation against combinations of the kind in the history of the State, which has been prominent in the insurance business for so many years, and (2) that the bill was passed over the unanimously unfavorable report of the Insurance Committee. At the time of going to press the Senate had not considered the measure, but there was said to be a strong sentiment in that body favorable to its becoming a law.

Those who speak with authority on the subject of insurance are strong in the opinion that the effect of the bill would be to disorganize the insurance business, and that it would not only close out the smaller companies but would seriously injure the larger ones by subjecting them to disastrous competition by outside companies not affected by the law. Attention is called to the fact that the interests of the insurance companies are those of the insured and that whatever interferes with the prosperity of the companies lessens the value of the protection that they offer. There is apparently no complaint of unreasonable rates; they are said to be lower than those of almost any other State, and lower than a year ago; and it would seem to be unwise for Connecticut to discourage those who have developed the insurance business of the State into a science and whose experience enables them to conduct it for the best interests of all concerned. Whatever the final outcome, the success of the bill in the House of Representatives is a forcible example of what European writers have remarked as so characteristic of America and of American legislation in particular—the tendency to go to extremes, and at times, regardless of consequences, to carry matters beyond their logical conclusion. There is now much complaint against the great corporations and against combinations of wealth generally; therefore the idea of the lawmakers seems to be to legislate against them all, without distinction in favor of those with whose welfare that of the public is so closely connected.

COMMENT.

The United States Supreme Court, in its decision of March 22d, in the case of *U. S.* v. *Trans-Missouri Freight Ass'n*, declares that combinations of railways formed for the purpose of maintaining rates are illegal under the Sherman Anti-Trust Act of 1890, and in contravention of the Interstate Commerce Act of 1887. This decision, involving as it does such great questions both of economics and of law, ranks in the opinion of the press "scarcely second in its wide-reaching importance to any other decision of the Supreme Court." The case arose in 1892, when the United States District-Attorney of Kansas brought suit to dissolve the Trans-Missouri Freight Association as a conspiracy in restraint of trade under the Sherman Act. The defendant association was composed of eighteen competing railway companies which entered into a contract by which they agreed "not to compete, to charge non-competitive rates on all competing roads between the same termini, and to divide upon a certain ratio all freights shipped by these routes not especially designated by the shipper to one road in preference to the others." Although the association in its original form was dissolved during the progress of litigation, the agreement on rates was maintained by the roads and upheld by the Circuit Courts (53 Fed. Rep. 440; 19 U. S. App. 36). The Supreme Court reversing the judgments of the lower courts, decides, by the narrowest majority, that such agreements are an unlawful restraint of trade, and an attempt to monopolize interstate commerce.

The majority opinion of Mr. Justice Peckham regards as the two important questions demanding consideration, (1) whether the Sherman Act applies to common carriers by railroad, and (2) if so, whether the traffic agreement violated any provision of the Act. As to the first question the court says, "The language of the Act includes every contract, combination in the form of trust or otherwise, or conspiracy in restraint of trade or commerce, among the several States, or with foreign nations. Unless it can be said that an agreement, no matter what its terms, relating only to transportation, cannot restrain trade, we see no escape from the conclusion that the agreement is condemned by this act. It cannot be denied that those who are engaged in the transportation of persons or property from one State to another are engaged in interstate commerce, and it would seem to follow that if such persons enter into agreements between themselves in regard to the compensation to be secured from the owners of articles transmitted, such agreement would at least relate to the business of commerce, and might more or less restrain it." The court also holds that the Interstate Commerce Act does not authorize an agreement of this nature. In discussing the second question as to the true construction of the statute, Mr. Justice Peckham denies the position of the defendant association that the common-law meaning of the phrase "contract in restraint of trade" includes only such contracts as are in unreasonable restraint of trade. He calls attention to the difficulty of judging as to what is a "reasonable rate" for transportation, and contends that to say that the Act does not cover agreements which are not in unreasonable restraint of trade and which tend simply to keep up reasonable rates, is substantially to leave the question of reasonableness to the companies themselves. In reply to defendant's argument that the prohibition of agreements as to rates results in rate-cutting and prejudices public interest, the court says, "It is a matter of common knowledge that agreements as to rates have been continually made of late years, and that complaints of each company in regard to the violation of such agreements by its rivals have been frequent and persistent. * * * Competition will itself bring charges down to what may be reasonable, while in the case of an agreement to keep prices up, competition is allowed no play; it is shut out, and the rate is practically fixed by the companies themselves by virtue of the agreement, so long as they abide by it."

Toward the close of the majority opinion Mr. Justice Peckham distinguishes the English case of the *Mogul Steamship Co. v. MacGregor* (1892) App. Cas. 25, emphasized by the defendant and the courts below, by the fact that that case was governed by the common law, while the case at bar involves the interpretation of a statute. Thus the court's decision is made on the ground that it must construe the law according to the language used and not read into a statute what it may take to be the intention of Congress.

The strong dissenting opinion of Mr. Justice White holds that the traffic agreement was only such as looked to the uniform classification of freight, by which secret under-cutting was avoided and rates secured against arbitrary and sudden changes. His main argument was that to define the words "in restraint of trade" as embracing every contract which in any degree produced that effect would be violative of reason, because it would include those contracts which are the very essence of trade and every contract or combination by which workingmen seek to peaceably better their condition.

In reversing the greater part of the decision of Judge Locke of the Southern District of Florida (78 Fed. 175), the Supreme Court, in the case of the steamer *Three Friends* (17 Sup. Ct. 495), has rendered a decision decidedly favorable to Spain, especially considering the treatment some Americans have recently undergone at the hands of Spanish subjects. The steamer was seized by the Collector of Customs of St. Johns, Florida, on the charge that she was a filibustering steamer which had violated the neutrality laws in assisting the Cuban insurrectionists against Spain. The main question turned upon the interpretation of Rev. St. §5283, forbidding the fitting out and arming of a vessel with intent that she be employed in the service of any Prince or State, "or of any colony, district or people"—as to whether these latter words included any insurgent body of people acting together in conducting hostilities, although their belligerency had not been recognized.

Chief-Justice Fuller, delivering the opinion of the court, stated that it was true that in *Wiborg* v. *U. S.*, 16 Sup. Ct. 1127, 1197, the court had referred to Sec. 5283 as dealing "with fitting out and arming vessels in this country in favor of one foreign power as against another foreign power with which we are at peace"; but that was matter of general description only. The bill is headed "Neutrality," which the Chief-Justice defines as "abstinence from any participation in a public, private or civil war, and in impartiality of conduct toward both parties; but the maintenance unbroken of peaceful relations between two powers when the domestic peace of one of them is disturbed is not neutrality, when the disturbance has acquired such a head as to have demanded the recognition of belligerency." As Attorney-General Hoar pointed out (13 Op. Attys. Gen. U. S. 178), the Act was not alone intended to secure neutral action, but also to punish offenses against the United States. The crucial words, "colony, district, or people," were said to have been inserted in the original Act drawn by Hamilton in 1793, on the suggestion by the Spanish Minister in 1817 that the word "state" might not include the South American Provinces in revolt, and not yet recognized as independent. The reasonable conclusion is, that the inserted words were intended to include communities whose belligerency had not been recognized, and Chief-Justice Marshall in *The Gran Para*, 7 Wheat. 471, 489, seems to have been of this opinion. While the word "people" may mean the entire body of the inhabitants of a state, its meaning in this branch of the section, taken in connection with the words "colony" and "district" covers any insurgent body of people acting in concert, although its belligerency has not been recognized. It belongs to the political department to determine when belligerency shall be recognized, but the present case sharply illustrates the distinction between recognition of belligerency and recognition of political revolt; for here the political department has not recognized the existence of a *de facto* belligerent power, but has, by many proclamations and messages, judicially informed the court of the existence of an actual conflict of arms in resistance of a government with which the United States is on terms of peace and amity.

Justice Harlan, dissenting, considered that a very strained construction had been put upon the statute—one not justified by its words, or by any facts disclosed by the record, or by any facts of a public character (*i. e.*, documents issued by the Executive Branch of the Government) of which the court might take judicial notice. He concurred entirely with the opinion of Judge Locke of the District Court, whose main contentions were, that the words "or of any colony, district or people" were added simply as further description of both parties contemplated, and that the courts were bound by the actions of the political branch of the Government in the recognition of the political character and relations of foreign nations, and of the conditions of peace and war.

In the case of *Henderson Bridge Co.* v. *Commonwealth of Kentucky*, 17 Sup. Ct. Rep. 532, the United States Supreme Court rendered a decision on a question relative to interstate commerce which may prove far-reaching in its consequences. The main issue was as to the right of a State to tax the property of a company which by virtue of a State charter owned and operated a bridge over the Ohio River, connecting the States of Kentucky and Indiana. It appeared that the company derived its profits from outsiders who used the bridge in the transaction of interstate business and paid tolls for this privilege. The court took a technical view of this fact and decided that as it was not the company but its customers who were engaged in interstate commerce, a tax levied on the company by the State was legal and valid. Mr. Justice White in a dissenting opinion, speaking for three other justices, forcibly combats the position taken by the majority of the court and maintains that inasmuch as the interstate commerce was carried on over the bridge, the company owning the bridge and deriving its income from tolls paid by the carriers of such commerce was engaged in interstate commerce, and therefore that the tax on its property was unconstitutional and void. He holds, apparently with much reason, that the contention of the majority of the court is a mere distinction without a difference. The consequences of this decision, if the rule laid down is extended in its application to other means of interstate commerce, may well be disastrous. To quote from the dissenting opinion: "A large portion of the interstate commerce business of the country is carried on by freight lines. These lines arrange with the railways for transportation, pay them a charge or toll and upon this basis afford the public increased business facilities. Under the supposed distinction all this interstate commerce traffic ceases to be such, and the whole of the gross receipts become taxable in every State through which the business passes. The freight lines do not transport the merchandise; the railways do. Therefore, the receipts of the freight lines as to such lines are not interstate commerce receipts." The same reasoning would seem to apply to sleeping-car companies and express companies.

RECENT CASES.

CONTRACTS.

Contract—Breach of Promise of Marriage.—Yale v. *Curtiss,* 45 N. E. Rep. 1125 (N. Y.). The New York Court of Appeals, in this case, takes a view at variance with that of courts generally and refuses to infer an engagement to marry from such circumstances as usually attend an engagement.. In the language of Judge Haight, "A formal offer and acceptance is not necessary, but there must be an offer and acceptance ' sufficiently disclosed or expressed to fix the fact that they were to marry as clearly as if put in formal words.' * * * Mere courtship, or even intention to marry, is not sufficient to constitute a contract." There must be a meeting of the minds as in any other contract. 24 N. Y. Sup. 981, reversed.

Insurance—Breach of Conditions—Assignment for Benefit of Creditors.—Milwaukee Trust Co. et al. v. *Lancashire Ins. Co. et al.,* 70 N. W. Rep. 81 (Wis.). Conditions in insurance policies providing that they shall be void in case of assignments, unless provided by agreement indorsed on the policies, cover assignments for the benefit of creditors, even though such assignments may be void for fraud or by statute.

Pawnbrokers—Usury—Collateral Contracts.—Stich et al. v. *Sarnek,* 43 N.Y. Sup. 1068. A contract by which a coat is pledged to a pawnbroker at the maximum legal rate of interest, and providing for an additional charge of twelve cents for insurance against moths is valid if made in good faith.

CONVEYANCES.

Deeds—Delivery—Deputy Clerk.—Robbins v. *Rascoe,* 26 S. E. Rep. 807 (N. C.). A deed of gift was handed by the grantor to a deputy clerk of court to be proved and registered before the clerk, but was recalled by the grantor before probate or registration. The grantee was ignorant of the deed until after its recall. Held, that the delivery of the deed was complete on its commission to the deputy clerk, an acceptance by the grantee not being essential to complete delivery.

Mortgages—Assumption—Remedy of Mortgagee—Statute of Frauds.—*Flint* v. *Winter Harbor Land Co.*, 36 Atl. Rep. 634 (Me.). A deed conveyed land subject to a mortgage, "which said mortgage this grantee, by acceptance of this deed, hereby assumes and agrees to pay and fully discharge." Held, that the mortgagee could hold both the mortgagor and the grantee liable in equity or either liable in assumpsit and that after foreclosure, if the property was of less value than the debt, he could recover the deficiency from either or both in equity. The debt is part of the purchase money and the promise is not to pay the debt of another within the Statute of Frauds.

Chattel Mortgage of Sheep.—*First Nat. Bank of Santa Ana* v. *Errica et al.*, 47 Pac. Rep. 926 (Cal.). A chattel mortgage upon sheep does not extend by implication to wool growing upon them after the mortgage, nor to lambs in gestation at date of mortgage, according to an extension of the principle in *Shorbert* v. *DeMotta*, 112 Cal. 215, 44 Pac. 487, where such a mortgage was held not to cover lambs subsequently born.

Joint Will—Probate.—*In re Davis' Will, Ia. Appeal of Hodges*, 26 S. E. Rep. 636 (N. C.). An instrument purporting to be the joint will of two parties cannot be probated as a joint will during the life of one of the parties. Such writing may be proved as the separate will of one of the parties on his death, while the other is living.

DAMAGES.

Common Carriers—Delay in Delivery—Damages.—*Mitchell* v. *Weir*, 43 N. Y. Sup. 1123. Plaintiff shipped by defendant company a bicycle to be used by her during her vacation, she being unable to use it at any other time. There was a failure to deliver the bicycle; at the close of her vacation company offered to deliver it, which was refused. Plaintiff was unable to get another bicycle to ride. Held, that the above facts brought the case within the rule of damages for failure to deliver on the part of the carrier and that damages to the value of the bicycle should be assessed.

Action—Damnum absque Injuria—Expenses of Litigation.—*Andrus* v. *Bay Creek Ry. Co.*, 36 Atl. Rep. 826 (N. J.). A railway company, after having instituted condemnation proceedings to secure certain land for its use, discontinued such proceedings, thereby putting the owner of the land to needless expense for counsel fees and other incidentals. An action in tort was brought to recover damages for this loss to the landowner, and the case was held to be one of *damnum absque injuria.* The English courts maintain, in similar cases, a rule quite as stringent as this (2 Addison on Torts, § 863).

Assessment—Rule in Assessment of Mill Property.—Troy Cotton & Woolen Manufactory v. *City of Fall River,* 46 N. E. Rep. 99 (Mass.). It is found that the land, buildings and machinery of a mill, which are subject to local taxation, are in the aggregate more valuable when kept together and used for mill purposes, than if one is separated from the other, and when all are owned by the same person or corporation each item should be valued as it is used in connection with the others, though the land alone would be more valuable for other purposes. The court extends the rule declared in *Tremont and Suffolk Mills* v. *City of Lowell,* 163 Mass. 283, 39 N. E. 1028, to the machinery used in manufacturing establishments which is locally taxable in connection with the land and buildings thereon.

Master and Servant—Wrongful Discharge.—Tickler v. *Andrae Manuf'g Co.,* 70 N. W. Rep. 292 (Wis.). In an action for wrongful discharge a servant cannot recover his expenses in seeking other employment, even though his wages in such other employment are charged in reduction of his damage.

NEGOTIABLE PAPER.

Check—What Constitutes—Indorsement on Architect's Certificate.— Industrial Bank of Chicago v. *Bower,* 46 N. E. Rep. 10 (Ill.). An architect's certificate recited that a certain sum was due the contractor, the E. B. Co. P. H. & Co. had made a building loan to the owner which was drawn on such certificates as needed. The owner wrote on the back of the certificate: "P. H. & Co., Pay to the order of the E. B. Co., John R. Bowes." Held, that although the drawees were not bankers, the indorsement constituted a check and not a bill of exchange. 64 Ill. App. 300 reversed.

Note—Sufficiency of Consideration.—Irwin v. *Lombard University,* 46 N. E. Rep. 63 (Ohio). A note given for certain defined educational purposes, which were carried out, is upon a sufficient consideration. *Johnson* v. *Otterbein Univ.*, 41 Ohio St. 527, disapproved. *Methodist Episcopal Church* v. *Kendall* (Mass.) holds the contrary.

MISCELLANEOUS.

Constitutional Law—Right to Jury Trial—Liquor License—Forfeiture.—Voight v. *Board of Excise Commissioners of City of Newark*, 36 Atl. Rep. 686 (N. J. Sup.). A statute providing for the forfeiture of liquor licenses and that the body which granted the license shall on the complaint of three resident voters investigate the acts alleged to have worked such forfeiture, and if defendant is found guilty, revoke his license, does not contravene the constitutional right of trial by jury, and the licensing body need not wait for the action of the criminal courts. See *People* v. *Board of Commis., etc., of Brooklyn*, 59 N.Y. 96, for a somewhat similar statute upheld.

Anti-Trust Act—Interstate Commerce.—United States v. *Addyston Pipe and Steel Co.*, 78 Fed. Rep. 712. Where several corporations engaged in the manufacture of cast-iron pipes formed an association whereby they agreed not to compete with each other in regard to work done or pipes furnished in certain states and territories, and to make effectual the objects of the association, agreed to charge a bonus which was to be added to the real market price of the pipe sold by those companies, the combination was not a violation of the "Anti-Trust" act, as it affected interstate commerce only incidentally.

Trade Marks—Infringement.—City of Carlsbad v. *Schultz*, 78 Fed. Rep. 469. One who sold artificial "Carlsbad" water five years before the importation of the real article has a right to continue his business and cannot be restrained from using the name "Carlsbad," provided it is accompanied with an adjective such as "artificial" printed as conspicuously.

Customs Duties—Vessels or Yachts.—The Conqueror, 17 Sup. Ct. Rep. 510. Vessels and ships are not dutiable under tariff act of Oct. 1, 1890 (26 Stat. 567), not being scheduled *eo nomine* under "articles;" nor can the fact that a pleasure yacht was purchased abroad and brought to this country by an American be applied as a test of dutiability.

BOOK NOTICES.

Domesday Book and Beyond: Three Essays in the Early History of England. By Frederick William Maitland, LL.D:, Downing Professor of the Laws of England in the University of Cambridge. Cloth, 543 pp. Little, Brown & Company, Boston, Mass., 1897.

It is a practice far too common among our modern lawyers to confine themselves to the study of the law as it exists to-day, leaving untouched the great field of its historical development. Nevertheless the few whose tastes lead them to investigate the causes which have led to the present state of English and American law find the subject one of fascinating interest. Such a pursuit, however, is not without its difficulties. After we have passed through the period which extends back from the present time to the twelfth or thirteenth century, we become at once involved in uncertainty. It is at this point that a work like that of Prof. Maitland's is of the greatest assistance. Facts and authorities far beyond the reach of the average student are collated and applied to the subject in a way which leaves no room for criticism. So reasonable are the theories of the author that we almost forget that they are theories at all; they appeal to us as realities. Prof. Maitland's method is retrogressive. Beginning with matters upon which there is little controversy he leads us back through the times subsequent to the Norman Conquest, into the hazy region beyond. In the first essay he shows the true aspect and character of the great land survey of William the Conqueror; in the second, the different sorts of land tenure are treated, and in the third is a detailed account of the systems of land measurement and taxation. We echo the confidence which the author expresses in his closing lines that the darkness which surrounds these early times will be soon dissipated, and desire to add that the bulk of the advance which has been made in this direction in late years has been due to Prof. Maitland's own efforts.

MAGAZINE NOTICES.

The Green Bag, April, 1897.

    Daniel Doherty and the Philadelphia Bar (with portrait),   A. Oakey Hall
    Why Thomas Bram was Found Guilty, . . Charles E. Grinnell
    The Supreme Court of Wisconsin, IV. (illustrated),   Edwin E. Bryant
    The Legal Aspect of the Maybrick Case, . . . Clark Bell
    London Legal Letter.
    Editorial Department.

Central Law Journal. Leading Articles.

    Mar. 5.   Liability of Common Carriers to Passengers carried Gratuitously, . . . Charles Hebberd
    Mar. 12.   Negotiability of Guaranties, . . Cyrus J. Wood
    Mar. 19.   Imputed Wrong as the Same Affects Railway Law, ... Linton D. Landrum
    Mar. 26.   Setting Aside Conveyances of Real Estate on Account of False and Fraudulent Representations by the Vendee or his Agent, . S. S. Merrill
    April 2.   Liability of a Sleeping Car Company for Loss of Effects of its Passengers, . . . W. C. Rodgers
    April 9.   Responsibility of Insurance Company for Misstatement of its Agent as to Health of the Insured, . . . Flora V. Woodward Tibbits
    April 16.   What Constitutes a Broker, . . Nathan Newmark

The Albany Law Journal, 1897.

    Mar. 13.   The Cuban Question, . . . George A. Benham
    Mar. 20.   The Assignability of Bills of Lading, . Business, New York
    Mar. 27.   Women as Pleaders, . . *Canadian Law Journal*
    April 3.   Pleading Negligence, . . . Landon D. Sandrum
    April 10.   The Alienation and Hypothecation of Corporate Franchises and Corporate Property,   John C. Kleber

American Law Review, March-April, 1897.

    The Present State of the Law.
    American Lawyers and their Making.
    The Late Constitutional Convention and Constitution of South Carolina.
    Courts versus Clearing Houses.
    The Evolution of the American Fee Simple.
    Pooling Contracts and Public Policy.
    Notes.
    Notes of Recent Decisions.
    Correspondence.
    Book Reviews.

SUPPLEMENT

CONTAINING

MEMORABILIA ET NOTABILIA.

[Graduates are requested to contribute to this column and address their communications to YALE LAW JOURNAL, box 1341, New Haven, Conn.]

Judge Baldwin will deliver an address before the annual meeting of the Georgia Bar Association at Warm Springs, Ga., June 30.

* * *

The latest volume of the *American and English Encyclopedia of Law* contains an article by Professor Beers on "Benevolent or Benefit Associations."

*

The following seniors have been chosen as competitors for the Wayland Prize by the committee of juniors appointed for that purpose: C. L. Avery, R. S. Baldwin, H. C. Bartlett, N. Candee, T. H. Cobbs, M. F. Hatcher, M. A. Kilker, H. W. Merwin, E. C. Snyder, R. C. Stoll.

*

Prof. Beers and Talcott H. Russell have formed a partnership, with offices in the First National Bank building, New Haven.

* * *

The final trials of the Yale-Princeton debate was held April 13. N. Candee, '97, T. H. Cobbs, '97, and C. L. Avery, '97, spoke as representatives of the Kent Club, chosen in competitive debate. Mr. Avery was chosen one of the alternates.

* * *

Mr. John W. Hendric of Sound Beach, Conn., has given the Law School $10,000 toward the completion of the Law School building. This gift makes the total of Mr. Hendric's contributions to this fund $35,000. The amount necessary to complete the building is from $75,000 to $80,000.

Prof. Thos. Thacher of the New York Bar, was tendered a reception on March 18, by the faculty of the Law School, preparatory to his course of lectures on Corporation Law before the senior class.

The *Yale Shingle* will be edited this year by N. Candee, '97. It will be published about May 1 and will contain the following articles: "Class Poem," E. C. Snyder; "Junior Year," Henry W. Merwin; "Senior Year," Francis Parsons; "Kent Club," Roger S. Baldwin; "Social," J. D. Thomson; "Religious," R. J. Thompson; "Athletics," C. L. Avery, Jr.; "Moot Court," G. B. Thayer; also an article by a member of the faculty.

The semi-annual meeting of the Kent Club for the election of officers was held Monday, April 12, and the following were elected: President, T. H. Cobbs, '97; Vice-President, R. G. Pleasant, '99; Secretary, T. F. Noone, '99; Treasurer, M. A. Kilker, '97. It was voted to present a gavel to R. C. Stoll, '97, the retiring president, and to C. L. Avery, the president during the first term.

1849. Edwin L. Barney, of New Bedford, Mass., died recently. He was born in Swansea, Mass., in 1827. In 1847, after graduation from Brown, he entered the Yale Law School. In 1865 he was a senator in the Massachusetts legislature, and in 1870 was appointed by President Grant U. S. district attorney for the Western District of Texas. Afterwards Mr. Barney was the law partner of Gen. B. F. Butler, and when General Butler was governor of Massachusetts he was appointed judge advocate on his staff.

1861. Hon. Washington F. Wilcox of Chester, has been appointed to the Board of Railroad Commissioners for the State of Connecticut.

1872. W. A. Wright has formed a law partnership with W. S. Pardee, 1884, with office in the First National Bank building, New Haven.

1875. C. La Rue Munson, who for several years past has lectured in the Law School on "The Beginnings of Practice," is the author of *A Manual of Elementary Practice*, just published by the Bowen-Merrill Co., of Indianapolis.

1878. Hon. John S. Seymour, Commissioner of Patents under President Cleveland, is reported to have taken an office at 30 Pine street, New York, where he will practice law with Edward Harmon, brother of Attorney-General Harmon.

1881. Epaphroditus Peck has been appointed associate judge of the Hartford, Conn., Common Pleas Court.

1881. Frank E. Hyde, who has been United States Consul at Lyons, France, since 1893, has resigned and formed a co-partnership in the law firm of Valois de Folord and Harper, of Paris.

1883. Carter H. Harrison was recently elected mayor of Chicago on the regular democratic ticket by a large majority.

1887. H. T. Shelton has retired from the firm of Stoddard, Bishop & Shelton, Bridgeport, Conn.

1891. Roger S. Newell has been appointed judge of the town court of Bristol, Conn.

1893. James K. Blake has an article in the March number of the *Bachelor of Arts* entitled: "The Calcium Light Parades at Yale."

1894. A. C. Baldwin has been appointed prosecuting attorney for Derby and Milford, Conn.

1895. Elmore S. Banks has been elected judge of the Probate court at Southport, Conn.

1895. George W. Klett is clerk of the city court at New Britain.

Ex.-1895. The marriage of Wm. R. Begg to Miss Spencer of Hartford, Conn., took place Wednesday, April 21, at Hartford.

1896. John L. Hall has recently entered the law office of Benton & Choate of Boston, Mass.

1896. The engagement is announced of James S. Jenkins to Miss Phoebe Vail of Stamford, Conn.

Ex.-1896. Alfred J. Brumder died of consumption at his home in Milwaukee, Wis., on April 23d.

Ex.-1897. James J. Hickey was married on April 21st to Miss Marie Stoddart Cooke, of New Orleans, La.

YALE LAW JOURNAL

VOL. VI   JUNE, 1897   No. 6

BRIEF FOR THE UNITED STATES IN THE CASE OF THE UNITED STATES OF AMERICA *v.* THE TRANS-MISSOURI FREIGHT ASSOCIATION.

STATEMENT.

The United States filed its bill in the circuit court for the district of Kansas against the Trans-Missouri Freight Association and the eighteen railroads composing it, to enjoin further execution of the agreement whereby such association was formed, on the ground that it was in violation of the act of July 2, 1890, entitled "An act to protect trade and commerce against unlawful restraints and monopolies." The case was heard on the bill and answers. The court dismissed the bill. The Government appealed to the circuit court of appeals for the eighth circuit, which, by a majority (Judges Sanborn and Caldwell), affirmed the judgment, Judge Shiras dissenting. Both opinions are reported[1]. The case comes here on the Government's appeal.

ADMITTED FACTS.

The bill averred[2] that the lines of the railway companies, defendants, were engaged in interstate commerce, were separate and distinct in ownership and operation, and—

furnish to the public and to persons engaged in trade, traffic, and commerce between the several States and Territories and countries aforesaid *separate, distinct, and competitive lines* of transportation and communication, extending among and between the States and Territories of the United States lying westward of the Missouri and the Mississippi rivers to the Pacific Ocean; and that the construction and maintenance of such *separate, distinct, and competitive*

---

[1] 58 Fed. 58.
[2] Record, bottom p. 3 and p. 4.

lines of railroads as aforesaid had been encouraged and assisted by the United States of America and by the States and Territories in the region of country aforesaid, and by the people of said several States and Territories, by franchises and by grants and donations of large amounts of land of great value, and of money and securities for the purpose of securing to the public and the people engaged in trade and commerce throughout the region of the country aforesaid *competitive lines of transportation and communication.*

The answers, which are alike in substance, expressly admit these averments. I quote from that of the Chicago, Rock Island and Pacific Railway Company:[3]

Further admitting, this defendant admits that the railroad companies, parties hereto, severally own, control, operate, and use *distinct and separate lines* of railroad, fitted up for carrying on business as common carriers of freight *independently and disconnectedly with each other*, * * * and it says that the other companies mentioned in said bill, and the combinations of interest above enumerated, are each *separate and distinct* in their organization, ownership, and management, *and are active competitors each with the others* for all common business at all points where such competition is possible. It further admits that the lines enumerated as above are lines of transportation and communication engaged in freight traffic between and among the States and Territories of the United States, having through lines for said freight traffic in that region of the country lying to the westward of the Mississippi and Missouri rivers and east of the Pacific Ocean. * * * It admits that the said lines of railroad, prior to the organization of the Transmissouri Freight Association, furnished to the public and to persons engaged in trade, traffic, and commerce between the several States, Territories, and countries named in the bill, *separate, distinct, and competitive lines* of transportation, extending among and between the States and Territories of the United States lying westward of the Missouri and Mississippi rivers to the Pacific Ocean, and it says that they still continue to do the same.

It admits that the construction of some lines owned by defendants was encouraged and assisted by the United States, and by some of the States and Territories in the region of country aforesaid, by means of land grants, loans of credit, donations of depot sites and rights of way, and, in a few cases, by investments of money; and that people of the said States and Territories to a limited extent made investments in the stocks and bonds of said railroad companies, while other of such lines were almost entirely constructed by capital furnished by non-residents of said region.

It believes that the purpose of the said land grants, loans, donations, and investments was *to obtain the construction of said competitive lines* of transportation and communication to the end that

[3] Record, bottom p. 14 and p. 15.

the public and the people engaged in trade and commerce throughout said region of country might have facilities afforded by railways in communicating with each other and with other portions of the United States and of the world. * * * It also admits that prior to March 15, 1889, and subsequent to the present time, all of said defendants have. been and are engaged as common carriers in the railway freight traffic connected with the interstate commerce of the United States.

The answers also admitted[4] that the defendants had made the agreement set out in the bill,[5] and that they were operating their respective lines under its provisions.

THE AGREEMENT.

The preamble recites that the agreement is—

for the purpose of mutual protection by establishing and maintaining reasonable *rates*, rules, and regulations on all freight traffic, both through and local.

Article I provides that—

1. The traffic to be included in the Transmissouri Freight Association shall be as follows: *All competitive traffic* between points in the following-described territory, commencing at the Gulf of Mexico on the ninety-fifth meridian, thence north to Red river, thence via that river to the eastern boundary of the Indian Territory, thence north by said boundary line and the eastern line of the State of Kansas to the Missouri river at Kansas City, thence via said Missouri river to the point of the intersection of that river with the eastern boundary of Montana, thence via the said eastern boundary line to the international line, the foregoing to be known as "The Missouri River Line;" thence via said international line to the Pacific coast, thence via the Pacific coast to the international line between the United States and Mexico, thence via said international line to the Gulf of Mexico, thence via said gulf to the point of beginning, including business done between points on the boundary line as described.

2. All freight traffic originating within the territory as defined in the first section when destined to points east of aforesaid Missouri river line.

Article II provided for the election of a chairman, for regular and special meetings, at which each party was to be represented by some one authorized to act definitely for it, and also that—

3. *A committee* shall be appointed *to establish rates*, rules, and regulations on the traffic subject to this association, and to consider changes therein, and *make rules for meeting the competition of outside lines*. Their conclusion, when unanimous, shall be made

---
[4] Rec., p. 15.
[5] Rec., pp. 5-9.

effective when they so order; but if they differ, the question at issue shall be referred to the managers of the lines parties hereto, and if they disagree, it shall be arbitrated in the manner provided in Article VII.

4. At least five days' written notice, prior to each monthly meeting, shall be given the chairman of any proposed reduction of any rates or change in any rule or regulation governing freight traffic.

5. At each monthly meeting the association shall consider and vote upon all changes proposed, of which due notice has been given, and all parties shall be bound by the decision of the association so expressed, unless then and there the parties shall give the association definite written notice that in ten days thereafter they shall make such modification, notwithstanding the vote of the association, provided that if the members giving notice of the change shall fail to be represented at the meeting no action shall be taken on its notice, and the same shall be considered withdrawn. Should any member insist upon a reduction of rate against the views of the majority, or if the majority favor the same, and if in the judgment of said majority the rate so made affects seriously the rates upon their traffic, then the association may, by a majority vote upon such other traffic, put in effect corresponding rates to take effect upon the same date. By unanimous consent any rate, rule, or regulation relating to freight traffic may be modified at any meeting of the association without previous notice.

6. Notwithstanding anything in this article contained, each member may *at its peril* make at any time without previous notice such *rate*, rule, or regulation as may be necessary to meet the *competition of lines not members of the association*, giving at the same time notice to the chairman of its action in the premises. If the chairman upon investigation shall decide that such rate is not necessary to meeting competition, of lines not members of the association and shall so notify the road making the rate, it shall immediately withdraw such rate. At the next meeting of the association, held after the making of such rate, it shall be reported to the association, and if the association shall decide by a two-thirds vote that such rate was not made in good faith to meet such competition, the member offending shall be subject to the penalty provided in section 8 of this article. If the association shall decide by a two-thirds vote that such rate was made in good faith to meet such competition, it shall be considered as authority for the rate so made.

7. All agreements with connecting lines for a division of through rates, relating to traffic covered by this agreement, shall be made by authority of the association; provided, however, that when one road has a proprietary interest in another, the division of such rates shall be what they may elect, and shall not be the property of the association. Provided, further, that as regards traffic contracts at this date actually existing between lines not having common proprietary interest, the same shall be reported,

so far as the divisions are concerned, to the association, to the end that divisions with competing lines may, if thought advisable by them, be made on equally favorable terms.

Paragraph 8 of Article II provided the penalty as follows:

It shall be the duty of the chairman to investigate all apparent violations of the agreement and to report his findings to the managers, who shall determine by a majority vote (a member against whom complaint is made to have no vote) what, if any, penalty shall be assessed, the amount of each fine not to exceed $100, to be paid to the association. If any line party hereto agrees with the shipper, or anyone else, to secure a reduction or change in the rates, or change in the rules and regulations, and it is shown upon investigation by the chairman that such arrangement was effected and traffic thereby secured, such action shall be reported to the managers, who shall determine, as above provided, what, if any, penalty shall be assessed.

For the purpose of detecting violations of the agreement, the chairman was given authority to examine all books, papers, and contracts.[6] He was to be furnished with copies of all waybills for freight when called for.[7] It was also provided[8] that—

The chairman shall be empowered to authorize lines in the association to meet the rates of any other lines, or other lines in the association, when, in his judgment, such action is justified by circumstances.

The reference in the agreement to outside competing lines will be understood by reading the averment of the answers:[9]

But it is not correct to state, as alleged in the bill, that they are the only such lines, there being several others, to wit: The Northern Pacific, the Great Northern, the Southern Pacific, the Texas and Pacific, and others which would be properly included in said description.

These were all lines within the same territory as those of appellees, but not controlled by members of the association.

AVERMENTS OF THE INTENT, EFFECT, ETC., OF THE AGREEMENTS.

I contend that the various averments and denials in the bill and answers as to the real intention of the parties to the agreement, and as to its actual operation and effect, are entirely irrelevant, save in so far as they are based upon the necessary tendency and effect of the agreement itself as shown by its terms; and that,

---

[6] Record, bottom p. 7.
[7] Art 3. §5.
[8] Art 3. §8.
[9] Record, bottom p. 14.

therefore, the statements of the answers as to the lawful intent of the parties to the agreement and its actual effect on rates of freight are not to be taken as admitted by setting the case down for hearing on bill and answer. But it will be more convenient to treat of this subject hereafter.

QUESTIONS INVOLVED.

It appears, therefore, that the defendants are all common carriers engaged in interstate commerce, owning and operating lines which were intended to be, and in fact were, naturally and actually competing, and whose construction was authorized and aided by the government and by others for that reason; that they have surrendered to a committee of the association control over the making of rates and the conduct of their business, binding themselves by penalties to obey the orders of this committee. And the questions raised in the courts below, which will no doubt be raised here, are—

(1) Does the act of July 2, 1890, entitled "An act to protect trade and commerce against unlawful restraints and monopolies,"[10] apply to railroad companies?

(2) Is the agreement in question a violation of that act?

Some minor questions have been raised which I do not think it necessary to mention here.

I maintain the affirmative of both the questions above stated.

ARGUMENT.

I.

The act of July 2, 1890, applies to railroad companies as well as to all other persons.

Its terms are sufficiently broad to include such companies, and are not to be restricted by reason of what was said or proposed in Congress while the law was pending.

Such companies are not to be excluded from its operation because they are also governed in some respects by the act to regulate commerce passed February 4, 1887.

The provisions of the act of July 2, 1890, which have been considered in the case, are as follows:

SEC. 1. Every contract, combination, in the form of trust or otherwise, or conspiracy in restraint of trade or commerce among the several States or with foreign nations is hereby declared to be

---

[10] 26 Stat. at Large, 209, ch. 647.

illegal. Every person who shall make any such contract or engage in any such combination or conspiracy shall be deemed guilty of a misdemeanor, and, on conviction thereof, shall be punished by fine not exceeding five thousand dollars, or by imprisonment not exceeding one year, or by both said punishments, in the discretion of the court.

SEC. 2. Every person who shall monopolize, or attempt to monopolize, or combine, or conspire with any other person or persons to monopolize any part of the trade or commerce among the several States, or with foreign nations, shall be deemed guilty of a misdemeanor, and, on conviction thereof, shall be punished by fine not exceeding five thousand dollars, or by imprisonment not exceeding one year, or by both said punishments, in the discretion of the court.

SEC. 4. The several circuit courts of the United States are hereby invested with jurisdiction to prevent and restrain violations of this act; and it shall be the duty of the several district attorneys of the United States, in their respective districts, under the direction of the Attorney-General, to institute proceedings in equity to prevent and restrain such violations. Such proceedings may be by way of petition setting forth the case and praying that such violation shall be enjoined or otherwise prohibited. When the parties complained of shall have been duly notified of such petition, the court shall proceed, as soon as may be, to the hearing and determination of the case; and pending such petition and before final decree, the court may at any time make such temporary restraining order or prohibition as shall be deemed just in the premises.

It is manifest from the reading of this act that its terms are as broad as the language affords. *Every contract* and *combination*, in form of a trust or *otherwise*, or *conspiracy* is declared to be illegal *when it is in restraint* of trade or *commerce* among the several States, etc. The use of the word "commerce" as well as the word "trade" indicates a plain intention to give the act a scope which goes beyond the mere mercantile community which may be said to be engaged in trade, and includes all persons or combinations of persons, natural or artificial, which are in any way engaged in or may undertake to affect *commerce* among the several States.[11]

---

[11] *In re* Debs, 64 Fed., at page 749; also United States *v.* Joint Traffic Association (Appendix D of brief for appellees, where it is cited on other points from which the Government dissents and has appealed), wherein Judge Wheeler said (p. 127):

The restraint and monopoly act expressly authorizes such a proceeding in equity as this to prevent its violation, and this suit is well maintained if this contract is within it. Railroads are not expressly named in this act and are said in argument not to be within its terms. No one is so named, but it applies to all combinations in restraint of trade or commerce among the States. Railroads do not trade among the States, but they carry for those who do, and what would restrain their so carrying would be a restraint of such commerce.

That transportation is commerce within the meaning of the Federal Constitution and of the various laws of Congress is now settled beyond dispute.

Commerce includes intercourse between the citizens of the several States.[12] It extends to transportation of goods and passengers.[13] It embraces the vehicles as well as the articles of commerce.[14] It includes the operations of telegraphy.[15]

It is useless to multiply citations. Considering the fact that railways are the chief instruments of commerce among the States, absolutely controlling it with respect to transportation, it seems to me that, taking the language of the act as it reads, the intention to include railroad companies within its operation is not

---

[12] 9 Wheat. 1; 114 U. S. 196, 203.

[13] 7 How. 283; 91 U. S. 275; 15 Wall. 232; 92 U. S. 275; 95 U. S. 465, 470.

[14] 7 Wall. 646; 8 Wall. 123; 24 How. 169; 154 U. S. 204, 218.

[15] Pensacola Telegraph Co. *v.* Western Union Tel. Co., 96 U. S. 1; Telegraph Co. *v.* Texas, 105 U. S. 460; Western Union Tel. Co. *v.* Pendleton, 122 U. S. 347, 356.

In the last case cited the court, by the Chief Justice, said (p. 464):

A telegraph company occupies the same relation to commerce as a carrier of messages, that a railroad company does as a carrier of goods. Both companies are instruments of commerce, *and their business is commerce itself.*

In the County of Mobile *v.* Kimball, 102 U. S 691, the court, by Mr. Justice Field said (p. 696):

That power is indeed without limitation. It authorizes Congress to prescribe the conditions upon which commerce in all its forms shall be conducted between our citizens and the citizens or subjects of other countries, and between the citizens of the several States, and to adopt measures to promote its growth and insure its safety.

In the State Freight Tax Case, 15 Wall. 232, the court, by Mr. Justice Strong, said (p. 275):

Beyond all question the transportation of freight, or of the subjects of commerce, for the purpose of exchange or sale, is a constituent of commerce itself. This has never been doubted, and probably the transportation of articles of trade from one State to another was the prominent idea in the minds of the framers of the Constitution, when to Congress was committed the power to regulate commerce among the several States. A power to prevent embarrassing restrictions by any State was the thing desired. The power was given by the same words and in the same clause by which was conferred power to regulate commerce with foreign nations. It would be absurd to suppose that the transmission of the subjects of trade from the State to the buyer or from the place of production to the market, was not contemplated, for without that there could be no consummated trade either with foreign nations or among the States. In his work on the Constitution (sec. 1057) Judge Story asserts that the sense in which the word commerce is used in that instrument includes not only traffic, but intercourse and navigation. And in the Passenger Cases, 7 How. 416, it was said: "Commerce consists in selling the superfluity, in purchasing articles of necessity, as well productions as manufactures, in buying from one nation and selling to another, or in transporting the merchandise from the seller to the buyer to gain the freight." Nor does it make any difference whether this interchange of commodities is by land or by water. In either case the bringing of the goods from the seller to the buyer is commerce. Among the States it must have been principally by land when the Constitution was adopted.

open to debate. In fact, in the light of U. S. *v.* E. C. Knight Co., 156 U. S. 1, it is difficult to imagine what Congress meant the act to affect if not railroads.

The circuit court held that the act did not apply to railroad companies. The circuit court of appeals assumed that it did. The question was expressly left open in *In re* Debs, 158 U. S. (see p. 600), and by Mr. Justice Harlan in Arthur *v.* Oakes, 63 Fed. (see p. 329). The act has been held in labor cases to apply to railroads by Judges Billings, McCormick, and Toulmin;[16] by Judges Thayer and Philips;[17] by Judges Taft and Lurton;[18] by Judge Baker[19] and by Judge Ross.[20]

SCOPE NOT AFFECTED BY SECTION 6.

The claim is that, as railroad property does not come within the provisions of section 6 for seizure and forfeiture, contracts by railroad companies are not covered by the earlier sections. There are obvious public and other reasons why railroad property should be omitted from the seizure provided for—that is, the property used in the business of common carriage—leaving the companies subject only to the other penalties of the act. But, if I concede that section 6 does not apply to railways, I fail to see the connection between premise and conclusion. By what principle is it assumed that such additional penal provisions are intended or operate as a limitation of the remainder of the act to such offenders as, from the nature of their business, may possibly become liable to such added penalties? I presume it will not be denied that the act applies to telegraph and telephone companies, yet they never have property "in the course of transportation" which can be seized.

PROCEEDINGS IN CONGRESS.

It is said, however, that the proceedings in Congress during the pendency of the bill show that it was not so intended. A large part of the briefs for the various defendants has been devoted to reprinting portions of the Congressional Record with much emphasis of lead and italics.

---

[16] U. S. *v.* Workingmen's Amalgamated Council of New Orleans, 54 Fed. 994; 57 Fed. 85.
[17] U. S. *v.* Elliott, 62 Fed. 801; 64 Fed. 27.
[18] *In re* Phelan, 62 Fed. 803, 821.
[19] U. S. *v.* Agler, 62 Fed. 824.
[20] *In re* Grand Jury, 62 Fed. 840. See *dictum contra* by Judge Putnam in U. S. *v.* Patterson, 55 Fed. 605.

When the language of an act is clear the court does not look elsewhere to ascertain its meaning. Reference to the debates and proceedings of the legislative body could at most be merely an aid to construction where the meaning is doubtful. Where the meaning of a statute is plain it is the duty of the court to enforce it according to its obvious terms. In such a case there is no necessity for construction.[21] Even if the debates could in any case be properly resorted to, this could not be done where there is no necessity for construction. But expressions in debate, or proposed amendments, cannot be permitted to control or vary the language used in the final enactment.[22]

The reasons for this well settled rule have an apt illustration in the proceedings now invoked.

The bill, as originally introduced, is printed in Appendix C of the brief for the Union Pacific Railway Company and others, herein (p. 99). It was in much more specific terms than those finally adopted. It mentioned "transportation" as well as "im-

---

[21] Thornley v. United States, 113 U. S. 310–313.

[22] In United States v. Union Pacific Railway Company, 91 U. S. 72, the court, by Mr. Justice Davis, said (p. 79):

In construing an act of Congress, we are not at liberty to recur to the views of individual members in debate, nor to consider the motives which influence them to vote for or against its passage. The act itself speaks the will of Congress, and this is to be ascertained from the language used.

In District of Columbia v. Washington Market Co., 108 U. S. 243, the court, by Mr. Justice Matthews, said (p. 254):

Nor are we willing to accept the debates that are reported as occurring in Congress at the time of the passage of the deficiency appropriation act of March 3d, 1873, as evidence of the meaning of the clause on which the controversy in this case depends.

The question is whether, according to its correct construction, that clause authorized the parties to execute the agreement into which they entered.

The subject is treated more fully in the opinion of the supreme court of the District of Columbia in the same case, 3 MacArth., at page 571.

In Mitchell v. Great Works Milling and Manufacturing Company, 2 Story, at page 653, Mr. Justice Story said:

At the threshold of the argument, we are met with the suggestion that when the act was before Congress, the opposite doctrine was then maintained in the House of Representatives, and it was confidently stated that no such jurisdiction was conferred by the act as is now insisted on. What passes in Congress upon the discussion of a bill can hardly become a matter of strict judicial inquiry; and if it were, it could scarcely be affirmed that the opinions of a few members, expressed either way, are to be considered as the judgment of the whole House, or even of a majority. But, in truth, little reliance can or ought to be placed upon such sources of interpretation of a statute. The questions can be, and rarely are, there debated upon strictly legal grounds, with a full mastery of the subject and of the just rules of interpretation. The arguments are generally of a mixed character, addressed by way of objection, or of support, rather with a view to carry or defeat a bill, than with a strictness of judicial decision.

But if the House entertained one construction of the language of the bill, *non constat*, that the same opinion was entertained either by the Senate or by

portation" and "sale." It enumerated "arrangements" and "agreements" as well as "contracts," "trusts," and "combinations." It was made expressly applicable to "corporations" as well as to "persons." Various constitutional objections were raised and considered, and finally, on April 2, 1890, the bill was reported as subsequently passed, all the original bill after the enacting clause was stricken out.[28]

In the House various amendments were offered, some of which were intended to specify contracts for preventing competition in transportation. An amendment to this effect, containing a proviso, was adopted by the House. Various changes in the amendment were discussed in conference and by the Senate, and it was finally adopted by the Senate in the language found at page 116, Exhibit C, above cited. The House amendment forbade all contracts for any restraint of competition in transportation. The Senate added the clause "so that the rates of transportation may be raised above what is just and reasonable." The House

---

the President; and their opinions are certainly, in a matter of the sanction of laws, entitled to as great weight as the other branch. But, in truth, Courts of justice are not at liberty to look at considerations of this sort. We are bound to interpret the act as we find it and to make such an interpretation as its language and its apparent objects require. We must take it to be true, that the Legislature intend precisely what they say, and to the extent which the provisions of the act require for the purpose of securing their just operation and effect. Any other course would deliver over the Court to interminable doubts and difficulties; and we should be compelled to guess what was the law, from loose commentaries of different debates instead of the precise enactments of the Statute. Nor have there been wanting illustrious instances of great minds, which, after they had, as legislators or commentators, reposed upon a short and hasty opinion, have deliberately withdrawn from their first impressions when they came upon the judgment seat to re-examine the statute or law in its full bearings.

See also Aldridge v. Williams, 3 How. 9, 24.

In County of Cumberland v. Boyd. 113 Pa. St., at page 57, the court said:

In giving construction to a statute we cannot be controlled by the views expressed by a few members of the Legislature who expressed verbal opinions on its passage. Those opinions may or may not have been entertained by the more than a hundred members who gave no such expression. The declarations of some and the assumed acquiescence of others therein cannot be adopted as a true interpretation of the statute. Keeping in mind the previous law, the supposed evil and the remedy desired, we must consider the language of the statute and the fair and reasonable import thereof.

To the same effect see the opinion of Mr. Justice Field in Leese v. Clark, 20 Cal. 387, 425.

In The Queen v. Hertford College, 3 Q. B. D., at page 707, the Lord Chief Justice (Coleridge) said:

We are not, however, concerned with what Parliament intended, but simply with what it has said in the statute. The statute is clear and the Parliamentary history of a statute is wisely inadmissible to explain it, if is not; but in this case, if it could be referred to, it would appear beyond all controversy *Parliamentum voluisse quod dicit lex.*

[28] See Appendix C, above cited, p. 107.

having disagreed, the amendment was modified in conference, but the clause about just and reasonable rates was retained. The House having refused to agree, a further conference resulted, in which the House conferees were instructed to recede from the original amendment. Finally the bill was passed and approved as it originally passed the Senate.

The argument now made from all this is that the intention of both bodies was—the Senate in its change of the original form of the bill, and the House in receding from its amendments specifically mentioning agreements respecting transportation—to exclude carriers from the operation of the bill.

The same argument would necessarily lead to the conclusion that it was also the intention to exclude corporations from the operation of the law, as well as "arrangements" and "agreements" which for any technical reasons might not be considered "contracts." A comparison of the language of the bill as introduced with that of the bill as passed will show other similar consequences to which the argument leads.

But the futility, not to say danger, of resorting to such means of ascertaining legislative intent, is demonstrated by a portion of the proceedings to which counsel do not refer. In reporting the bill again from the Judiciary Committee of the Senate with the House amendment amended, as aforesaid,[24] Senator Hoar, who it will be remembered, was a member of the conference committee, said:[25]

The other clause of the House amendment is that contracts or agreements entered into for the purpose of preventing competition in the transportation of persons or property from one State or Territory into another shall be deemed unlawful. That the committee recommend shall be concurred in. *We suppose that it is already covered by the bill as it stands; that is, the transportation is as much trade or commerce among the several States as the sale of goods in one State to be delivered in another, and, therefore, that it is covered already by the bill as it stands.* But there is no harm in concurring in an amendment which expressly describes it, and an objection to the amendment might be construed as if the Senate did not mean to include it. So we let that stand.

How can counsel show that the final result, leaving the bill as it originally passed the Senate, was not due to general concurrence, at last, in the view of Senator Hoar, which applies as well to the

---

[24] Reports, it appears, stand on a somewhat different footing from debates, Holy Trinity Church *v.* United States, 143 U. S., at p. 465, The Delaware, 161 U. S., at p. 472.

[25] Cong. Rec., vol. 21, pt. 5, pp. 4559-60.

entire change of the bill in the Senate as to the amendment proposed by the House ?

The same line of reasoning applies to the portions of the debate in the House relating to the effect of the proposed amendment upon, and the general relation of the bill to, the interstate-commerce act.[26]

EFFECT OF INTERSTATE-COMMERCE ACT.

The act of July 2, 1890, is not prevented from applying to railroad companies by reason of the provisions of the previous act of February 4, 1887, relating to them.

Counsel admit[27] that the principle of the rule of construction for which they contend is that repeals by implication are not favored, and that therefore an act in general terms sufficiently broad to include the subject of a prior special act will be held not to repeal such special act in the absence of a repealing clause or other indication of intention to repeal.

Counsel accordingly recognize the necessity of showing irreconcilable inconsistency between the general and the special act, being fully aware of the application of the still higher rule which requires that both acts be given their full natural scope and effect, if possible. They therefore seek (p. 25) first to establish the premise that contracts and agreements in restraint of trade and commerce are permitted by the act of February 4, 1887, so as to prepare the way for the contention that the act of July 2, 1890, forbidding such contracts and agreements should be held inapplicable to railroads.

I maintain, however—

First. That the act of February 4, 1887, does not authorize associations of competing railways for the purpose of fixing and maintaining rates.

Second. That there is no inconsistency whatever between the act of 1887 and that of 1890, but that both can be given full scope and effect according to their terms.

While counsel say (p. 27), "if the *articles of agreement* in question are *authorized* by the interstate-commerce *act*, as we have endeavored to show," the endeavor to show (p. 25) is merely that "*associations* similar to the one in question have been repeatedly recognized by the Interstate Commerce *Commission.*"

---

[26] See the following cases as to reference to the original form and amendments of bills: Legal Tender Cases, 12 Wall., at p. 559; Blake *v.* National Banks, 23 *Id.*, at p. 317; United States *v.* Burr, 159 U. S., at p. 85.

[27] Page 27 of brief for Union Pacific Railway Company, *et al.*

Even if it should be conceded that the Commission may put a construction upon the law which would affect the judgment of this court, it does not appear that it has put upon the law the construction contended for, much less that it has done so with the uniformity and for the time required to invoke the rule as to departmental construction. It has never approved in any way an agreement between competing lines fixing rates. So there has been no action to create a rule of practical construction. No one has ever held or contended that the mere theories of an executive officer or body can ripen into a rule of construction, no matter how long they have been held nor how often they have been uttered. The quotation from the first annual report of the Commission, which is given on the last named page of the brief, does not relate at all to associations among competing railroads for the fixing of rates, but only to associations to secure uniformity in classification. Nor can I agree to the statement on page 15 of the brief that "Tariff agreements of the general nature of that which the present bill attacks were universally known to exist among railway companies at the times, respectively, of the passage of the interstate-commerce and the anti-trust acts," if the expression "general nature" is intended to apply to agreements between competing lines for the fixing and maintaining of rates.[28]

An examination of the act of February 4, 1887, shows plainly that it does not attempt to deal with the relations of competing lines save in the single section (five) which forbids pooling. The other sections are all intended to secure to the public from each line and its connections, considered separately, charges which are reasonable, just and uniform, and equal facilities to all. Sched-

---

[28] The views of the Commission, as well as the historical fact about such agreements, will be found in the following extract from the report of the Commission filed December 1, 1895, at page 96 in the chapter on "Traffic agreements:"

While the interstate commerce act permits and encourages the establishment of joint tariffs by carriers operating *continuous* lines, there is no authority in that act for the joint establishment and maintenance of rates by *competing* carriers operating substantially parallel lines. On the contrary, the tenor of the fifth section seems plainly opposed to any arrangement tending to limit railroad competition. The act, however, contains no express prohibition of contracts to maintain rates unless that purpose is accomplished by a pooling of freights or division of earnings. Prior to the passage of the act the plan adopted by the carriers to regulate competition and to maintain agreed rates was the pooling system, under which, whenever it was effective, each of the competing lines secured an agreed percentage of the total traffic, or in default of that an equivalent in money paid out of the pool. After the passage of the act many railroad companies apparently sought to maintain rates by such adjustment of tariffs as would in effect produce an apportionment of traffic among competing lines, and agreements containing provisions to this end were from time to time filed with the Commission.

ules of rates are required, with notice of all changes therein (sec. 7). But all penalties are imposed upon individuals and none upon corporations.

Sec. 10. That any common carrier, * * * or whenever such common carrier is a corporation, any director or officer thereof * * * shall wilfully do, or cause to be done, * * * any act, matter, or thing in this act prohibited * * * shall be deemed guilty of a misdemeanor, etc.

This section was so construed in United States v. Michigan Central Railroad Company (43 Fed. Rep. 26), which decision has, I believe, been generally accepted.

That the act was not intended to be a final and complete treatment of the subject to which it relates in all aspects appears from the reference in section 15 to "any law cognizable by said Commission."

We have, then, a law regulating commerce in certain respects, which does not profess to be exclusive, and which deals with railroads in the relation of competitors in one respect only, viz: by forbidding a specific form of agreement under penalties imposed upon individuals only.

If the question were between this act and the one which afterwards prohibited pooling generally, the question would arise which should prevail; and probably the decision would be that the specific provision as to pooling by railroads would be held not to be repealed by the general one; but I am quite unable to perceive how, by the application of any principle, a subsequent general act is to be so treated with respect to additional provisions entirely consistent with those of the former act. Assuming that pooling contracts are contracts in restraint of trade and commerce, so that the act of July 2, 1890, would apply to them, corporations might be subjected to penalties it imposes on individuals without in anywise interfering with the operation of the former act.

It certainly would not have affected the act of February 4, 1887, if a subsequent act had in terms forbidden all contracts in restraint of trade and commerce by railroad companies. The one would have supplemented and not contradicted or overthrown the other. Then how can it be claimed that a general act including railroad companies operates otherwise?

Counsel do not properly put the contention which they must make to sustain this point. If they did, its mere statement would be the best answer to it. It is this: The act of February 4, 1887, prohibited only one form of agreements among competing lines, viz: pooling. Congress intended, therefore, to legalize all other forms of agreement relating to rates or division of business between such lines. The act of July 2, 1890, can not be held to apply to railroads, because its effect would be to repeal this implied authorization.

No decision or other authority has been cited, and I know of none, which sustains the proposition that any such supposed legislative negative pregnant is to be considered in construing subsequent laws. The inconsistency must always be between different positive enactments.

Nor is there any better support for the unexpressed proposition which underlies the argument of appellees, viz: that partial treatment of a subject precludes the operation upon that subject of subsequent general legislation whose terms would naturally include it, and whose effect is to supplement only.

It is a fact so well known that the court will take judicial notice of it, that the chief if not the only form of contract and combination among competing railroads for the purpose of lessening or preventing competition which was known at the time the act of 1887 was passed, was that called pooling. It is fair, therefore, to assume that in designating this form of contract in its prohibition, Congress really intended to forbid the evil itself rather than a particular form of it, but unfortunately used terms which described the particular form only. In the enormous extension and multiplication of contracts and combinations which afterwards ensued, aimed at the suppression of competition, it was found that managers of railroads had enough fertility of resource to devise other methods than pooling. Congress later, in the act of 1890, in dealing with this subject which is of such great concern to the public, considered both as individuals and as a body politic, used apt language to forbid contracts and combinations of every nature and by all persons whatsoever, whose natural tendency and effect are to restrain freedom of trade and commerce.

It seems to me a gross perversion of legal principles which are intended to facilitate the ascertainment and effectuation of the will of Congress to apply them in support of such a claim as that now made.

I conclude, therefore, that the act of July 2, 1890, applies to all contracts, combinations, and conspiracies by railroad companies in restraint of trade and commerce, as well as to those made by others—certainly to all except pooling contracts.

II.

THE AGREEMENT IN QUESTION, IN SO FAR AS IT RELATES TO THE FIXING AND MAINTAINING OF RATES, IS A VIOLATION OF THE ACT OF JUNE 2, 1890.

(A) The act stands on its terms without reference to the Common Law, and those terms forbid all contracts, etc., in restraint of commerce among the States.

(B) If reference be had to the Common Law, the agreement in question must be condemned, because it is made by corporations charged with duties to the public of the highest importance.

(C) In either case the contract is to be judged by its natural tendency and effect and not by the intention of the parties, or by its actual effect on rates so far as known down to the time of suit or trial. Such intention and effect being, therefore, irrelevant, are not subjects of either pleading or proof.

A.

Counsel for appellees cite authorities to show that there is no Common Law of the United States.

What is known as commerce among the States is a subject peculiar to the United States, which is committed to the sole and absolute control of Congress. The act of 1890 must, therefore, be taken as it reads, and is not subject to definitions or implied limitations or qualifications borrowed from the Common Law.

While the title of the act speaks of "unlawful" restraints and monopolies, the term obviously refers to such as are made unlawful by the act itself. As there is no Common Law of the United States, and as the peculiar subject in hand is not known to the Common Law of England, those restraints and monopolies are unlawful which the act condemns, and no others.

The arguments of counsel and the decisions below proceed on the theory that only those contracts, combinations, and conspiracies are unlawful which are in *unreasonable* restraint of trade or commerce. But there is no qualification whatever in the act.

Every contract * * * *in restraint of trade or commerce* among the several States, or with foreign nations, is hereby declared illegal. *Every* person who shall make *any such contract* * * * shall be deemed guilty of a misdemeanor. * * *

I do not think the intention of this section was to forbid *bona fide* transfers of property among persons engaged in the same lines of trade or commerce, although the result may be to reduce the number of competitors. Such transactions are "contracts" in the broadest sense of the term; but the word was used in its ordinary meaning—agreements which merely created continuing relations between the parties and deal directly with the freedom of trade or commerce. This is borne out by the companion words "combination," "trust," and "conspiracy."

But what warrant is there for excluding from the operation of the act any contract of the class which its language fairly and naturally describes, whether the restraint imposed be great or small, reasonable or unreasonable?

The court below, and other inferior courts, have held that this act creates no new offense, but merely adds penal sanctions to the making of such contracts as by the rules of the Common Law the courts had, before the passage of the act, refused to recognize or enforce. But, in view of what I have already said, which counsel will hardly venture to gainsay in view of the plain terms of the act and their own admissions, it appears clearly to follow that the act bears no relation to the Common Law.

The title of an act can never prevail against its express language. Even if it be proper ever to refer to the title to aid in ascertaining the meaning of the act itself, this can be done only in case of doubt and uncertainty and affords little aid.[29]

But there is no doubt or uncertainty here. The language is broad, sweeping, and unqualified by reference or otherwise. It forbids every contract which in any manner or to any extent is "in restraint of trade or commerce" among the States. There is no escape, therefore, from the conclusion that the intention of Congress was to keep trade and commerce among the States and with foreign nations absolutely free from all the artificial restraints which are created by contract or combination of every kind and form. Counsel contend, and sustain the contention by quotations from public writers, that competition is, under some circumstances at least, hurtful to trade and commerce. The same claim is often made on behalf of trusts and other commercial combinations. If this should be conceded, the answer would be that Congress, acting for the people, and in this instance representing their almost universal sentiment, did not think so. It evidently believed that competition is the life of commerce as well as of trade, and therefore imposed on the courts no duty of inquiry as to reasonableness or justifiability, but condemned all restraints. For it will be noted that counsel do not attempt to deny, but virtually, if not

---

[29] Hadden v. The Collector, 5 Wall., at page 110; The King v. Williams, 1 W. Bl. 95.

expressly, admit that the prevention of competition, entire or partial, is a restraint of the trade or commerce in which it exists.

It is incredible that Congress, dealing in obedience to the popular demand for relief from a great and growing evil which affected the entire people, intended to qualify the relief it granted by leaving its enforcement to depend on the varying views of other tribunals as to public policy. No such intention is expressed, nor is there the slightest ground for implying it. On the contrary, Congress declared in no uncertain terms the public policy with respect to the trade and commerce committed to its care and control, instead of leaving it to be discovered or pieced out from the multitude of conflicting decisions, of which the briefs afford abundant examples.

It would be hard to add anything to what Judge Shiras has said on this subject in his dissenting opinion below, to which I refer the court.[30]

RELATION OF INTERSTATE-COMMERCE ACT.

It is said that the act must be considered in connection with the "act to regulate commerce," which prescribes that rates shall be "reasonable and just." But the latter act gave no definition of those terms and prescribed no rule by which reasonableness and justness of rates are to be determined. They were plainly to be left to the operation of the natural influences which decide all commercial values, whether of property or service, and the chief, or one of the chief, of these influences is competition.[31]

Reasonableness and justness were certainly considered by Congress with reference to the public as well as with reference to the carriers (162 U. S., at pp. 219, 233), though this view of the matter seems to be overlooked or slighted by counsel. Supply and demand, which are only another name for competition, can not fairly be disregarded in considering what rates are "reasonable and just" from the point of view of the public. If folly unduly increase the supply of means of transportation, or if bad management lead to excessive investment or cost of service, there is nothing to show that Congress intended to save carriers from the consequences at the expense of the public, even if it might properly have done so.

It is said that, by reason of the act of 1887 as well as of the general duty of common carriers to treat all alike, the business of

---

[30] 58 Fed., pp. 90, 91.
[31] Mr. Justice Brewer in C. & N. W. R. R. Co. *v.* Osborne, *supra*.

public carrying is not subject to competition like other business. This is a clear misconception. The only difference is that carriers are required, in competing with each other, to deal with the public as a whole and not with individuals. But the operation and effect of the competition are just the same. Public carriers must treat all alike; but they may, and do, when not restrained by such agreements as that now in issue, vie with each other in seeking patronage by the excellence of their service and the rates they charge. Competition with lines not covered by the agreement is expressly provided for by Article II, section 6.

It does not appear whether the appellees are or are not subject to laws fixing maximum rates, as is the case with some railway companies, at least as to passengers; but if they are, this affords no reason for exempting them from the operation of the act which forbids contracts to stifle or restrain free competition. Such a consideration could properly be addressed only to the law-making power.

It appears to me to follow from what I have said that the act of 1887 does not affect in anywise the operation of the act of 1890 upon railroad companies, but that the two acts are entirely consistent and capable of complete enforcement together.

B.

But if we must go to the Common Law to discover what contracts, etc., in restraint of trade or commerce among the States are forbidden by the act, we must, in this court and country, reach the conclusion that the agreement in question, in so far as it affects competition among the appellees, is one of them.

RESTRAINTS UPON ORDINARY TRADE.

The numerous cases relating to restrictions of *trade*, which I agree is not synonymous with *commerce*,[32] deal with the questions under what circumstances contracts may impose such restrictions and to what extent of time, territory, etc. Many of them are cited and discussed in the opinions below and in the briefs.

It is true that under certain circumstances and limitations such restraints may lawfully be imposed, and that the Common Law has somewhat relaxed its strictness so as to meet new conditions. But whatever may be the rule elsewhere, I believe it to be settled in this country, by the great weight of authority, that there can be no restriction whatever upon competition in trade except as an

---

[32] *In re* Debs and United States *v.* Joint Traffic Assn., *supra.*

incident to some transaction between the parties which creates rights to whose full enjoyment or protection the restraint is necessary. The usual instances are the transfer of property, business, or good will. In such cases the restriction may go to whatever extent is necessary for the protection of the right, and no further. *But the question whether the restraint is reasonable can never arise unless and until it appear that the rights so created make it proper that there should be some restriction.*

It must appear that—

"The partial restraint is not the *primary object* but a *mere incident* of the agreement." "The consideration and special circumstances inducing the arrangement must be shown to the court and approved by it." There must not only be a consideration, "but a good reason shown for the contract" (viz: the covenant in restraint of trade). If it be on the purchase of a business, the covenant must be made "intending still to pursue the business." "A man can not for money alone, where he has no other interest in the matter, purchase a valid contract in restraint of trade."[83]

No matter how limited, contracts in restraint of trade are not valid *when they are the main object of the parties.*[84]

Judge Sanborn, in the opinion below, recognized this rule, after reviewing many cases. The restraint must not be "*the main purpose*" (bottom of p. 70). "If *the main purpose* or natural and inevitable effect of a contract was to suppress competition or create a monopoly, it was illegal" (bottom of p. 72).

There was no such relation between the parties to this association as justified them in entering into any agreement whatever affecting their full freedom to seek business by offering better rates than others, and in this way deprive the public of actual or possible advantage. They were merely competitors and nothing more. They had no other relations whatever to each other. The error into which the circuit court and the majority of the circuit court of appeals fell was in assuming that because, in the class of cases above mentioned, the question is whether the restraint is reasonable, therefore the question of reasonableness arises and is decisive in all cases involving restraints upon competition created by agreement or combination of parties.

I am not willing to admit, as Judge Shiras seems to do in his dissenting opinion, that this agreement among natural competitors, made for the mere purpose of fixing rates and thereby to that extent putting an end to competition by means thereof, would

---

[83] Lange *v.* Werk, 2 O. S. 532 *et passim*). Also, W. W. W. Ass'n *v.* Starkey (84 Mich. 76).

[84] Grasselli *v.* Lowden, 11 O. S. 355; Alger *v.* Thacher, 19 Pick. 51.

be sustainable even if they were private companies engaged in ordinary trade. The few cases which apparently tend to justify it are against the weight of authority. Three cases are cited on page 77 of the brief for the U. P. R. R. Co. and others already mentioned. The first two, Central Shade Roller Co. *v.* Cushman (143 Mass. 353), and Gloucester &c., Co., *v.* Russia Cement Co. (154 Mass. 92), go on the ground that the subjects of the agreements were not staple articles, but were covered by patents or secret processes to which, of course, a different rule may well apply. The third, Kellogg *v.* Larkin, 3 Pinney (Wis.) 123, was to recover rent upon the lease of a mill which contained a stipulation forbidding the lessor to deal in wheat. It was sought to defeat recovery by showing that there was a scheme to control the wheat market in Milwaukee, to which lessor and lessee were parties, and in furtherance of which the lease was made.

It is unnecessary, however, to discuss the case on the principles which apply to persons and companies engaged in ordinary trade, because none of these companies are of that class. They are all

QUASI PUBLIC CORPORATIONS.

Not only are appellees corporations of this nature, but it is admitted that they were chartered and given public aid for the very purpose of securing independent and competing lines of railway.

In Gibbs *v.* Baltimore Gas Co. (130 U. S., at pp. 408, 409) the court, by the Chief Justice, stated the distinction between such companies and private organizations and persons:

The supplying of illuminating gas is a business of a public nature to meet a public necessity. It is not a business like that of an ordinary corporation engaged in the manufacture of articles that may be furnished by individual effort [citing cases]. Hence, while it is justly urged that those rules which say that a given contract is against public policy, should not be arbitrarily extended so as to interfere with the freedom of contract (Printing, etc., Registering Co. *v.* Simpson, L. R., 19 Eq. 462), yet in the instance of business of such character that it presumably can not be restrained to any extent whatever without prejudice to the public interest, courts decline to enforce or sustain contracts imposing such restraint, however partial, because in contravention of public policy [citing cases].

It will be observed that the justification alleged in that case for an agreement between rival companies to fix the price of gas was excessive competition resulting in loss (p. 397).

I deem it unnecessary to cite any of the many other decisions to the same effect. Some of them will be referred to in discussing the alleged admissions on the pleadings as to the intention of the parties and the actual effect of the agreement on rates.

MONOPOLY.

It is said by counsel that nothing can be claimed in this case on the ground of monopoly, because the companies, notwithstanding the agreement for fixing rates, were still to continue competing for business. It appears to be claimed, too, that the principles relating to monopolies, real or attempted, can not, from the nature of things, apply to railroad companies.

All this might have been and doubtless was said of the agreement between gas companies which was the subject of the case last cited. One of the chief elements of evil in monopolies is the destruction of competition and the consequent prevention of the operation of ordinary commercial causes upon prices. When this result is reached by any form of agreement or combination, courts, which look at substance rather than form, do not hesitate to apply the wise rule above stated, whether a technical monopoly is created or not.

A monopoly, in the modern sense of the word, ordinarily consists in requiring control, more or less complete, of a business which is open to all who choose to engage in it.[85] A railroad company has, by reason of physical causes, control of the business of transportation by land between distant points which it connects. If more than one line of railway be built through the same territory, then the various companies have among them control of the business as against all the world, because the number which may engage in it is necessarily limited. This may be said to be a natural monopoly of the right to supply citizens with such transportation. In so far as concerns this control which arises from natural causes no one can lawfully complain. But when the companies which enjoy this natural monopoly of supply extend its effect artificially by an agreement fixing rates, or otherwise stifling competition among themselves, they are guilty of exactly the same public wrong as ordinary trusts or combinations. It is, in fact, more harmful in effect, though the same in principle, because it is easier to stifle competition which is limited by natural laws. When but little competition is possible, such as there is becomes all the more important and should be the more zealously guarded.

---

[85] United States *v.* E. C. Knight Co., *supra*, at p. 10.

The fact that the agreement does not purport to prevent the parties to it from competing by affording greater facilities, such as better service or quicker time, does not tend in any degree to excuse the express suppression of all competition in rates which was plainly its main object. Lowering of prices is the chief means of competition the world over. There can be no real competition without it. The right of the public to procure slower or less convenient transportation at a lower rate, which is a valuable right in these days of sharp and close competition in all lines of business, is entirely taken away by this agreement. It operates upon rates exactly as an ordinary trade trust does upon prices; and the argument now advanced would apply to most if not all of the combinations among rival dealers to fix the price of commodities, which were involved in the many cases in which they have been held invalid. Each was generally left at liberty to get all the business he could at the rates fixed. This is necessarily so, except in cases of pooling.

This answer to the charge of creating a restraint, under a rule of law which forbids all restraints, "*however partial,*"[86] is that the restraint is *only partial*.

C.

But it is contended that the question of the validity of the agreement as to fixing rates is affected by certain portions of the answers which stand admitted by submitting the case on bill and answer.

The matters so relied on are set out at page 66 *et seq.* of the brief already mentioned. They consist in denials of the unlawful intent charged in the bill, in averments of a mere purpose to further the objects of the act of 1887, and in allegations that rates have not been increased, but on the contrary have in fact been lowered, under the operation of the agreement. By so setting the case for hearing, only such averments are admitted as are well pleaded.[87]

That is to say, only such as are relevant and open to issue and proof, for an averment upon which, if denied, evidence would not be heard, can not be the subject of admission, which is merely a mode of proof.[88] As the court said, speaking of an agreement in

---

[86] Gibbs *v.* Baltimore Gas Co., *supra*.

[87] Story's Eq. Pl., 10th ed., pp. 741-742, 413; Interstate Land Co. *v.* Maxwell Land Co., 139 U. S. 577; Taylor *v.* Barclay, 2 Sim. 220, quoted at 137 U. S. 215.

[88] Louisville & Nashville R. R. Co. *v.* Palmes, 109 U. S. 244, 253.

restraint of trade, in Kellogg *v.* Larkin, 3 Pinney (Wis.), at p. 135—a case cited by appellees on others points—

Therefore no averment could give to the agreement a character which it had not, and no admission could take from it the character which it had.

The character, business, and relations of the various companies, appellees, being admitted, as well as the making of the contract, its terms, and entry upon its performance, the sole question before the court arises upon the contract itself. The only intention which is material is that which the law implies from the instrument.[39]

That in such agreements the actual effect, so far as it can be known at the hearing, is irrelevant, and that they are to be judged by their natural tendency and effect, is well settled.[40]

In the former case the court said, by Mr. Justice Brown, at p. 676:

Whether the consolidation of competing lines will necessarily result in an increase of rates, or whether such consolidation has generally resulted in a detriment to the public, is beside the question. Whether it has that effect or not, it certainly puts it in the power of the consolidated corporation to give it that effect—in short, puts the public at the mercy of the corporation. There is, and has been for the past three hundred years, both in England and in this country, a popular prejudice against monopolies in general, which has found expression in innumerable acts of legislation. We can not say that such prejudice is not well founded. It is a matter upon which the Legislature is entitled to pass judgment. At least there is sufficient doubt of the propriety of such monopolies to authorize the Legislature, which may be presumed to represent the views of the public, to say that it will not tolerate them unless the power to establish them be conferred by clear and explicit language.

In the latter case the court said, by the Chief Justice:

Again, all the authorities agree that in order to vitiate a contract or combination it is not essential that its result should be a complete monopoly; it is sufficient if it really tends to that end and to deprive the public of the advantages which flow from free competition.[41]

---

[39] Interstate Land Co. *v.* Maxwell Land Co., *supra;* Pearsall *v.* Gt. Northern Ry. Co., 161 U. S. 646.

[40] Pearsall *v.* Gt. Northern Ry. Co., *supra;* United States *v.* E. C. Knight Co., 156 U. S. 16.

[41] See also the passage quoted by Mr. Justice Harlan, dissenting on other points, from Central Ohio Salt Co. *v.* Guthrie, 35 O. S. 672 (*id.*, 27). In addition to the various cases cited by him to the same effect, see—People *v.* Sheldon, 139 N. Y. 251; Judd *v.* Harrington, *id.* 110; People *v.* Milk Exchange, 145 *id.* 267; Anderson *v.* Jett, 89 Ky. 375; Anheuser-Busch Brewing Ass'n *v.* Houck, 27 S. W. Rep. 696; Moore *v.* Bennett, 140 Ill. 69; Chapin *v.* Brown Bros., 83 Ia. 156.

The reasons are obvious and are stated in many of the cases, why agreements involving subjects of public concern must be judged by what *may* be done under them and not by what the parties may have chosen to do down to the time of the inquiry.

I submit that this agreement put the public "at the mercy" of appellees with respect to freight rates; that its natural tendency and effect were to deprive the people of a great region of advantages which both they and Congress believe flow or may flow from competition among railroads; and that it therefore should be condemned by this court and the judgment below reversed.

CASES CITED BY THE COURT OF APPEALS.

The majority of the court of appeals disposed of Gibbs *v.* Gas Co., and similar cases, by saying:

But we think, in view of the state of facts on which the decisions were predicated, and the points actually adjudicated, it would be unwise to deduce an unbending rule that any and every contract between two railway companies which enjoins or contemplates concert of action in the matter of establishing freight or passenger rates between competitive points is against public policy, and an unlawful restraint of trade. No case, we believe, has yet gone to that extent, or has declared that the business of transporting freight and passengers by rail is of such character that no restraint whatever upon competition therein is permissible. On the contrary, contracts between common carriers which impose some restrictions upon competition have been frequently sustained by our highest courts, and the rule has been often applied that the test of their validity was not the existence, but the reasonableness, of the restriction imposed.

I will notice briefly in the margin the cases cited by the court in support of its statement. [42]

---

[42] Navigation Co. *v.* Winsor, 20 Wall. 64, involved a stipulation in a contract for the sale of a steamboat that it should not be used in certain waters, which the court held (p. 69) "was necessary to protect the former company (the seller) from interference with its own business," *i. e.*, by the use of the steamboat sold.

Chicago, etc., R. R. Co. *v.* Pullman Car Co., 139 U. S. 79, was an action by the latter company to recover from the former the value of two cars which had been destroyed by fire while in use by the former. One of the defenses was that the agreement under which the cars were so used was void, as being against public policy, because it gave the Pullman Company the exclusive right for fifteen years to furnish drawing-room and sleeping cars to the railroad company. But the court said, by Mr. Justice Harlan (p. 89): "We cannot perceive that such a contract is at all in restraint of trade."

Wiggins Ferry Co. *v.* C. and A. R. R. Co., 73 Mo. 389, belongs to the same class of cases as the last cited. It involved merely an agreement by a railroad company for the ferriage of its passengers and freight across the Mississippi.

REPORTS OF INTERSTATE COMMERCE COMMISSION.

In addition to the cases I have mentioned, the court of appeals also cited certain extracts from reports of the Interstate Commerce Commission, which, it is claimed, show that, in the opinion of that body, the intention of Congress was, by the act to regulate commerce, "to place important restraints upon competition." (58 Fed. 75).

It will be remembered that the Commission is not charged with any duty with respect to the act of July 2, 1890, and that whatever may have been said in its reports must be considered without reference to that act.

There are undoubtedly many purposes for which railroad companies may make agreements or form associations, such as continuous carriage, interchange of cars, use of uniform coupling appliances, classification of freights, etc. But the fact that such companies form an organization which they call an association does not entitle them to add to such proper purposes others which the law condemns. As to the latter, the agreement, whatever it be, must be considered as though it stood alone.

What the Commission has said in its annual reports or otherwise with respect to such associations should be read in light of the fact that there are lawful purposes, such as those above enumerated, for which they may properly exist; and it is not just to assume that whatever may have been said in general approval of the efforts of such associations to accomplish proper purposes was intended to be in approval of all other purposes, of specific provisions in any of their agreements, or of any unlawful act they may commit.

The quotation from page 19 of the Fourth Annual Report,

It was analogous to an agreement with a connecting line, not to an agreement with a competing one.

While some of the language used in the opinion in Manchester, etc., R. R. Co. *v.* Concord R. R. Co., 66 N. H. 100, read without regard to the case decided, might be taken, as the court below took it, as meant to justify agreements among companies *actually operating* competing lines to put an end to all competition in rates, yet, in view of the facts upon which he was passing, the judge who delivered the opinion must be absolved from any such intention. The suit was for accounting and recovery under contracts and leases by virtue of which the defendant company had been for many years in possession and operation of the railroad of the plaintiff company. The defendant sought to defeat recovery by pleading, among other things, that the contracts and leases were against public policy because the lines of the two companies were competing.

The subject of the action was *an actual lease and transfer of property*, not a purely executory agreement or combination, as in the case at bar. There

given by the court at page 75, does not profess to be a construction of the law, but merely a statement of fact with reference to such associations. The quotation from page 21 of the same report, made at page 76, is simply an utterance against what are known as "rate wars" and their consequences, and can not, in even a remote degree, be said to approve association agreements like that in question. On the contrary, in the same paragraph, on page 22 of the report, will be found this statement:

was no agreement whatever as to rates, but control of them and the consequent ending of competition resulted from an executed transaction which brought about change of possession and control of property.

It is fair to infer that the desire to terminate the competition was the motive which led to the transaction. But the common law has at no time undertaken to question actual leases or purchases of property on the ground that they were intended to result, or did result, in the cessation of competition between the parties. The right to acquire and dispose of property has always been too highly considered to be in anywise restricted. The natural limitations of the power of acquisition and the risks and liabilities which result from actual ownership of property, or its control by *bona fide* lease, or otherwise, have always been deemed sufficient protection to the public; or it has been thought unwise to seek prevention of restraint of trade by imposing a restraint upon property which would prove the greater evil. In fact the law has always encouraged the transfers of property by permitting restraints of trade as incidents thereto which it would condemn, if independent because it has always considered wholesome the restriction on the right of *mere executory contract* which forbids restraint of trade thereby. I know of no authority, ancient or modern, which would have justified the court in refusing to adjudge to the lessor company its rights for any such reasons as those invoked with respect to public policy or restraint of trade. The case would have been different if the lease had been a sham, without actual transfer of possession, to cover a mere agreement between the companies to prevent competition. But the *bona fides* of the lease in this regard was not questioned. It had not only been made, but its covenants had been fully performed by the lessor.

Assuming the corporate power of the companies to enter into the lease, there was, at the time it was made, no law forbidding the purchase or leasing of competing railroads, and without such a law there was no limit upon the right of acquisition. Recognizing this, a law was afterwards enacted in New Hampshire, as in most if not all other States, forbidding railroad companies to acquire competing lines by lease or otherwise.

The case does not justify the position in whose support it is cited. Surely the court would not have decreed an accounting and recovery upon an agreement involving no sale, lease, or other transfer of property, but simply engaging two rival railroad companies, both remaining in active operation of their lines, not to compete in rates.

The passages cited by the court from Morawetz Priv. Corp., Sec. 1131, and Redfield Law of Railways, Sec. 146, appear to be founded on a failure to observe the distinction which I have endeavored to point out between stipulations against competition which are merely incidental to sales, leases, etc., and those which are made for the sole purpose of preventing competition, and

Agreements between railroad companies which from time to time they have entered into with a view to prevent such occurrences have never been found effectual, and for the very sufficient reason that the mental reservations in forming them have been quite as numerous and more influential than the written stipulations.

The quotation from page 25 of the second annual report, made at page 76, used in the connection in which it is used, is entirely

---

also on ignoring the distinction between purely private and *quasi* public companies pointed out in Gibbs *v.* Gas Co., *supra.* They also depend on English cases which are not only contrary to the weight of authority in this country, but also are affected more or less by English statutes, and are therefore of little aid.

See A. T. & S. R. R. *v.* D. & N. O. R. R., 110 U. S. at p. 684.

Judge Redfield says in the section cited:

But when it is considered that these companies have to a very great extent a monopoly of the traffic and travel of the country, the power to regulate fares and freight by arrangement between the different companies is certainly one very susceptible of abuse.

I quote this here, out of its regular order, as bearing on the intention and scope of the act of July 2, 1890. The object of the act was to prevent this liabilty to abuse, against which the very difficult inquiry as to the reasonability of such agreements was an inadequate protection.

Mogul Steamship Co. *v.* McGregor, upon which the court rely as sustaining the validity of the agreement, was wholly unlike the case now before the court, and is not at all in point.

A number of ship owners, engaged in the carriage of tea from China, entered into an agreement to drive competitors from the market by offering rebates, etc. Those competitors having been by that means compelled to carry at a loss, sued for damages. The question was not whether the agreement was or was not one which would have been enforceable as among defendants themselves, but whether the alleged loss caused plaintiffs by the *too severe competition* of defendants was an injury for which they could recover damages. The case was the same as that which would be presented here if the outside lines, for competing with which by means of lowering rates the agreement specially provided (section II. § 6), had lost their business at common points or had been compelled to do it at a loss, and had then sued the members of the association for damages. The only bearing which the character of the agreement of the defendants, as among themselves and as against the public generally, was claimed to have, was that if it were unlawful, so considered, it was a conspiracy which would make whatever was done in furtherance of it actionable.

But the Lord Chief Justice said in deciding the case on its trial (21 Q. B. D., at p. 553) " Restraint of trade, with deference, has in its legal sense nothing to do with this question."

He gave judgment for defendants, not on the ground that the agreement among them was or was not invalid as in restraint of trade because the object was eventually to control the trade by driving the plaintiffs out of it, but because the loss occasioned to plaintiffs by the severe competition of defend-

misleading. As will be seen by reference to the chapter from which it is taken, the subject discussed is the unity of railroad interests. The following passage from the same connection as that quoted shows the injustice of the use to which the latter is applied:

One of the chief perplexities encountered in dealing with complaints against railroad companies arises from the fact that to the public mind the railroad interest of the country seems to be in

---

ants was not an injury in law. It was freedom and not restraint of trade which the decision vindicated.

On appeal the three judges divided. Lord Esher, M.R., was for reversal, chiefly on the ground that defendants were guilty of "an act beyond the limits of fair trade competition" which prevented plaintiffs from exercising their "full right to a free course of trade" and "leads to an irresistible inference of an indirect motive" (23 Q. B. D., at p. 609). He thererore held that "the act of the defendants in lowering their freights far beyond a lowering for any purpose of trade * * * was an act done evidently for the purpose of interfering with * * * the plaintiffs' right to a free course of trade, and was, therefore, a wrongful act," etc. (p. 610).

Bowen and Fry, L. J.J., voted to affirm. The former (p. 615) ridiculed the idea that a court should undertake to decide what is "reasonable" or "fair" competition or rates of freight. He maintained the right to the utmost freedom of competition (p. 617). In answer to the claim that the agreement of the defendants was illegal as among themselves, because in restraint of trade, he says (p. 619):

The term "illegal" here is a misleading one. Contracts, as they are called, in restraint of trade, are not, in my opinion, illegal in any sense, except that the law will not enforce them. It does not prohibit the making of such contracts. It merely declines, after they have been made, to recognize their validity. The law considers the disadvantage so imposed upon the contract a sufficient shelter to the public. * * * No action at common law will lie or ever has lain against any individual or individuals for entering into a contract merely because it is in restraint of trade.

He therefore held that—

If peaceable and honest combinations of capital *for purposes of trade competition* are to be struck at, it must, I think, be by legislation, etc. (p. 620).

See Fry, L. J., to same effect at pp. 626-7. He said, p. 627:

It is plain that the intention and object of the combination before us is to check competition, but the means it uses is competition, and it is difficult, if not impossible, to weigh against one another the probabilities of the employment of competition on the one hand and its suppression on the other.

In short, the decision was that mere competition, even though combined, gives no right of action to those who suffer loss thereby. The court was not concerned with the question whether an agreement among parties not to compete with each other was valid *inter sese* or not.

The affirmance of the judgment in the House of Lords (1892), App. Cas. 1, was upon the same lines.

It will be noted that the business of ocean navigation, which is free to all, has not the same *quasi* public character as that of transportation by rail. The former requires neither the grant of franchises nor the right of eminent domain.

some sense a unity, so that when there is cause for complaint in the system anywhere, the whole interest is chargeable with some degree of moral if not legal responsibility.

After setting forth the fact that Congress has not attempted to deal with railroads as a unity, but treats them as separate entities in the exercise of its power to regulate commerce, the report undertakes to state some of the difficulties *that would be* encountered in an effort to enforce regulation upon the theory of unity, and in this connection uses the language quoted, which is in the nature of an argument against the unit theory of regulation. Yet this was cited by counsel below, and adopted by the court, as an approval of association agreements like that now in question. The other quotation from the same report is subject to the same criticism.

It seems to me unnecessary to notice the various quotations from the reports of the Commission which appear in the opinion and in the briefs. What I have said applies with more or less aptness to all of them. But we should look for construction by the Commission to what they have done with reference to association agreements.[43]

III.

RIGHT OF THE GOVERNMENT TO SUE.

(a) If, as I have tried to show, the act of July 2, 1890, applies to railroad companies, and the agreement among the appellees is in violation of that act, then it seems conclusively to follow that the right to sue to enjoin further performance of the agreement is given to the United States by section 4 of the act.

---

[43] See Cincinnati Freight Bureau *v.* The Southern Railway and Steamship Association and The Chicago Freight Bureau *v.* The C. N. O. and T. P. Railway Company and others, decided May 29, 1894, in which it was held by the Commission that certain provisions of the agreement were tantamount to pooling and therefore illegal, and also certain other provisions, such as that " to apply full local rates upon all traffic subject to the association agreement coming from or going to such offending lines." At the conclusion of the case the Commission said:

The mere combination or agreement to thus discriminate is not, however, made an offense under the act, and no actual discrimination of this kind has been shown in these cases. As to whether such combination or agreement alone, in the absence of an overt act, would be indictable at Common Law *or under some other statute*, it is unnecessary, and perhaps, improper, for this Commission to express an opinion.

See also Blanton Duncan *v.* The A., T. & S. F. R. R. Co, and others, decided November 3, 1893.

See also in this connection quotation (*supra*, p. 308) from the report of the Commission for 1895.

The control of interstate commerce, and the consequent duty of protecting it, made it entirely competent for Congress to add the preventive remedy by injunction to the penal provisions of the act, because the civil remedy and the criminal sanction are entirely independent and not inconsistent. This seems to me to be settled by the decision *In re Debs*, 158 U. S. 564.

In reply to the attempt to anticipate the use of that decision in this connection (brief above named, p. 86), I will only say that I understand it to go on broader lines than "the property right in its mails." I see no such gross materialism in that magnificent exposition of Federal law. The only "property interest" the Government had was in the mail bags. Surely the court was not simply protecting these, but was defending the right of the public, of which the Government was guardian and trustee, to have Federal functions proceed without impediment. The right of the whole people to free passage of the mails is chiefly valuable because they are an instrument of interstate commerce, which, as well as the mail service, is committed to the care of Congress by the Constitution. The Government does not operate the mails as a source of revenue and therefore has no pecuniary interest in them. The general public, however, for whose benefit this suit is brought, have a direct pecuniary interest in having commerce free from restrictions. By the same right it has to protect from interruption the mails, which are a mere means or incident of commerce, it may protect the latter also by preventing as well as by punishing interference or restraint.

The case of U. S. *v.* U. P. R. R. Co., 98 U. S. 569, which is cited at page 81 of the brief already named, does not seem to me relevant. The court did not deny the right of the Government to sue as provided in the act under which the suit was brought, but simply held that it made out no case for recovery. The company on whose behalf the Government might have recovered appeared and disclaimed. The Government itself had, as the court found, neither public interest nor property right in the subject of the suit. It has an interest, and the people on whose behalf it sues have a direct pecuniary interest, in maintaining the freedom of interstate commerce from unlawful restraints, and the act expressly gives it the remedy by injunction to protect such interests.

(*b*) But apart from the right to sue given by the act, the Government has a right to maintain this suit.[44]

---

[44] C., N. O. & T. P. Rwy. Co. *v.* Interstate Commerce Commission, 162 U. S. 184; Texas Pacific R. R. Co. *v.* same, *id.*, 197; *In re* Debs, 158 U. S. *supra*.

The passage quoted from the Texas Pacific case (brief, p. 86) mentions the absence of persons complaining of the rates in question simply as bearing on the *fact of unreasonableness*, which had to to be found to justify action by the court, and not as affecting the *jurisdiction* without which it could not proceed to any inquiry at all.

The right of the Government to sue under the interstate commerce act is not limited to the mere protection of the interest of individuals.[45]

JUDSON HARMON.

---

[45] U. S. *v.* M. P. R: R. Co., 65 Fed. Rep. 903, 906. That the State has a right to sue to enjoin acts contrary to public policy, etc., see Pomeroy's Eq. Jur., secs. 934, 1093, and note; L. & N. R. R. Co. *v.* Commonwealth, 31 S. W. Rep. 477; Stockton, Atty. Gen., *v.* Central R. R. Co. *et al.*, 50 N. J. Eq. 52. In XI. Am. R. R. & Corp'n Rep., p. 485 (note 2 to case of People *v.* Milk Exchange, *supra*), the cases on the subject are collected.

PERSONAL INJURY LITIGATION.

A writer in the *North American Review* of February, 1897, has performed a public service by calling attention to the enormous increase of actions claiming damages for personal injuries or for death resulting therefrom. Crude and limited as are the statistics he gives enough is shown to startle the ordinary reader who is not familiar with the subject. Yet there are considerations not adverted to by him which are quite as interesting to one seriously thinking out some remedy for an obvious evil. That evil is the corrupted public sentiment in favor of looting any public or quasi-public treasury in aid of private suffering or private want, if not private greed. Its expression is not confined to the jury-box nor to personal injury verdicts. It appears in constitutional conventions, legislatures and in Congress.

Its operation is sometimes bold, as in pension legislation of high and low degree, appropriations for private benefit under the disguise of public needs, in many forms, and in all kinds of legislation to make this species of pillage easy by removing whatever barriers are found in the ancient law and the repugnance of our ancestors; and sometimes it is more insidious and crafty, as in proposed reforms of practice which have the purpose of ousting the bench from all power to hinder the plundering process. If a legislator wishes by statute to direct how the judge shall instruct the jury generally you will find in him or those who are behind him the speculators, runners and brokers in damages for personal injuries mentioned by the writer in the *North American Review*.

Nor is it strange that men coming into the jury-box from the flood tides of a periodical literature devoted to an agitation for relief from individual suffering by socialistic combinations of the poor against the rich, should find the verdict of a jury against "a corporation" a most convenient sort of combination to mitigate the suffering at least in this one case. Are not all corporations a trust organized by capital to oppress labor? And this being so is not the denial by this corporation of its liability to this plaintiff a part of the conspiracy of the rich to oppress the poor? It will only "average up things" if we take every occasion to distribute some of this dangerous aggregation of wealth to those who sorely need it, and the "corporation" will never feel the loss. Perhaps not a single juryman is conscious of this reasoning in the given instance of its exercise; indeed, he does not, in fact, go through this formula in reaching his verdict and is, therefore, not guilty of the implied corruption there is in it; nevertheless, his state of mind is such that the process works itself by the callous indifference he indulges towards the case of the "corporation," and the supersensitive sympathy he feels towards a poor laborer or anyone injured by violence, causes him to do an injustice he does not recognize as such. But this state of mind is chronic with him and the result of a pernicious education. The strong men who resist or resent any influence of this kind are not generally found in the jury-box.

Nor is there wanting a very considerable justification for a good deal of this ill feeling towards railroads, mostly the victims of personal-injury verdicts, arising out of their own conduct in the premises. Almost without exception everywhere they adopt the policy of "fighting" every claimant for damages, no matter how clear their liability, unless it may be they will "compromise" when they can pay a nominal and wholly inadequate sum; they ridiculously search the injured man's smallest actions with hypercritical minuteness for some trace of contributory negligence and in directions that they must know are unjust, because the conduct complained of is in their own interest or with generous fidelity was supposed by the employee to be so, or else was taken with a human thoughtlessness in those engaged in earnest and faithful labor that is practically unavoidable; they even make rules that they know cannot be enforced, such as that a brakeman shall never go between moving cars to couple or uncouple them when it is certain that under some circumstances the cars cannot be coupled unless they are moving, and when they know that a want of courage in this respect would result in dismissal because it would be in fact inefficiency; doing this in order that the rules may be used in stress of weather as a harbor of refuge—a pretext for a counter-claim of contributory negligence; they even send their "runners," in the shape of claim agents, local lawyers, doctors, surgeons and nurses, to take "statements" that are, to say the least, if not perverted to suit their interests, with great injustice made to speak most favorably for the company, and these are sometimes used as impeaching testimony under circumstances that shock the commonest sense of humanity; as in one case where the amputation was delayed after the ether had been partially administered until the "statement" could be taken, amid protests from the by-standers that it was not fair; and so there often appear many evidences of injustice on the part of the companies that jurors are quick to notice and resent, resulting in a general prejudice against the companies that makes verdicts against them all too easy.

Again, in the struggle against the well-founded belief that it is almost impossible to have juries do right towards the defendants in personal injury cases, there is a possibility of "straining the timbers of the law" and pressing perilously near the danger line in rulings upon contributory negligence, fellow-servant law and the like defenses, and in directing the verdicts of juries. He need not be a very old lawyer to know that to send up to an appellate court a bill of exceptions containing all the testimony was until recently almost unknown in any well-regulated jurisdiction; the Supreme Court of the United States for a hundred years forbade it because under our Federal Constitution an appellate court cannot have the jurisdiction to re-try a question of fact. Yet, nowadays, the feeblest whisperings and the most inconsequential givings out of all the witnesses must go up that the appellate court may say whether the case ought to have been submitted to the jury or ought not to have been so submitted, and whether the trial judge should not have directed the verdict always asked of him by the railroad company, as if there never were a case when it should not be done; certainly it is never admitted by the railroad lawyer that a case against a railroad company can be one for the jury; if he grants this motion the railroad company feels that it has escaped the peril of the jurybox; if he refuses, it feels that there is another chance that other judges may save it that peril. And so there beat about the constitutional guaranty of trial by jury strong forces whose activities are dangerous beyond all question.

It is mostly this personal injury litigation that has developed so actively the practice of directing verdicts by the court. That the power exists there can be and never was any question, but that it was for a long time, and until this evil of jury injustice to railroads invoked it, almost dormant in this country is also true. It stands in the way of personal-injury speculators and lawyers, and they are engaged everywhere in every way in hostile array against it—saying that the judgment of judges whether railroad companies shall pay damages is not more to be trusted than the verdict of juries, and here we have in the struggle against the practice of directing verdicts another startling effect of the growth of personal-injury litigation as shown by the article in the *North American Review.*

Nor is this all, for in the Constitutional Conventions and Legislatures the influences hostile to the railroad companies are assiduously engaged in digging out and casting away almost every vestige of the law of contributory negligence, of fellow servant, of defective machinery known to be so, and like defenses, and turning these companies into delightful accident and life insurance companies, with no fine-print restrictions and without premiums for the risks, except such as they levy on the public by increase of transportation rates in their schedules.

Shall we loosen or abandon the guaranty of trial by jury, abrogate all just protection to the master as against claims of compensation for an injury to his servant while in his service and all laws protecting railroads in the rightful use of their tracks as against trespassers and those using the crossings, merely because jurors will not do the right thing towards "corporations," and because there are so many cormorants' and their trainers interested in having them levy contributions on corporation treasuries in aid of the suffering poor? No. It is not essential to do any of these things, but it is necessary that public opinion—that great corrector of all social evils—shall be aroused and educated to the right way of thinking on this subject. The railroad companies can help by doing right themselves and paying without litigation every just claim. If they would organize in their own legal department "a court" to which the claimant might himself resort if he found it fair to him, and which at all events would make a perfectly impartial investigation in all cases, and whenever the claim was just fix the reasonable compensation which the law itself would give, tendering this without litigation, the prejudice against them in the jury-box might almost disappear and then the juries would make short work of the speculators in unjust and fabricated claims. Many companies might combine to maintain such a tribunal, and as an adjunct to it organize for a uniform and systematic defense against wrongful claims, tendering the money into court in all that were fair and honest when the offer of compensation should be rejected. Such a plan as this may not be practicable but if it be it is worth a trial to check the evil tendencies of that now in use. It would require big lawyers to sustain it but big lawyers are at the service of corporations to meet this demand. Compulsory arbitration by statutory methods would afford no better tribunals than existing courts, but the voluntary offer to pay fair demands for injuries sustained would soon do its work of restoring a sense of justice in the jury-box. The work cannot all be done by the bench.

It is a long jump from 4 Edw. III., C. 7, which abrogated the rule that personal actions die with the person even as to injuries to property to Lord Campbell's Act, giving an action for the wrongful killing of another to those who suffer by the death; but this space of time and growth in legal remedies has witnessed a corresponding enlargement of the importance of the law of torts. If people are more civilized they are less inclined to submit to injuries that entail pecuniary loss when they can obtain redress, not by retaliation in kind, but by a kind of recoupment in money damages. Love of money and love of the remotest and most questionable chances to get it have grown with the civilization we boast and there is nowhere a more disagreeable exhibition of it than the uses made of slight wrongs or injuries that ordinarily were never noticed hitherto, but now are made the foundation for building up by perjury, and all the arts and devices of sharp practice, claims for enormous damages. The sharp practices of two professions, legal and medical, are called in to aid the money-raid upon the unfortunate tort-feasor. The personal-injury lawyer and the personal-injury doctor, with his "traumatic neurosis," stand in the ring and fight the railroad doctor and the railroad lawyer, with his "contributory negligence," from "start to finish" with a jury for the referee and a judge who is reduced by legislation, if possible, to be a mere official time-keeper. The "Marquis of Queensberry rules" provided by constitutional conventions and Legislatures are all one-sided and in favor of the *Plaintiff*. The comparisons for ferocity now raging between the prize-ring and the college foot-ball game should not ignore the combat between the "Master and Servant" in a personal injury case in a court of law.

Eli Shelby Hammond.

RECENT LEGISLATION AFFECTING PATENTS.

The American Bar Association, a year or more ago, appointed a special committee to draft and report amendments to the United States Statutes relating to patents, for the purpose of correcting certain recognized defects. The work of this committee resulted in the introduction in the last Congress of a bill known as H. R. Bill 3014. This bill in essentially the form prepared by the Bar Association committee was enacted by Congress and was approved March 3d, 1897.

The first of the amendments limits the time within which an invention which has been patented or has been described in a printed publication, may be made the subject of an application for a patent in the United States. Before discussing this amendment in detail, it will be useful to review certain peculiar developments of patent practice which have resulted from the efforts of patent lawyers to secure for their clients broad and controlling patent protection, subsequently to the full development of an industry. Three methods were devised of availing of the provisions of the patent laws, in a manner which could scarcely have been contemplated when the laws were framed. They may be appropriately termed the re-issue method, the divisional application method, and the early publication and foreign patent method. The first of these has been effectually regulated by decisions of the courts; the second is partially regulated by recent court decisions and is further restricted in effect by the new act; the third is the subject of the first amendment above referred to.

The re-issue method, which was at one time extensively practiced, consisted in re-issuing patents with claims much broader in scope than those originally contained in the patents. The task of properly patenting an invention frequently calls for as great an exercise of ingenuity on the part of the patent lawyer, as was required on the part of the inventor in devising the invention which is to be made the subject of the patent. While it may not be difficult to describe and claim the average invention in such manner that the specific device is fairly well protected, it is impossible to foresee all the various ways which others may devise to circumvent the patent, when practical use has demonstrated the value of the invention. It is the aim of the patent lawyer to secure for his client all possible avenues by which the same or equivalent results may be obtained. Frequently, however, patents are found to be inadequate to secure the protection which the inventor is manifestly entitled to; moreover, in the prosecution of applications for patents, mistakes and errors are often made of a character which in justice to the inventor should admit of correction. Section 4916 of the Revised Statutes was designed to provide for such emergencies by the re-issue of a patent, if the specification was defective or insufficient or if the patentee had claimed as his own more than his own invention, and "the error arose through accident or mistake and without fraudulent or deceptive intention."

Exactly what constituted error or mistake in the sense used in the law was not clear, and the Patent Office became very liberal in allowing re-issues, so much so that upon the surrender of an unexpired patent it was possible to re-mould the entire specification, broaden the claims and receive from the Patent Office a re-issued patent, far more comprehensive than the original, and this process might take place at any time before the expiration of the seventeen years term of the original patent.

For many years this provision of the laws was taken advantage of to re-issue patents under the following circumstances: A valuable industry having been developed, the records upon being searched might disclose some obscure patent which, in the light of the present development, would afford foundation for a claim of sufficient scope to broadly cover the industry to which, however, it may itself have practically contributed nothing. Such a patent would then be re-issued with claims commensurate with the developed art, provided it appeared that this patent contained earliest disclosure of the invention. The requisite "error" was found in the fact that the original claim was not sufficiently broad and comprehensive. Manifestly, however, it was not the intent of the law that a patentee should permit an announcement to stand for years that he claimed a particular limited invention, and, after others had embarked in an enterprise, free from infringement of the patent, that the claim of that patent should be so re-constructed as to bring the new enterprise within its scope. Nevertheless, the Patent Office was in the habit of thus re-issuing patents with enlarged claims, until the decision of the Supreme Court in Miller *v.* Brass Co., in 1881, emphatically declared that a re-issue patent should not contain claims of enlarged scope, unless there were clear evidence of the error and steps were taken within a reasonable time to correct it. This decision effectually closed the door to the subordination of vested interests by re-issue of old patents. The practical effect of this decision upon the Patent Office practice is forcibly shown by the fact that in 1880 the number of re-issues was 506, whereas in 1882, the year after the decision, there were but 271, and the number has steadily decreased until during the year 1896 there were but 54 patents re-issued.

The practice of thus covering subsequent developments by re-issue having been terminated, the divisional application method of obtaining in a measure the same result was brought into use. An application, after it is filed, may be divided and a patent issued upon the divisional application, the original application being kept alive in the Patent Office for years, and eventually issued with claims worked out with care in the light of subsequent developments in the art. In many instances this practice is perfectly harmonious with the law, but frequently the practical effect has been to prolong the effective protection afforded, by as many years as intervene between the issue of the two patents.

As illustrating the extent to which the division of applications may be carried, an instance was found, not long since, where, from an application, filed seven years before, as many as sixteen divisions had been drawn and issued as patents, the original application still remaining in the Patent Office. While there is no proper objection to be made to the division of applications for the purpose of claiming clearly separable inventions in separate patents, the practice of claiming the same invention or different functions of the same device in separate patents is clearly objectionable. The decision of the Supreme Court in Miller *v.* Eagle Company, which was ably discussed in the April number of the YALE LAW JOURNAL, has served to, in a measure, regulate this practice. It was there held that a second patent may not be had for an invention inseparably involved in the first patent.

There remained, however, the third method of securing controlling patents, after the development of an art, provided public use had not existed more than two years. This consisted in acquiring the United States rights to some unexpired foreign patent, or to an invention described in some printed publication, and founding thereon a United States patent with broad controlling claims. If based upon a foreign patent, the term of the

United States patent would be limited by the term of the prior foreign patent, but if based upon a mere published description, no such limitation was imposed, even though the publication had existed many years. It is manifestly inequitable, that an obscure published description or a forgotten foreign patent, which itself made no impression upon the art, but which, when viewed in the light of later developments, might be found to contain the essence or germ of a subsequently-developed invention of practical importance, should be dragged from the archives and permitted to check or control the industry which has developed and existed for years in entire ignorance thereof. To prevent this, however, it was necessary that the laws themselves should be revised, and the amendments relating to Sections 4886 and 4920 of the Revised Statutes accomplish this. These amendments provide that no patent for an invention shall be granted, if the invention has been patented or described in any printed publication for more than two years prior to the application for a patent therefor. Two years public use of an invention in this country, prior to the application for a patent, has always been a bar to the grant of a United States patent, but no limit was formerly placed upon the time that it might have been described in a printed publication or in some other patent. The amendments seek to render two years existence of knowledge of the invention, through publication or patent, equally effective with two years public use in this respect. This, while allowing a proper period for the true inventor to apply for his patent, practically prevents a continuation of the practice of resuscitating and revamping forgotten or ignored descriptions of inventions, years after they have been published or patented elsewhere.

The law as amended will also prevent a second claimant from appearing in the United States Patent Office two years after a United States patent has issued upon an invention and, by interference proceedings, contesting the patentee's right thereto. With reference to these amendments the House Committee on Patents, in reporting the bill, made the following statements setting forth some of the reasons why the amendments should be adopted:

"As the law now stands, an invention may be published and patented abroad, and years after be patented to the foreign inventor in this country. The same reasons that compel the applicant for a patent under the present law to apply within two years after the invention has gone into public use in this country make it reasonable that he should apply for his patent within two years after it has been patented or published abroad."

Section 4920 of the Revised Statutes, which relates to the defenses which may be proved in an action for infringement, is amended, by the second section of the act, to include the two years publication or patenting, prior to the application for patent, as a defense which may be proved in such actions, when the action is based upon a patent applied for after January 1, 1898, the date when the amendments are to take effect.

The third section of the act deals with Section 4887 of the Revised Statutes. This section has been a most fruitful source of litigation. It relates to the limitation of the term of a United States patent by the term of a prior foreign patent. The last two or three years of the term of a patent often cover the most valuable period of its life, hence no means were left untried to distinguish individual cases from the prior decisions of the courts. The Supreme Court, by their decision in the well-known Bate Refrigerator case, gave a final interpretation to this statute. The endeavor, in framing the law, was to permit foreigners to patent their inventions in this country, but to guard against their United States patents outliving the corresponding foreign patents. Americans, however, patent a great many of their inventions abroad, particularly such inventions as they consider of special value. It was difficult to so arrange matters that neither the United States patent should be shortened by a prior foreign patent, nor the foreign patent rendered void by a prior publication of the United States patent in the foreign countries. The practice had therefore arisen of filing the foreign patents in the various countries upon the same day that the United States patent issued, so that all the patents should bear the same date. This required a preärranged concert of action on the part of the solicitors in the several countries and involved many difficulties. The inconvenience was in measure overcome by the provisions of the International Convention Act, permitting a certain latitude in applying for patents in various countries, but this was not quite adequate. The amendment now adopted provides that the life of the United States patent shall not be affected by a prior foreign patent "unless the application for said foreign patent was filed more than seven months, prior to the filing of the application in this country, in which case no patent shall be granted in this country." By this amendment the date of *filing* of the United States patent and not its date of issue, determines its relation to a foreign patent, and hence it is free from all the difficulties which surrounded the old law. Mr. Draper, the chairman of the House Committee on Patents, in presenting the bill, made the following explanatory remarks regarding this amendment:

"This Section as amended would not apply to any American patent that has been granted prior to the passage of this Act or to any applications now pending in this country for a patent, or to any patent granted on any pending applications."

Reference has been made to the practice of holding back applications in the Patent Office, and of issuing divisional applications, while the original application was retained in the Patent office for many years. This was rendered easy of accomplishment because two years were allowed between successive actions in the Patent Office. Section 4894 of the Revised Statutes, relating to the prosecution of applications in the Patent Office, is by the new act amended to require the applicant to prosecute his application within one year after any action by the Patent Office, the aim being to compel reasonable diligence in completing the application for final action, and thus render it much more difficult to purposely delay an application in the Patent Office.

Section 4898 relating to assignments of patents is amended by providing that a proper assignment, bearing a certificate of acknowledgment under the hand and official seal of a notary or other proper officer, shall be *prima facie* evidence of the execution of such assignment. This is a useful provision, for while formerly it was customary to accept Patent Office certified copies of assignments as such evidence, recent decisions have held that such certified copies are not competent. The need of an amendment of this character has long been recognized, for it has not been customary for the Patent Office to require proof that an assignment, presented to it for record, had been executed by the party purporting to have executed it; therefore, it was possible that a fraudulent assignment might be recorded, and, under the old practice, a certified copy thereof might, by oversight, be received as *prima facie* evidence of a valid transfer of title. Under the law as amended, the better practice will be to have the execution of all assignments of patents and applications for patents properly acknowledged before a notary or other proper officer.

Section 4921 of the Revised Statutes, relating to the powers of courts to grant injunctions and estimate damages, is amended so that, in an infringement suit, there shall be no recovery of profits or damages for infringement committed more than six years before the filing of the bill of complaint or the issuing of the writ. This amendment places actions in equity upon a parity with actions at law in this respect. The patent committee in their report to the House, remarked that "under the decisions of the Supreme Court the State statutes of limitation apply to actions for infringement of patents upon the law side of the court. It seems to your committee desirable that there should be a uniform statute of limitation." The provisions of this amendment will apply to existing causes of action, when the Act goes into effect in January, 1898.

One other amendment is contained in the act, it relates to the method of procedure in cases where any head of a department of the Government shall request the Commissioner of Patents to expedite the consideration of any particular application for a patent. This amendment was not proposed by the Bar Association, but originated after the bill had been reported by the patent committee and it has no special bearing upon the general patent practice.

The final section of the act provides that the amendments shall take effect January 1, 1898, and that the amendments to the sections relating to the two years prior publication or patenting, the interdependence of United States and foreign patents and the prosecution of applications in the Patent Office, shall not apply to patents granted upon applications filed prior to January, 1898.

Contemporaneously with the Act above referred to, Congress passed a bill defining the jurisdiction of the United States Circuit Courts in cases brought for the infringement of letters patent. Heretofore, when it has been desired to sue a manufacturer of an infringing device, it has been necessary to bring the suit at the home of the manufacturer. To do this often involves serious inconvenience and hence suits are frequently brought against users of infringing devices, rather than against the manufacturer, particularly in cases where the home of the manufacturer is remote from the residence of the owner of the patent. Usually the effect of such a suit against a user, is to bring the manufacturer actively into the defense, although not a party thereto. The act has special bearing upon manufacturing corporations, as will appear from the following extract from the remarks made by Senator Platt of Connecticut in advocating the bill before the Senate:

"Corporations in these days that are using patented inventions go into various States and obtain charters or acts of incorporation and then do business in other States. Now, to sue for an infringement of patent it is necessary that suit be brought in the State where the act of incorporation is obtained. In some of the States there is no provision for service upon anyone, and the corporations thus have an opportunity to infringe upon patents and almost escape any responsibility for it by reason of the difficulty of finding them in order to sue them, for it is very inconvenient to travel across the continent to sue them when they are infringing in a business established near the plaintiff or the owner of a patent."

The new act provides that a suit may be brought in a district of which the defendant is not an inhabitant, but in which the defendant has committed acts of infringement and has a regular and established place of business, and service may be made upon an agent of the defendant conducting the business in that district.

This change in the laws is useful in making it possible to reach the manufacturer of infringing devices in any circuit in which he may have sold infringing devices; it also relieves the complainant from resorting to the sometimes unpleasant course of suing a mere user.

The patent bar is to be congratulated upon the fact that the legislation effected by these two acts has been brought about, and that neither act militates against the true interests of the inventor or of the general public, but will have the result of furthering the real object of all proper patent legislation, which is to promote the progress of science and useful arts by securing for limited times to inventors the exclusive right to their respective discoveries.

Charles A. Terry.

THE CONCLUSIVENESS OF DECREES OF DISMISSAL.

The fact that a final adjudication in favor of the defendant in chancery results in a decree that the bill be dismissed, instead of the more precise and definite language of a judgment in favor of the defendant at law, has sometimes caused uncertainty as to whether the dismissal intended amounted to a mere withdrawal of the case in its then form, or an adjudication which would prove a bar to a reopening of the issues. The opportunity for misunderstanding is, perhaps, increased by the fact that the word dismiss is in common use in reference to suits at law, to mean simply the discontinuance of a cause, with the right to begin it over again and litigate the same matters.

Where the decree is properly drawn and shows clearly the grounds on which the court acted, there is little room for doubt. In general, decrees of dismissal, with language aptly worded, because the action has been prematurely brought,[1] or for lack of jurisdiction,[2] or for want of proper parties,[3] or for merely formal or technical defects,[4] do not constitute a bar to a subsequent suit. And so, too, voluntary dismissals by the complainant, and dismissals for want of prosecution, are in general no bar, unless when entered in an advanced stage of the cause, as will be hereafter considered. And on the other hand, unqualified decrees of dismissal, which clearly show on their face an adjudication of the merits, whether on demurrer or plea, on bill and answer, or on pleadings and evidence, as obviously do constitute a bar. This must, of course, be understood subject to the usual rules in regard to identity of parties and issues, and bearing in mind that an adjudication that the complainant has no case in chancery does not necessarily deprive him of the right to sue at law, if, for example, his bill has been dismissed solely for the reason that he has an adequate remedy at law.

In the middle ground between decrees which clearly do not constitute *res adjudicata*, and decrees which clearly do, lie cer-

---
[1] Foster *v. The Richard Busteed*, 100 Mass. 409.
[2] Walden *v.* Bodley, 14 Pet. 160.
[3] St. Romes *v.* Levee Cotton Press Co., 127 U. S. 614.
[4] Gilmer *v.* Morris, 30 Fed. Rep. 476.

tain classes of decrees not so summarily to be disposed of, which it is the purpose of this article to examine, having in view the ascertainment of the law as it has been applied in various jurisdictions, rather than the reconcilement of the different authorities.

The general rule for the construction of unqualified decrees of dismissal is thus stated by Chief Justice Shaw in the case of Foote *v.* Gibbs, 1 Gray 412:

"The authorities, both in England and this country, are decisive that a general entry of 'bill dismissed,' with no words of qualification, such as 'dismissed without prejudice,' or 'without prejudice to an action at law,' or the like, is conclusively presumed to be upon the merits, and is a final determination of the controversy." To the same effect are numerous other cases, the most apposite of which are cited in the margin.[5]

With but slight exception there is a general concurrence of the authorities in this doctrine. In one case in Maryland [6] it was said that a decree of dismissal was not a bar unless it was shown that there was an absolute determination that the party had no title, and that the matter was *res adjudicata*, but the point was outside the questions actually decided, and the case cannot be considered an authority in conflict with the prevailing view.

In cases where the record discloses that the dismissal might well have been on grounds not going to the merits, some courts have been reluctant to apply the principle of presumptions in all its strictness. For example, in an Ohio case [7] where the issues had not been closed, either by setting down the plea for hearing, or by a replication, it was said that the bill might have been dismissed for want of prosecution, and that no presumption would be indulged that the merits had been passed on. The court said, however, that where it appears that the dismissal was upon a hearing of the case, it is to be inferred that it was upon the merits.

So in the case of Foster *v. The Richard Busteed,* 100 Mass. 409, where the court considered the effect of the entry "Petition

---

[5] Durant *v.* Essex Co., 7 Wall. 107; Lyon *v.* Perin Mfg. Co., 125 U. S. 698; Bigelow *v.* Winsor, 1 Gray 299; Tankersly *v.* Pettis, 71 Ala. 179; Taylor *v.* Yarbrough, 13 Gratt. 183; Curts *v.* Bardstown, 6 J. J. Mar. 536; Kelsey *v.* Murphy, 26 Pa. St. 78; Adams *v.* Cameron, 40 Mich. 506; Burton *v.* Burton, 58 Vt. 414; Garrick *v.* Chamberlain, 97 Ill. 620; Knowlton *v.* Hanbury, 117 Ill. 471; Stickney *v.* Goudy, 132 Ill. 213; Armstead *v.* Blickman, 51 Ill. App. 470.

[6] Chase's Case, 1 Bland Ch. 206, 17 Am. Dec. 277.

[7] Loudenback *v.* Collins, 4 O. St. 251.

dismissed," in an action for the purpose of enforcing a lien on a vessel. The answer set up that the petition had been prematurely filed (which appeared to be a fact), and also grounds going to the merits. The court said that where in an answer several matters of defense were set forth, some of which related to the maintenance of the suit, and some to the merits, and there was a general decree of dismissal, the merits could not be assumed to have been passed on, and the decree would not be held to be a bar.

Decrees of dismissal which show on their face that the complainant consented to a dismissal on the merits,[8] and also those made because of failure of proof,[9] are considered a bar.

The proper form of the decree, and the only one which can be relied upon to put beyond the possibility of doubt its construction, where the court intends to permit a simple discontinuance of the suit, without concluding the parties on the issues, is to dismiss the bill "without prejudice." Where a bill is dismissed without prejudice, the grounds for the reservation cannot be reëxamined in another suit, and the decree is not subject to collateral attack to show that in fact the merits were involved on the hearing, and that the provision that the decree should be without prejudice was erroneous.[10]

An appeal lies, however, directly from such a decree, and if the decree should clearly have been absolute it will be reversed and ordered so modified.[11]

Where an absolute decree of dismissal has been entered, the decree may be amended on appeal so as to read without prejudice.[12]

Uncertainty is sometimes liable to arise where a decree of dismissal in chancery is pleaded to an action at law. For example, in an Ohio case [13] the court had before it a question of this sort, and held that where a demurrer for want of equity was sustained, and the decree was that the complainant was not entitled to the relief sought and that the bill be dismissed, it would not be assumed that anything but the right to equitable

---

[8] Pelton v. Mott, 11 Vt. 148, 34 Am. Dec. 678; Donnelly v. Wilcox, 113 N. C. 408, 18 S. E. Rep. 339.

[9] Cochran v. Couper, 2 Del. Ch. 27, McWhorter v. Norris (Ind. App.), 34 N. E. Rep. 854.

[10] Wanzer v. Self, 30 O. St. 378.

[11] Wanzer v. Self, *supra*.

[12] Durant v. Essex Co., 7 Wall. 107, and cases cited. See Gove v. Lyford, 44 N. H. 525, where a motion to add "without prejudice" was denied.

[13] Lore v. Truman, 10 O. St. 45.

relief was adjudicated, and that an action at law was not barred. And later cases in the same court [14] indicate that a decree of dismissal without qualification simply determines the right to equitable relief, and does not bar a suit at law for the same cause of action.

It is obvious, however, that a chancery suit may adjudicate not only the right to equitable relief, but particular points or the precise question which may afterwards be presented in a suit at law. A decree on the merits puts an end to all further controversy concerning the points thus decided between the parties to the suit.[15] Where the reservation of the right to sue at law, or the reason of the court's action, does not affirmatively appear from the record, there may be much difficulty in determining how far there has been an adjudication of the issues which are subsequently raised at law—a question which does not seem to have been particularly examined except in these Ohio cases, which present only one phase of it.

We come now to cases dismissed for want of prosecution, or voluntarily dismissed by the complainant. In regard to these two classes, and especially the latter class, a difference in practice between courts of law and chancery has sometimes misled the practitioner. Under the common law, as modified by the statute of 2 Hen. IV., ch. 7, a voluntary nonsuit could be taken up to the time that the jury announced its verdict, and under the practice as it exists in most of the States at the present day a nonsuit can be taken up to the time that the jury retires from the box, without creating any bar to a subsequent suit based on the same cause of action. In chancery, however, according to the weight of recent authority, a voluntary dismissal of a case cannot be entered after the cause has been set down for final hearing, without incurring the risk of the decree of dismissal operating as a conclusive adjudication of the merits, and dismissals for want of prosecution stand very much on the same footing.

There is some conflict of authority on this subject, much of it traceable to differences in the chancery rules of different jurisdictions.

Under the English chancery practice as it existed prior to 1845 there was no rule of court explicitly providing for the effect of dismissals of this character. The cases are not all in accord, but in general the doctrine prevailed that if a complainant

---

[14] Cramer v. Moore, 36 O. St. 347; Porter v. Wagner, *ib.* 471.
[15] Bank of U. S. v. Beverly, 1 How. 148; Smith v. Kernochen, 7 How. 198.

obtained leave to dismiss his bill on payment of costs, even at the hearing, and at any time up to the decree, or if the bill was dismissed at the hearing for failure of the complainant to appear, the dismissal would not operate as a bar.[16]

In the case of Pickett *v.* Loggon, 14 Ves. 232, Lord Eldon said:

"At the same time, if a party thinks proper to bring his cause to a hearing upon examination of witnesses, publication passed, and the cause capable of being opened, and then makes default, it is very difficult, and would be rather mischievous, to treat such conduct merely as a non-suit at law."

And in a case in the Irish court of chancery [17] it was held that a dismissal by the complainant at the final hearing, after publication had passed, was a bar.

Among the chancery rules adopted in England in 1845 was a rule providing that a dismissal on the plaintiff's motion or on his default, after the cause has been set down to be heard, unless the court otherwise orders, is equivalent to a dismissal on the merits, and may be pleaded as a bar.[18]

Wherever this rule has been adopted the practice is freed from considerable doubt. In at least one State, and probably in others, the rules provide that after a cause has been set down for a hearing, either party may have the cause heard on notice, and if one or the other of the parties does not attend, the cause may nevertheless be proceeded in, and such decree rendered as the right and justice of the case may require.[19]

The rules prescribed by the Supreme Court of the United States for the Federal courts of equity have no provision on the subject. It was accordingly held by Justice Clifford, that in the absence of any special rule of the circuit court, the procedure must be governed by the English practice as it existed in 1842, when the general equity rules were adopted, which practice he construed to permit a withdrawal of the case at any time before decree.[20]

The United States Supreme Court has not passed on the precise point, though two cases are instructive as to the general principles. In Lyon *v.* Perin Manufacturing Company, 125 U. S. 698, the complainant introduced evidence to show that a prior

---

[16] Carrington *v.* Holley, 1 Dick. 280.
[17] Byrne *v.* Frere, 2 Molloy 157.
[18] Ord. XXIII. 13—see 1 Dan. Ch. Pl. & Pr. (5th ed.) 659.
[19] Fla. Eq. Rules 86.
[20] Badger *v.* Badger, 1 Cliff. 237.

decree of dismissal was entered for failure of the complainant to appear upon the call of the case, after answer and replication had been filed, and after the time for taking testimony had expired without any testimony having been taken. The decree recited that the cause being submitted upon bill, answer and replication, the court decreed that the equities were with the defendant, and that the bill be dismissed. The court held that the decree, being absolute in its terms, must be considered a bar.

In Durant v. Essex Company, 7 Wall. 107, the circuit court made a decree on final hearing as to some of the defendants in favor of the complainant, who was dissatisfied with the relief accorded him, and declined to accept it. The court thereupon dismissed the bill. This decree being affirmed on appeal by a divided court, the complainant moved in the circuit court for leave to discontinue the suit, or that the bill be dismissed without prejudice, which motion was denied. The Supreme Court held that these proceedings constituted a bar to the maintenance of a new bill.

In one case in a United States circuit court,[21] the doctrine of Durant v. Essex Company was invoked to justify a plea of *res adjudicata*, based on an order noting the death and striking the name of one out of several defendants, on complainant's motion, before the taking of testimony was closed. It is doubtful if this case can be sustained on principle.

The earlier cases in the court of chancery of New York held that a complainant might get leave to dismiss his bill on payment of costs, before an interlocutory or final decree, without losing the right to begin his case over again,[22] and that a dismissal for failure to prosecute at the final hearing did not constitute a bar.[23] In a later case decided by the Court of Appeals,[24] however, the court held, Justice Bronson doubting, that a decree of dismissal where the cause had been set down for hearing after replication and an order closing the proofs, was a bar, although no proofs were in fact introduced, and the decree was taken by default at the hearing. The case of Byrne v. Frere, *supra*, was cited as authority, and Chancellor Kent's ruling in Rosse v. Rust was overruled. I cannot find that the authority of Ogsbury v. LaFarge has since been called in question in New York.

In Massachusetts the question was considered incidentally in

---

[21] Howth v. Owens, 30 Fed. Rep. 910.
[22] Cummins v. Bennett, 8 Paige 79.
[23] Rosse v. Rust, 4 Johns. Ch. 300.
[24] Ogsbury v. LaFarge, 2 N. Y. 113.

the case of Bigelow *v.* Winsor, 1 Gray 299, 301, where Chief Justice Shaw said:

"Sometimes, indeed, a party plaintiff in equity who, because he is not prepared with his proofs, or for other reasons, desires not to go into a hearing, but rather to have his bill dismissed, in the nature of a discontinuance or non-suit, in an action at law, may be allowed to do so; but we believe the uniform practice in such case is to enter 'dismissed without prejudice.'"

Later, the point was decided in Borrowscale *v.* Tuttle, 5 Allen 377. Here a bill to redeem, requiring an answer under oath, was dismissed on motion of the plaintiff, without the knowledge of the defendant, after answer, and after the expiration of the time allowed by the rules of the court for the plaintiff to file his replication. It was held that this decree must be conclusively presumed to have been upon the merits, and must be held a bar to a subsequent bill. The authority of this case, which was cited with approval by Judge Story,[25] does not appear to have been doubted, but in the later case of Kempton *v.* Burgess, 136 Mass. 192, the court made some remarks which seem to countenance a different theory. Here, before the hearing on the merits, the plaintiff moved for leave to discontinue, which motion was overruled, and a decree made dismissing the bill in general terms. On the plaintiff's appeal, the decree was ordered modified so that the bill should be dismissed without prejudice. Chief Justice Morton, in delivering the opinion, took occasion to say:

"If, at the time of the hearing, a plaintiff in equity is not ready to go on, and the court refuses to grant further time, he may move for an order dismissing his bill, which will be granted upon payment of the costs; if he does not do so, the defendant is not entitled to a decree upon the merits, but can only have the bill dismissed for want of prosecution, and such a dismissal, like a dismissal upon plaintiff's motion, is not a bar to a new bill."
Borrowscale *v.* Tuttle does not seem to have been called to the attention of the court, though Foote *v.* Gibbs and Bigelow *v.* Winsor are cited with approval, together with Cummins *v.* Bennett, 8 Paige 79, whose authority was shaken, if not destroyed, by Ogsbury *v.* LaFarge. If the decree as it stood had been pleaded in another suit, a different question would have been raised. The distinction is clearly pointed out in a Kentucky case, where it was held that an absolute decree of dismissal for

---

[25] Story Eq. Pl., § 793 *a.*

want of parties would be reversed and modified on appeal so as to read without prejudice, but that if not revised on appeal, it would be held a bar to another suit.[26]

The subsequent case of Bradley *v.* Bradley, 160 Mass. 258, treating of a decree on a libel for divorce, cited Borrowscale *v.* Tuttle with approval, the court thus stating the law of estoppels by decree:

"The entry 'Libel dismissed,' without the addition of the words 'without prejudice,' purports to be a final judgment upon the merits. It is a bar to any further proceedings upon the cause of action set out in the libel. In collateral proceedings it is not conclusive by way of estoppel, or as evidence, except upon matters actually tried and determined, but as a final disposition of that for which the suit was brought, it is, like a judgment by default, conclusive as well in regard to the matters which might have been pleaded as those which were formally put in issue."

In other States the decisions are not altogether in unison. In Michigan it was held [27] that an absolute decree of dismissal upon the plaintiff's consent, upon a hearing on pleadings and proofs, was a bar, the court saying that the effect of a voluntary dismissal of a complainant's bill was the same as an adverse one, if made upon the hearing, when the merits were involved.

In a case in Iowa [28] in which the Massachusetts cases were examined, the decree considered recited that the complainant's solicitors withdrew their appearance, and that the bill was dismissed upon the pleadings and proofs. This decree was held to be a bar.

In Mississippi the court said in one case:[29] "It is true that the complainant may, at any time before final decision by the chancellor, dismiss his bill, but if the dismissal is made after the cause is set down for final hearing, it will have the effect, unless otherwise ordered by the chancellor, of a dismissal on the merits, and may be pleaded in bar to another suit."

In a later case in the same State,[30] the decree showed that the case came on for final hearing, and the complainant failing to appear, on motion of the defendant the bill was dismissed. The court held here that the defendant might have submitted the cause for final hearing, in which case the decree would have been

---

[26] Thompson *v.* Clay, 3 T. B. Mon. 359. 16 Am. Dec. 108.
[27] Edgar *v.* Buck, 65 Mich. 356.
[28] Scully *v.* C. B. & Q. R. R., 46 Ia. 528.
[29] Phillips *v.* Wormley, 58 Miss. 398.
[30] Baird *v.* Bardwell, 60 Miss. 164.

a bar, but having moved to dismiss for want of prosecution, the decree was not a bar. The court refused to follow Byrne *v.* Frere and Ogsbury *v.* LaFarge.

In Vermont, in a case [81] citing the overruled case of Rosse *v.* Rust as one of its authorities, the court held that no bar was created by a decree which recited that the case being called to be heard on the merits, the solicitor for the orator appeared and declined a hearing, and thereupon it was ordered that the bill be dismissed.

In a recent Florida case,[82] where on the complainant's motion a decree of dismissal without prejudice was entered at the final hearing, the court refused to reverse the decree and make it absolute on the defendant's appeal, the special circumstances apparently contributing largely to the decision arrived at.

After looking over the field that we have hastily surveyed, it will be noticed what a very important part the words "without prejudice" play. It has been said in connection with propositions of compromise that there is no magic in these words, but as applied to decrees the observation loses force. A consideration of the various cases, if it does not lead to any definite conclusion as to universally applicable principles, at least points one moral, which all the cases tend to illustrate, and that is that the form of a decree of dismissal is worthy of the closest scrutiny and the most watchful care of counsel.

Thomas Mills Day, Jr.

---

[81] Porter *v.* Vaughn, 26 Vt. 624.
[82] Robbins *v.* Hanbury, 37 Fla. 468.

YALE LAW JOURNAL

SUBSCRIPTION PRICE, $2.00 A YEAR   SINGLE COPIES, 35 CENTS

EDITORS:

ROGER S. BALDWIN, *Chairman.*
HUGH T. HALBERT, *Treasurer.*

CHRISTOPHER L. AVERY, JR.   GEO. JAY GIBSON,
SAMUEL F. BEARDSLEY.   JOHN MACGREGOR, JR.
MICHAEL GAVIN, 2D.   HENRY W. MERWIN.

Published six times a year, by students of the Yale Law School
P. O. Address, Box 1341, New Haven, Conn.

If a subscriber wishes his copy of the JOURNAL discontinued at the expiration of his subscription, notice to that effect should be sent; otherwise it is assumed that a continuance of the subscription is desired.

AN Act of the Legislature of Utah, approved March 10, 1892, provided that "In all civil cases a verdict may be rendered on the concurrence therein of nine or more members of the jury," and although sustained by the trial and Supreme courts of the Territory, the opinion of the United States Supreme Court, rendered recently by Mr. Justice Brewer in the case of The American Publishing Company *v.* A. Fisher and Aaron Keyser, has held the Act to be unconstitutional. The principle which arose in that case was the important but well established one as to the extension of the United States laws over the Territories of the United States and the consequent right to trial by jury as that right existed at common law. The power of a State as distinguished from a Territory to abridge or amend the right to jury trial had been decided before and was not touched upon in the opinion.

This decision renews interest in the discussion of the better adaptation of the jury system to the present conditions and requirements of our society and emphasizes the need of a suggested change which has recently been much debated. The origin and growth of the jury is perhaps better suited for an academic than a practical discussion and yet to many the present rule of unanimity in civil cases seems so at variance with our other institutions and customs that they are driven to the supposition that it grew up and developed under conditions and circumstances other than our own. The duty of the juror, it is said, has changed from the giving to the weighing of evidence and yet this rule has been preserved in spite of the change. A majority controls in other cases, the most important affairs of nations are determined by majority votes and it is asked why a different rule should be applied to civilians in their relations with one another. Indeed, the question does not seem an idle one when it is remembered that unanimity is not required to determine law although the correctness of law is perhaps even more important than the correct finding of facts, for to the law other facts are applied. Under our present system, moreover, five Justices of the United States Supreme Court may overrule four of their associates who agree with three additional judges in the court below and yet the law, thus decided by a minority of five to seven of those who passed upon it, is considered sufficiently certain and settled. Indeed, if unanimity were to be required on the bench the future determination of law would be most dubious.

This wide and frequent disagreement in our courts is sometimes sought to be explained by the previous training of our judges in different States where differing principles prevail, but if this be true it seems then reasonable that the same result should be expected in the case of our jurymen. It is not to be presumed that a body of men taken from various employments and stations in life should unanimously agree upon any point as to which there might be any opportunity for a difference of opinion, and the consequence of the rule of unanimity is either to often leave the issue undecided or to force its decision by means of perjured ballots. The gravity of both of these alternatives is apparent.

It is said by some that the moral effect of a verdict will be weakened by a dissenting vote and that a loss of unanimity will mean a loss of discussion. It might be suggested, however, in reply that the defeated litigant will never be satisfied and that the loss of moral force in the verdict, if the means by which unanimous verdicts are obtained are rightly understood, will hardly be appreciable, should any in fact ensue. But in order to insure discussion a certain time might be prescribed before which nothing but a unanimous verdict would be received and after which a majority of four or six would prevail. Indeed, if the opinions of the jurors should be formed only upon that evidence which has been produced in court it might be asked with apparent reason whether those opinions should not also in the main be formed before leaving the jury box, uninfluenced by the persuasiveness or eloquence of a fellow juror. The value of jury trial seems to be enhanced by the safety in numbers but the safety in numbers is dependent upon preserving the individuality of the jurymen.

In criminal cases, on the other hand, especially those involving capital punishment, the circumstances are open to a different construction and it seems to be generally agreed that the apparent popular aversion to the taking of life requires, at least for the present, a unanimous verdict. This, however, would only be recognizing the rule of evidence which in criminal cases requires the proof of guilt to be beyond a reasonable doubt, but in civil suits allows the verdict to follow the preponderance of evidence. The Act of the Legislature of Utah, although held to be unconstitutional, is interesting as evidence of the tendency and desire to break away from the old common law rule of unanimity and to make an adaptation to present needs and conditions which in the eyes of some seems most necessary if the jury system is to be maintained.

* * *

THE recommendation of a new course in a law school already abundantly supplied is not to be made in a thoughtless moment and yet the ease with which much good might be accomplished persuades us to offer a suggestion as to a possible addition to the curriculum of this as well as other law schools where such a course as we have in mind has not been instituted. The average apprentice in the study of the law is as ignorant of the tools with which he is to work as is the beginner in other arts, and yet a practical acquaintance with the tools of his profession is almost as important, although not so difficult to obtain, as the theories which should control their use. Next to a knowledge of the law, therefore, we would place a knowledge of the means by which to discover what the law may be, and to obtain that a few hints as to the best use of law libraries and law books would be of the greatest value. The use of the various digests and encyclopedias, the method of tracing a case from its inception to its final determination, and the best manner of collating and verifying authorities is surely of sufficient importance and interest to warrant some practical suggestions early in a course of law instruction. A few lectures on Library Procedure might with advantage be added to the curriculum of a law school.

* * *

WITH this number the YALE LAW JOURNAL completes its sixth volume and passes into the care of other editors. The past year has seen a slight enlargement in the size of the magazine and a slight increase in the number of contributions; the future should see a still stronger growth and development. The three years' course in the School will offer opportunity for a much-needed connecting link between succeeding editorial boards and give the benefit of some experience to those who will assume control. The thanks of the Board are due to Prof. E. G. Buckland and Dr. W. Frederic Foster for so kindly serving upon the committee to judge the competitive essays submitted by the Junior candidates for editorial positions on the JOURNAL. For the kindness of those who have contributed to the JOURNAL or otherwise aided in making this volume possible the present editors express their sincere appreciation; for those who are to succeed us we wish an experience as pleasant as ours has been and the success which should result from their efforts.

* * *

THE editorial board of the YALE LAW JOURNAL for the ensuing year will be composed as follows: Charles Frederic Clemons, Chairman; Edward William Beattie, Jr., Secretary and Treasurer; William Ansel Arnold, William Bradford Boardman, Frederick Stephen Jackson, Addison Strong Pratt, Ernest Clyde Simpson and Harrison Graw Wagner.

In the competition for the JOURNAL Essay the successful essay was written by Charles Frederic Clemons.

COMMENT.

The use of the injunction as a panacea for legal ills has led to an attempt to make it practically a substitute for *quo warranto* proceedings against private corporations illegally organized. The fact that a trust was involved made the attempt more plausible in *Stockton* v. *American Tobacco Co.*, 36 Atlantic (N. J. Eq.) 971. When companies which manufactured ninety-five per cent of the cigarettes of the United States were incorporated into the American Tobacco Co., they issued its stock in exchange for the property of the several manufactories thus merged. Little money was actually paid in. It then set out to keep other manufacturers from getting a foothold in the market by making jobbers sign a contract not to sell the cigarettes of any other company, and its own only at a certain high price. The jobbers, deprived of the profit from selling other goods, then asked that the trust be restrained from causing this special injury, and also moved the Attorney-General to ask for an injunction restraining the alleged public injury. The court expressed no doubts that the acts were within the chartered powers of the corporation. Being a legal entity, "a trading corporation has the same authority as an individual to sell or consign its goods, to select its selling agents, and to impose conditions as to whom they shall sell, and the terms upon which they shall sell." Then quoting from Chancellor Vroom, in the leading case of *Attorney-General* v. *Stevens*, 1 N. J. Eq. 369, the decision proceeds: "They are a corporation *de facto*, if not *de jure*. * * * I do not feel at liberty in this incidental way to declare all their proceedings void, and treat them as a body having no rights and powers." The purpose of the contract to form the corporation may have been to create a monopoly. As such it was unenforceable, and might have been annulled upon a bill filed by the Attorney-General. But to enjoin it from exercising its powers would be equivalent to taking away its powers. For this there is an adequate remedy at law, by *quo warranto*. To enjoin the agents of the corporation from doing acts within its powers is practically to enjoin the corporation from transacting any business, and this is the equivalent of a judgment on *quo warranto*. Although such a prayer will not be granted in the case of private corporations it is well settled that where a quasi-public corporation exceeds its corporate powers and its acts tend to public injury a bill will lie to restrain it. Such are the cases of *Raritan and D. B. R. Co.* v. *Del. and R. Canal*, 18 N. J. Eq. 547, and *Atty. Gen.* v. *Great Eastern Ry. Co.*, 11 Cho. Div. 450.

A few years ago to break up the coal "trust" a bill was recognized to annul the lease of the New Jersey Central to the Philadelphia and Reading (*Stockton* v. *Ry. Co.*, 50 N. J. Eq. 52; 24 Atlantic 964). But in that case the lease was distinctly *ultra vires*, and its annulment in no way curtailed any corporate powers. It is interesting to note in this connection that in New York the officers and agents of the American Tobacco Co. have been indicted for conspiracy in doing acts in furtherance of the contract tendered to its agents and referred to above. The acts were held to amount to "intimidation," and therefore were unlawful, and a combination of the officers of the corporation to carry them out amounted to conspiracy (*People* v. *Duke*, 44 N. Y. Sup. 336).

The Supreme Court of Missouri in the recent case of *Glencoe Sand and Gravel Co.* v. *Hudson Bros. Commission Co.* (40 S. W. Rep. 93), has decided that no action will lie against one who induces a third party to break a contract with another, unless the relation of master and servant was created by such contract. In reaching this conclusion the court has departed from the English doctrine as laid down in *Lumley* v. *Guy* (2 El. & B. 216), and *Bowen* v. *Hall* (62 B. Div. 333), and from *Walker* v. *Cronin* (107 Mass. 555), *Haskins* v. *Royster* (70 N. C. 601), *Jones* v. *Stanley* (76 N. C. 355), and *Jones* v. *Blocker* (43 Ga. 331), the early decisions of this country following the English decisions.

Lumley v. *Guy*, *supra*, decided in 1853, was the first English case to extend the doctrine and hold that an action would lie for the procurement of a breach of contract even though the strict relation of master and servant did not exist. *Bowen* v. *Hall*, *supra*, followed and affirmed this in 1881. *Walker* v. *Cronin*, *supra*, and cases following it, held that the action did not rest upon the relation of master and servant alone, but was founded upon the legal right derived from the contract, and that it applied to all contracts of employment if not to contracts of every description. The later American decisions, which are relied upon by the court in the present case, hold directly the reverse. In *Chambers* v. *Baldwin* (91 Ky. 122) and *Bourlier* v. *Macauley* (*id.* 135) decided in 1891, it is held that there are only two exceptions to the rule that an action cannot be maintained against one who maliciously procures the breach of a contract, viz:

(1). Whereby a contract of employment the relation of master and servant exists, and (2), where the party has been procured to make the breach against his will by deception and coercion *Boyson* v. *Thorn* (98 Cal. 579), decided in 1893, holds that the action will not lie unless the relation of master and servant exists, or there were threats, violence falsehood, deception, etc., used in procuring the branch.

In the present case which was an action brought for procuring a railway company to break a contract of carriage with the plaintiff, the learned judge thought it not pertinent to inquire whether the relation of master and servant existed between the plaintiff and the railroad for "to hold that a carrier is the servant or employe of the shipper would revolutionize the whole law relating to the duties, obligations, and liabilities of common carriers."

When a doctrine which has been almost continuously upheld since the foundation of the common law, is overturned, it is worthy of notice. Such a case is that of *Clayton* v. *Clark et al.*, 21 South. Rep. 565, which was founded upon a few simple facts. A written agreement of release had been given, upon receipt of $1,000, for a past-due note of $2,789. Upon an attempt to recover the balance, the Supreme Court of Mississippi, in a very clear and logical opinion, containing a *resumé* since its foundation of the doctrine involved, reversed the rule almost continually held hitherto, that "an agreement by a creditor with his debtor to accept a smaller sum of money in satisfaction of an ascertained debt of a greater sum is without consideration and is not binding upon the creditor, even though he has received the smaller sum agreed upon in the new contract." The court also overruled the cases of *Jones* v. *Perkins*, 29 Miss. 139, and *Jones* v. *Perkins*, 50 Miss. 251, in setting up this new rule as the doctrine of the State of Mississippi.

A Connecticut case of special importance is that of *Canastota Knife Co.* v. *Newington Tramway Co.*, lately decided by the Supreme Court of that State. This case involved the interesting question of "additional servitude," and while the court agreed in its conclusions, there were two views raised as to whether a street railway may be built in a highway without compensation to the owners of the adjoining land. The majority of the court hold that circumstances may determine that point, while two dissenting judges are of the opinion that the owner is entitled to compensation. Judge Baldwin, in the majority opinion, maintains that the common law of Connecticut is somewhat more favorable to the rights of the public as against the land owner than the common law of England, and that New York is the only State in the country which has accepted the position that a railway not operated by steam imposes new servitude upon the soil of a city or village street. While the courts of Connecticut have regarded the railway structure as the private property of the company and in the nature of real estate, they also hold that its right to pass over the streets is no greater than that of any other member of the community, at the most a limited, qualified property right; and no owner of the soil, subject to the highway, had set up a claim to compensation for the construction of a street railway upon it, before the present suit was brought. The majority of the court hold that there is no substantial impediment to public travel or proximate cause of special damage of a new description to the owner of the soil, and that the public right has for some time been recognized as extending not only to the laying of water pipes, gas pipes, etc., but to street railways as well. "Two rights are to be guarded with equal care; that of the individual land owner, and that of the public at large; but his estate is the servient tenement. He has no rights which are incompatible with the fullest enjoyment of the public easement."

The dissenting judges, however, regard the street railway as creating a new right against the owner of the fee in favor of persons with whom he before had no legal relation whatever, and as burdening the land with a peculiar use for one person exclusive of any rights in others to that use.

RECENT CASES.

RAILROADS.

Railroads—Intersection.—Carolina Cent. R. Co. v. Wilmington St. Ry. Co., 26 S. E. Rep. 913 (N. C.) A railroad company, having built a bridge over its tracks, of sufficient strength for travel by foot and horse and ordinary vehicle transportation, is not obliged to render same safe for passage of street railway cars, said passage being an additional servitude and necessitating the contribution by the street railway company to the maintenance thereof.

Street Railroads—Nuisance—Injunction Against—Right of Individuals.—Central Crosstown Ry. Co. v. Metropolitan St. Ry. Co., 44 N. Y. Sup. 752. Although the unauthorized construction and operation of a street railroad in a public street by defendant company is a public nuisance, plaintiff railroad company, which already had a line in operation in the same street, may enjoin the operation of defendant railroad, where it is shown that it will come into competition with plaintiff line, thus causing it special and irreparable damage, the amount thereof not being capable of ascertainment (see Sec. 102 of the Railroad Law). The case is not essentially different from *Forty-Second Street R. R. Co. v. Thirty-Fourth St. R. R. Co.*, 52 N. Y. Super. Ct. 252, where the action was brought previous to the construction of defendant's road.

Street Railroads—Paralleling Railroad—Ultra Vires.—New England R. R. Co. v. Central Railway and Electric Company, et al., 36 Atl. Rep. 1061 (Conn.) A railroad company which does not have an exclusive franchise is not injured in any of its legal or equitable rights by the construction of a street railway parallel to its lines even though such street-railway is to be constructed by *ultra vires* acts.

Additional Servitude—Occupation of Streets by Railroads.—Chicago & N. W. Ry. Co. v. Milwaukee, R. & K. Electric Ry. Co., 70 N. W. Rep. 678 (Wis.). Upon an application for an injunction against a street railway it was held that a commercial railway upon public streets and highways which engaged to carry besides passengers, merchandise, personal baggage, mail and express matter, would tend to obstruct and interfere with the ordinary uses of a street and highway and impose an additional servitude upon the lands of abutting owners.

TELEGRAPH.

Telegraph Companies—Failure to Deliver—Notice of Special Circumstances—Measure of Damages.—Western Union Tel. Co. v. Carver, 39 S. W. Rep. 1021 (Texas). Where a telegram directs the person addressed to purchase cattle at a specific price per head and to "get all you can," it is sufficient to put the telegraph company on notice as to the incidental facts of the transaction and to render it liable to the sender for loss resulting from non-delivery; and where there was a subsequent permanent advance in the price of the cattle, the measure of damages is the difference between the price named in the message and the price at which they could have been bought at the time when it was learned of the non-delivery of the telegram.

Telegrams—Insufficient Address.—Western Union Tel. Co. v. Birchfield, 39 S. W. Rep. 1002 (Texas). It is no excuse for negligence in delivering a telegram that it had no specific address, but was directed "care some hotel," since, in the absence of any address, it would have been the duty of the telegraph company to ascertain if the party was at any hotel in that city.

RIGHTS OF CREDITORS.

Power to Dispose of Property by Will—Effect of Execution—Rights of Creditors of Testator.—Freeman's Adm'r et al. v. Butters et al., 26 S. E. Rep. 845 (Va.). Where the personal property of a widow is not sufficient to satisfy her debts, and she has willed to volunteers, during her widowhood, property left to her by her husband with absolute power of disposal by will, her creditors may levy on said property in satisfaction of their claims.

Partnership—Rights as to Third Persons—Payment of Individual Debts.—In re Lafferty's Estate, appeal of Linde, 37 Atl. Rep. 113 (Penn.). Where an executor wrongfully uses funds of an estate and repays them with money belonging to a firm of which he is a member, the estate is not liable to the firm when it was unaware that it was partnership money.

PROCEDURE.

Appeal—Abatement.—Nickerson v. Nickerson, 48 Pac. Rep. 423 (Ore.). The death of a husband, who has appealed from a decree for divorce whereby his wife became entitled to one-third of his property, does not abate the appeal. It survives to his heirs, and they may prosecute the cause in order to determine whether the divorce was rightfully granted and to settle conflicting property rights between them and the appellee.

Cities—Improvements in Streets—Discrimination.—Larned v. City of Syracuse et al., 44 N. Y. Sup. 857. Where a petition for the pavement of a street prayed that the materials be purchased from a certain firm and the city council passed a resolution granting the petition the entire proceedings are void as preventing free competition.

Action by County to Recover Land Limitation—Adverse Possession.—Johnston v. Llano County, 39 S. W. Rep. 995 (Texas). Although the statute of limitation does not run against a county, as a subdivision of the State, as to any "road, street, side-walk, or grounds," yet the right of the county to recover lands not acquired or used for public purposes may be barred.

MISCELLANEOUS.

Navigable Waters—Control by the United States—Incidental Damage—Compensation—Constitutional Law.—Gibson v. U. S., 17 Sup. Ct. Rep. 578. In accordance with United States River and Harbor Acts, a dike was built at a point in the Ohio River off Neville Island, nine miles west of Pittsburg, for the purpose of concentrating the water-flow in the main channel. The change of flow which followed this improvement, prevented the access of boats to the landing place of the plaintiff, a lower riparian owner, except at high stages of water in the Spring and Fall. The obstruction greatly reduced the value of the plaintiff's land and he petitioned the Court of Claims for the recovery of damages. The Supreme Court upholds the Court of Claims (29 Ct. Cl. 18) in finding the claimant not entitled to recover, there not being in this case a taking of private property for public use, without compensation, but the injury being a mere incidental consequence of the lawful exercise of Governmental power.

Negligence—Proximate Cause—Contributory Negligence—Assisting Person in Danger.—Saun v. H. W. Johns Manf. Co., 44 N. Y. Sup. 641. Plaintiff's intestate, a workman in defendant's factory, had been directed to repair the pipes of a certain felt-washing machine; after so doing he and another workman made several unsuccessful attempts to put a belt upon the machine, when a third workman volunteered to assist them by holding the belt so as to relieve it from the friction of the shaft from which it hung and which was revolving at full speed. In so doing the belt slipped and caught the volunteer workman in a sort of loop which carried him around the shaft. Deceased seeing the workman in this perilous position succeeded in rescuing him from it, but in the attempt was himself caught in the belt and whirled over the shaft, sustaining thereby injuries from which he died. Held, that as plaintiff had not been directed to adjust it, the condition of the belt was not the proximate cause of the injury, and although it is not contributory negligence to attempt to rescue a person in peril, no matter whether it was the result of the person's own negligence (*Eckert* v. *Railroad Co.*, 43 N. Y. 502; *Spooner* v. *Railroad Co.*, 115 N. Y. 22, 21 N. E. 696; *Gibney* v. *State*, 137 N. Y. 1, 33 N. E. 142), yet no action would lie against defendant in this case, as its negligence was not the proximate cause of intestate's death.

Attorney and Client—Liability for Negligence—Overlooking First Lien.—Larrall v. *Groman*, 37 Atl. Rep. 98 (Penn.). An attorney searching the record in regard to certain property, held liable to his client for overlooking prior liens, wherein client loaned money on a mortgage of said property on the strength of his stating there were no prior liens.

Gift to Infant—Engagement Ring—Conditions of Marriage—Breach. —Stramberg v. *Rubenstein*, 44 N. Y. Sup. 405. A man cannot recover during the infancy of his former fiancée an engagement ring given her, on the ground that she had broken the engagement.

Monopolies—Combination in Restraint of Trade—Promissory Note.— Milwaukee Masons and Builders Ass'n v. *Nieserowski*, 70 N. W. Rep. 166 (Wis.). The private by-laws of a masons' and builders' association, which consists of most of the mason contractors in a city, are void as in restraint of trade, when they require the members to pay six per cent on all contracts performed by them, and that all bids for work must be first submitted to the association, and six per cent must be added by the lowest bidder to his price before he submits it to the owner or his architect. A note given by a contractor to such an association, of which he was a member, for the percentage due under the by-laws, on a contract for building, is invalid and will not be enforced.

Criminal Law—False Pretenses.—Jules v. *State*, 36 Atl. Rep. 1027 (Md.). A false representation by one that he has supernatural power to cure is as to an existing fact and a promise to exercise this power in the future does not overthrow the consequences attached to the false representation.

Collision—Steamships in Harbor.—The Bowden v. *The Decatur H. Miller*, 78 Fed. Rep. 649. The obligation to use care in avoiding collisions is as incumbent upon a vessel lying in harbor and not under sail or steam as upon a moving vessel, and failure to warn approaching vessels of her helpless condition constitutes negligence. In this case the court also held that the approaching steamer, having failed to obtain answer to her signals, was bound to neglect no precaution to prevent risk of collision, even from the fault of the other vessel.

Divorce—Jurisdiction—Domicile.—Dickinson v. *Dickinson*, 45 N. E. Rep. 1091 (Mass.). A husband abandoned his wife, whom he had shortly before married under compulsion, and moved into another State. As soon as the statutory residence had been acquired there he applied for a divorce in that State, and the divorce was granted. The Massachusetts court holds that the fact of the abandonment and the early application for divorce, together with the circumstances of the marriage, warrant the inference that the husband's residence in the foreign State was not a *bona fide* one and that he went there purely for the purpose of obtaining a divorce. Therefore, that other State had no jurisdiction. *Looker* v. *Gerald*, 157 Mass. 42, 31 N. E. 709, distinguished.

Schools—Police Power—Power of State Board of Health—Compulsory Vaccination of Children—Delegation of Legislative Power.—State ex. rel. Adams v. *Burdge et al.*, 70 N. W. Rep. 347. A statute authorizing a State board of health to make such regulations "as may in its judgment be necessary for the protection of the people," from contagious disease and leaving it to decide as to what diseases are contagious, is an unwarranted delegation of legislative power. In the absence of a statute making vaccination a condition precedent to the right to attend public schools, a rule to that effect by the board of health is unreasonable and cannot be sustained as an exercise of the police power of a State, being made when there is no danger of epidemic.

BOOK NOTICES.

Handbook of the Law of Partnership. By William George, of the St. Paul Bar. Law sheep, 618 pp. West Publishing Company, St. Paul, Minn., 1897.

Mr. George has succeeded, we think, in accomplishing the difficult task of reducing the somewhat intangible law of Partnership to a series of concrete propositions. His style is clear and forcible, and his arguments on doubtful points are logical and convincing. A new feature is introduced in the typographical form of the foot-notes, the names of the States from whose reports cases are cited being printed in large letters, so that the value of the book as a digest of the law in the different States is increased.

The Historical Development of Code Pleading in America and England. By Charles M. Hepburn of the Cincinnati Bar. Cloth, 334 pp. W. H. Anderson & Company, Cincinnati, O., 1897.

The author sets forth in a very interesting and instructive manner the different steps in the reforming process which has been employed in respect to the cumbersome common law pleading. The book covers the present codes of all the States and is very complete and accurate.

A Treatise on the American Law of Guardianship. By J. G. Woerner, author of "The American Law of Administration." Law sheep, 581 pp. Little, Brown & Company, Boston, 1897.

The law of guardianship has been treated to some extent by text writers on domestic relations and kindred subjects, but always as a mere division or section of the main subject. Mr. Woerner's work is the first, we believe, to deal exclusively with the care of minors and persons of unsound mind. This branch of the law is discussed as it is administered in courts of probate in the United States, and the trend of the whole volume is toward the concrete and practical rather than the abstract and theoretical. It is thus a valuable manual for the practitioner, while it is complete and exhaustive enough to serve as an admirable reference work. Many of the statements of legal principles are founded upon the writer's own experience and their truth and accuracy has therefore been proven.

The True Doctrine of Ultra Vires in the Law of Corporations. By Reuben A. Reese of the Colorado Bar. Law sheep, 338 pp. T. H. Flood & Company, Chicago, 1897.

Conflicting decisions in the courts have left the meaning of the expression "*ultra vires*" so hazy that perhaps Mr. Reese has as much reason as any other writer for calling his own doctrine the "true" one. His whole treatise proceeds upon the principle that a corporation, being entirely a creature of the law, absolutely *cannot* commit an act unauthorized by its charter. When he comes into contact with decided cases where acts of this nature have been sanctioned by courts of undoubted authority he experiences no little difficulty. A similar obstacle is encountered when he discusses the liability of a corporation for a tort committed by its officers or agents. While recognizing Mr. Reese's courage in so vigorously attacking a subject which has worsted so many good men, and his exhaustive study of the subject, as shown by his careful and elaborate annotations, we are yet compelled to say that in our humble judgment his doctrine is far from being the "true" one, and that his treatise has thrown very little light on this dark and involved subject.

A Treatise on the Criminal Law. By Emlin McClain, A.M., LL.D. Law sheep, two vols., 725 and 785 pp. Callaghan & Company, Chicago, 1897.

A new and valuable feature is introduced in the above work, which consists in treating along with any particular crime the forms of pleading proper to the case, and the evidence which may be adduced by prosecution or defense. The reader is thus enabled to review almost at a glance the corresponding portions of criminal law, criminal procedure, and evidence. The book is well written and the typographical work irreproachable.

The General Digest, New Series, Volume Second. Law sheep, 1,329 pp. Lawyers' Coöperative Publishing Company, Rochester, N. Y., 1897.

The volume just issued is the second in the new series, and covers the latter part of the year 1896. The size is smaller than that of the volumes in the former series and the book is much easier to handle. The digesting is as thoroughly done as in former issues and this is the highest praise we could give it.

MAGAZINE NOTICES.

The Green Bag, May, 1897.

    John Randolph Tucker, - - - - Susan P. Lee.
    Condemned to the Noose.
    An Unpublished Letter of Chancellor James Kent.
    Tear Shedding before the Jury.
    The Supreme Court of Wisconsin, - - - Edwin E. Bryant.
    Lawyers and Law Practice in England and the United
        States Compared. I.
    The Burgomaster of Amsterdam (verse), - - John Albert Macy.
    Election Petition Trials in England, - - - Edward Porritt.

Central Law Journal.

    Apr. 23. The Power of a Court of Equity to Authorize the
        Issue of Receivers' Certificates, - - Charles A. Hardy.
    Apr. 30. Liability for the Sale of Intoxicants, John D. Shackleford.
    May 7. Right of a Creditor to Sue and Attach before
        Expiration of the Credit, - - Chapman W. Maupin.
    May 14. Answers in Insurance Suits, - - S. S. Merrill.

Albany Law Journal.

    Apr. 17. Mr. Ellsworth's Anti-Cartoon Bill, - - Ben. S. Dean.
    Apr. 24. Infringement of Copyright by Reviews (*Law
        Times*, London).
    May 1. Imprisonment for Debt, - - Marshall VanWinkle.
    May 8. Imprisonment for Debt (continued), Marshall VanWinkle.
    May 15. Imprisonment for Debt (concluded), Marshall VanWinkle.

SUPPLEMENT

CONTAINING

MEMORABILIA ET NOTABILIA.

[Graduates are requested to contribute to this column and address their communications to YALE LAW JOURNAL, box 1341, New Haven, Conn.]

"The anniversary exercises of the Law School will be more complete this Commencement than heretofore. The annual meeting of the alumni will be held in the Law School Building at 1 o'clock on Monday, June 28th, when a luncheon will be served. The alumni will march in procession to College Street Hall, where the Townsend prize speaking will take place, followed by an address to the graduating classes by Mr. Justice Harlan of the United States Supreme Court. An innovation will be the delivery of the doctor's oration by Tokichi Masao of the D. C. L. class."

* * *

The Announcement of the Townsend speakers was made May 22d. The men and their subjects are: Christopher Lester Avery, Yale '93, of Groton, on "The Rise and Future of the Hawaiian Republic"; Roger Sherman Baldwin, Yale '95, of New York City, on "The Adaptation of the Jury System to the Conditions of Modern Society"; Joseph Edwin Proffit of Lloyd, Va., on "Lynching: its Cause and Cure," and John Walcott Thompson, Dartmouth '95, of New Haven, on "Daniel Webster as a Lawyer."

* * *

The Wayland Prize Debate was held in the College Street Hall on the evening of May 20th. The judges were Hon. Thomas M. Waller of New London, the Hon. S. E. Merwin of New Haven, and the Hon. S. O. Prentice of Hartford. The subject for debate was, "Resolved, That Congress ought to pass a National Bankrupt Law, with provisions for compulsory as well as voluntary proceedings." The contestants spoke in the following order: Affirmative, Edgar C. Snyder, John W. Thompson, Richard C. Stoll, Christopher S. Avery, Jr., Henry W. Merwin; negative, Marshall F. Hatcher, Nehemiah Candee, Herbert C. Bartlett, Roger S. Baldwin and Thomas H. Cobbs.

The first prize of $50 was awarded to R. S. Baldwin, the second prize of $30 to H. W. Merwin, and the third prize of $20 to H. C. Bartlett.

* * *

Dean Wayland is President of the Baptist Social Union and acted as toast-master at the annual banquet held at Calvary Baptist Church, New Haven, Conn., Tuesday, May 11th.

* * *

Hon. A. F. Judd, Chief-Justice of the Supreme Court of Hawaii, visited the Law School Saturday, April 24th.

* * *

The Wurts Moot Court Club of the Senior Class gave a dinner in honor of Prof. Wurts at Traeger's Saturday, May 8th. Prof. W. K. Townsend was the guest of honor.

* * *

Rev. Edwin P. Parker of Hartford delivered a lecture in the Kent Club course at the College Street Hall Thursday, April 29th. The subject was "The Gentler side of Puritan Character." On May 6th Hon. St. Clair McKelway, editor of the Brooklyn *Eagle*, lectured, under the same auspices, on "Representative Americans." The last lecture of the course was delivered on May 27th by the Hon. Andrew D. White, his subject being "Evolution against Revolution in Politics."

* * *

The Yale Moot Court Club has been organized by members of the Junior class. A. J. Raney, '99, is President, and F. E. McDuffee, '98, is Secretary. Prof. Wurts presides at the weekly meetings.

* * *

The Edward Thompson Co. of Northport, L. I., has offered to the Law School an annual prize of a set of its "Encyclopedia of Pleading and Practice," or of its "Cyclopedia of Law" (first edition), or of the "Cyclopedia of Law" (second edition) as may be elected by the successful competitor. The prize is to be awarded to that member of the Senior class who shall write the best thesis on some legal subject. On account of the lateness of the announcement the prize will this year be awarded to the member of the Senior class who shall be voted most faithful and successful in his legal work throughout the year, Seniors being allowed one vote and members of the Faculty five votes each.

A new Yale club has lately been formed in New York City. Any person is qualified for membership who has received a degree from the University, or who, being twenty-one years of age and upwards, has been connected with any department of Yale as a student or instructor for at least one year. The annual dues are to be twenty dollars for resident members who have been five years out of the University and ten dollars for all others, resident or non-resident.

1866. Major Bradley David Lee, one of the most prominent lawyers of St. Louis, died at his home on Monday, May 10th, of heart disease. He was born in Litchfield County, Conn., March 24, 1838, and received his preliminary education in the public schools and at Williston Academy. He read law for two years, and then entered the army as First Lieutenant of the Nineteenth Regiment, Connecticut Volunteer Infantry. Later he was assigned by President Lincoln to general staff service of the United States Volunteer Army with the rank of Captain. He served in the Army of the Potomac, and at the close of the war was breveted Major for meritorious conduct. Upon his return to Connecticut Major Lee entered the Yale Law School from which he was graduated in 1866. Soon after he went to St. Louis, where he practiced until the time of his death. He was counsel for a number of railroads and insurance companies.

1875. C. LaRue Munson, who for several years past has been a lecturer in the school on "The Beginnings of Practice," is the author of "A Manual of Elementary Practice," recently published by the Bowen-Merrill Company of Indianapolis.

1881. Col. Lucien F. Burpee has been elected Judge of the City Court at Waterbury, Conn.

1882. John A. Stoughton has been appointed Judge of the newly-established Town Court of East Hartford, Conn.

1883. Walter Pond was married to Miss Linna E. Downs of Westville, Conn., Thursday, April 22d, 1897.

1885. Hon. John G. Tod has been elected Judge of the Civil District Court of Houston, Texas.

1888. C. D. Rinehart of Jacksonville, Fla., has dissolved his present partnership and will, in future, conduct the business in his own name.

1890. N. W. Bishop is Assistant Treasurer of the American Ordnance Company of Bridgeport, Conn.

1891. Thomas M. Cullinan has an office at 94 State street, Bridgeport, Conn.

1891. Percy L. Johnson is in the law firm of Hall & Johnson with offices at 403 Main street, Bridgeport, Conn.

1892. Herbert A. Hill has an office at 37 Main street, Bridgeport, Conn.

1892. Sanford B. Martin has an office at room 2, 116 Church street, New Haven, Conn.

1893. Jas. D. Dewell, Jr., is prosecuting agent for New Haven County.

Ex.-1893. J. G. Estill is the author of "Numerical Problems," written with special reference to the Yale entrance requirements in Geometry. The book is published by Longmans, Green & Co.

1893. Cards are out for the wedding of Wm. T. Hincks and Miss Maud Morris of Bridgeport, Conn., June 25, 1897.

1893. Jesse A. Stewart has an office at 403 Main street, Bridgeport, Conn.

1894. The class of '94 of the Law School will hold a triennial celebration on Tuesday, June 29th. The affair will consist of a banquet and the class will attend the Yale-Harvard baseball game in a body. Judge James F. Torrance of Derby is Secretary of the class.

1894. H. O. Bowers was married to Miss Lillian Estella Shepard on Wednesday, May 12, 1897, in the Congregational Church, West Hartford, Conn. F. E. Healy, '93, and Harold R. Durant, '95 M. S., were ushers.

1894. Harold F. Durant has been appointed Prosecuting Attorney of the City Court at Waterbury, Conn. He has retired from the law office of Col. Lucien F. Burpee.

1894. Geo. R. Montgomery was arrested by the Greeks while doing newspaper work near their camp at Pharsala.

1894. M. A. Reynolds and J. F. Donovan have formed a partnership with offices in the First National Bank Building, New Haven.

1894. Henry E. Ferris has been appointed Prosecuting Attorney in the Norwalk Town Court.

1895. Frank J. Brown has been appointed Prosecuting Attorney of the City Court of New Haven.

1895. Howard C. Webb has been appointed Assistant Prosecuting Attorney of the City Court of New Haven.

1895. Frederick A. Hill has been appointed Clerk of the Norwalk Town Court.

1895. Henry C. Burroughs has an office in the *Standard* Building, Bridgeport, Conn.

1895. Messrs. Wm. T. Hincks and John Banks, '95, have formed a partnership with officers at 94 State street, Bridgeport, Conn.

Lightning Source UK Ltd.
Milton Keynes UK
UKHW010652291118
333182UK00015B/906/P